REPORT WRITING

FOR CRIMINAL JUSTICE
PROFESSIONALS

LARRY S. MILLER
JOHN T. WHITEHEAD

FOURTH EDITION 4

ELSEVIER

AMSTERDAM • BOSTON • HEIDELBERG • LONDON
NEW YORK • OXFORD • PARIS • SAN DIEGO
SAN FRANCISCO • SINGAPORE • SYDNEY • TOKYO
Anderson Publishing is an imprint of Elsevier

Acquiring Editor: Elisabeth Ebben
Project Manager: Paul Gottehrer
Designer: Dennis Schaefer

Anderson Publishing is an imprint of Elsevier
30 Corporate Drive, Suite 400, Burlington, MA 01803, USA

Notices
Knowledge and best practice in this field are constantly changing. As new research and experience
broaden our understanding, changes in research methods or professional practices, may become
necessary. Practitioners and researchers must always rely on their own experience and knowledge in
evaluating and using any information or methods described herein. In using such information or
methods they should be mindful of their own safety and the safety of others, including parties for
whom they have a professional responsibility.

To the fullest extent of the law, neither the Publisher nor the authors, contributors, or editors, assume
any liability for any injury and/or damage to persons or property as a matter of products liability,
negligence or otherwise, or from any use or operation of any methods, products, instructions, or ideas
contained in the material herein.

Library of Congress Cataloging-in-Publication Data
Application submitted

British Library Cataloguing-in-Publication Data
A catalogue record for this book is available from the British Library.

ISBN: 978-1-4377-5584-8

Printed in the United States of America
    11 12 13 14 10 9 8 7 6 5 4 3 2

Working together to grow
libraries in developing countries

www.elsevier.com | www.bookaid.org | www.sabre.org

ELSEVIER   BOOK AID International   Sabre Foundation

For information on all Anderson publications visit our website at www.andersonpublishing.com

DEDICATION

This Fourth Edition of *Report Writing for Criminal Justice Professionals*
is dedicated to:

Ruth Miller & Pat Whitehead

ACKNOWLEDGMENTS

Acknowledgment is given to Jerrold G. Brown and Clarice R. Cox, authors of the first and second editions of this text. Their vision and work have made *Report Writing for Criminal Justice Professionals* a leading text in the field, used in many academic and training institutions. John Whitehead and I are extremely proud to be associated with this work.

Others who have contributed significantly to the text include William S. Sessions, former Director of the Federal Bureau of Investigation; John Lowry, Chief, Johnson City Tennessee Police Department; Ed Graybeal, Sheriff, Washington County Tennessee Sheriff's Office; Russell Jamerson, Major, Washington County Tennessee Sheriff's Office; Michael S. Nakamura, Chief, Honolulu Police Department; Karl Godsey, Captain, Honolulu Police Department; Nathan Matsuoka, Statistical Analyst, Honolulu Police Department; Sumie Hayami, Secretary, Honolulu Police Department and Heidi Harralson, Spectrum Forensic International.

Special thanks are extended as well to Michael Foley, retired captain of the Honolulu Police Department and owner of Pacific Systems; Warren Ferreira, Corporate Director of Security, Outrigger Hotels, Hawaii and Dr. David Mellinkoff, Professor Emeritus, UCLA.

In addition, gratitude is expressed to Allan L. Abbott, Director-State Engineer and Robert A. Grant, Risk Management Supervisor, Nebraska Department of Roads; Matt L. Rodriguez, Superintendent and Charles B. Roberts, Assistant Deputy Superintendent, Chicago Police Department; Fred Moeller, Captain, San Diego Police Department Regional Law Enforcement Training Center; and Sylvester Daughtry, Jr., Chief, and L.M. James, Lieutenant, Greensboro Police Department.

The authors wish to acknowledge O. Leanne Smith, Miami-Dade Police Department; Michael Pentory, Bellevue Police Department, Washington; Tammy

Garig, Louisiana Department of Corrections; Robert Ramiz, Handy Fender-Bender Corp.; Janice White, The CAD Zone, Inc.; Bennie F. Brewer, Chief, and Nancy Carnes, Writer-Editor, Programs Support Section of the Criminal Justice Information Services Division, Federal Bureau of Investigation; Philip Arreola, Chief, Richard McCrea, Lieutenant, and Kenneth A. Zilke, Field Training Coordinator, City of Tacoma Police Department; John F. Nichols, Sheriff, Barnett Jones and Michael McCabe, Captains, Oakland County Sheriff's Department, Pontiac, Michigan; Michael W. McLaughlin, Sheriff, Thomas B. Gallagher, Administrative Undersheriff, and Gail E. Dolson, Sergeant, Camden County Sheriff's Department, Camden, New Jersey.

Thanks to Larry W. Tolliver, Chief, and Gary L. Barr, Deputy Chief, Anne Arundel County Police Department; Richard L. Stalder, Secretary, and Johnny Creed, Assistant Secretary, Louisiana Department of Safety and Corrections; Michael Magill, Director, Loss Prevention, Longs Drug Stores, Inc.; Al A. Philippus, Chief of Police, Joseph MacKay, Sergeant, and Bob Sills, Special Projects Officer, San Antonio Police Department.

Thanks to William K. Finney, Chief, and Gary C. Briggs, Lieutenant, Saint Paul Police Department, Saint Paul, Minnesota; T.W. Connen, Executive Officer, David A. Felix, Captain, and Patsy DiBenedetto, Arizona Department of Public Safety; Carlos Alvarez, Director, Metro-Dade Police Department, Miami, Florida; and David L. Michaud, Chief, and Kay Davidson, Technician, Denver Police Department.

Thanks also go to Larry Ackerman, Milt Ahlerich, James E. Bender, Sherman Block, William J. Brennan, Alice Brown, Paul Brown, William Brown, Anthony V. Bouza, Lee P. Brown, Bobby R. Burkett, Michael Carpenter, Michael P. Chabries, William Chur, W.R. Coffey, Tom Corbett, Sarah Cortez, Letha DeCaires, Timothy R. Delaney, A.F. Diorio, Gregory J. Eilers, Leilani Fukuhara, Wanda Fukunaga, Russell B. Garris, Douglas G. Gibb, Don Gorham, Chester Hazlewood, George R. Hess, Edward Y. Hirata, Jean Johnson, Norm Johnson, Glen Kajiyama, Harold Kawasaki, Gerry Keir, Barbara Krauth, Mike Kroner, Delta Letney, Doric Little, Elden Loeffelholz, Michael Magill, Mark Mikami, Al Mitterer, John Moran, Mark J. Murphy, Jamie Napuunoa-Beppu, Norman D. Osthoff, Ralph D. Pampena, Cordon Parks, Turner Pea, Billy D. Prince, Morris G. Redding, David Rendell, Thomas H. Teal, Maurice T. Turner, Catherine R. Vallone, Mary Victoria Pyne, William R. Waller, and Aristedes W. Zavares.

Special thanks go to Dr. Michael Braswell, acquisitions editor for Elsevier and to Elisabeth Roszmann Ebben, J.D., our editor at Elsevier.

Larry S. Miller and John Whitehead

INTRODUCTION

A young officer comes back from a frustrating day in court and tells his "old-timer" partner about his experience. The young officer tells his mentor,

> The defense attorney asked me if I had taken a course in report writing at the academy. When I said I did, he asked me what they taught us. I told him that they stressed the importance of writing neat and legible reports that are submitted in a timely manner. He then asked if they taught us anything else, and I testified that they taught us to include all relevant information and to be accurate. He then asked if I write my reports in that way. When I told him that I did, he asked, "Why then, officer, did you not include in your report many of the facts that you testified about today?" I told him that I must have forgotten to put them in or thought that they weren't important at the time.

> By the follow-up questions he asked, it was clear that he was trying to make the jury believe that at best I'm incompetent, and at worst I'm a liar. There are so many things to do at a crime scene. Who can remember to put everything in the report? And besides, it's hard to determine what the attorneys are going to be interested in.

> "Well you know what they say," replies the old-timer, "If it's not written down, it doesn't exist."

A condominium board of directors wants to keep costs to a minimum and to do so skimps on security officer training and pay. As one board member says, "How hard is it to write a report? It should be simple enough, fill out a log line by line, note the time, any dangerous conditions, or suspicious occurrences. For that you need a Ph.D.?" When a poorly trained, poorly supervised, or just plain lazy security officer completes his log ahead of time, filling in the time and location of where he is expected to be and then fails to check that area, the board members learn the cost of such an action when a woman is assaulted in the unchecked area and sues the condominium.

In a courtroom across town, a single mother nervously peels red nail polish from her stubby fingers as she watches the judge read the probation officer's report. Her background includes charges of runaway, drinking, and marijuana possession, but this time it was cocaine. If she goes to prison, who will take care of her daughter? Not her father, who had abused her as a child. Not her mother, who is more often drunk than sober. Her future and that of her young daughter is dependent on the information included in the probation officer's report. The majority of the information that the judge uses in making a decision about sentencing comes from that report.

What ties all of these incidents together? What are the differences? What are the responsibilities of writers in each part of the criminal justice system?

These cases are tied together by the responsibility for precise documentation. The handling of an incident is not complete until the best possible report is filed, in whatever format required by the agency.

Format of Reports

The format of the reports will vary according to the writers' responsibilities:

1. *Law enforcement officers* write just about the facts. They are not expected to offer opinions on the *why* unless the answers emerge from evidence, including statements of witnesses, victims, and suspects. The *who*, *what*, *when*, *where*, and *how* are the basic questions to answer. Law enforcement officers are not expected to testify in court to things that are not in their reports. While the young officer's mentor's statement in the first scenario is not completely true, there is a lot of truth to it. Attorneys whose clients will be damaged by information an officer presents in court that is not documented in his or her report will attack the officer's credibility by implying that the officer is mistaken or even intentionally lying.

2. *Security personnel* — ranging from security officers (also known as loss prevention officers) to highly trained investigators — protect not only people and property but also focus on protecting the reputation of employers. They report first to their employers who are often hotels, hospitals, airports, and businesses. Sometimes called private police, they number far more than sworn law enforcement officers. Security officers maintain logs, cooperate with law enforcement, and write incident and other reports. Investigative

units may write complex and detailed reports on incidents from fraud cases to industrial espionage.

3. *Corrections officers* write many types of reports including shift logs and incident, use of force, and injury reports. They also include information on the *who*, *what*, *when*, *where*, and *how* in their reports, including information on the *why* only when substantiated by the evidence, including statements.

4. *Probation officers* report not just on the *who*, *what*, *when*, *where*, and *how*, but also on the *why*. They do very thorough background checks and are expected to give opinions, even conjectures, and recommendations based on facts and evidence. Often judges read the Presentence Investigation Reports (PSIs or PSIRs) in the short time available, interact briefly with the defendants, and make decisions. The same is true for many of the reports written by *parole officers*, whose reports are often the basis of decisions made by parole boards or corrections administrators. The results of both types of reports may result in problems that affect not only defendants but also the community. The decision for probation or parole may result in crime headlines, but failure to give the offenders a chance results in overcrowded facilities.

5. *Forensic and Scientific personnel* report on findings from crime laboratory and forensic pathology laboratories. These reports may entail traffic crash analysis, DNA, trace evidence, questioned documents, firearms and ballistics and autopsy examinations. These reports are read and used by police, prosecutors, judges, and juries in understanding how physical evidence was examined and the opinion of the expert. It is imperative that these types of reports are clear, understandable and provide an uncomplicated description of how evidence was processed and what probative value it holds in a case.

While law enforcement, security, corrections, probation and parole officers, and forensic specialists are the main focus of this text, the importance of good documentation now applies to many other agencies. For example, some Forest Service personnel also have powers of arrest as crime increases in the national forests. The same is true of other agencies. Their actions must be fully documented to avoid repercussions.

It should also be noted that persons involved in the criminal justice system all may be called on to write administrative or research reports that have slightly different formats and may call for personal opinions and recommendations, areas which are normally left out of case reports.

Not only should people and property be protected by those working in the criminal justice system. It is also important to remember that the persons writing the reports have their reputations and jobs on the line as well. Few people realize the importance of a well-written, accurate, brief, and complete report as a defense against charges of brutality, incompetence, or other misconduct. Report writing is not something to be done grudgingly and carelessly. It can be critical to success or failure in the criminal justice system.

New Trends in Reporting

While preparing to write this text the authors contacted more than 100 law enforcement, security, forensics, and corrections agencies. Several provided information about new systems that have been developed by their agencies. Some have computer systems with screens that ask for specific information in completing reports. The systems then provide templates with major headings for which information must be gathered for completion of the narrative section of the report. Other agencies have systems where investigators at crime scenes or other incidents complete their investigations and then call in by telephone either directly to a clerk who types up the report as dictated, or to a recording device so that the information can be typed later by clerks. You may be thinking that if this is the direction toward which things are heading then you don't need to study report writing. The authors believe that even if you are fortunate enough to be employed by one of these agencies, this text will be helpful to you in organizing the information you obtain before you call it in. In addition, most of these agencies still require their employees to write or type their own administrative reports, memorandums, and letters of reply to inquiries.

A New Player in the Criminal Justice System

There is a recent player in the criminal justice system that has had a major impact on the system in the past few years. The player? The video camera. Whether in the courtroom or on the street, the video camera has changed the way people in the Western World look at the criminal justice system.

William Kennedy Smith was tried in a Florida courtroom, accused of rape. Television cameras were allowed in the courtroom and the trial was broadcast nationally. For the first time, millions of Americans saw the criminal justice system in action. They saw evidence and statements being presented in court. They saw police officers testifying about their actions at a crime scene, and saw them being questioned about their reports submitted about the case. Witnesses were cross-examined about information that was documented in police reports.

In 1991, Rodney King was stopped after a police pursuit through the streets of Los Angeles. The officers arrested King, wrote their reports, and didn't think much more about the case. A video recording by a nearby resident changed the way many citizens thought of their police department. The video was shown repeatedly by the news media. In addition to the video and the reports submitted by the officers, a new source of documentation was found. The transmissions between various officers using mobile data terminals were recovered in which officers described their actions using disparaging terms. The officers involved were tried for assault in state court and were found not guilty, and one of the largest riots in our nation's history followed with loss of life and tremendous property damage. The video was studied nearly frame by frame in the courtroom. The same video was used by federal prosecutors, and an officer and his supervisor were convicted of civil rights violations. King received a large settlement from the city of Los Angeles.

Nicole Brown Simpson and Ronald Goldman were murdered in an upscale Los Angeles neighborhood. Nicole Brown Simpson's ex-husband, former professional football player O.J. Simpson, was arrested and tried for their murders. The trial lasted months and every moment was televised. People around the world watched as a crime scene technician testified about his activities at the crime scene, including the collection of evidence. He referred to his notes and reports and testified that he was sure of the accuracy of his testimony. The defense then introduced a videotape of the technician collecting and placing the evidence in containers in a different manner from that to which he testified. Eventually O.J. Simpson was acquitted of the charges.

You can probably think of a number of other examples of high-profile cases in which statements given at crime scenes or early in investigations were then challenged on cross-examination. The trial and conviction of the Menendez brothers for the murder of their parents, Lorena Bobbitt's acquittal of cutting off her husband John's penis, his acquittal of sexually assaulting her, the Ruby Ridge incident, the Branch Davidians in Waco, Texas, the Oklahoma City bombing, and rapper Corey "C-Murder" Miller's shooting of a 16-year-old fan at a nightclub are just a few incidents that come to mind. The Federal Bureau of Investigation's crime laboratory, traditionally thought of as the best in the world, has come under attack recently in the media, in congressional hearings, and in high-profile court cases. Many of the problems stem from lack of, incomplete, or inaccurate documentation of the handling of evidence and the laboratory procedures conducted on the evidence.

All of these cases mentioned were followed by millions of people watching television. Guest commentators critiqued each step of the trial. It should be clear to the reader the importance of carefully written, accurate, brief, and complete reports. In a few high-profile cases, you, as the investigator, will have the luxury of knowing at the onset the importance of your report and the scrutiny it will receive. More often, though, it is the ordinary, run-of-the-mill report that ends up in a high-profile court case, on the front page of the newspaper, on the nightly television news, or on the desk of your agency's chief executive.

Improving Writing Skills

There are two things you can do to improve your writing skills. Once you improve your skills, your report writing will automatically improve.

1. Read. The more you read, the more you learn. In terms of vocabulary, each new word that is learned leads to knowledge of other words. In addition, reading helps you to learn sentence structure and to improve your knowledge of basic grammar. Find a little time each day to read. Don't say you don't have time to read. It is reported that just 10 to 15 minutes of reading a day will result in finishing 12 or more books in a year. It is important that

you read more than just the newspaper. Most newspapers are written at a seventh grade reading level and will have little impact on your skills.

2. Practice writing. Like any other skill that you seek to gain, you must actually practice it in order to improve. Think about learning to ride a bicycle. Can you really learn to ride without actually getting on one and trying? No. Writing is the same. The more you write, the easier writing will become, and the better you will be at it. If you really want to improve on your report writing skills, you can do so. Whenever you have the occasion to write, take a little extra time. Start early. Plan your writing. Reread your work and make revisions where necessary. Proofread your final product. If you take just a little time to proofread your writing and make corrections and revisions, your writing ability will quickly improve. Finally, use this text as a guide.

TABLE OF CONTENTS

TABLE OF FIGURES

SECTION ONE

The Nature of Report Writing

CHAPTER 1

The Why and How of Report Writing

What do you like least about working in the criminal justice system? If your answer is writing reports, you are not alone. Were you attracted to the criminal justice system because you enjoy writing reports? It is doubtful that many people were. Do you view report writing as a chore to do before you can either get on with the real work of the day or get home for fun or rest? If so, you are like many, if not most, of the people working in the criminal justice system. If you are already working in the system, you know that much of your time is spent writing reports. Many patrol officers report spending up to one-half of their workday completing reports. Some detectives report spending up to 75 percent of their day with reports. Big cases can wind up looking like volumes of books, with many people contributing to the final product.

Most criminal justice professionals receive little training in writing reports. Departments, agencies, academies, colleges, high schools — everyone expects someone else to do the training. With standards of writing falling fast even in newspapers and television, it is hard to recognize correct writing when you see it. You are not alone if you have a hard time writing reports.

With modern technology advancing so fast, why do you need report writing? Machines are a means used to complete reports. They cannot write or organize your work. They can help fill in forms fast, compare fingerprints and identifications, and speed information for law enforcement, security, corrections, and probation and parole personnel. They do not organize or think; they just do as they are told. They can speed misinformation as well. The spell-checking function on a computer or word processor will accept any word that is spelled correctly, e.g., *seen* for *scene*, *bale* for *bail*, *miner* for *minor*; anything goes, including your credibility.

3

DOI: 10.1016/B978-1-4377-5584-8.00008-6

Consider the O.J. Simpson case, arguably the most noted case of the twentieth century. The Los Angeles Police Department was an early user of technology, but how much did technology help to document the action? Other high-profile cases continue to benefit from the use of technology, often by comparing known factors in the various situations. Airports, hospitals, hotels, and businesses are helped by rapid exchange of information among security officers. Probation and parole officers depend on computerized information for short reports, often for monthly checking on observation of regulations.

Being computer literate is almost a given today, but the computer does not organize material, use correct grammar, or select the specific words to write an accurate and complete narrative. Your writing is important both to yourself and to the public, whether you are in law enforcement, probation or parole, corrections, security, or some other agency. The sooner you take a businesslike view of writing and develop a skilled approach, the faster you will progress in your writing — in both your own estimation and that of others. You are also less likely to wind up in court (usually long after the report is written) with insufficient material to aid the cause of justice. Knowing *why* you write will positively influence *how well* you write.

Why Do You Write Reports?

Just about everyone writes reports. Notes are written to our loved ones, bosses, co-workers, friends, enemies, and creditors. People write when they are happy, in love, angry, or sad. Most people learned to write while they were in school. Is what they learned applicable to law enforcement, probation, corrections, and security? Many people do not write much after leaving school unless their job requires it. Does yours? Stop and think of all of the reasons that you write. Some of the people you write to are very important to you, either in your personal or professional life. Errors in personal writing may cause laughter, but errors in professional writing can cause you to lose credibility, professional standing, and even your job.

In the criminal justice system, reports are written for many reasons. Recording information to ensure that it will be available in the future is one purpose. Reports are also an expeditious way to share information with other people without you having to be there. Few people, including those who write reports, actually stop to think about the many ways in which reports are used. The following are a number of operational and administrative uses of reports.

Law Enforcement Reports

Operational Purposes

1. Document actions taken by persons involved in crimes, incidents, and accidents, as well as actions taken by you and your fellow officers.

2. Give pertinent facts that will help determine if follow-up is required by you or anyone else.

3. Help the prosecutor decide whether to charge an individual, and if so, with what charge. (If the prosecutor charges the suspect with Crime X when testimony shows Crime Y was more important, the defendant may be released.)

4. Point out a pattern of action, a *modus operandi* or method of operation (MO) taken to commit the crime, or a trademark, a habit that may even slow down the action, but that is characteristic of a certain perpetrator. This can help to show similarities between crimes and is an important investigative aid.

5. Help you recall details of a case when you testify months or years later. Your report may also protect you against a civil suit.

6. Help you or others to keep track of what has been done on an investigation, what needs to be done, and to help coordinate activities between investigators and agencies involved in the investigation.

7. Pinpoint times and places with a high incidence of crime so that officers can be deployed to the best advantage. This can provide help for you when you need it most.

Administrative Purposes

1. Determine what type of administrative action or follow-up is needed.

2. Send materials to other agencies, states, or the federal government, and even to other countries. The FBI has been gathering statistics on a voluntary basis for the Uniform Crime Reports (UCR). There is a movement toward replacing this with the National Incident-Based Reporting System (NIBRS), which goes into even greater depth.

3. Assist in obtaining cooperation in community policing to better serve the area and enhance public relations.

4. To form the backbone of reports to the upper echelon in your city or state, including the mayor, governor, and members of the legislature. Such reports document problems, progress, and possible solutions, and the information is used to budget money. Your equipment, assistance, and paycheck may hang in the balance.

5. Help management determine training needs and to assist in quality control efforts within the agency.

6. To determine who receives advancements or transfers. People are often judged and selected for advancement or transfer based on their writing and communication skills.

Reports are also used by people outside of your agency and sometimes outside the criminal justice system. These people include attorneys, members of the public, insurance companies, and news agencies.

Security officers operate in many ways similar to law enforcement officers. Both groups protect people and property; however, their emphases may be different. Law enforcement, as its name implies, is expected to ensure that laws are upheld, and violations are referred to the proper agency for adjudication. Security officers are responsible first to their employers, and their reports are often used to provide employers with information required to make decisions and to protect the good name and financial interests of the employer.

The public has very little understanding of security officers, who are sometimes called private police. To some, "security" may refer to a guard or night watchman. To others, the word may suggest large organizations like Wackenhut or Burns. A local business may hire a few people off the street and give them scant training. On the other hand, the American Society for Industrial Security (ASIS) has high standards for certified public protection degrees. Duties vary from simple alarm sounding when danger threatens, to a whole assortment of work that can be done for large corporations. In addition to the protection of people and property, some organizations expect such things as reports on customer satisfaction, employee theft, narcotics, assault, sexual harassment, firearms possession, bomb threats, and more; the list goes on and on.

Security Reports

Operational Purposes

1. Note problems that may hinder the smooth working of the facility or business. (Pre-existing dangerous conditions that are not taken care of can form bases for lawsuits.)

2. Prevent employee theft and shoplifting from businesses.

3. Promote a favorable image of the company, facility, or organization by solving problems in-house, whenever possible.

4. Document courteous responses to public demands.

Administrative Purposes

1. Help protect stockholders by documenting specific needs and justifiable expenditures.

2. Help secure funds to support such places as museums, performing arts facilities, and colleges.

3. Can be used to cooperate with similar facilities such as other hotels and hospitals to share information about swindlers, drug dealers, con artists, and other threats to security.

Corrections Reports

Corrections writing sometimes differs from that of law enforcement and security. Logs are prepared, as are incident reports and memos, by corrections officers who work in many areas of correctional facilities. Admission and other forms are also filled out, as are investigative and incident reports.

Probation and Parole Officer Reports

Some of the most comprehensive investigations and report writing is done in Presentence Investigation Reports (PSIs or PSIRs). These reports are written by probation officers to assist judges, who often must make rapid decisions after only a brief exposure to the suspect involved. As defined by Clear, Clear, and Burrell (1989):

> The PSIR is designed to advise a judge of the offender's criminal behavior, the options available to the decision maker for disposal of the offender, and the risks to society and the offender for whichever option the judge might wish to choose. It is a momentous document, for the decisions it advises balance significant considerations of legal rights, human liberty and community values, among them community safety.

In a simple example, the judge with little time and a full docket sees both the probation officer's report and the offender. The judge forms a decision based on three points:

1. How serious the offense is and how likely it is to be repeated.

2. Options including incarceration, probation, parole, community service, and the many new alternatives, such as electronic monitoring.

3. How the judge's decision will affect the offender, his or her family, and society as a whole.

In smaller jurisdictions the probation officer and parole officer may be the same person. If the decision is made for probation, the probation officer must check to see if requirements are carried out and should report any infractions. If a person is incarcerated and then released, the parole officer supervises the return to the community, checking on the parolee and sometimes providing counseling. The reports documenting such checks and counseling may then have to be defended in court.

Forensic and Scientific Reports

Recent interest in the forensic sciences due to popular television and movie portrayals of forensic and crime scene investigations has increased the need for forensic evidence to be introduced in criminal proceedings. This has been termed "the CSI effect," because jurors now expect forensic evidence to be presented in court. Those in the forensic sciences normally write reports of their analyses and findings that are then made part of the court record. Police investigators, prosecuting attorneys, defense attorneys, judges, and jurors read these reports in support of testimony that may be given at trial. It is imperative that these reports are understandable to a layperson unfamiliar with scientific jargon or procedures.

Almost all forensic reports contain the most basic information regarding an analysis and examination result. These include:

1. Identifying agency requesting the examination (name, address, phone number)

2. Case style (case number, name)

3. Items submitted for examination (listed as Q for questioned and K for Known)

4. Request (specifically citing what is to be done to the evidence)

5. Procedures (a narrative explaining what was done to the evidence and how it was examined)

6. Summary of examination (a narrative explaining what was done to the evidence and what was found)

7. Opinion (a statement explaining what the results were of the examination and the opinion of the examiner regarding the evidence)

8. Signature and identification of the examiner

Most forensic reports adhere to Federal Rule of Court 26, which mandates that written reports:

1. Contain all opinions to be expressed in court and the basis and reasons therefor

2. The data or other information considered by the expert in forming opinions

3. Any exhibits to be used as a summary of or support for the expert opinion

4. Qualifications of the expert, including a curriculum vitae and publications authored within the past ten years

5. Any compensation paid for the examination and testimony

6. A listing of any other cases in which the expert has testified either at trial or deposition in the preceding four years

Care should be taken with forensic and scientific reports to refrain from using scientific and medical jargon. Technical and medical statements should be defined in parentheses to make the report clear to non-technical persons like jurors and judges. For example, a forensic autopsy report might include parenthetical words to describe "exsanguination" as "blood loss." A sample forensic laboratory report is shown in Appendix A.

Figures 1.1 through 1.4, as well as the directions for writing logs, illustrate some of the similarities and differences in reports for law enforcement, probation and parole, corrections, security, and forensics.

Writing reports is an integral part of your work. It is not as important as the face-to-face interactions and confrontations that occur in the field and in the office, but it is also not something to be done carelessly and inefficiently. You save your own time and that of others when you write reports well.

> Why do you write reports? You write them to record facts accurately, briefly, and completely to form the first line of information from which operational and administrative decisions are made.

How Do You Write Reports?

You assemble all the facts. In Figures 1.1 through 1.4 you can check whether you have the *who, what, when, where, how,* and *why* when it is applicable. The *why* is required in presentence investigation reports, where opinions and recommendations are used. In other reports, the *why* must be documented by evidence or signed statements.

Writing the Log

The simplest and most immediate form of writing is the log (see Figure 1.5). While used mainly by security guards, a log can be defined as a detailed record of any activity. Often kept in bound books with ongoing times listed, logs can be brought to court as significant evidence. Check for the form and directions used by your agency. The following is a common style:

1. Use black ink and take care to print or write legibly.

2. As you start a shift, print your name followed by "ON DUTY," and enter the time in military style in the place provided.

3. List the equipment you received from the person who just completed the previous shift. Your signature should follow the list as a receipt. The person you are replacing then prints his or her name and the words "OFF DUTY," adding his or her signature.

Figure 1.1
Information Typically Found in an Investigation Report (Law Enforcement)

BASICS		SPECIFICS	FURTHER DETAILS

WHO	Was the:	Complainant ___ Victim ___ Witness ___
		Individual ___Company ___Group ___
		Counsel for suspect___
			First information
			Description:
			  Physical Address
			  Facial Phone
			  Clothing Occupation
			Place of work

WHO or WHAT	Started your action:	Squad room assignment ___ Dispatch ___ All-points bulletin ___ On view ___ Citizen's request ___ Other ___	

WHEN	Your action occurred:
	Fellow officers came:
	You presented your
	  identification and/or
	  search warrant
		Sent ___ Arrived ___ Return ___
		Crime committed ___ Crime reported ___
		Complainant's actions:
		  prior to ___ during ___ after ___ the incident
		Victim's actions:
		  prior to ___ during ___ after ___ the incident
		Victim's actions:
		  prior to ___ during ___ after ___ the incident
			Important statements

WHAT	Crime against person: Crime against property: Accident: Abuse: Natural disaster: Missing person: Other:	Evidence: Objects found ___ Dusted for latents ___ Recovered prints ___ Negative ___ Secured ___ Booked ___ Receipt given ___ Chain of evidence maintained ___ Tests given ___ Breathalyzer ___ Lineup ___ Observations ___ Notification ___	Real, direct, circumstantial Amount, number, value Injuries to person Damage or theft of property Referral Aggravated circumstances
WHERE	Street, intersection: Exact address: Room or room part:	Building ___ Dwelling ___ Store ___ Other ___ Diagrams ___ Sketches ___ Photographs ___ Vehicle ___ Land ___ Water ___	
HOW	Objects used: Suspect arrived, departed: Words, spoken or written: Other inducements:	Instruments ___ Weapons ___ Gambling/con game objects ___Other ___ MO ___ Trademarks ___ Similar cases ___ Skill necessary ___ Strength ___ Knowledge ___	Main words quoted exactly General points briefly paraphrased
WHY	Statement of suspect: Accident: Disaster:	Motive ___ Intentional ___ Unintentional ___	No value judgment Additional facts must support opinions
CONCLUSION	Disposition:	Arrest ___ Charge placed ___ Pending further investigation ___ Assistance given ___ Case closed ___	Exact referral

Figure 1.2
Information Typically Found in a Presentence Investigation Report (Probation)

BASICS	SPECIFICS	FURTHER DETAILS
WHO was the defendant:	Court name ___ True name ___ Alias ___ SS# ___ DOB ___ Sex ___ Height ___ Weight ___ Complexion ___ Build ___ Marks ___ Birthplace ___ Nationality ___ Years in county, state, nation ___ Citizenship ___ Occupation ___ Place of employment ___ Marital status ___ Children ___ Mother's maiden name ___, birthplace ___, occupation ___ Father's birthplace ___, occupation ___ Siblings' addresses ___ Complainant ___ Victim ___ Witness ___ Individual ___ Company ___ Group ___ Counselor ___ Prosecutor ___ Defense lawyer ___ Probation officer ___ Parole officer ___	
WHAT is the:	Current charge ___ Describe: who ___, what ___, when ___, where ___, why ___ Victim impact ___ Restitution needed ___ Record of past offenses ___ Describe briefly ___ Social history ___ Family situation ___ Education ___ People who influenced ___ Marital history ___ Divorce ___ Children ___ Support ___ Employment history ___ Goals ___ Plans ___ Religious affiliation ___ Drug use ___ Seller ___ Present attitude ___ Drug tests ___ Pleas agreement ___ Probation plan ___ User's fee ___ Restitution ___ Court costs ___ Credit time served for each offense ___	Special circumstances Official version attached Losses Documentation Birth order Family atmosphere How defendant sees self School records Medical records Successes Failures Self-esteem Specific recommendations Felony Misdemeanor Class Length of probation Reports Job placement Education Counseling Electronic monitoring Community service Other alternatives

Figure 1.3

Information Typically Found in an Incident Report (Private Security)

BASICS	SPECIFICS	FURTHER DETAILS
WHO was the:	Complainant ___ Victim ___ Patient ___ Witness ___ Visitor ___ Guest ___ Shopper ___ Employee ___ Traveler ___ Customer ___ Doctor ___ Nurse ___	Description: name, sex, address, phone (home & business), occupation, physical, facial, clothing, SS#, license
WHAT started your action:	Foreseeable problem ___, describe ___ Location ___ Danger ___ Remedy ___	Precise details Repair or notification to person responsible
WHAT kind of problem:	Lost ___ Found ___ Criminal ___ Items listed ___ Non-routine ___ Trespassing ___ Accident ___, type ___ Person ___ Witness ___	Precise value claimed by owner Estimate Insurance
WHEN:	Notified ___ Viewed ___ Assistance given ___	Called maintenance Called police, arrival Called main office Called ambulance, arrival
WHERE:	Hospital ___ Hotel ___ Business ___ Museum ___ Other ___ Department ___ Room ___ Hall ___ Elevator ___ Office ___ Parking lot ___ Street ___ Restroom ___ Swimming pool ___ Other ___	Exact address and location of specific area
HOW:	Accidental ___ Presumed cause ___ Witnesses ___ Injuries ___ Damage ___ Help requested ___ Help given ___ Intentional ___ Criminal ___ Rape ___ Drugs involved ___ Burglary ___ Robbery ___ Unattended death ___	Statements Notifications Police called Precise list of items Value
WHY:	Statements by persons involved ___ Evidence: real ___, direct ___, circumstantial ___	No undocumented opinion

Figure 1.4
Information Typically Found in a Forensics Report

BASICS		SPECIFICS	FURTHER DETAILS
WHO	Was the:	Requesting agency	Address, phone
WHEN	The request was made	Date, Time, Method of evidence delivery	Chain of custody
WHAT	Was analyzed	Describe Questioned and Known material	List of evidence
WHERE	Was evidence examined	Describe location and procedures	Preliminary exam
HOW	Was evidence examined	Describe methodology used	Equipment, analysis
WHY	Were methods used	Describe accepted procedures	Follow protocols
CONCLUSION	Opinion of expert	Basis for conclusion	

4. List each subsequent entry on a separate line, noting the time and your initials.

5. Leave no space between entries, other than shift changes.

6. Do not use correction fluid, erase, or otherwise blot out. Draw a line through any mistake you make, make the correction, and initial it.

7. For patrols, list time and location, then record any routine or non-routine situations that could affect the safety or security of persons or property. Note any obstruction, malfunction, or unsafe situation so the appropriate person can correct it.

8. Any significant event or wrongful act requires an incident report, and such an event or act should have a brief synopsis in the log. Add the notation, "See incident report."

9. Complete the log *as* things occur. Never enter in advance any routine activities that you expect to occur and never wait until the end of your shift to complete the log.

10. Remember the log can be important evidence in court to back up your activities and those of others.

Figure 1.5
Security Officer Log

Security Officer Log

Security Department   Date _____

Location _____ Security Officer

Time	Signature	Unit #

Do Not Copy Randomly Chosen Models

Most people in the criminal justice system seem to learn documentation on their own, with little, if any, formal training. It is as if everyone assumes someone else is handling the "how to write" part of the profession. Colleges, academies, and departments routinely neglect this area. Some even protest that technology will make report writing unnecessary. Forms, whether on the computer or on paper, still do not always give additional details, and these must be expressed in a narrative form. In a world in which people have become accustomed to learning information from television sound bites, few people can write well, and fewer still are able to write good reports. As a result, most newly hired, transferred, or promoted employees go to the files to obtain copies of previously submitted work to use as models in completing reports. This works all right if the previous writers were superior. Too often, however, they are not, and their errors are repeated and passed on.

Many departments or agencies have vague and even contradictory directives. Realizing that this is true may help you find your way to a mentor whose work is respected.

If you are new to a position, find help from someone who writes well and completes thorough reports, or follow the example of some well-written sample reports. Ask your supervisor or other employees for help in choosing good samples.

How Do You Get Started?

Even in a world of so-called paperless publishing, you are still likely to need to know how to use a notebook, at least, to record your first observations. You may have a laptop in your car, but a notebook will fit in your pocket when you are checking the situation, interviewing witnesses or suspects, or even making preliminary sketches. What kind of notebook should you use? How much should you record? How will the notebook be used?

What Kind of Notebook Should You Use?

If your agency mandates the type of notebook to be used, your problem of choosing is solved. If not, select a notebook that is suited to your task. It should be a type with which you are comfortable. Many people who work in the field and are mobile choose a notebook that is about $3 \times 5''$ so that it can be easily carried in a pocket. If you need to choose between the bound and loose-leaf notebook, consider the following.

1. The bound notebook has pages that are fixed in an unchangeable continuity. The pages are not removable, so if you take the notebook to testify in court (an important use of notebooks is to refresh your memory on a case), the whole notebook must be submitted.

2. The loose-leaf notebook, with rings and a hard cover, is often used in law enforcement. The pages should be numbered consecutively, so that portions

may be removed for court appearances and the rest may be returned. Many departments consider this flexibility important. Others feel that the loose-leaf notebook opens you up to accusations of tampering with your notebook because pages can be easily removed, blown away, or accidentally lost.

For permanency and uniformity, write or print clearly using a black ball-point pen. Black ink results in a clear and clean reproduction. Blue ink does not reproduce as well, and pencil is totally unacceptable. If you are using a computer you should follow your agency's standard format, including the font type. Some writers are fortunate to have direct access to a computer, either a laptop at the scene, or a desktop at their offices, and may be able to complete their reports directly in the computer without having to take notes. When it is necessary to complete the report from notes taken at the scene, it is important to organize the notes based on the computerized format. This eliminates having to search through pages of notes to follow the computer protocol. Some agencies have note-taking report forms that are based on computer screens and the order of computer input.

How Much Should You Record in a Notebook?

Information is written in notebooks to help the report writer remember specific and detailed information. Most investigators cannot recall all of the details of an investigation. This is especially true for detailed information including the accurate recording of names, addresses, telephone numbers, ages, dates of birth, and other such information. Notebooks are also used to have ready access to information that was provided in roll call, in all-points bulletins (APBs) over the radio, and from other sources.

1. On the inside of the cover, put your name, rank, identification number, address of assignment, and name of your agency. This is imperative because the loss of your notebook can result in the loss of irretrievable information. Also include important phone numbers needed for your assignment. Cover these basics with plastic tape, because frequent fingering may fade them.

2. Your notebook is a permanent record and memory bank for you, as well as part of your first step to writing good reports. It may also be read by others, especially if you take it to court to corroborate your report. Even if you decide not to take it to court, attorneys in the case may be able to convince the judge to order you to bring it to court. You do not want them examining your doodling, personal phone numbers, comments, or grocery lists, so avoid placing personal information in your notebook. Have some loose 3 x 5″ cards in your notebook to write information on to be given out. This is so you do not have to tear pages out of your notebook. Also, the use of sticky-type notes is helpful in moving personal information in and out of notebooks. However, do not use removable notes to record

information from official cases. Write this information on the pages of your notebook.

3. Number the pages and include full details: case number, people involved, names, addresses, telephone numbers, ages, dates of birth, gender, ethnic origin, statements made, and actions taken by the people involved as well as by you and the other officers on the scene. (Consult Figures 1.1 through 1.4 for specifics.)

4. If you are in doubt about including something, put it in. Apparently irrelevant words or actions may be trademarks that are unnecessary to commit a crime — and may even hinder it — but may help you to identify the suspect.

5. Do not draw conclusions too soon and leave out details that might later turn out to be the key to the action. Minor details sometimes make a major contribution to the solution of a crime. If you have any doubt about the importance of information you have obtained, the rule is: "When in doubt *do not* leave it out." Minor details can often make the difference in administrative investigations into your conduct and in civil court cases against you or your agency.

6. Especially if you use a loose-leaf notebook, write on only one side of the page. If you have to hand over parts of your notebook in court, you will only be giving access to the relevant information.

7. File your notebooks in chronological order so that notes for a case coming up in months or even years can be easily located.

Investigate, Do Not Just Record

Keep in mind that the criminal justice report writer is not just a clerk or recorder of information. The writer is an investigator. A crucial portion of the investigation is the interview. It is usually best to allow persons being interviewed to tell their own stories. If you have to ask questions to start the interview or to keep it going, ask very general, open-ended questions. What happened? What did you see or hear? Then what happened? Do this without taking notes. Why? Nothing stops a person from talking or telling what is known faster than pulling out a tape recorder or a notebook. An exception to this is when you have to take notes on APB information to be immediately put out over the air.

Next, have the witness retell the story while you take notes. Again, ask general questions to keep the interview moving. This part of the interview and your questions should help you to determine the elements and the chronological order of the offense, and provide you with more detailed information about the incident. The last part of the interview involves asking more detailed questions. Even during the questioning phase it is better to ask general questions than to ask specifics.

Example: "How tall was he?" is better than, "Was he about six feet tall?" The investigator must look for inconsistencies and self-serving statements and follow up with direct questions. Again, remember that you are an investigator and not just a report taker. You must control the interview process.

An interview becomes an interrogation when you believe that the person is not forthcoming and forthright with you. Interrogations usually involve suspects, but are sometimes used with victims or witnesses who are not voluntarily providing the information needed.

Remember to listen the first time through, then start taking notes, asking questions to fill in information and to provide additional details. Notes are not expected to be complete reports of what was found, seen, or heard at the crime scene. They are meant to refresh your memory when you are writing your report. Take enough information so that you can write a complete and accurate report.

Do Not Use Legalese or Old-Fashioned Terminology

You can be perfectly adequate in getting your points across orally, but when faced with work on a paper or computer you may decide that simple terms may not sound "professional." This attitude may be partly due to exposure to lawyers. Resist the temptation to try to sound like a lawyer or legal documents you have read. For example, do not use a phrase such as "The party of the first part did knowingly and willfully . . . ." If Joe Jones did it, write it that way. You are not in a position to judge how much he knew or how willful he was.

In addition, do not use formal terms or the third person to refer to your work or yourself. A phrase such as "Pursuant to his duties, the undersigned did then proceed in his vehicle to the scene of the crime" is not clear. Is it possible to record the fact of getting there in a less stilted way? "Pursuant" means "in agreement or conformity to" and usually refers to duties or orders. It is understood that you are following orders or rules. What else would you be doing? "Proceed" has the connotation of a "formal and ceremonious manner." Is that really how you got there? "Vehicle" is defined as "any means by which someone or something is carried or confined" and can mean anything from a go-cart to a space shuttle.

Even the legal, banking, and insurance communities, the last bastions of formality, are slowly turning away from legalese and moving toward much better and more easily understood language.

Should You Use Abbreviations?

This is not easy to answer. Forms abound in every area of criminal justice, with most directives stating not to abbreviate. The same forms, however, make it impossible to write out terms in full. An example can be found on the face pages in Chapter 3. When using abbreviations, always make sure that you are consistent and that they are clear to your readers. Abbreviations are dealt with more fully in Chapter 13.

Add Sketches, Photographs, and Diagrams

"A picture is worth a thousand words," and in many cases had better be added to those words. Consider the measurements taken after a traffic accident, the position of a body in a homicide, the relation of rooms and objects in a burglary, the location of an injury-causing accident, and the place where contraband was found. In each of these cases, a sketch, photograph, or diagram can help your reader have a better understanding of the scene than would having only a written description.

Practice a consistent method of looking at a scene such as looking from left to right. Do not alter your original rough drawing, but you can use it to produce a more precise one to go with your professional report. See Figures 1.6 and 1.7 for templates available for use in traffic accidents and other situations, as well as sample diagrams. If you are using a computer to write your report, you may also have access to software programs that will allow you to transport photographs or drawings directly into your report. Computer-aided design or drawing systems can help you to complete professional-looking and accurate crime scene sketches. See Figure 1.8 for samples.

Be sure to use fixed objects from which to relate positions, either in writing or when sketching. For example, a body should be shown in relation to a door or wall corner rather than to a movable table or chair. Movable objects should be shown, but measurements should be made from unchangeable features. Include the direction in which the diagram is drawn (with north usually at the top).

Photographs are another reinforcement and, taking that concept further, there is also video. It is hard to argue with what you see. In many agencies there are specialists who handle pictures and videos, but it is becoming more popular in many areas to supply everything from cameras to camcorders to field personnel. Close-ups can be made of blood spatters, tool marks, writing on walls, and other important evidence, especially that which cannot be easily removed and submitted as evidence in its actual state. Be sure to record the direction in which the photograph is taken and the names of any people in the photographs, numbering and making a key, if necessary. Record the date and time the photograph is taken and the identity of the person taking the photograph. Many agencies have special supplementary report forms to use when submitting photographs as part of a report.

A staff artist is sometimes asked to make composite sketches from information given by victims and/or witnesses. Choosing features from a series can help assemble specifics. The artist can be helped by comments like "His nose was wider ... ," "Her face was thinner ... ," etc., until a resemblance appears. The Crime Zone, Identi-Kit, CompuSketch, and ComPHOTOfit are examples of commercially available products that can help you to include sketches, diagrams, and photographs in your reports.

Evidence for Law Enforcement

Evidence has been defined as anything that can be used to prove an unknown or disputed fact. Legal evidence is defined in *Black's Law Dictionary* (8th ed., 2004) as "a broad general term meaning all admissible evidence, including both oral and

Figure 1.6
Templates

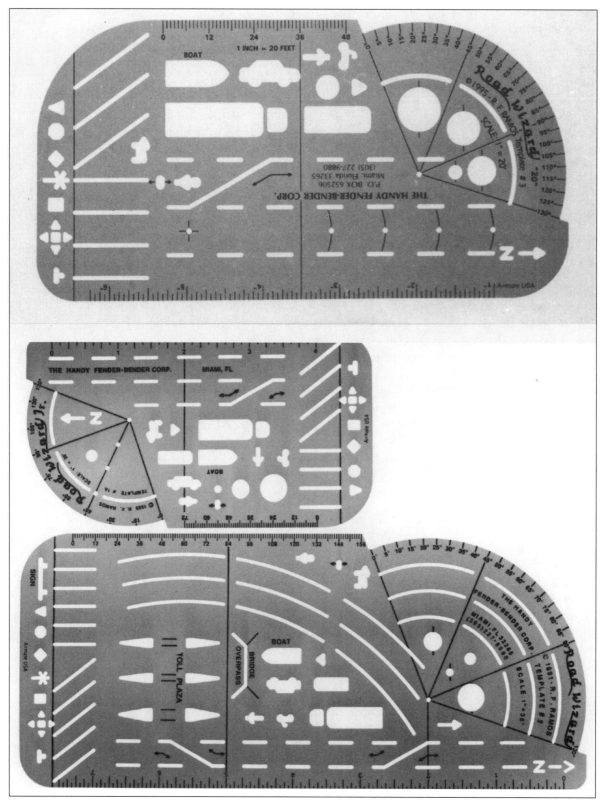

Figure 1.7
Diagrams

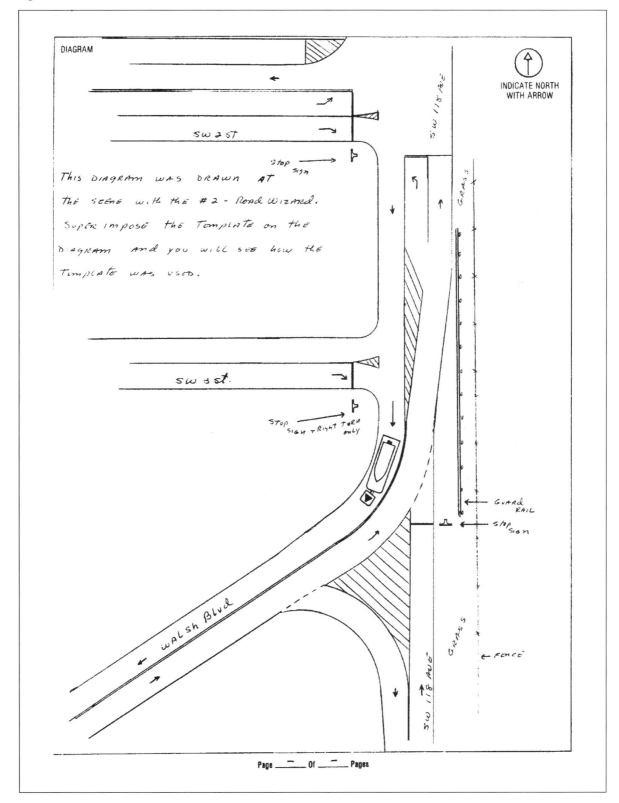

Continued

Figure 1.7—*continued*

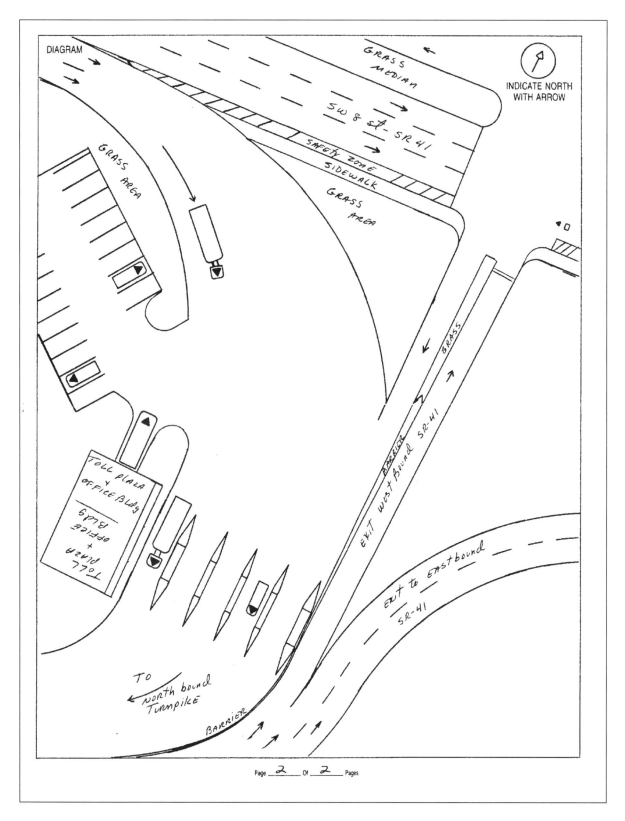

Figure 1.7—*continued*

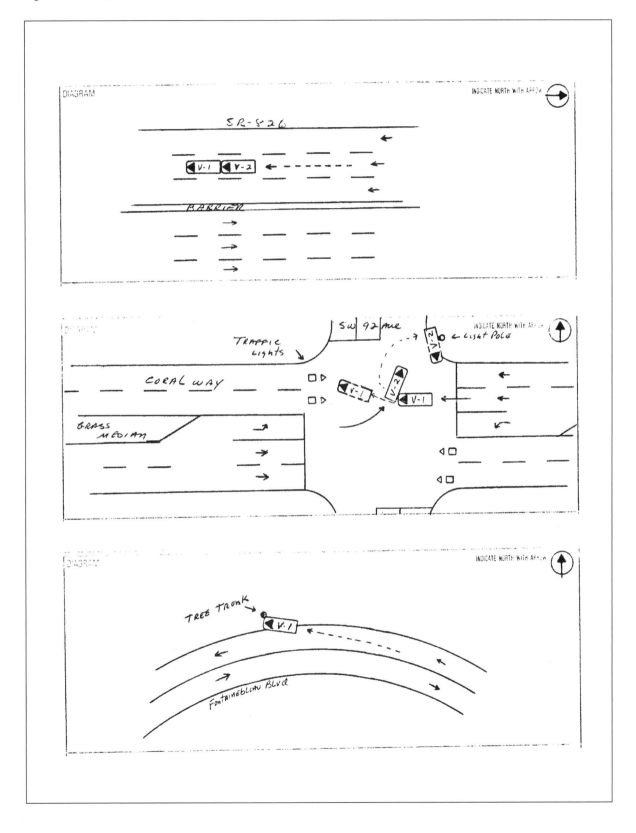

Figure 1.8
Computer-Aided Drawing Samples

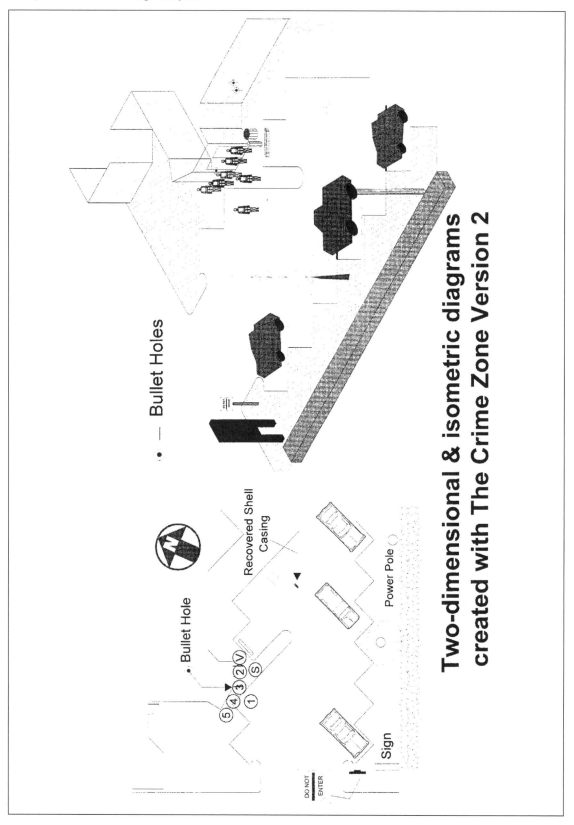

Two-dimensional & isometric diagrams created with The Crime Zone Version 2

Figure 1.8—*continued*

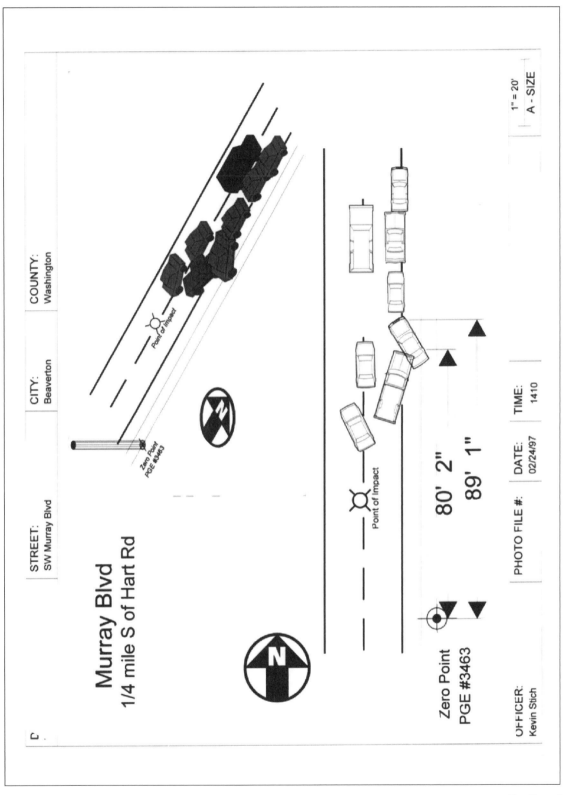

Continued

Figure 1.8—*continued*

| DESCRIPTION: Traffic Investigation | STREET: Macafee | CITY: Holmgren | COUNTY: White |

| OFFICER: Dotson | PHOTO FILE #: 12314 | DATE: 01/26/97 | TIME: 3:00 pm | 1" = 50' A - SIZE |

Figure 1.8—*continued*

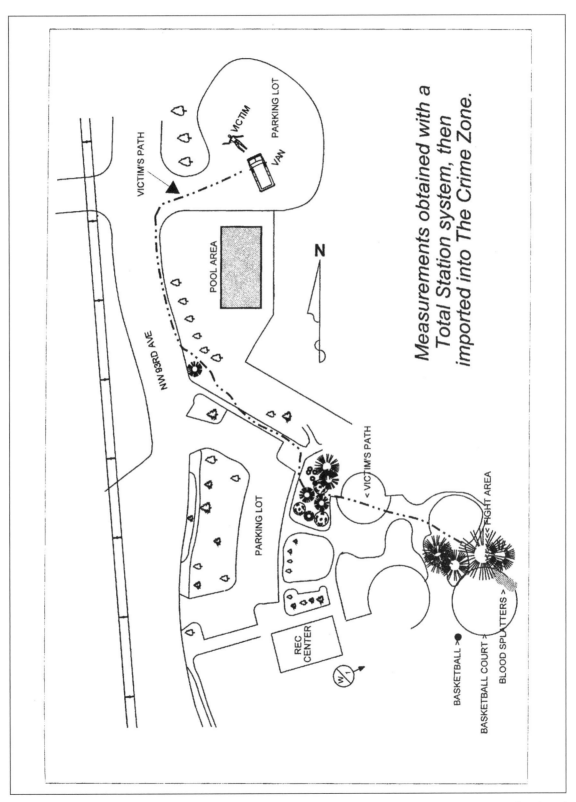

Measurements obtained with a Total Station system, then imported into The Crime Zone.

Continued

Figure 1.8—*continued*

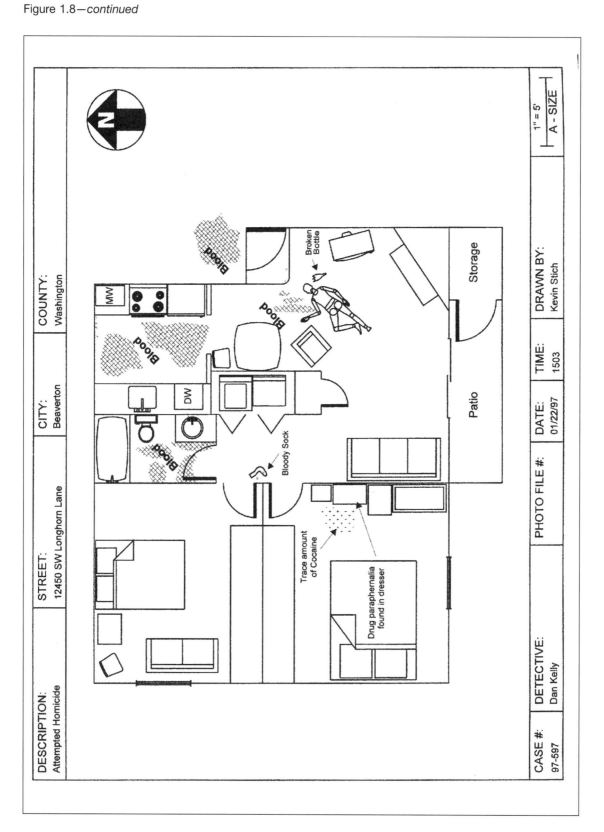

Figure 1.8—*continued*

The following is just a sample of the hundreds of investigation symbols available in The Crime Zone.

documentary, but with a further implication that it must be of such a character as tends reasonably and substantially to prove the point, not to raise a mere suspicion or conjecture." A lay dictionary defines evidence as "any species of proof, or probative matter, legally presented at the trial of an issue, by the act of the parties and, through the medium of witnesses, records, documents, exhibits, concrete objects, etc., for the purpose of inducing belief in the minds of the court or jury as to their contention."

Any evidence you find should be listed in your notebook and placed in appropriate containers so the integrity of the objects is not compromised. Separate objects to avoid contamination, place in containers that will prevent mold or drying out, and turn them in to the designated places as soon as possible. Maintain the chain of evidence as required by your agency and jurisdiction, get receipts for whatever leaves your hands, and note the time and place. The paper trail protects the victims, the integrity of the evidence, and your own reputation.

Types of Evidence

Real evidence for law enforcement, forensics, security, or corrections involves tangible, identifiable objects such as weapons, clothing, confiscated objects, semen, or blood. Be careful about listing evidence that appears to be blood, drugs, or precious metals. Common sense would suggest that it is what it appears to be, but you should list such evidence with phrases such as "appearing to be blood" or "substance appearing to be marijuana" or "yellow metal" or "gold in color." For example, a lost ring may look like platinum set with a diamond but may be silver set with a paste imitation.

Evidence records must be as accurate as possible. Remember the blood records found in the O.J. Simpson murder case and the difficulty proving the finding, as well as the decisions made through DNA testing? Identify who claims what the evidence is, but do not identify it yourself until so designated by laboratory examination.

Direct evidence includes what you or other persons know through the use of the five senses. Many people think that this is better than real evidence; however, people may lie or be mistaken. Tangible objects can be brought to court and can stand on their own. To be accurate, a witness must be in a position to make observations, must be physically competent, and must be unbiased, or biases must be known and explained in the report. For example, if a man waiting to be picked up by a friend sees a crash involving that friend, would his testimony be unbiased? Also remember that, in major cases, people may falsely claim to be witnesses.

Circumstantial evidence is evidence from which inferences can be drawn. These inferences can establish a fact or series of facts tending to prove the elements of a crime. The suspect's presence in the vicinity of a crime similar to one committed previously indicates that the person could have committed this crime, but it is not proof. Be very careful to examine the situation. Protect yourself as well as the suspect by presenting such material without drawing any conclusion from it. Many people believe that circumstantial evidence is the weakest type of evidence. This is not so if it is clearly documented and laid out for the court. Many criminal cases are successfully prosecuted based on circumstantial evidence.

Evidence Collected for Security

While much of the information on real, direct, and circumstantial evidence used in law enforcement applies to security, there are significant differences as well. Law enforcement personnel must focus on the possibility — however remote, in many cases — of a report going to court. That eventuality is much less likely for security personnel.

Retail stores may prefer to handle shoplifting on their own and call police when the matter goes over a certain dollar amount. They also must sometimes deal with violence, traffic problems in parking lots, even sexual assault. The same is true of hotels, hospitals, condominiums, airports, and the many places that use private security to protect people, property, and their public images. If a problem escalates, the preliminary report or log is very important, but security personnel rarely have to write reports that are as complicated as those done by criminal investigation divisions, which must include detailed explanations of how the evidence was found and handled.

Security personnel are especially concerned with the amount of evidence gathered to protect the public in advance: equipment malfunction, unsecured doors or windows, water damage, fire hazards, vandalism, safety hazards, trespassers, and many other things that could interfere with the orderly functioning of a facility (see Figure 1.3). Security personnel tend to be basically loyal to the employer rather than to the government, but both often benefit.

Evidence Collected for Probation and Parole

Probation officers are responsible for writing the PSIR, which many judges depend upon when determining a suitable sentence. These reports require much evidence: identifying the current offense as perceived by the police, the victim, and the offender; checking for a prior record; interviewing the offender, family, friends, teachers, neighbors, psychologists, and others influencing the offender; reviewing the past and present situation affecting responses and attitudes; giving sentencing recommendations; making recommendations regarding restitution, training, and job placement; and including information on other factors such as if, when, and how the best interests of the community and the individual are served.

Parole officers see an offender after he or she has been released from prison. The released individual must then report regularly to a parole officer, who often has too large a group to monitor and must see six or more persons a day. With information on the offense and the offender, along with conditions listed for parole, the officer must determine quickly if the parolee is following the rules imposed. This may involve testing for alcohol or drugs and checking on employment or community activities. The officer may visit the home or workplace and report on situations affecting return to prison, continued supervision, or termination of parolee status.

While opinions are valued in this type of report, it is still important to back up the *why* with evidence and statements whenever possible.

Need for Documentation

Documentation is the backbone of criminal justice. Without accurate records, action is incomplete. The investigator, whether a security guard, beat officer, corrections officer, or homicide detective, may handle an incident — from an injury report to purse snatching to murder — with the utmost competence. What must follow is an accurate, brief, and complete report, and that usually takes much longer than handling the original problem. Failure to document the investigation adequately could make the investigator look incompetent.

Periodically, criminal justice publications contain complaints about the lack of report writing skills among law enforcement officers. In one article, the headline was "Survey Says Rookies Lack the 'Write' Stuff." In preparing the second edition of this book, the authors wrote to more than 150 federal, state, municipal, and county law enforcement agencies, as well as to numerous corrections and private security agencies. Many of the chief executives and training officers responded, expressing their beliefs that poor or inadequate report writing continues to be one of their agency's major problems.

Writing used to be taught more rigorously, but current technology has lured people into thinking that machines can take much of the responsibility for composing and correcting information as it is recorded. A recent survey pointed out that of field training officers surveyed, 67 percent said that trainees could not handle basic report writing.

The dislike of and difficulty with the task of report writing seems to be almost universal among law enforcement, forensics, corrections, probation and parole, and security officers. The length of time on the job does not seem to determine either the ability to write reports or the dislike of the task. This points to a major problem for agencies, because writing takes up more than half of the workday and is an important function of the job. As our old-timer said in the introduction, "If it's not written down, it doesn't exist."

Added to these problems is the fact that, in some areas, little or no training is given before a badge is pinned on. Because report writing is so important and is a major duty of those in the criminal justice system, do not the individuals deserve thorough training in this important area of responsibility?

What Should Be Documented?

If you ask yourself whether you need to complete a report on an incident, you should already have an answer to the question. If you thought about it, then you need to submit a report documenting the situation. The report is often the first link in the criminal justice system. Criminal justice personnel are often hesitant to write reports, saying that nothing happened at a particular time or situation.

Sometimes a report saying nothing happened is crucial to the prosecution of a criminal case or in providing or disproving a civil case. One of the authors of this text investigated a robbery case when he was a detective. The case went to trial about one year after the incident and was built mostly on circumstantial evidence and a very weak eyewitness identification. The defendant took the stand in his own defense and claimed that he could not have been in the area of the robbery because one of his automobile's tires had gone flat on the other side of town at a particular intersection, and he had walked to a service station with the tire to have it repaired. He even provided a receipt from the service station for the repair of a tire. Fortunately, shortly after this case had been reported to the police, a supervisor had placed a number of officers at strategic check posts to watch for suspects. One of the intersections was the one at which the suspect claimed he had a flat tire. The officer had submitted a follow-up report saying he was on a check post, the time that he had arrived and was recalled, and that he had not noticed anything suspicious. Without the report, the prosecution would not have ever known that there was an officer at the intersection in question. The prosecution was able to call the officer to the stand to rebut the defendant's testimony. On cross-examination, the defense attorney questioned the officer on how he could be sure one year after the incident that the defendant's automobile was not at the intersection. The officer replied that if there had been a disabled vehicle at the intersection, he would have had to have helped with traffic control because of the design of the intersection and the heavy flow of traffic. He said that if he had to do that, he would have included it in his report to account for having been away from his assigned task. The prosecutor in the case later reported that the officer's testimony and the report documenting that nothing suspicious was seen on that assignment was crucial in obtaining a conviction. The moral of the story is that a report saying nothing unusual happened may be very important at some future time.

This is a reason why security officers keep shift logs of their workday. Such logs may go a long way in helping to defend their employers from a civil claim such as a "slip and fall" case when daily logs record the fact that a check of a location was made before and immediately after a reported fall, and no oil, water, or other reported causes of a fall were noted.

Keep in mind the purpose of your report, who will read the report, and all the possible ways the report may be used. In many traffic collision reports, the officers are only interested in having enough information to substantiate the issuance of a citation for the cause of the collision. Another equally important use of those reports is the documentation of facts that are important to the insurance and/or civil case that may develop. While this may not seem very important to officers at the time of the investigation, it may become important when they are called on to provide depositions or are called as witnesses in a civil case. The information will be extremely important to the family who has lost its vehicle or its ability to make a living as a result of the collision and is seeking just compensation. The information in a report may be crucial to a government agency or private landowner responsible for the location of the incident and can help in defending against a civil suit.

The ABCs of Report Writing (Whatever Your Field)

1. *Accuracy is important in word usage as well as in information.* Poor word choice will get you into trouble. One officer wound up in court on three occasions trying to explain what he meant when he said the suspect had "crowded" him. Was he pushed, shoved up against the wall, verbally intimidated, or what? *Value judgments and conclusory words must be avoided, and details should be given instead.* For example, do not say, "The child seemed afraid of his father." Instead, provide the facts that led you to the assumption: "When the father came into the room, the boy stopped talking and began to cry. The father smiled and offered the boy candy, but the son backed up to his mother and clung to her, crying harder." Specific statements and evidence will result in a stronger report and provide you with useful information when you testify in court.

2. *Brevity is important, as long as it is not used at the cost of losing accuracy or completeness.* Brevity is not addressing the length of the report but rather the style in which the report is written. Be concise in your writing. Never use a complicated word or phrase when a simple one will do. Use first person, active voice wherever possible: "I checked the door" is shorter and more to the point than using third person, passive voice: "The door was checked by this officer."

3. *Completeness is essential.* There is a story told of Abraham Lincoln as a young lawyer. According to the story, Lincoln won a case because he proved that the moon was not shining on a night that a presumed suspect was identified by the light of a full moon. You can't assume anything, even what seems most logical. A supposedly simple case of drunk driving made the front page in a paper in Australia. The report stated that the offender's eyes were bloodshot. "Both of them?" asked the defense attorney. Looking at the now clear-eyed defendant, the officer said firmly, "Yes, both of them," whereupon the defendant removed his clear artificial eye and rolled it on the table. Case dismissed.

Reports should be written in an objective manner (avoiding "slanting," which is the use of words with emotional or judgmental overtones) and should include all information, even that which might benefit the defense. Reports need to be written in a clear manner, a manner having the same meaning to all readers, and they need to be mechanically correct, using proper English. Reports need to be written legibly and submitted punctually.

Summary

1. Reports are written for operational and administrative purposes. For operational purposes, law enforcement reports document actions by persons involved in crimes, incidents, and accidents and actions by officers, give

facts for follow-up, help prosecutors decide on charges, indicate MO and trademarks, help you to recall the details of the case to testify in court, help to keep track of investigations, and pinpoint high incident-of-crime times and places. Administrative purposes of reports are to determine follow-up needed, send materials to other agencies, help get public cooperation and enhance public relations, form the backbone of reports to administrators to support budget requests, help management determine training needs, and determine who receives advancements and transfers. The operational needs of reports by security officers are to note dangerous conditions, prevent employee theft and shoplifting, promote a good public image, and document responses to public demands. Administrative needs are to protect stockholders, help secure funds, and cooperate with similar institutions. Probation officers thoroughly investigate offenders. Their reports include giving recommendations to the court about incarceration and probation. Parole reports include details on their investigations and recommendations about the release of persons serving prison sentences and the retake of persons who have violated the conditions of their parole.

2. Security operations vary from a single guard to large companies that provide a wide variety of security and investigative services. Security reports are usually directed to their employers.

3. The minimum information for reports includes the *who*, *what*, *when*, *where*, and *how* with necessary details. The *why* is not supposed to be given by law enforcement unless it is obvious from the evidence. The *why* may be a part of writing by probation and parole officers who are expected to make recommendations to the court or parole boards.

4. To get started in report writing you need a notebook and a black pen. If a notebook is not supplied, choose one, either loose-leaf or bound. Print or write clearly on only one side of the page and include identification, facts, and sketches to help write your formal report and refresh your memory if you go to court. File notebooks chronologically.

5. Remember that your job is to investigate, not just to record what people tell you. If someone gives you what seems to be a self-serving statement, document it first and then ask about and record the answers about inconsistencies and his or her explanations about the inconsistencies.

6. Look over the crime scene, make a rough sketch in your notebook, and use the sketch to help you prepare a more precise one in your report.

7. List the evidence found and maintain the chain of custody. Preserve its condition. When you turn evidence in, get receipts, lab reports, statements, and whatever else is needed to keep a complete record and provide documentation of the chain of custody.

8. There are three kinds of evidence: (1) real evidence, which is made up of tangible objects such as marijuana or blood; (2) direct evidence, which includes what you or any witnesses know through the use of the five senses; and (3) circumstantial evidence, which involves known facts from which inferences can be made.

9. Accuracy, brevity, and completeness are the ABCs of report writing.

Chapter 1—TEST

1. Operational uses of law enforcement reports include these: documenting the actions by persons involved in _____, _____, _____, and give pertinent facts to determine if a _____ is required, help prosecutors _____, point out _____ and _____ to show similarities between crimes, help you recall _____, help to keep track of _____ on an investigation, and pinpoint _____.

2. Administrative uses of law enforcement reports include determining what kind of _____ is needed; sending _____ to other agencies, states, and the federal government; assisting in obtaining _____ in community policing; forming the backbone of reports to the _____, _____, and _____ legislature for budgeting purposes, determining training needs; and determining who receives _____ or _____.

3. The _____ _____ completed by security personnel follows the pattern for law enforcement writing.

4. The notebook may be loose-leaf or bound, depending on your agency. It is usually 3 × 5″. _____ ink should be used. Notebooks should bear _____, which includes name and number, but they should not contain _____ material.

5. Minimum information on a report includes the _____, _____, _____, _____, and _____, such as news accounts contain. The *why* of the case must be treated carefully to avoid making a value _____ unless a suspect tells why in a _____. The *why* is addressed in the _____.

6. There are three kinds of evidence: _____, _____, and _____.

7. A picture is worth a thousand words. _____, _____, and _____ are integral parts of an incident report.

8. Sketches made on the scene should not be _____. Use _____ points from which to relate bodies or objects. In diagrams and pictures identify _____, _____, and _____.

9. Maintain the chain of custody of evidence. List what was _____, its condition, and what was done with it. Request _____ when you turn over material, and be sure to give a _____ when you accept anything from others.

10. Taking a notebook to court is _____. If you do so, you may be required to _____ it to the court. File notebooks by date of _____ and _____, and by _____, so that you will have a memory bank.

11. The ABCs of report writing are _____, _____, and _____.

CHAPTER 2

Starting to Write

As mentioned in Chapter 1, people write for many different reasons. Many people simply sit down and start writing, whether they are writing a simple note, a long report, or a term paper. In this chapter you will learn a simplified method that can be used anytime you need to write — on the job, at home, or for school.

Planning Your Writing

Most people spend time planning their work or pleasure activities. They would not think of going on a road trip without a map and a travel plan, yet, when they sit down to write something out, they dive right into it without having done any planning. They often wonder why the finished product does not come out in the form or order they desired.

Writing a well-written report requires planning. You may have heard the old military saying about the five "Ps": Pre-Planning-Prevents-Poor-Performance. That saying holds *very* true in writing.

Writing a report of any length or importance requires several steps. These steps start prior to writing the report, and they continue during the writing phase and after. This chapter will teach you a method of organizing your reports that can be used for any type of writing that you need to complete.

Completing the Face Page

Many reports start with the completion of the face page. The face page often provides the basic identifying information about the who, what, when, where, and how of an incident. Many people new to the criminal justice field recount that they believed that report writing involved completing forms with a number of check

DOI: 10.1016/B978-1-4377-5584-8.00009-8

blocks. As has been mentioned previously, it is common for those in the field to spend a good part of their workday completing reports. Filling out forms is just one part of the process. The difficult part of the job involves writing the narrative report. The face page is covered in-depth in Chapter 3. The narrative is discussed in Chapter 4.

Review Your Notes

The first step of writing the narrative report involves reviewing the notes that have been taken. These notes may be from research gathered for a term paper, from interviews and investigations conducted, from meetings attended, or from telephone calls made. (See Chapter 1 regarding notebooks and note taking.)

Make a "Shopping List"

Read through your notes and make a "shopping list." How do you make a shopping list? Just like you do when you are going to go to the store. Let's say you are going to go to Goodnow's Drug Store, the grocery market, and the gas station. You do not write yourself a note that says:

> My Shopping List
>
> I am going to go to the store today. I will arrive there by my personal automobile at about 5 p.m. When I get to Goodnow's Drug Store, I will first pick up some toilet paper. I will then move to the area where the toothpaste is displayed and purchase the most inexpensive fluoride toothpaste. I hope to purchase the largest sized tube. Oh, I need to put gas in my automobile before I go to Goodnow's. I then plan to go to the aisle . . .

No one writes out a list like that. You would write the list perhaps something more like this:

Shopping List

Goodnow's
t.p.
toothpaste
cola
film
scrub pads . . .
Groceries
meat
potatoes
milk
ice cream
sugar

flour
corn
Gas
fill-up
oil
windshield washer fluid

The "shopping list" for your report is written in the same way. You will need to use a word or two to describe each point that is in your notes or that you learned in conducting your investigation until you have a list of all of the ideas covered in your notes. Names, addresses, and other such facts should be written out completely. The facts that you gathered and are now making a list out of will not be in the order that you will use them in your report. They are in the order that you wrote them in your notebook. By making your shopping list, you have put the information from your notes into a manageable form.

Graphically, it should look something like this:

info
info
info
info
info
info
info
info
info
info
info
info

Place Information in Groups

Now you are ready for the next step. On a piece of paper, start grouping your shopping list by similar ideas or facts or information that logically fits together. Statements made by a particular person should almost always be placed in a group by themselves. Give yourself plenty of room in which to work. Using a pencil and eraser can make the task easier, but do not worry about neatness. This is for your use only in planning your report.

Graphically, your groupings will now look something like this:

info
info
info

info
info
info

info
info
info
info

info
info

Label the Groups

Your next task is to name or label each of the groups that you established. Use from one to five words to describe the major topic of the group. Statements will usually be labeled as such (e.g., Victim's Statement or John Smith's Statement).

Graphically, your labeled groups should look something like this:

LABEL
info
info
info

LABEL
info
info
info

LABEL
info
info
info
info

LABEL
info
info

Place Groups in Order

You are now ready for the final phase of the planning process: placing the labeled groups in a logical order. The groups should be put in an order that makes the most sense, assists your reader in understanding the report, or puts emphasis on the message that you are trying to impart. Often, the groups are arranged in chronological order.

Keep in mind that every report needs three things: an introduction, a body of information, and a conclusion. In both writing and in speech making you want to tell your readers or audience what you are going to tell them, you then tell them what you want them to know, and then finally you tell them what you told them. The body of your report comes from your labeled groups. So, graphically, your plan will now look something like this:

INTRODUCTION

LABEL
info
info
info

LABEL
info
info
info

LABEL
info
info
info
info

LABEL
info
info

CONCLUSION

Notice the white space that is left by skipping a line between each heading. This really aids your reader and makes your report more presentable.

Writing the Report

At this point, you have a very good plan or road map to follow in writing your report. You may have to refer to your original notes often to fill in all of the facts needed to complete your report. Use subheadings for groupings that are too long or have related information. Do not forget that the information under the headings you have created should be arranged in a logical order. As you write your report, you need to write the information in its proper order.

The beautiful thing about this method is that it works for any writing, whether it is a few paragraphs long or a few hundred pages long.

Subheadings

When you start writing and you find that information under a particular heading is too long — usually more than about two paragraphs — determine if the information can be split into further groups, either as additional headings or as sub-headings. Subheadings come under a main heading and are indented. If subheadings are used, it is suggested that there be at least two subheadings under any one heading.

Proofreading and Revisions

In any writing that you do, it is very important that you proofread your work. Read your writing twice: once for content and once for spelling and punctuation errors. Use whatever references you need to help you. If you ask yourself if a word is spelled or used correctly, you probably need to look it up. If you are unsure of a grammatical or punctuation rule, either change the sentence or look up the rule in a reference. Make any required revisions. Will the reader understand what you are trying to communicate based on only the information contained in your report? Clarify if necessary. Chapter 7 will cover proofreading in detail.

Sample Writing Exercise Using the Shopping List Method

In college and criminal justice academy classrooms in which the students or recruits have not had many real-life experiences, newspaper articles or simulations can provide the facts to use in practicing report writing. Newspaper articles often give several versions of a situation, just like those in real-life situations.

Here is an example of a newspaper article, the facts of which were actually reported in a major city's daily newspaper. Students in a law enforcement writing class were assigned to take the information read to them from the newspaper article and submit a report about the incident. The students were permitted to use only the facts presented in the newspaper. The article is as follows:

The Mooseville Reporter Wednesday, March 4, 2010.

Drinking, Littering Suspect Hangs Himself in Cell Block

A 45-year-old man who couldn't post bail on a misdemeanor charge committed suicide yesterday by hanging himself with his jacket from the bars in the Mooseville Police Department cell block, police said.

Police said the man, who was arrested at 5 p.m. at First and Elm streets for public drinking and criminal littering, was extremely violent and was being held in the disorderly cell.

The man had been checked 10 minutes prior to 7:35 p.m., when he was discovered hanging. Officers said they were just about to strip him and place him in a padded cell. The officer who found him took him down and attempted to revive him but could not.

Video monitors of the cell block area where the hanging occurred do not show the interior of the cell, police said.

Police said the man had told them he was a truck driver and had given a Pine Street address as his residence.

Police declined to name the man pending notification of relatives.

Creating a Shopping List from Notes

drinking, littering suspect
found hanging by jacket
cell block
male
45 yrs. old
no bail $
3-3-10
arrested 5 p.m.
First & Elm
public drinking
crim. littering
violent
put in disorderly cell
checked 10 min. prior 7:35 p.m.
found hanging by jacket
about to strip
padded cell
officer found
took down
misdemeanor charge
attempted to revive
couldn't revive
monitor doesn't show cell
truck driver
Pine St.
police won't name next of kin

Grouping the Shopping List

drinking, littering suspect
male
45 yrs. old
truck driver
Pine St.
police won't name next of kin

public drinking
criminal littering
misdemeanor charge
arrested 5 p.m.
First & Elm
3-3-10

cell block
no bail $
violent
put in disorderly cell

about to strip
padded cell
officer found
found hanging by jacket
takes down
attempt to revive
couldn't revive

checked 10 min. prior to 7:35 p.m.
monitor doesn't show cell

Labeling the Shopping List

<u>SUSPECT INVOLVED</u>
drinking, littering suspect
male
45 yrs. old
truck driver
Pine St.
police won't name next of kin

<u>SUSPECT ARRESTED</u>
public drinking
criminal littering
misdemeanor charge
arrested 5 p.m.
First & Elm
3-3-10

<u>HELD IN CELL BLOCK</u>
cell block
no bail $
violent
put in disorderly cell

<u>OFFICER DISCOVERED SUSPECT HANGING</u>
about to strip
padded cell
officer found
found hanging by jacket
takes down
attempted to revive
couldn't revive

<u>PRIOR CHECKS</u>
checked 10 min. prior to 7:35 p.m.
monitor doesn't show cell

Placing the Labeled Shopping List in Order

At this point, the body of the report is outlined and the information needs to be put in the order in which it is to be presented. Notice that the headings "Introduction" and "Conclusion" are added.

<u>INTRODUCTION</u>

<u>SUSPECT ARRESTED</u>
public drinking
criminal littering
misdemeanor charge
arrested 5 p.m.
First & Elm
3-3-10

SUSPECT INVOLVED
drinking, littering suspect
male
45 yrs. old
truck driver
Pine St.
police won't name next of kin

HELD IN CELL BLOCK
cell block
no bail $
violent
put in disorderly cell

OFFICER DISCOVERED SUSPECT HANGING
about to strip
padded cell
officer found
found hanging by jacket
takes down
attempted to revive
couldn't revive

PRIOR CHECKS
checked 10 min. prior to 7:35 p.m.
monitor doesn't show cell

CONCLUSION

Final Report

The final report is now written, using the ordered groupings as a road map. It is necessary to place the information under the headings in a chronological or logical order because in the previously listed steps, the information is in the order that came from the notes, which may not be in such an order. It will probably be necessary and useful to refer often to your notes for details needed for the report. Some information in the shopping list included under one heading may sometimes be repeated under another heading. Information about the source of the information is included in the introduction or as needed under specific headings.

INTRODUCTION
The March 4, 2010 edition of *The Mooseville Reporter* reported on the death of a male held in the Mooseville Police Department cell block in an article titled "Drinking, Littering Suspect Hangs Himself in Cell Block." The article was read to AJ138, Police Reporting Class by the class instructor Mr. Foley at about 5:35 p.m. on March 5, 2010, and we were instructed to write a report on the article using the shopping list method of report writing.

SUSPECT ARRESTED

On March 3, 2010, at about 5:00 p.m., a male was arrested for the offenses of criminal littering and public drinking at the corner of First and Elm Streets. Both of the offenses are misdemeanors.

MALE IDENTIFIED

The male suspect was reported to be a 45-year-old truck driver who lived in the Pine Street area. Police will not release the man's name pending notification of his next of kin.

SUSPECT HELD IN CELL BLOCK

The suspect was placed in a disorderly cell due to his extremely violent behavior and his inability to post bail.

OFFICER DISCOVERED SUSPECT HANGING

As officers were just about to strip the suspect and place him in a padded cell, an officer found him hanging by his jacket from the bars in the cell block. The officer who found the suspect took him down from the bars and began an unsuccessful attempt at resuscitation.

PRIOR CHECKS

The man had been checked 10 minutes prior to 7:35 p.m., when he was discovered hanging. Police said the video camera monitors of the cell block area where the hanging occurred do not show the interior of the cell.

CONCLUSION

A 45-year-old truck driver arrested for public drinking and criminal littering hanged himself in the Mooseville Police Department cell block on March 3, 2010. Police declined to identify him until his family is notified.

Notice that the introduction clarifies the source from which the information was obtained. It is always important to remember to document in your report where each piece of information came from. If you do not provide this documentation, you are assuming responsibility for the information. In a courtroom setting you may or may not be allowed to testify about that information, based on the rules of evidence and court decisions that vary from jurisdiction to jurisdiction. Also notice that the conclusion summarizes the information for us. The information in the conclusion is almost always information that is already in the actual report. The conclusion also is the place to tell the reader what will happen next if such information is available. Agencies may require a conclusion, summary, disposition, or combination thereof.

Do not forget the importance of proofreading, making revisions, and looking up or changing areas about which you are unsure. Remember that you are judged by the quality of the reports you submit.

If you are thinking that this process takes too long to use with every report you write, you are absolutely correct. If you follow these procedures a number of times, you will find that you can start skipping steps. You will get to the point that you can start with making the headings that will be used in your report, place them into their chronological or logical order, and then write your report using the headings as your road map. Hopefully, by that point you will also be in the habit of proofreading your report and making revisions as necessary.

Basic Recommendations for Writing Reports

Spelling, Jargon, and Abbreviation

When you are ready to begin writing, you should have a good dictionary nearby and you should use it. If you have to ask yourself whether something is right, you should look it up. Avoid writing reports that are full of jargon and abbreviations. Use words rather than initials, abbreviations, or symbols. Remember that while you and most of your immediate co-workers will understand what you write, the report may be read by people outside of your agency who may be completely unfamiliar with your agency's jargon and abbreviations. Keep your language and format simple and to the point. The facts presented must be clear to the reader. Do not use penal or traffic code sections unless they are specific to crimes listed and defined in your report. For example, do not use: I arrested the suspect for 187. Instead, write: I arrested the suspect for Homicide, a violation of Section 187 of the California Penal Code. Use slang only when giving an exact and necessary quote. These concepts will be covered further in Chapters 3, 11, 12, and 13.

Verb Tense

There are three major tenses used in criminal justice reporting: present, past, and future.

Present tense: I am notifying my insurance company of the theft.
Past tense: I notified my insurance company of the theft.
Future tense: Tomorrow I will notify my insurance company of the theft.

Most reports are written in the past tense. Attempt to use only one tense in your report and avoid switching back and forth between tenses. An exception, of course, is when you are taking a statement, and you are accurately reporting the statement. Example: "The robber then said, 'Give me the money!'" This will be covered further in Chapter 8.

Active versus Passive Voice

Reports are best when written in the active voice, because such sentences are clear and normally require fewer words. In sentences written in the active voice, the subject of the sentence is doing the acting. Example: The officer saw the two suspects trespassing on the school grounds. In the passive voice the subject is acted upon. Such statements normally take more words and are often confusing. Example: The two suspects in the case were observed by the officer trespassing on the school grounds. Who was trespassing on the school grounds? The officer or the suspects? The use of active voice will be covered further in Chapter 8.

Pronoun Agreement

A major problem in reports is the failure of the pronouns to agree with the subject. If the subject is singular, the pronoun that replaces it must also be singular. Examples: Brent Smith stated that he damaged the property. The two suspects Smith and Jones admitted that they damaged the property. It is also extremely important that the reader be able to understand to whom the pronoun is referring. Often the use of pronouns confuses the situation. This can be clarified by using the names of the persons. Example: Smith and Jones fought. He then punched him in the mouth. Who was punched in the mouth, Smith or Jones? Clarify by writing that Smith and Jones fought. Smith punched Jones in the mouth. The use of pronouns in reports will be covered further in Chapter 9.

Third Person versus First Person

Many criminal justice agencies traditionally required employees to write reports in the third person. Example: The undersigned officer arrived at the scene at 1238 hours (or "this officer," "the undersigned," "this writer," etc.). The theory was that such writing made the report more objective. Objectivity is shown by writing factual reports, not by using the third person in an attempt to sound objective. The authors of this text recommend that criminal justice personnel use first person "I" statements to describe their own actions in reports. Example: "I arrested John Smith for the burglary of the Hotel Street Bakery" rather than "The undersigned officer arrested the suspect for the Hotel Street Bakery burglary." The use of the first person will be discussed further in Chapter 5.

Gender-Neutral Language

It is important for reports to remain gender neutral. In traditional writing, the use of *he* and *him* was considered "universal" and applied to both men and women. Most criminal laws were written in such a fashion and it was convention to write criminal justice reports in that way. This is no longer acceptable. Many traditional terms are easily replaced by gender-neutral terms. Examples: *personnel* for *manpower*, *mail carrier* for *mailman*, *police officer* for *policeman*. Use the proper pronoun for the sex of the person(s) involved. If there are both male and females involved or you are writing in generic terms, make the sentence plural and use gender-neutral plural pronouns. Example: "Each officer should inspect his weapon," can be rewritten as "Officers should inspect their weapons." Remember, you cannot use plural pronouns such as *their* in sentences when the subject is singular. The use of gender-neutral language will be discussed further in Chapter 12.

Superfluous Words or Legalese

As discussed in Chapter 1, avoid using superfluous words or so-called legalese in an attempt to sound "professional." Such usage often has the effect of interfering with the reader's ability to understand what you are trying to communicate. Remember the "KISS" rule: Keep it short and simple. In addition, remember the saying, "Write to express, not impress." This will be covered further in Chapters 9 and 12.

Accurate and Factual Reporting

Report what happened based on statements and physical evidence. Facts are verifiable. Anything other than facts, including inferences, suppositions, and opinions, must be labeled as such to avoid confusion. Always include information about where you obtained the information. Avoid writing subjective or conclusory statements, such as, "He made a furtive movement." Instead, describe the actions that led you to believe that he was making a movement that you considered to be furtive.

Conciseness

Conciseness is related to the concept of brevity in the ABCs of report writing. Say as much as is necessary with as few words as possible. Avoid the use of unnecessary words and phrases. Avoid the use of run-on or extremely long sentences and paragraphs that have a tendency to confuse both you as the writer and your readers.

Promptness

Reports must be completed in a timely manner. Failure to submit arrest reports or reports on judicial determination of probable cause will result in the dismissal of criminal cases.

> Remember that writing is a skill. It develops over time through repeated practice. There are few "natural" writers. Remember to plan your writing, proofread your work, make corrections, and use references, including dictionaries and grammar books.

Summary

1. Plan your writing. Remember the five "Ps": Pre-Planning-Prevents-Poor-Performance.

2. Review your notes from research gathered for a term paper, or from interviews, investigations, meetings, or telephone conversations. Make a "shopping

list" that describes each idea or point in one or two words based on the information in your notes.

3. Place the ideas on the "shopping list" in groups based on similarity of facts.

4. Label each of the groups by using only a few words to describe the major topic.

5. Place the groups in either logical or chronological order, whichever is appropriate for your writing. Add an introduction and conclusion if these are not already included in the groupings.

6. You now have a road map with which to start writing your report. Fill in the facts by using your notes and use subheadings as necessary.

7. Be careful with the use of abbreviations and jargon, and check your spelling for correctness.

8. Most reports are written in the past tense, with the exception of direct quotations. Keep your writing in the first person, using an active voice if your agency allows it.

9. Check for correct pronoun agreement and use gender-neutral language.

10. Avoid the use of superfluous words or legalese.

11. Complete reports that are accurate and factual as well as concise. Turn them in on time.

12. Proofread your work twice: once for content, and once for spelling and punctuation. Make revisions as necessary. Remember that you are judged by the reports that you submit.

Chapter 2 — TEST

1. In order to write properly, you should plan before starting to write.

   The five "Ps" refers to: _____

   _____

2. The shopping list method involves several steps. The first step is to
   _____. Next you take the information and place it
   in groups, which are then _____ by using a few words to describe
   each group. Now you need to place the groups in _____ or
   _____ order. Add a(n) _____ and
   _____ if these are not included in the groupings. Now you write
   your report by filling in the _____ and referring to your notes
   as necessary.

3. After completing your report, do not forget to _____ and make
   _____ as necessary.

CHAPTER 3

The Face Page

Trying to explain the typical face page of a report (the form with blocks in which facts are to be entered) is like trying to draw a blueprint. Different states, agencies, and departments vary in the number and specifics of the forms they use. In addition, these forms are frequently supplemented, revised, or eliminated by the various agencies. Basic information is included on all face page reports. Each agency has its own policy regarding the number of different forms used. Some agencies use one form for all criminal cases except those for recording motor vehicle collisions. Many agencies have specialized forms for particular types of cases. The variations in the number of forms used by agencies is diverse. For example, the Tucson, Arizona Police Department uses more than 100 different forms; the Washoe County, Nevada Sheriff's Office reports utilizing more than 200 different forms; the Department of Corrections of the Commonwealth of Kentucky uses several hundred different forms; and the County of Suffolk, New York Police Department uses 933 different forms.

Just as the forms vary, so do laws and ordinances. As a result, it is often very difficult to compare statistical compilations between jurisdictions. Tying together this bewildering collection of information is the Uniform Crime Reporting (UCR) Program, through which the various states voluntarily submit material to the Federal Bureau of Investigation (FBI). These statistics are submitted using the UCR standard classifications and definitions of crimes. (This does not mean that the classifications and definitions contained within the UCRs are accepted by the participating states. The Uniform Crime Classifications are categorized only for the purpose of the monthly voluntary reporting system.)

Bear in mind that the examples given here, even the Uniform Crime Classification, are not necessarily accepted for action in every jurisdiction. It is advisable to request forms and compare them. For example, to the uninitiated, burglary and sexual assault would appear to be easily classifiable crimes. Not so. Interpretation of these crimes and the face pages on which to report them vary widely from state to

57

© 2011 Elsevier Inc. All rights reserved.

state and even within states. In certain jurisdictions, burglary refers only to homes; in others, the term includes business establishments. In still others, burglary can occur within any enclosed area. This would include vehicles such as cars and some types of boats, but not motorcycles (although telephone booths would qualify). Sexual assault varies in degree based on the victim's age or mental status, degree of consent, and a number of other factors dependent upon the laws of a particular jurisdiction.

The value of the face page is that it offers a quick checklist for the writer and a fast survey for the reader. Sometimes certain sections are specially marked (usually by shaded areas) for information that is to be fed into computers. With some automated reporting systems, the face page is actually formatted in the computer and appears on the screen when a report is being typed.

A well-organized face page orders the material and prompts the memory so that the writer is not so dependent on his or her own memory, and the busy reader can see at a glance whether vital information has been omitted. Although recordings of oral reports have been and will continue to be utilized, it is advisable to learn how to handle the face page.

This chapter includes information about the Uniform Crime Reporting Program and examples of the Uniform Crime Classification system. There are examples of multipurpose and single-purpose face pages (sometimes called face sheets or initial incident reports), methods of gathering information, and some basic information and general rules about filling in the blanks on face pages. Also included is information about writing synopses, along with suggestions of mistakes to avoid.

UCR Crime Definitions

The following information was obtained from the *Uniform Crime Reporting Handbook* by the FBI. The International Association of Chiefs of Police (IACP) formed a Committee on Uniform Crime Records in the 1920s to develop a uniform system to report and record crime statistics. A plan for crime reporting was completed in 1929 and became the foundation of the Uniform Crime Reporting Program.

Seven criminal offenses were used to define the Crime Index, which is used to judge the crime picture in a jurisdiction and for comparison purposes between jurisdictions. The Index Offenses, called Part I offenses, include murder, rape, robbery, aggravated assault, burglary, larceny, and motor vehicle theft. In 1979, Congress mandated that arson be included as an Index Offense. All other criminal offenses except traffic violations are considered Part II offenses.

To allow comparison of statistics between jurisdictions, it was necessary to develop standardized definitions of offenses so that all crimes reported as one type of offense were of the same nature, without regard to differences between definitions in local laws or ordinances.

Crime reporting by states and cities began in 1930. Congress then enacted legislation that gave the responsibility for gathering crime statistics to the Attorney General, who in turn designated the FBI as the responsible agency.

Each month, law enforcement agencies report all known Part I offenses, as well as all cases cleared via prosecution or by exceptional means. "Exceptional means" includes cases in which the law enforcement agency knows the identity of the offender and has enough information to prosecute the offender, but is prevented from prosecuting by some reason outside the control of the agency. Examples of exceptional means closings include cases in which the offender is dead, in which extradition is denied, or in which the victim refuses to prosecute.

In addition, law enforcement agencies report each month the arrests of all persons for both Part I and Part II offenses. The program now gathers statistics from nearly 16,000 law enforcement agencies.

While this system was originally based on the recommendations of the 1920s report of the Committee on Uniform Crime Records, it is not static — there have been committees, conferences, and surveys of the Uniform Crime Reporting Program. The "Blueprint for the Future of the Uniform Crime Reporting Program" was released in 1985. More extensive information is expected to be collected in the future by the National Incident-Based Reporting System (NIBRS, pronounced Ni-bers). According to the Criminal Justice Information Services (CJIS) of the FBI, "NIBRS collects data on each single incident and arrest within 22 offense categories made up of 46 specific crimes called Group A offenses. For each of the offenses coming to the attention of law enforcement, various facts about the crime are collected. In addition to the Group A offenses, there are 11 Group B offenses for which only arrest data are reported." As can be seen, NIBRS collects much more data than UCR. Figure 3.1 is a sample incident report that can be used to collect NIBRS information. The FBI has handbooks available to assist agencies in reporting Uniform Crime Reporting and NIBRS data.

As of 2008, almost 40 percent of reporting law enforcement agencies were participating in NIBRS, including the state Uniform Crime Reporting systems of 31 states. Thus, the FBI is collecting both NIBRS data and traditional UCR data. The FBI continues to publish crime data for the country, although it discontinued printed versions of its crime data reports in 2006 and switched to online versions only. Three annual UCR series are *Crime in the United States, Law Enforcement Officers Killed and Assaulted,* and *Hate Crime Statistics* (for more information, go to www.fbi.gov/ucr/).

In the meantime, law enforcement agencies will continue to submit statistics following the original UCR program using the following definitions.

PART I OFFENSES:

1. Criminal Homicide
   a. Murder and non-negligent manslaughter
   b. Manslaughter by negligence
      This classification does not include attempts to kill (aggravated assault), suicides, accidental deaths, or justifiable homicide.
2. Rape
   a. Rape by force
   b. Attempts to commit forcible rape
      This does not include statutory offenses, in which no force is involved and victim is under the legal age of consent.

Figure 3.1
Incident Report

ORI #:

INCIDENT #:

REPORT TYPE: ☐ INITIAL REPORT ☐ SUPPLEMENT

INCIDENT REPORT
(EXAMPLE)

INCIDENT STATUS:
☐ UNFOUNDED
☐ CLEARED BY ARREST
☐ CLEARED EXCEPTIONALLY

A ☐ DEATH OF OFFENDER
B ☐ PROSECUTION DECLINED
C ☐ EXTRADITION DECLINED
D ☐ REFUSED TO COOPERATE
E ☐ JUVENILE, NO CUSTODY
N ☐ NOT APPLICABLE

EXCEPTIONAL CLEARANCE DATE:

OFFENSE

COMPLAINANT: (Last, First, Middle)   **PHONE:** (Home) (   )

ADDRESS: (Street, City, State, Zip)   (Business) (   )

LOCATION OF INCIDENT: (Address Or Block No.)

OFFENSE:	(Check If Bias Motivated)	OFFENDER:
1.	1. ☐	1.
2.	2. ☐	2.
3.	3. ☐	3.

UCR OFFENSE CODE: 1. 2. 3.   **DATE(S) OF INCIDENT:**   **TIME(S) OF INCIDENT:**

BIAS MOTIVATION: (Check one for Offense #1)

RACIAL
11 ☐ ANTI - WHITE
12 ☐ ANTI - BLACK
13 ☐ ANTI - AMERICAN INDIAN / ALASKAN NATIVE
14 ☐ ANTI - ASIAN / PACIFIC ISLANDER
15 ☐ ANTI - MULTI - RACIAL GROUP

ETHNICITY / NATIONAL ORIGIN
31 ☐ ANTI - ARAB
32 ☐ ANTI - HISPANIC
33 ☐ ANTI - OTHER ETHNICITY / NATIONAL ORIGIN

RELIGIOUS
21 ☐ ANTI - JEWISH
22 ☐ ANTI - CATHOLIC
23 ☐ ANTI - PROTESTANT
24 ☐ ANTI - ISLAMIC (MOSLEM)
25 ☐ ANTI - OTHER RELIGION
26 ☐ ANTI - MULTI - RELIGIOUS GROUP
27 ☐ ANTI - ATHEISM / AGNOSTICISM

SEXUAL
41 ☐ ANTI - MALE HOMOSEXUAL (GAY)
42 ☐ ANTI - FEMALE HOMOSEXUAL (LESBIAN)
43 ☐ ANTI - HOMOSEXUAL (GAYS AND LESBIANS)
44 ☐ ANTI - HETEROSEXUAL
45 ☐ ANTI - BISEXUAL

ENTER BIAS MOTIVATION CODE IF DIFFERENT FROM OFFENSE #1
#2 [ ][ ]
#3 [ ][ ]

OFFENSE STATUS: (Check Only One Per Offense)
1. A ☐ ATTEMPTED C ☐ COMPLETED
2. A ☐ ATTEMPTED C ☐ COMPLETED
3. A ☐ ATTEMPTED C ☐ COMPLETED

OFFENDER(S) USED: (Check As Many As Apply)
A ☐ ALCOHOL
C ☐ COMPUTER EQUIP.
D ☐ DRUGS
N ☐ NOT APPLICABLE

(For Burglary Only)
NUMBER OF PREMISES ENTERED: _____
METHOD OF ENTRY: F ☐ FORCIBLE   N ☐ NO FORCE

LOCATION OF OFFENSE: (Check Only One) (Enter Code Number for Offense #2 ____ #3 ____)
01 ☐ AIR / BUS / TRAIN TERMINAL
02 ☐ BANK / SAVINGS & LOAN
03 ☐ BAR / NIGHT CLUB
04 ☐ CHURCH / SYNAGOGUE / TEMPLE
05 ☐ COMMERCIAL / OFFICE BUILDING
06 ☐ CONSTRUCTION SITE
07 ☐ CONVENIENCE STORE
08 ☐ DEPARTMENT / DISCOUNT STORE
09 ☐ DRUG STORE / DR'S OFFICE / HOSPITAL
10 ☐ FIELD / WOODS
11 ☐ GOVERNMENT / PUBLIC BUILDINGS
12 ☐ GROCERY / SUPERMARKET
13 ☐ HIGHWAY / ROAD / ALLEY
14 ☐ HOTEL / MOTEL / ETC.
15 ☐ JAIL / PRISON
16 ☐ LAKE / WATERWAY
17 ☐ LIQUOR STORE
18 ☐ PARKING LOT / GARAGE
19 ☐ RENTAL / STORAGE FACILITY
20 ☐ RESIDENCE / HOME
21 ☐ RESTAURANT
22 ☐ SCHOOL / COLLEGE
23 ☐ SERVICE / GAS STATION
24 ☐ SPECIALTY STORE (TV, FUR, ETC.)
25 ☐ OTHER / UNKNOWN

TYPE CRIMINAL ACTIVITY: (Check Up To Three)
B ☐ BUYING / RECEIVING
C ☐ CULTIVATING / MANUFACTURING / PUBLISHING
D ☐ DISTRIBUTING / SELLING
E ☐ EXPLOITING CHILDREN
O ☐ OPERATING / PROMOTING / ASSISTING
P ☐ POSSESSING / CONCEALING
T ☐ TRANSPORTING / TRANSMITTING / IMPORTING
U ☐ USING / CONSUMING

TYPE WEAPON / FORCE INVOLVED: (Check Up To Three) (Enter A In Box If Automatic)
11 ☐ FIREARM (type not stated)
12 ☐ HANDGUN
13 ☐ RIFLE
14 ☐ SHOTGUN
15 ☐ OTHER FIREARM
20 ☐ KNIFE / CUTTING INSTRUMENT
30 ☐ BLUNT OBJECT
35 ☐ MOTOR VEHICLE
40 ☐ PERSONAL WEAPONS
50 ☐ POISON
60 ☐ EXPLOSIVES
65 ☐ FIRE / INCENDIARY
70 ☐ NARCOTICS / DRUGS
85 ☐ ASPHYXIATION
90 ☐ OTHER
95 ☐ UNKNOWN
99 ☐ NONE

VICTIM

VICTIM # 1: (Last, First, Middle)   **PHONE:** (Home)

ADDRESS: (Street, City, State, Zip)

TYPE OF VICTIM: (Check Only One)
I ☐ INDIVIDUAL   G ☐ GOVERNMENT   O ☐ OTHER
B ☐ BUSINESS   R ☐ RELIGIOUS   U ☐ UNKNOWN
F ☐ FINANCIAL   S ☐ SOCIETY / PUBLIC

RACE:
W ☐ WHITE
B ☐ BLACK
I ☐ INDIAN
A ☐ ASIAN
U ☐ UNKNOWN

SEX:
M ☐ MALE
F ☐ FEMALE
U ☐ UNKNOWN

AGE:
DOB:
NO. OF VICTIMS:

RESIDENT STATUS:
R ☐ RESIDENT
N ☐ NONRESIDENT
U ☐ UNKNOWN

ETHNICITY:
H ☐ HISPANIC
N ☐ NON - HISPANIC
U ☐ UNKNOWN

AGGRAVATED ASSAULT / HOMICIDE CIRCUMSTANCES: (Check Up to Two)
01 ☐ ARGUMENT
02 ☐ ASSAULT ON LAW OFFICER
03 ☐ DRUG DEALING
04 ☐ GANGLAND
05 ☐ JUVENILE GANG
06 ☐ LOVERS' QUARREL
07 ☐ MERCY KILLING
08 ☐ OTHER FELONY INVOLVED
09 ☐ OTHER CIRCUMSTANCES
10 ☐ UNKNOWN CIRCUMSTANCES

INJURY TYPE: (Check Up to Five)
N ☐ NONE
B ☐ BROKEN BONES
I ☐ POSS. INT. INJURIES
L ☐ SEVERE LACERATION
M ☐ MINOR INJURY
O ☐ MAJOR INJURY
T ☐ LOSS OF TEETH
U ☐ UNCONSCIOUSNESS

VICTIM CONNECTED TO OFFENSE NUMBER ABOVE:
1. ☐
2. ☐
3. ☐

RELATIONSHIP OF VICTIM TO OFFENDER: (For multiple offender relationships enter offender number[s] in space)
SE ___ SPOUSE
CS ___ COMMON - LAW SPOUSE
PA ___ PARENT
SB ___ SIBLING
CH ___ CHILD
GP ___ GRANDPARENT
GC ___ GRANDCHILD
IL ___ IN-LAW
SP ___ STEPPARENT
SC ___ STEPCHILD
SS ___ STEPSIBLING
OF ___ OTHER FAMILY
AQ ___ ACQUAINTANCE
FR ___ FRIEND
NE ___ NEIGHBOR
BE ___ BABYSITTEE (baby)
BG ___ BOY / GIRL FRIEND
CF ___ CHILD OF "BG" ABOVE
HH ___ HOMOSEXUAL REL.
XS ___ EX-SPOUSE
EE ___ EMPLOYEE
ER ___ EMPLOYER
OK ___ OTHERWISE KNOWN
ST ___ STRANGER
VO ___ VICTIM WAS OFFENDER
RU ___ RELATIONSHIP UNKNOWN

Page _____ of _____

Figure 3.1—*continued*

PROPERTY

TYPE PROPERTY LOSS / ETC.	CODE	QUANTITY	PROPERTY DESCRIPTION INCLUDE MAKE, MODEL, SIZE, TYPE, SERIAL #, COLOR, ETC.	VALUE	DATE RECOVERED Month / Day / Year
1 ☐ NONE					
2 ☐ BURNED					
3 ☐ COUNTERFEITED / FORGED					
4 ☐ DAMAGED / DESTROYED					
5 ☐ RECOVERED					
6 ☐ SEIZED					
7 ☐ STOLEN					
8 ☐ UNKNOWN					

PROPERTY DESCRIPTION CODE TABLE:
(Enter Number In Code Column Above)

01 AIRCRAFT	14 GAMBLING EQUIPMENT	28 RECREATIONAL VEHICLES
02 ALCOHOL	15 HEAVY CONSTRUCTION / INDUSTRIAL EQUIPMENT	29 STRUCTURES - SINGLE OCCUPANCY DWELLINGS
03 AUTOMOBILES	16 HOUSEHOLD GOODS	30 STRUCTURES - OTHER DWELLINGS
04 BICYCLES	17 JEWELRY / PRECIOUS METALS	31 STRUCTURES - OTHER COMMERCIAL / BUSINESS
05 BUSES	18 LIVESTOCK	32 STRUCTURES - INDUSTRIAL / MANUFACTURING
06 CLOTHES / FURS	19 MERCHANDISE	33 STRUCTURES - PUBLIC / COMMUNITY
07 COMPUTER HARDWARE / SOFTWARE	20 MONEY	34 STRUCTURES - STORAGE
08 CONSUMABLE GOODS	21 NEGOTIABLE INSTRUMENTS	35 STRUCTURES - OTHER
09 CREDIT / DEBIT CARDS	22 NONNEGOTIABLE INSTRUMENTS	36 TOOLS - POWER / HAND
10 DRUGS / NARCOTICS	23 OFFICE-TYPE EQUIPMENT	37 TRUCKS
11 DRUG / NARCOTIC EQUIPMENT	24 OTHER MOTOR VEHICLES	38 VEHICLE PARTS / ACCESSORIES
12 FARM EQUIPMENT	25 PURSES / HANDBAGS / WALLETS	39 WATERCRAFT
13 FIREARMS	26 RADIOS / TVs / VCRs	77 OTHER
	27 RECORDINGS - AUDIO / VISUAL	88 PENDING INVENTORY
		99 (_____)

OFFENDER

NUMBER OF OFFENDERS: _____

1.   ADDRESS: (Street, City, State, Zip)

AGE:	SEX: M ☐ MALE / F ☐ FEMALE / U ☐ UNKNOWN	RACE: W ☐ WHITE / B ☐ BLACK / I ☐ INDIAN / A ☐ ASIAN / U ☐ UNKNOWN	HEIGHT: ___ feet ___ inches	WEIGHT:	EYES:	HAIR:	CLOTHING:

2.   ADDRESS:

AGE:	SEX: M ☐ MALE / F ☐ FEMALE / U ☐ UNKNOWN	RACE: W ☐ WHITE / B ☐ BLACK / I ☐ INDIAN / A ☐ ASIAN / U ☐ UNKNOWN	HEIGHT: ___ feet ___ inches	WEIGHT:	EYES:	HAIR:	CLOTHING:

3.   ADDRESS:

AGE:	SEX: M ☐ MALE / F ☐ FEMALE / U ☐ UNKNOWN	RACE: W ☐ WHITE / B ☐ BLACK / I ☐ INDIAN / A ☐ ASIAN / U ☐ UNKNOWN	HEIGHT: ___ feet ___ inches	WEIGHT:	EYES:	HAIR:	CLOTHING:

ARRESTEE

NUMBER OF ARRESTEES: _____   **MULTIPLE CLEARANCE INDICATOR:**   M ☐ MULTIPLE   C ☐ COUNT ARRESTEE   N ☐ NOT APPLICABLE

ARRESTEE #1: (Last, First, Middle)   ADDRESS: (Street, City, State, Zip)

AGE:	SEX: M ☐ MALE / F ☐ FEMALE	RACE: W ☐ WHITE / B ☐ BLACK / I ☐ INDIAN / A ☐ ASIAN / U ☐ UNKNOWN	DOB:	ARRESTEE ETHNICITY: H ☐ HISPANIC / N ☐ NON-HISPANIC / U ☐ UNKNOWN	RESIDENT STATUS: R ☐ RESIDENT / N ☐ NONRESIDENT / U ☐ UNKNOWN

ARRESTEE WAS ARMED WITH: (Check Up To Two) (Enter A In Box If Automatic)

01 ☐ UNARMED	14 ☐ SHOTGUN	
11 ☐ FIREARM (type not stated)	15 ☐ OTHER FIREARM	
12 ☐ HANDGUN	16 ☐ LETHAL CUTTING INSTRUMENT (e.g. Switchblade Knife, etc.)	
13 ☐ RIFLE	17 ☐ CLUB / BLACKJACK / BRASS KNUCKLES	

TYPE OF ARREST:
O ☐ ON-VIEW
S ☐ SUMMONED / CITED
T ☐ TAKEN INTO CUSTODY

DISPOSITION OF ARRESTEE UNDER 18:
H ☐ HANDLED WITHIN DEPARTMENT
R ☐ REFERRED TO OTHER AUTHORITY

HEIGHT: ___ feet ___ inches	WEIGHT:	EYES:	HAIR:	ARREST NUMBER:	ARREST DATE:	UCR ARREST OFFENSE CODE:

WITNESS

	NAME: (Last, First, Middle)	ADDRESS: (Street, City, State, Zip)	RESIDENTIAL PHONE:	BUSINESS PHONE:
#1				
#2				

NARRATIVE

☐ continued on supplement

3. Robbery
   a. Firearm
   b. Knife or cutting instrument
   c. Other dangerous weapon
   d. Strong-arm — hands, fists, feet, etc.
4. Aggravated assault
   a. Firearm
   b. Knife or cutting instrument
   c. Other dangerous weapon
   d. Hands, fists, feet, etc. — aggravated injury
5. Burglary
   a. Forcible entry
   b. Unlawful entry — no force
   c. Attempted forcible entry
      This includes any unlawful entry to commit a theft or a felony, even though no force was used to gain entrance, as well as attempts at same. Does not include shoplifting or theft from an automobile or telephone booth. For UCR purposes, these offenses are classified as larceny-theft.
6. Larceny-Theft (except motor vehicle theft)
7. Motor Vehicle Theft
   a. Autos
   b. Trucks and buses
   c. Other vehicles
8. Arson
   a. Structural
   b. Mobile
   c. Other

PART II OFFENSES:

9. Other assaults: assaults and attempted assaults
10. Forgery and counterfeiting: includes bad checks except forgeries and counterfeiting; includes attempts
11. Fraud: fraudulent conversion and obtaining money or property by false pretenses
12. Embezzlement: misappropriation or misapplication of money or property
13. Buying, receiving, or possessing stolen property: includes attempts
14. Vandalism: destruction, injury, disfigurement, or defacement of property
15. Weapons: carrying, possessing, etc.
16. Prostitution and commercialized vice: sex offenses of a commercial nature (and attempts)
17. Sex offenses: except forcible rape, prostitution, and commercial vice

18. Drug abuse violations: violations of state and local laws. Includes all attempts to sell, manufacture, or possess
19. Gambling
20. Offenses against the family and children
21. Driving under the influence: operating a motor vehicle or common carrier while drunk or under the influence of liquor or narcotics
22. Liquor laws: State or municipal liquor law violations, except drunkenness or driving under the influence
23. Drunkenness
24. Disorderly conduct
25. Vagrancy
26. All other offenses: all violations of state and local laws except those offenses already classified
27. Suspicion: arrest for no special charge and released without formal charge being placed
28. Curfew and loitering laws (persons under 18)
29. Runaways (persons under 18)

Methods of Gathering Information

Material compiled by large and small police departments on sophisticated or simple forms is thus codified for the FBI. Experiments are being conducted in many places to try to save time and money and increase accuracy. Methods being studied or implemented include the use of word processing, laptop computers, combinations of computer-aided dispatch and records management systems, and the redesigning of report forms (see Chapter 14). Other methods include using notebooks, videotaping or audiotaping either at the station or scene, transcribing by clerks or officers, and writing directly on forms (with duplication made of the original). Some stations are trying methods that have been discarded elsewhere. A review of the advantages and disadvantages of each method may help you or your agency decide which method to use. Only you and your colleagues can decide what is appropriate for your agency.

Estimates of time spent writing reports averages up to 50 percent of a patrol law enforcement officer's day, and the accuracy of reports is often questioned. This makes report writing techniques important to administrators, employees, and the public.

Notebooks (discussed in Chapter 1) include prior information provided in the squad room, on-scene facts, and sometimes follow-up. They refresh the writer's memory when he or she appears in court. However, time and even accuracy may be lost in transcribing, and the notebook may be lost or held against the officer if brought to court.

Examples of face pages in this chapter come from areas varying in size and location throughout the United States (see Figures 3.2 through 3.13). Notice that while the forms may look very different they all basically ask for detailed information about the who, what, when, where, and how of the incident. Some agencies have report writing manuals that explain block by block what is needed to complete the face page report (see Appendix B for an example).

Figure 3.2
Sampling Police Incident Report Form, Tacoma Police Department

GENERAL REPORT
AGENCY:
[ ] TPD   [ ] PCSO
OTHER: _____

1 Public Disclosure Act   PAGE _____ OF _____

INCIDENT NO.

| 2 Arrest | 3 Vehicle | 4 Juvenile | 8 Report Name/Offense |
| 5 Property | 6 Medical | 7 Domestic Viol. | |

9 Type of Premise (For Vehicles State Where Parked)

10 Entry Point

11 Method

12 Weapon/Tool/Force Used

| 13 Date Report'd | 14 Time Rept'd. | 15 Date Occur. | 16 Time Occur. | 17 Day of Week |

18 Location of:
Incident   [   ]
Address   [   ]

19 Census   20 Dist.

PERSONS/BUSINESS INVOLVED

CODE   C (Person Reporting Complaint)   V (Victim)   W (Witness)   P (Parent)   VB (Victim Business)   O (Other)

21 Code	22 NAME: Last First Middle (Maiden)	23 Race/Sex	24 Date of Birth	25 Home Phone
26 PDA	27 ADDRESS: Street City State Zip	28 Place of Employment/School		29 Business Phone
21 Code	22 NAME: Last First Middle (Maiden)	23 Race/Sex	24 Date of Birth	25 Home Phone
26 PDA	27 ADDRESS: Street City State Zip	28 Place of Employment/School		29 Business Phone
21 Code	22 NAME: Last First Middle (Maiden)	23 Race/Sex	24 Date of Birth	25 Home Phone
26 PDA	27 ADDRESS: Street City State Zip	28 Place of Employment/School		29 Business Phone

[ ] Additional Persons On Report Continuation Sheet (People) Form No. Z-556

PERSON NUMBER 1

CODE: A (Arrest)   S (Suspect)   SV (Suspect Verified)   R (Runaway)   M (Missing Person)   I (Institutional Impact)

30 Code	31 NAME: Last First Middle (Maiden)	32 Home Phone	33 Business Phone
34 ADDRESS: Street City State Zip	35 Occupation	36 Place of Employment/School	37 Relation to Victim
38 Date of Birth	39 Race	40 Sex	41 Height	42 Weight/Bld.	43 Hair	44 Eyes	45 Clothing, Scars, Marks, Tattoos, Peculiarities, A.K.A.
46 [ ] Booked [ ] Cited Number	47 Charge Details (Include Ordinance or R.C.W. Number)

PERSON NUMBER 2

30 Code	31 NAME: Last First Middle(Maiden)	32 Home Phone	33 Business Phone
34 ADDRESS: Street City State Zip	35 Occupation	36 Place of Employment/School	37 Relation to Victim
38 Date of Birth	39 Race	40 Sex	41 Height	42 Weight/Bld.	43 Hair	44 Eyes	45 Clothing, Scars, Marks, Tattoos, Peculiarities, A.K.A.
46 [ ] Booked [ ] Cited Number	47 Charge Details (Include Ordinance or R.C.W. Number)

[ ] Additional Persons On Report Continuation Sheet (People) Form No. Z-556   Juvenile Arrests – Block No. 109 MUST Be Completed

VEHICLE

48 Stolen*	49 Victim	50 Impound	54 License No.	55 Lic. State	56 Lic. Year	57 Lic. Type	58 Vin.
51 Recovry	52 Suspect	53 Hold					
59 Year	60 Make	61 Model	62 Body Style	63 Color	64 Peculiarities	65 Hold Requested By/For	
66 Ori. & Case No.	67 Registered Owner: Name Address City State Zip	68 Home Phone	

RECOVERY

69 Condition
[ ] Drivable   [ ] Stripped
[ ] Not Drivable   [ ] Wrecked

70 Inventory

70 Inventory (Cont.)

71 Tow Co. & Signature

NOTICE

| 72 Enter | 73 Date | 74 Time | 75 WACIC | 76 LESA | 77 Initial | 78 Release Info | 79 Date | 80 Time | 81 Release No. | 82 Releasing Authority |
| 83 Clear | 84 | 85 | 86 | 87 | 88 | 89 Owner Notified | 90 | 91 | 92 Operator's Name | |

| 93 Signature & I.D. No. of Reporting Officer(s) | 94 Approval | 95 Distribution Excp. |

| REPORT PROCESSING (Records Personnel Only) | DISTRIBUTION: DATE _____ BY _____ | Microfilmed | Filed |
| | INDEXED: DATE _____ BY _____ | Initials _____ | Initials _____ |

Z-555a

Figure 3.2—*continued*

96 STOLEN *		PAGE _____ OF _____	INCIDENT NO.

Divorce/Separation In Progress? [ ] Yes [ ] No   Payments Delinquent? [ ] Yes [ ] No   Car Locked? [ ] Yes [ ] No

Key In Switch? [ ] Yes [ ] No   Key Needed? [ ] Yes [ ] No   Permission To Drive Given? [ ] Yes [ ] No

STATEMENT OF PERSON REPORTING

I, the undersigned, declare this to be a true and correct report. I will testify, in court, under oath, to the facts herein. I understand that I may be charged with violation of R.C.W. 9A.76.020 "Obstructing a Public Servant" if filing a false report. If reporting a stolen vehicle, I understand I am liable for all towing and storage costs incurred in the recovery of this vehicle.

Date _____ Time _____ Signature _____

MEDICAL	97 Type of Injury or Illness		98 Hospital Taken	99 By?	100 [ ] Employee [ ] On Duty
	101 Extent of Injuries		102 Attending Physician	103 Suicide Note Found? [ ]	104 Hold Placed By

105 PROPERTY	Stolen	Evidence	Recovered	Theft Inventory Att.	106 Total Theft $	107 Total Damaged $
	Lost	Damaged	Narrative	Theft Inventory Left		

108 Damage and Minor Property Loss

Insurance Company

PARENT/GUARDIAN NOTIFICATION	109 Name and Relationship of Person Notified	110 Date & Time Notified	111 Notified By:

INDEX	NARRATIVE

112   HAZARD SECTION
Complete the Hazard Section of this report only if the officer encounters combative resistance or physical aggression. More passive resistance or attempts to break free do not require completion of this section. If suspect threatens officer, check box "Threats Only".

	OFFICER ASSIGNMENT		RESPONDING TO:	
1 [ ] Combative Resistance				23 [ ] Mentally Deranged
2 [ ] Physical Aggression	9 [ ] Uniform	14 [ ] One Officer Car	18 [ ] Ambush — No Warning	24 [ ] Handling Prisoner
3 [ ] Threats Only	10 [ ] Non-Uniform	15 [ ] Two Officer Car	19 [ ] Attempting Other Arrests	25 [ ] Robbery In Progress
4 [ ] Officer Injured	11 [ ] Detective	16 [ ] Officer Alone	20 [ ] Burglary In Progress	26 [ ] Suspicious Circumstances
5 [ ] Firearm	12 [ ] Foot	17 [ ] Officer Assisted	21 [ ] Civil Disorder (Riot)	27 [ ] Traffic Stops
6 [ ] Knife	13 [ ] Off-Duty		22 [ ] Disturbance Call	28 [ ] All Others
7 [ ] Other Dangerous Weapon				
8 [ ] Hands, Fists, Feet, Etc.			Suspect Involved In Hazard 29 [ ] Number 1 30 [ ] Number 2	

Z-555b

Figure 3.3
Sample Sheriff's Incident/Prosecution Report Form, Oakland County Sheriff Department

OAKLAND COUNTY SHERIFF DEPT.
1201 N. Telegraph Rd., Pontiac, MI 48341
Phone: 248-858-5011   ORI # MI6316300

INCIDENT / PROSECUTION REPORT

PO # _____
☐ PRIMARY   ☐ SUPP   PAGE ____ OF ____

01 | DATE | DAY | SHIFT | PLAT | BADGE 1 | BADGE 2 | UCR | ADMIN | YEAR | INCIDENT #

02 | RECEIVED | DISPATCHED | ARRIVED | COMPLETED | DATE(S) OCCURRED | TIME(S) OCCURRED | HOUR | DAY

03 | LOCATION / ADDRESS (DIRECTION, STREET, SUFFIX, QUALIFIER) | LOCATION 2 (INTERSECTING STREET)

04 | CITY | STATE | ZIP | CODE | BUSINESS NAME | BUSINESS PHONE

05 | ESTAB CODE | ORIGIN ☐ PHONE ☐ PERSON ☐ 911 ☐ FOP ☐ OTHER | HOW ACTIVATED ☐ FOP ☐ PERSON ☐ MDT ☐ DISP ☐ OTHER | REPORT TAKEN ☐ SCENE ☐ STATION ☐ PHONE ☐ OTHER | REC BADGE | DISP BADGE | UNIT 1 | UNIT 2

06 | NATURE OF INCIDENT #1 | ATT ☐ | CRIME CLASS | ALC ☐ DRUGS ☐ COMP ☐ | BIAS | WEAPON | # PREM | ACTIVITY | POINT OF ENTRY / ATTACK

07 | NATURE OF INCIDENT #2 | ATT ☐ | SEC CLASS | ALC ☐ DRUGS ☐ COMP ☐ | BIAS | WEAPON | # PREM | ACTIVITY | METHOD OF ENTRY / ATTACK

08 | NATURE OF INCIDENT #3 | ATT ☐ | SEC CLASS | ALC ☐ DRUGS ☐ COMP ☐ | BIAS | WEAPON | # PREM | ACTIVITY | TOOL / OBJECT / WEAPON

09 | NATURE OF INCIDENT #4 | ATT ☐ | SEC CLASS | ALC ☐ DRUGS ☐ COMP ☐ | BIAS | WEAPON | # PREM | ACTIVITY | OTHER CHARACTERISTICS

CODES (1)REPT'D BY (2)OWNER (3)VICT (4)PERS INTERV (5)ARREST (6)SUSP (7)MISS'G (8)WITN (9)SECUR'D BY (O)JUV ARREST (D)DRIVER (P)PASSNGR (R)RESPONSIBLE (S)SUMMONED (X)MISC

10 | CODE | VICT # | ACTUAL VICTIM (LAST, FIRST, MIDDLE, SUFFIX) | RAC | SEX | DOB | AGE | VICTIM TO RECEIVE CVRA NOTICE

11 | CODE | NAME (LAST, FIRST, MIDDLE, SUFFIX) (ACTUAL VICTIM'S REP) | RAC | SEX | DOB | AGE | RELATION TO ACTUAL VICTIM

12 | ADDRESS | (DIRECTION, STREET, SUFFIX, QUALIFIER) | CITY | STATE | ZIP

13 | HOME PHONE | BUSINESS PHONE | STATE | DRIVER'S LICENSE # | CONN ☐1 ☐3 ☐2 ☐4 | TYP | REL TO OFN # | INJ | V CIRC | JHC

14 | PE | CODE | OFN # | NAME (LAST, FIRST, MIDDLE, SUFFIX) | RAC | SEX | DOB | AGE

15 | ADDRESS | (DIRECTION, STREET, SUFFIX, QUALIFIER) | CITY | STATE | ZIP

16 | HOME PHONE | BUSINESS PHONE | HEIGHT | WEIGHT | EYES | HAIR | LENGTH | STYLE | BUILD | SKIN TONE

17 | STATE | DRIVER'S LICENSE # | SOC SEC # | SID # | FBI # | MISC #

18 | ALIAS (MAIDEN NAME, LAST, FIRST, MIDDLE, SUFFIX) | COMMENTS / CLOTHING / ETC | VIOLATION

19 | ARREST CHRG 1 | ARREST DATE | PLAT | BADGE 1 | BADGE 2 | FM | DIS | ARREST CHRG 2 | ARREST DATE | PLAT | BADGE 1 | BADGE 2 | FM | DIS

20 | OST | MCN | CLR | ARMED AT ARREST | ORIGIN ☐ FOP ☐ MDT | ☐ DISP ☐ PER ☐ TEL | STATUS 1 ☐ JAILED 3 ☐ APPEARANCE TCKT 2 ☐ RELEASED 4 ☐ NOT ARRESTED | FINGERPRINTS ☐ YES ☐ NO | CHR ☐ YES ☐ NO | ACTION REQUESTED 1 ☐ ARREST WARRANT 3 ☐ PADLOCK 5 ☐ FORFEITURE 2 ☐ SEARCH WARRANT 4 ☐ INJUNCTION 6 ☐ OTHER

CODES (H)HOLD (S)STOLEN (Y)COUNTERFEIT (E)EVIDENCE (L)LOST (A)ATTACKED (R)RECOVERED (F)FOUND (C)CONFISCATED (X)IMPOUNDED (V)SUSPECT VEHICLE (B)BURNED

21 | CODES | DESCRIPTION | PROP TYPE | QUANTITY | YEAR | MAKE | MODEL

22 | STYLE | COLOR(S) | MONTH | YEAR | STATE | LICENSE | SERIAL / VIN #

23 | STOLEN $ | DAMAGED $ | RECOVERED | PROPERTY TAG # | LOCATION PROPERTY | LEIN REF # | NIC #

24 | COMMENTS / INSURANCE COMPANY / LIEN HOLDER / BANK | REC BADGE 1 | REC BADGE 2 | LEO | RECOVERY DATE | DG TYPE | DRUG AMOUNT | MEAS

25 | BRIEF SUMMARY OF OFFENSE (TITLE / SUMMARY)

26 |

27 |

28 |

YEAR   INCIDENT #

Form 102 4-96 | INVESTIGATING OFFICER(S) | REVIEWED BY | ATTENTION TO | I affirm the above information is true and correct. O.I.C. Signature _____

Figure 3.4
Sample Sheriff's Incident Investigation Report Form, Camden County Sheriff's Department

OFFICE OF THE SHERIFF CAMDEN COUNTY		INCIDENT ☐	INVESTIGATION ☐	SO-1

1. Unit:	2. Phone Number:	3. Prosecutor's Case Number:	4a.Case Year: 4b.Case Number: 4b.Case Unit 05

5. Crime/Incident:	6. N.J.S.A.:	CHECK ALL THAT APPLY	7. Domestic Violence ☐	8. Bias Incident ☐	9. Co-op ☐

CHECK ALL THAT APPLY	10. Alcohol Involved ☐	11. Drugs Involved ☐	12. Evidence Report ☐	13. Supplemental Report ☐	14. Arrest Report ☐	15. Tow Report ☐	16. Other ☐

INCIDENT / INVESTIGATION LOCATION

17. Complete Address:	18. Municipality:	19. County: Camden	20. Mun. Code:	21. Type Of Premise:

VICTIM'S INFORMATION

22. Victim Name (first,last):	23. Victim's Complete Address:	24.Phone Number:	Ext:

25. Soc Sec Number:	26. D.O.B.:	27. Sex:	28. Race Code:	29. Juvenile: ☐

30. Guardian Name (first,last)	31. Guardian's Complete Address:	32. Phone Number:	Ext:

REPORTING PERSONS INFORMATION

33. Person Reporting Crime/Incident:	34. Complete Address :	35. Phone Number:	Ext:

36. Reported Date:	37. Reported Time:	38. Day Code:	39. Juvenile: ☐

40. Guardian Name (first,last)	41. Guardian's Complete Address:	42. Phone Number:	Ext:

List Arrested/Summoned - List and Identify Additional Victims - Describe Perpetrators/Suspects - Date Action Taken - Include Findings and observations of Investigator - Physical Evidence Found - Where - By Whom - Disposition and Technical Services Performed - Interview of Victims, Witnesses, Persons Contacted - Suspects - Attach Statements - Court Action - All NCIC Entry/Inquiries - Prisoner Disposition

43. Narrative:
SEE CONTINUATION PAGE

44. Rank/Name/Badge:	45. Page 1 of : 2	46. Date of Report:	47. Reviewer/Badge:

48. Signature:	49. Supervisor Signature/Date:

SO#1 1/1/04   649

Figure 3.5
Sample Police Incident Report Form, Anne Arundel County Police Department

ANNE ARUNDEL COUNTY POLICE DEPARTMENT, MILLERSVILLE. MD.	Incident Report	Page 1 of 2

1. OFFENSE	2. BUSINESS/VICTIM NAME (LAST, FIRST, MIDDLE	3. CASE NUMBER

4. DATE AND TIME OCCURRED	5. BUSINESS/VICTIM ADDRESS	CITY	6. RESIDENCE PHONE

7. DATE AND TIME REPORTED	8. VICTIMS EMPLOYMENT	CITY	9. BUSINESS PHONE

10. DAY OF WK OCCURRED	11. DAY OF WK REPORTED	12. DOB	RACE	SEX	AGE	13. OCCUPATION	14. ALCOHOL DRUG USAGE

15. WEATHER AT TIME OF OCCURRENCE CLEAR RAIN FOGGY CLOUDY COLD UNK. SNOW SEVERE WIND WARM OTHER	16. REPORTING PERSON (LAST, FIRST, MIDDLE)	17. DOB	18. RESIDENCE PHONE

19. DISTRICT POST SHIFT	20. REPORTING PERSON ADDRESS	CITY	21. BUSINESS PHONE

22. PRIMARY VICTIM VULNERABILITY

23. LOCATION OF OFFENSE	24. TOTAL LOSS VALUE	25. DESCRIBE LOCATION

26. TOOLS/WEAPON USED	27. ENTRYPOINT/EXIT POINT/ENTRY LOCATION

28. ROUTE/METHOD OF ESCAPE	29. METHOD OF OPERATION/INTENT

30. PHYSICAL INJURY/MENTAL CONDITION (VICTIM, SUSPECT, MISSING PERSON)	31. HOSPITALIZED? WHERE	32. HOW TRANSPORTED

32. VEHICLE CODES (CHECK APPLICABLE CODES)
ABANDONED, DAMAGED, EVIDENCE, IMPOUNDED, RECOVERED STOLEN, STOLEN, SUSPECT, THEFT FROM, TOWED, USED IN CRIME

34. RELEASE YES NO	35. BODY TYPE	36. YEAR	37. MAKE	38. MODEL	39. COLOR	40. TAG	41. STATE	42. EXPIRES

43. VIN NUMBER	44. VALUE	45. CONDITION/IDENTIFYING MARKS

46. LOCATION STOLEN, TOWED, RECOVERED	47. OWNER NOTIFIED BY	48. PERSON/OTHER DEPT. NOTIFIED	49. DATE AND TIME NOTIFIED

50. TOW CO.	51. TOWED TO	52. RADIO NOTIFIED - DATE AND TIME	TTY #	53. LOCKED: DOORS WINDOWS TRUNK KEYS IN CAR RADIO SPARE TIRE

54. ENTER WITNESS, VICTIM, SUSPECT, RUNAWAY/MISSING PERSON INFORMATION BELOW: (USE LETTER 'CODE' BLOCK)
WITNESS (W), VICTIM (V), SUSPECT (S), RUNAWAY (R) OR MISSING PERSON (M)

CODE	55. NAME	DOB	SEX	RACE	EYES	HAIR	WEIGHT	HEIGHT
	ADDRESS			PHONE (home)		PHONE (work)		
	IDENTIFIERS							

CODE	56. NAME	DOB	SEX	RACE	EYES	HAIR	WEIGHT	HEIGHT
	ADDRESS			PHONE (home)		PHONE (work)		
	IDENTIFIERS							

59. WAS INCIDENT RACIAL, ETHNIC, RELIGIOUS, SPOUSAL ASSAULT, N/A	60. REPORT TAKEN SCENE, STATION, PHONE, OTHER	61. EMERGENCY RUN YES NO

62. DISPOSITION OPEN, CLOSED, SUSPENDED, ARREST UNFOUNDED, FALSE REPORT, FOLLOW-UP NEEDED	63. OPERATION IDENTIFICATION YES NO N/A

64. FIRST OFFICER	ID	65. SECOND OFFICER	ID	66. SUPERVISOR	ID	67. REVIEW OFFICER	ID

Form # 09-40-7-1

Figure 3.6
Sample Police Incident Report Form, Honolulu Police Department

Honolulu Police Department

INCIDENT REPORT

Page____of____pages
☐☐ / ☐☐☐ - ☐☐☐
Year   Six Digit Report Number

BASIC

Incident Type | Code | Reclassify ☐ Yes | Key Report ☐ Yes ☐ No | F/U ☐ | Status ☐Open ☐Closed | Disposition | HRS Section Number

Location Of Offense (Must Have Street Number And Street Name, Or Names of Two Streets That Intersect)

Domestic Violence Yes ☐ No ☐

Responsible Officer Last First | I D Number | Division | Beat of Offense | Location Code

Date / Time / Day Reported | Date / Time / Day Occurred From | Date / Time / Day Occurred To

Related Reports or Comments

1. Residence 2. Apart / Condo 3. Hotel 4. Street 5. Non-Beach Parks 6. Beach-Parks 7. Scenic Pt. 8. Gas Stn. 9. Restaurant 10. Bar 11. Store 12. Bank, etc. 13. Jewelry 14. Liquor 15. School 16. Commercial 17. Taxi 18. Other

PERSON · HOSP

☐ Complainant ☐ Victim ☐ Reporting Person ☐ Finder ☐ Witness ☐ Suspect

☐ White ☐ Black ☐ Am Ind ☐ Chnse ☐ Jpnse ☐ Korea ☐ P Rican ☐ Hawn ☐ Samoa ☐ Tonga ☐ Vietn ☐ Filpn ☐ Unk ☐ Other | Name Last First Middle | Age | DOB | Sex

☐ Blood Test ☐ Breath Test ☐ Refuse | Results | S S N | Occupation / For Juvenile - School Attending | ☐ Visitor ☐ H P D ☐ Military | Juv ☐Yes ☐No

Home Address City - Country - State - Zip

Business Address City - Country - State - Zip | Local Address (for visitors)

At Local Address Until / Date | Home Phone ( ) | Business Phone ( ) | Work Hours | Local Phone

Injured ☐Yes ☐No | Treated ☐Yes ☐No | S I D # (if appropriate) | Hospital | Transported By | Victim Relationship to Suspect | Will Prosecute ☐ Yes ☐No

☐ Mental ☐ Suicide ☐ I C F ☐ S C F ☐ Other ☐ Intox ☐ Drugs ☐ Indust ☐ Uncon ☐ Resisted Assist | Voluntary ☐ Yes ☐No | ☐ Good/Fair ☐ Ser/Guard ☐ Fatal | Attending Physician | ☐Confined ☐Refused ADM ☐Sent Home | ☐ Refused Tmt ☐ Tr / Released

A K A | Who Described | Peculiarities

Height | Weight | Build | Hair Color | Hair Char | Eyes | Compl | Voice | Facial Hair Color | Facial Hair Char | Clothing

PERSON · HOSP

☐ Complainant ☐ Victim ☐ Reporting Person ☐ Finder ☐ Witness ☐ Suspect

☐ White ☐ Black ☐ Am Ind ☐ Chnse ☐ Jpnse ☐ Korea ☐ P Rican ☐ Hawn ☐ Samoa ☐ Tonga ☐ Vietn ☐ Filpn ☐ Unk ☐ Other | Name Last First Middle | Age | DOB | Sex

☐ Blood Test ☐ Breath Test ☐ Refuse | Results | S S N | Occupation / For Juvenile - School Attending | ☐ Visitor ☐ H P D ☐ Military | Juv ☐Yes ☐No

Home Address City - Country - State - Zip

Business Address City - Country - State - Zip | Local Address (for visitors)

At Local Address Until / Date | Home Phone ( ) | Business Phone ( ) | Work Hours | Local Phone

Injured ☐Yes ☐No | Treated ☐Yes ☐No | S I D # (if appropriate) | Hospital | Transported By | Victim Relationship to Suspect | Will Prosecute ☐ Yes ☐No

☐ Mental ☐ Suicide ☐ I C F ☐ S C F ☐ Other ☐ Intox ☐ Drugs ☐ Indust ☐ Uncon ☐ Resisted Assist | Voluntary ☐ Yes No | ☐ Good/Fair ☐ Ser/Guard ☐ Fatal | Attending Physician | ☐Confined ☐Refused ADM ☐Sent Home | ☐ Refused Tmt ☐ Tr / Released

A K A | Who Described | Peculiarities

Height | Weight | Build | Hair Color | Hair Char | Eyes | Compl | Voice | Facial Hair Color | Facial Hair Char | Clothing

MO

A | B | C | D | E | F | G | H | I | J | K | L | M | N | O | P | Q | R | S

Misc. | ☐Dusted & Submitted ☐Dusted & Negative ☐Not Dusted

PROP · SYNOPSIS

Property Status Codes: ST=Stolen OV=Overdue LS=Lost DM=Damaged FN=Found RC=Recovered OT=Other **Type Codes:** I = Item B = Building V = Vehicle L = Land

Item #	Status	Type	Serial / Other I D	Description or Manufacturer / Model / Gun Make / Type Cal Ga	Property Codes	Qty	Value

VEHICLE

Vehicle Status Codes: ST = Stolen OV = Overdue WV = Wanted SV = Suspect RC = Recovered IM = Impounded OT = Other **Veh Type Codes:** ☐ Auto ☐ Const ☐ Farm ☐ Trailer ☐ M / C ☐ Truck ☐ Other

Who Described | Status | Year | Make | Model | Body Type | Color | State | License No.

VIN | Emblem | Characteristics | Towed By | Vehicle Value

Held At | Tow Date / Time | Owner Name | Phone

Owner Address | Owner Notified By Date / Time | Person Notified | Returned By Date / Time

Recovered Date / Time | Recovering Officer | Recovered Location | Beat Rec

Writer | I D Number | Date / Time | Approved By | I D Number

HPD-192 (R-7/95)

Continued

Figure 3.6—continued

INCIDENT TYPE AND UCR CODES

Abuse		**Opium, Cocaine**		Court-Ordered Surrender 426	**Motor Vehicle Collision**	**Sex Offense** 170
Suspected 482		Distribution or Sale . . 185		Weapons Offense . . . 150	Major MVC 550	**Stolen Property, Receiving** 130
Warning 481		Possession 189		Fire Call 443	Minor MVC 551	**Suicide** 434
Alarm Call 444		**Marijuana, Hashish**		Forgery 100	Major Non-traffic Acc. . 552	Attempted Suicide 433
Argument, Domestic 483		Distribution or Sale . . 186		Found Property 428	Minor Non-traffic Acc. . 553	**Theft**
Assault		Possession 190		Fraud 110	**Motor Vehicle Theft** . . 077	Pickpocket 061
Aggravated 040		**Non Narcotic**		**Gambling**	Motor Vehicle Recovery . 078	Purse-snatch 062
Simple 080		Distribution or Sale . . 187		Bookmaking 252	Negligent Manslaughter . . 213	Shoplift 063
AWOL 445		Possession 191		Numbers or Lottery . . . 253	**Order**	From Vehicle 064
Bribery 132		**Synthetic**		Other Illegal Gambling . 254	Protective 465	Vehicle Parts 065
Burglary 050		Distribution or Sale . . 188		Harassment 083	Temporary Restraining . 464	Bicycle 066
Possession of Burg. Tools 131		Possession 192		Hit & Run 212	Violation 260	From Building 067
Delinquent Child		**Drug Paraphernalia** 193		Homicide 010	Overdue Rental 282	From Coin Machine . . . 068
Beyond Parental Control 307		**DUI**		House Check 440	**Perjury** 127	Other 069
Curfew 305		Liquor 210		ICF/SCF 430	**Pornography** 176	**Threatening, Terroristic** . . 081
Injurious Behavior 306		Drugs 211		Indecent Exposure . . . 175	**Property Damage** 140	**Tow Abandoned Vehicle** . 533
Truancy 310		**Embezzlement** 120		Kidnapping 230	Arson 079	**Traffic Violation** 535
Runaway 327		**Escape** 281		Liquor Law 220	Graffiti 141	**Traffic Incident** 560
Disorderly 240		**Extortion** 195		Lost Property 429	**Prostitution** 160	**Trespass** 280
Drowning 447		**Extradition** 446		Misc. Crime 299	**Rape** 020	Warning 480
Near Drowning 448		**Family Offenses** 200		Misc. Public 432	**Reckless Endangering** . . 082	**Unattended Death** 442
Drugs		**Firearm**		Missing Person 441	**Robbery** 030	**Warrant** 297

RELATIONSHIP OF VICTIM TO SUSPECT

AQ	Acquaintance	EE	Employee / Employer	GP	Grandparent	OF	Other Family	SP	Step Parent
BE	Baby Sittee	FR	Friend	IL	In-Law	PA	Parent	SC	Stepchild
CF	Child of "FN"	FN	Girl / Boyfriend	MR	Married / Spouse	SB	Sister / Brother	ST	Stranger
CL	Common-Law Spouse	GC	Grandchild	NE	Neighbor	CH	Son or Daughter	XS	Ex-Spouse
								RU	Unknown

PHYSICAL CHARACTERISTICS

BUILD	Auburn	Blond	Kinky	Blk	**COMPLEXION**	Olive	Local	Goatee
Small	Dk Brn	Sandy	Wavy	Gray	Brn	Pale	Mumbled	Shaven
Thin	Brn	Other	Long	Green	Tan	Ruddy	Other	Sideburns
Medium	Lt Brn	Unk	Strght	Blue	Blk	Yellow	Rapid	Mustache
Heavy	Red	**HAIR CHAR**	Other	Hazel	Dark	Other	Soft	MOUST
Muscular	Blk	Bald	Unk	Pink	Medium	Unk	Southern	LM (large)
Unk	Gray	Thin	**EYES**	Mixed	Fair	**VOICE**	Unk	SM (small)
HAIR COLOR	Wht	Short	Brn	Other	Light	Foreign	**FACIAL HAIR**	MB (&beard)
				Unk	Albino	Impediment	Beard	Other
								Unk

M.O.

A. FORCE OR WEAPON USED
1 = Blunt Object (club, hammer)
2 = Explosives, Incendiary Device
3 = Fire
4 = None
5 = Other
6 = Unknown
7 = Knife
8 = Screwdriver
9 = Drugs, Narcotics, Sleeping Pills
10 = Rifle
11 = Shotgun
12 = Pistol
13 = Hands, Feet, Teeth
14 = Threat of Force
15 = Other Threat
B. VEHICLE LOCKED
Y = YES   N = NO
C. TYPE OF ENTRY
1 = Attempt
2 = Forcible
3 = Unlocked Point
4 = None
5 = Other
6 = Unknown
7 = Lawful
D. KEY IN IGNITION
Y = YES   N = NO
E. ENTRY POINT
1 = Door
2 = Sliding Door

3 = Louvered Window
4 = None
5 = Other
6 = Unknown
7 = Other Window
8 = Roof
9 = Wall
10 = Floor
11 = Fenced Area
F. NO. OF LOUVERS REMOVED
G. ENTRY AREA
1 = Front
2 = Rear
3 = Side
4 = None
5 = Other
6 = Unknown
7 = Above
8 = Below
9 = Within
H. METHOD OF ENTRY / ATT
1 = Bodily Force
2 = Hid in Building
3 = Punched or Cut Lock
4 = None
5 = Other
6 = Unknown
7 = Unlocked
8 = Broke Glass
9 = Cut Glass
10 = Pried or Jimmied
11 = Drilled
12 = Twisted Knob

I. SUSPECT ACTION TO PREMISES (4)
1 = Vandalized
2 = Ransacked
3 = Disabled Alarm
4 = None
5 = Other
6 = Unknown
7 = Knew Cash Location
8 = Neat Search
9 = Disabled Phone
10 = Shut Off Power
11 = Drilled
J. SUSPECT ACTION ON VICTIM (4)
1 = Rip or Cut Clothes
2 = Blindfolded Victim
3 = Used Victim's Name
4 = None
5 = Other
6 = Unknown
7 = Threatened Retaliation
8 = Struck Victim
9 = Took Victim's Vehicle
10 = Bound or Gagged Victim
K. SUSPECT PERSONAL & (4) OTHER RELATED ACTIONS
1 = Smoked
2 = Ate / Drank
3 = Masturbated
4 = None
5 = Other
6 = Unknown
7 = Partly Disrobed

8 = Totally Disrobed
9 = Defecated
10 = Had Been Drinking
11 = Had Been Using Drugs
12 = Demanded Money
13 = Used a Demand Note
14 = Used Bag/Put Property in Bag
15 = Attempt
16 = Fired Weapon
17 = Used Lookout
18 = Used Driver
19 = Possibly Drinking
20 = Possibly Using Drugs
21 = Use of Mace/OC (by anyone)
22 = Gang on Gang Crime
23 = Gang on Other Crime
L. SUSPECT SOLICITED OR OFFERED (4)
1 = Food / Drink / Candy
2 = Money
3 = Sex
4 = None
5 = Other
6 = Unknown
7 = Drugs
8 = Phone
9 = Ride
10 = Light / Match / Cigarette
M. INSTRUMENT USED
1 = Bolt Cutter
2 = Brick or Rock
3 = Glass Cutter

4 = None
5 = Other
6 = Unknown
7 = Pipewrench / Vise Grip
8 = Hammer / Sledge / Ax
9 = Key or Slip Lock
10 = Pry Bar
N. ALARM
1 = Inoperative
2 = Inactive
3 = Activated
4 = None
5 = Other
6 = Unknown
O. PRECIPITATING CIRCUMSTANCES
1 = Hitchhiking
2 = Voluntarily with Suspect
3 = Allowed Suspect in Vehicle
4 = None
5 = Other
6 = Unknown
7 = Allowed Suspect in Home
8 = Victim Abducted from Premises
9 = Victim at Social Event
10 = Domestic Quarrel
11 = Non-Domestic Quarrel
12 = Occurred During Another Crime
P. VICTIM CONDITION

4 = None
5 = Other
6 = Unknown
1 = Sober
2 = Influence of Drugs /Alcohol
3 = Mental /Senile
4 = None
5 = Other
6 = Unknown
Q. VICTIM'S ACTIVITY WHEN ATTACKED
1 = Working
2 = Sleeping
3 = Opening Business
4 = None
5 = Other
6 = Unknown
7 = Closing Business
8 = Arriving Home
9 = Shopping
10 = At Home
11 = Jogging or Running
R. OBJECT OF ATTACK (4)
1 = Money
2 = Safe
3 = Jewelry
4 = None
5 = Other
6 = Unknown
S. ARSON
1 = Occupied
2 = Unoccupied

PROPERTY CODES

AUTOMOBILE ACCESSORIES
AENGINE   Engine Parts
AEXTERI   Exterior Parts
AINTER   Interior Parts
AOTHER   Misc. Parts
ASTEREO   Auto Stereo
BICYCLE
BBICYCL   Bicycle (2 wheels)
BOTHER   Mopeds / Other
CAMERA EQUIPMENT
CACCESS   Camera Access.
CCAMERA   Camera
CLENS   Camera Lens
COTHER   Other
EQUIP & TOOLS
ECOMPRE   Compressor, A/C
EDRILL   Drill
EGENER   Generator, Battery

EHAND   Hand Tool
EHEAVY   Farm, Garden
ELIFT   Lift, Ladder, Hoist
EMEASUR   Meter, Sorter
EOTHER   Other
EPOWER   Power Tool
ESAW   Saw, Sander, Lathe
FIREARMS
GAMMUN   Ammunition
GGUN   Gun
FOOD
FFOOD   FFOOD
HOUSEHOLD APPLIANCES
HCLEANER   Washer, Vacuum, Dryer
HCOOKER   Stove, Grill, Microwave
HFREEZER   Freezer, Refrig., Cooler
HFURNIT   Furniture
HOTHER   Other Household
HPROCE   Food Processor, Cutter
HSILVER   Silverware

JEWELRY
JBADGE   Badge, Shield
JBRACEL   Bracelet
JEARRIN   Earring
JMETALS   Precious Metals
JNECKLA   Necklace
JOTHER   Other Jewelry
JPENDAN   Pendant, Locket, Medal
JPIN   Pin
JRING   Ring
JWATCH   Watch
MUSICAL INSTRUMENTS
MOTHER   Other Musical
MPERCU   Piano, Percussion
MSTRING   String Instrument
MWIND   Wind Instrument
CURRENCY & DOCUMENTS
NFOREIGN   Foreign Currency

NOTHER   Documents
NUS   US currency
OFFICE EQUIPMENT
OCOMPUT   Computer, Monitor, etc.
OOTHER   Other Office
OPRINTR   Copier, Typewriter
OTELEPH   Answering Device
PERSONAL ACCESSORIES
PBAG   Bag, Purse, Luggage
PCLOTHE   Clothing
POTHER   Other Personal
AUDIO / VIDEO EQUIP
ROTHER   Other Audio / Video
RPORTAB   Radio
RSENREC   2-way Radio, Scanner
RSTEREO   Stereo
RTV   Television
RVCR   Video Recorder

SPORTS EQUIPMENT
SBALL   Ball, Golf, Racket
SFISHIN   Fishing, Scuba
SGUN   BB or Pellet Gun
SOTHER   Other Sports
SWATER   Surfboard, Skis
VIEWING EQUIPMENT
VBINOCU   Binoculars
VLIGHT   Light, Flashlight
VMICROS   Microscope
VOTHER   Other Viewing
MISCELLANEOUS
YDRUGS   Drugs
YOTHER   Other
YPETS   Pets
YSERV   Services
YSTOCK   Livestock
YSTRUCT   Structure

Figure 3.7
Sample Corrections Incident Report, Louisiana Department of Public Safety and Corrections

---

LOUISIANA DEPARTMENT OF PUBLIC SAFETY AND CORRECTIONS
INCIDENT REPORT

INSTITUTION: _____

1. Name of Inmate		2. Number	3. Date of Incident	4. Time of Incident

5. Place of Incident	6. Job Assignment (Inmate)	7. Housing Assignment (Inmate)

8. Nature of Incident

9. Description of Incident (Include all relevant information — "unusual inmate behavior, staff witnesses, physical evidence & disposition, immediate action including use of force"; use other side, if necessary)

_____
_____
_____
_____
_____
_____
_____
_____
_____
_____
_____
_____

10. Signature of reporting employee	11. Name, Title, Assignment (Print)

12. Date of Report	13. Time of Report	14. Report (copy) given to above inmate by:	15. Inmate's Signature:

16. Plea by Inmate: ☐ Not Guilty ☐ Guilty   17. Verdict: ☐ Not Guilty ☐ Guilty

18. Date of Hearing:	19. Counsel Substitute: DOC #:

20. Motions: _____
_____

21. **Reasons for Disposition:**
☐ Report is clear and precise.   ☐ Lack of a credible defense/little or no defense.   ☐ Based on his statement.
☐ The officer's version is determined to be more credible than the inmate's.   ☐ Pled guilty/accepted guilty plea.
☐ Only defense is denying contents of report.   ☐ The inmate presented no evidence to refute the charges.
☐ The investigative officer's testimony was deemed more truthful and accurate than the inmate's.   ☐ Plea bargain.
☐ The inmate's demeanor led the board to believe that the inmate's testimony was untrue.
☐ Other_____

22. **Reasons for Sentence:**
☐ Seriousness of offense.   ☐ The need to protect the institution, employees, or other.
☐ Poor Conduct record. A total of _____ rule violation(s). A total of _____ Schedule B violations since _____.
      A total of _____ # _____ rule violations since _____.
☐ Other_____

23. Sentence:
           Suspended ☐   _____ Days
           Imposed ☐

24. Sentence:
           Suspended ☐   _____ Days
           Imposed ☐

25. **DISCIPLINARY BOARD:**

Cost may be imposed for any property loss, damage, or medical expense occasioned through the fault of an inmate who in so causing the loss, damage, or medical expenses also is found guilty through the disciplinary process of violating one or more of the rules set out in the Disciplinary Rules and Procedures for Adult Inmates.

CHAIRMAN (DISCIPLINARY OFFICER) _____

MEMBER _____

Figure 3.8
Sample Loss Prevention Report Form, Longs Drugs Stores, Inc.

Longs Drug Stores, Inc.

CASE NUMBER

G. O. # _____

Store # _____

P. D # _____

LOSS PREVENTION DEPARTMENT

_____ REPORT

Store Location and Number _____

Reporting Person _____

Badge # _____

Date of Occurrence _____

Day of week: S   M   T   W   T   F   S

		LAST	FIRST	MIDDLE		S#	LAST	FIRST	MIDDLE
SUBJECT	S#								
ADDRESS	NUMBER		STREET			NUMBER		STREET	
	CITY		STATE	ZIP		CITY	STATE		ZIP
PHONE	( )					( )			
OCCUPATION									
EMPLOYER									

	RACE		SEX	ADULT/JUV.		RACE		SEX	ADULT/JUV.
DESCRIPTION	A. Asian/Oriental B. Black H. Hispanic I. American Indian	P. Polynesian W. White O. All Others	M / F AGE D.O.B.	A / J		A. Asian/Oriental B. Black H. Hispanic I. American Indian	P. Polynesian W. White O. All Others	M / F AGE D.O.B.	A / J
	HT	WT	HAIR	EYES		HT	WT	HAIR	EYES
	CLOTHING					CLOTHING			
IDENTIFICATION	SSN		D/L			SSN		D/L	

	M.O. (Enter Number)	1. Purse 4. Clothing 7. Other 2. Shopping Bag 5. Price Switch 3. Pocket 6. Cart/Basket		1. Purse 4. Clothing 7. Other 2. Shopping Bag 5. Price Switch 3. Pocket 6. Cart/Basket

DEPARTMENT (Enter Number)	1. RX Drugs 5. Pho Pros 9. Tobacco 14. Toys 2. OTC 6. Pho 10. Bks/Mags 15. Stn/Cards 3. COS 7. Food/Candy 11. Hseware 16. Auto 4. App 8. LIQ 12. House Suppls. 17. Hdwre 13. Sptg. Gds. 18. Sundry		1. RX Drugs 5. Pho Pros 9. Tobacco 14. Toys 2. OTC 6. Pho 10. Bks/Mags 15. Stn/Cards 3. COS 7. Food/Candy 11. Hseware 16. Auto 4. App 8. LIQ 12. House Suppls. 17. Hdwre 13. Sptg. Gds. 18. Sundry

	$ Cash	Check Book	Credit Card	$ Cash	Check Book	Credit Card
CASH ON PERSON		YES / NO	YES / NO		YES / NO	YES / NO

		Adult		Juvenile			Adult		Juvenile	
DISPOSITION (circle)	DETAINED	Arrested	Released	Police	Released To Parents	DETAINED	Arrested	Released	Police	Released To Parents

LOSS	LM	LC	TL	LM	LC	TL
RECOVERY	RM	RC	TR	RM	RC	TR

CIVRES (Circle)	DO NOT SEND	WAS PURCHASE MADE IN STORE?*	YES	NO	DO NOT SEND	WAS PURCHASE MADE IN STORE?*	YES	NO

TIMES	BEGAN SURV		TIME INCIDENT OCCURRED	TIME OF CUSTODY	TIME POLICE/ PARENTS NOTIFIED		TIME POLICE/ PARENTS ARRIVED		TOTAL HANDLING TIME	

TOTALS	TOTAL NUMBER ADULTS & JUV. DETAINED	ADULTS ARRESTED	ADULTS RELEASED	JUVENILES REFERRED TO POLICE	JUVENILES RELEASED TO PARENTS
	LOSS OF MERCHANDISE	$	LOSS OF CASH	$	TOTAL LOSS	$
	RECOVERED MDSE	$	RECOVERED CASH	$	TOTAL RECOVERY	$

WITNESSES (print)	DESCRIPTION OF MERCHANDISE	VALUE
_____	_____	$ _____
_____	_____	_____
_____	_____	_____
_____	_____	_____
_____	_____	_____
	TOTAL	$ _____

Figure 3.8—*continued*

Name of Responding Police Officer(s) _____ Badge Number(s) _____

SUBJECT'S FIRST WORDS AT TIME OF DETENTION: _____

NARRATIVE   (Include Who, What, Where, When, Why and How. Include subject's explanation in detail. Attach written
statement of subject(s) and *copies of pertinent cash register receipts.

_____

_____

_____

_____

_____

_____

_____

_____

_____

_____

_____

_____

_____

_____

_____

_____

_____

_____

_____

_____

_____

_____

_____

_____

_____

_____

17-01 Rev 8/89

_____
SIGNATURE OF REPORTING PERSON

Figure 3.9

Sample Field Interview/Recovered Vehicle/Offense Continuation Report, San Antonio Police Department

San Antonio Police Department ☐ OFFENSE ☐ INCIDENT ☐ SUPPLEMENTAL REPORT	(1) Weather Conditions at Time of Offense ☐ Warm ☐ Cool ☐ Dry ☐ Wet ☐ Unknown	(2) Case Number

| ☐ Gang Related   ☐ Suspected Hate Crime
☐ Domestic Violence ☐ Drive-by Shooting | Routing of Reports ☐ Homicide ☐ Robbery ☐ Forgery ☐ Intelligence ☐ Arson ☐ Youth ☐ T. I. D.
Check Appropriate Box (Original to Records) ☐ |

(3) Offense/Event	(4) Location of Offense (Number and Street)	Apt. #	(5) District

(6) Dates of Occurrence (MM/DD/YY)	(7) Hours of Occurrence	(8) Reporting Officer (Name/Badge)	Signature	Reporting Date

(9) Firm Name Address Phone	(10) Approving Authority (Name, Badge Date)

(11) Code   C – Complainant   R – Reporting Person   M – Manager/Owner   D – Day
              W – Witness   G – Guardian   O – Other   N – Night
                                                                              B – Both

Code	Name (Last, First, MI) Title	Race – Sex - DOB	Best Address Phone	
			Res.	
	Race	Sex	DOB	Bus.
			Res.	
	Race	Sex	DOB	Bus.
			Res.	
	Race	Sex	DOB	Bus.
			Res.	
	Race	Sex	DOB	Bus.

Inj. Per.	Code	(12) Victim Taken to	(13) Transported By	(14) Describe Injuries	(15) Condition

Codes   S- Stolen   D – Damaged   L – Lost   F – Found   R – Recovered   E – Evidence

Property Section

Code	Description (Brand/Make) Article	Model/Caliber/Color	Serial Number	OAN Number	Estimated Value

List Additional Items on SAPD Form 2-PCU

above listed date and time, had legal custody, and was the legal owner of the property listed here-in, which corporeal, personal property was wrongfully taken, without my consent, and I desire to prosecute the party, or parties, responsible.

X _____   X _____ Date: _____
         (Signature of Owner/Manager)   (Signature of Reporting Officer)

Forgery Evidence

One Forged Check/Card on the Account of
Check Number _____ Dated _____ _____
In the Amount of $ _____ Drawn on the _____ Pay to the order of _____ Bank _____
Account/Card Number _____ And signed with the Makers Signature of _____

(16) Property Tag Number	(17) Property Receipt Made ☐ Yes ☐ No	(18) Photograph Taken ☐ Yes ☐ No	(19) OAN applied it (TYPE) ☐ DL ☐ SSN ☐ DOB ☐ OTHER	(20) Total Stolen Value

(21) Size of Property Taken Was ☐ Concealable ☐ Hand Carried ☐ Needed Assistance	(22) Obvious Property Not Taken ☐ Personal Accessories ☐ Jewelry ☐ Money ☐ Furs ☐ Guns ☐ Radio/TV/Stereo ☐ Other:

Vehicles/Bicycle Information

(23) ☐ Stolen ☐ Crim. Misch. ☐ Burg Vehicle ☐ Unauth. Use ☐ Access. Theft ☐ Theft LPO ☐ Impound Veh. ☐ Abandoned Veh.	License Number	State/Yr/Type	Year	Make	Model	Style	VIN

Bicycle Serial Number	Make	Model	Type Frame ☐ Boys ☐ Girl	Type Brake ☐ Hand ☐ Foot	Wheel Size	Speed

(24) Color 1 (Solid or Top)   (25) Special Vehicle Features   Enter Number(s) From Below
     Color 2

1 Beige	9 Cream	17 Pink
2 Black	10 Gold	18 Red
3 Blue/Light	11 Gray	19 Silver
4 Blue	12 Green/Light	20 Tan
5 Blue/Dark	13 Green	21 Turquoise
6 Bronze	14 Green/Dark	22 White
7 Brown	15 Maroon	23 Yellow
8 Copper	16 Orange	24 Other

1. Level Altered
2. Sticker/Decal on Body/Bumper
3. Sticker/Decal on Window
4. Rust or Primer
5. Decorative Paint
6. Window Broken
7. Missing Parts
8. Loud Mufflers
9. Damage to Front
10. Damage to Rear
11. Damage to Side
12. Painted Inscription on Body
13. Vinyl Top
14. Door Panel(s) Removed
15. Torn Seat(s).Headliner
16. Camper Top
17. Special Wheels/Tires
    (Mags, Wide Tires, Etc.)
18. Extra Antenna(s)/Mirrors
19. Tinted Windows
20. Other

(26) Further Vehicle/Bicycle Description:

(27) Insurance Company	Policy Number	(28) Value of Vehicle/Bicycle	(29) Vehicle/bicycle insured? ☐ Yes ☐ No

SAPD Form 2-2 Rev. (Sep 04) PC

Figure 3.9—*continued*

2	San Antonio Police Department		Case Number

(30) Type Premises:

1. Single Family House	5. Chain/Convenience Store	9. Bar/Lounge	13. Car/Bus/Truck	17. Park
2. Apartment	6. Liquor Store	10. Bank/Saving & Loan	14. Office	18. Parking Lot
3. Hotel/Motel	7. Gas/Service Station	11. Finance Company	15. Street/Roadway	19. Restaurant
4. Other Residential	8. Other Retail Sales	12. Other Commercial House	16. School/Public Building	20. Other

CRIME AGAINST PROPERTY M. O.

(31) Direction

Entry Only
1. North
2. South
3. East
4. West

(32) Location

Entry Only
1. Front
2. Right Side
3. Left Side
4. Rear

(33) Entry/Exit Description

Point of Entry/Exit   /
1/1 Door
2/2 Window
3/3 Wall
4/4 Garage
5/5 Fence
6/6 Roof
7/7 Floor
8/8 Skylight
9/9 Fire Escape
10/10 Duct/Vent
11/11 Sliding Glass Door
12/12 Adjacent Building

13/13 Unknown
14/14 Other
15/15 N/A

(Burglary M. V.)
Entry Only
16. Vent Window
17. Door Window
18. Door
19. Hood
20. Trunk
21. Windshield/Back Glass

(34) Method of Entry

1. Pried
2. Broke
3. Cut
4. Chop/Pound
5. Remove
6. Concealment
7. Threats
8. Fraud
9. Attempt Only
10. Unlocked
11. Open For Trade
12. Unknown
13. Other
14. N/A

(35) Instrument/Tool Used for Entry

1. Blackjack/Club	11. Key/Pick/Plastic
2. Bodily force	12. Knife
3. Bolt Cutter	13. Lock-Puller
4. Chain, Locks/Vice Grips	14. Pliers
5. Coat Hanger/Wire	15. Pry Bar
6. Cutting Torch	16. Rock/Brick
7. Drill	17. Screwdriver
8. Explosives/Chemicals	18. Unknown
9. Glass Cutter	19. Other
10. Gun (Describe)	20. N/A

(36) Suspects Actions

1. Ate/Drank on Premises	6. Malicious Destruction
2. Attempted Defeat/ Defeated Alarm)	7. Removed Prints/Gloves
	8. Tripped Alarm/Returned Later
3. Crime not Complete	9. Turned Lights on/off
4. Crime Skillfully Done	10. Used Tools Found at Scene
5. Knew Location of Hidden Valuable	11. Other
	12. N/A

(37) Complainant Was

1. At Funeral/Church/Wedding
2. At Home
3. At Work/School
4. Absent (Ad in Paper)
5. Moving
6. Out of Town
7. Place of Entertainment
8. Present
9. Shopping
10. Other
11. N/A

(38) Crime Elements

1. Alarm Inoperative
2. Victim of Similar Crime
3. Object of Attack- Abandoned or Under Construction
4. N/A

Forgery and Credit Card Abuse

(39) I. D. Presented by Actor   I. D. Numbers

1. Drivers License
2. Social Security
3. Credit Card
4. Other

(40) Witness's Statement   List Witnesses on Front

1. Can Teller/Cashier Identify Actor?	☐ Yes ☐ No
2. Is Teller/Cashier Known?	☐ Yes ☐ No
3. Does Teller/Cashier Recall Transaction?	☐ Yes ☐ No
4. Are There Witnesses Who Can identify Actor?	☐ Yes ☐ No

Pin Number / Initials

Service Agent	/
Crime Analyst	/
Data Entry Clk.	/

(41) Explain "Other" Responses by Box Number

(42) List Significant M. O. by Box Number   1.   2.   3.   4.   5.

(43) Details of the Offense/Event:

Check one
Yes – Victim Notified of Provision of Victim Compensation Act (Art 8309 – 1V.T.C.S
No – Explain in Details)

PRTS Sergeant   Badge #   Date   Time   Supplement Attached ☐   ☐☐

Figure 3.10
Sample Missing Person Report Form, Bellevue Police Department

DISCLOSE INFO YES☐ NO☐

City of Bellevue POLICE

☐ RUNAWAY
☐ MISSING PERSON
☐ KIDNAPPING
☐ UNLAWFUL IMPRISONMENT
☐ CUSTODIAL INTERFERENCE

MISSING PERSON REPORT

CASE NO. | UCR | DIST | NBHD

PAGE ____ OF ____

REPORTED: MO | DAY | YR | DOW | TIME
OCCURRED: MO | DAY | YR | DOW | TIME

USE ONE OF BELOW LISTED UCR CODES
KIDNAPPING 26.11.02 | JUV RUNAWAY 29.00.00 | MISSING PERSON 47.01.00

LOCATION | APARTMENT / BUSINESS NAME

COMPLAINT INFO: LAST NAME | FIRST NAME | MIDDLE NAME | DOB | RESIDENCE ( )

ADDRESS | CITY | STATE | ZIP CODE | RELATIONSHIP TO MISSING PERSON | BUSINESS ( )

EMPLOYER / SCHOOL | RACE | SEX | HAIR | EYES | HGT | WGT | DRIVER'S LIC / ID CARD / SOCIAL SEC / ALIEN ID | STATE

MISSING PERSON INFORMATION

☐ ENDANGERED ☐ VOLUNTARY ADULT
☐ DISABLED ☐ JUVENILE (MKE)
☐ DISASTER VICTIM ☐ INVOLUNTARY

VICTIM LAST NAME | FIRST NAME | MIDDLE NAME | SEX | RACE

PLACE OF BIRTH | DOB | DATE EMANCIPATION | HEIGHT | WEIGHT | EYE COLOR | HAIR COLOR | SKIN TONE (CIRCLE ONE) ALB BLK DRK DBR FAR LGT LBR MED MBR OLV RUD SAL YEL

SCARS, MARKS, TATTOO, ETC (SMT) | NCIC FINGERPRINT CLASSIFICATION (FPS)

OTHER IDENTIFYING NUMBER (MNU) | SOCIAL SECURITY (SOC) | OPERATOR LICENSE NUMBER (OLN) | STATE (OLS) | YR EXPIRE (OLY)

DATE LAST CONTACT (DLC) | MISSING PERSON'S ADDRESS | BLOOD TYPE (CIRCLE ONE) (BLT) A-POS B-POS AB-POS A-NEG B-NEG AB-NEG O-NEG | HAS MISSING PERSON EVER DONATED BLOOD? ☐ YES ☐ NO

IF A BLOOD DONOR, WHERE AND WHEN? | PERSON CIRCUMCISED? (CRC) ☐ YES ☐ NO | ARE FOOT PRINTS AVAILABLE? (FPA) ☐ YES ☐ NO | ARE BODY XRAYS AVAILABLE? (BXR) ☐ YES ☐ NO

DOES THE MISSING PERSON HAVE CORRECTED VISION? ☐ YES ☐ NO ☐ GLASSES ☐ CONTACTS | CORRECTIVE VISION RX (VRX) | TYPE OF CONTACT LENSES AND COLOR (CIRCLE) HARD SOFT LONGWEAR SEMI BLUE GREEN GRAY CLEAR BROWN

HAS THE MISSING PERSON EVER BEEN FINGERPRINTED? ☐ YES ☐ NO | BY WHO OR WHAT AGENCY: | BUILD (CIRCLE) VERY THIN THIN MEDIUM MUSCULAR HEAVY/STOCKY OBESE (MIS)

DOES THE MISSING PERSON HAVE ANY BROKEN OR HEALED BONES, ARTIFICIAL BODY PARTS, OR MISSING BODY PARTS? ☐ YES ☐ NO | DESCRIBE:

ANY OTHER MISCELLANEOUS INFORMATION? (MIS) | RUNAWAY / MISSING PERSON: (MIS) IS A FIREARM MISSING? ☐ YES ☐ NO

BELOW IS A LIST OF CLOTHING AND PERSONAL EFFECTS. PLEASE INDICATE THOSE ITEMS THE MISSING PERSON WAS LAST SEEN WEARING. INCLUDE STYLE,TYPE,SIZE,COLOR,CONDITION, OR LABELS (MIST)

ITEM	STYLE/TYPE	SIZE	COLOR	MARKINGS	ITEM	STYLE/TYPE	SIZE	COLR	MARKINGS
HEAD GEAR					SHOES/BOOTS/SNEAKERS				
SCARF/TIE/GLOVES					UNDERWEAR				
COAT/JACKET/VEST					BRA/GIRDLE/SLIP				
SWEATER					STOCKINGS/PANTYHOSE				
SHIRT/BLOUSE					WALLET/PURSE				
PANTS/SKIRT					MONEY				
BELTS/SUSPENDERS					JEWELRY				
SOCKS					GLASSES				

LICENSE PLATE AND VEHICLE INFORMATION

PLATE (LIC) | STATE (LIC) | YEAR EXPIRES (LIY) | VEHICLE IDENTIFICATION NO (VIN)

PLATE TYPE (LIT) | YEAR (VYR) | MAKE (VMA) | MODEL (VMO) | STYLE (VST) | COLOR (VCO)

USE BELOW SECTION FOR SUMMARY OR TO START NARRATIVE | RELATED CASES

CASE DISPOSITION
☐ INACTIVE
☐ UNFOUNDED
☐ CLOSED/JUVENILE
☐ CLOSED/ARREST SUMMONS
☐ CLOSED/OTHER
☐ TRAINING

INVESTIGATED BY | PERSONNEL NO | DATE | APPROVED BY | DATE | ASSIGNED TO

Missing_0501

Figure 3.10—*continued*

REVERSE OF MISSING PERSON REPORT

CODES	V=VICTIM C=COMPLAINANT W=WITNESS S=SUSPECT IP=INVOLVED PERSON IB=INVOLVED BUSINESS	CASE NO. _____	PAGE ____ OF ____

CODE	LAST NAME	FIRST NAME	MIDDLE NAME	DOB Or Approx Age	RESIDENCE ( )
ADDRESS		CITY	STATE	ZIP CODE	BUSINESS ( )
EMPLOYER / SCHOOL		RACE	SEX	HAIR	EYES	HGT	WGT	DRIVER'S LIC / ID CARD / SOCIAL SEC / ALIEN ID	STATE	OTHER # or EMAIL

CODE	LAST NAME	FIRST NAME	MIDDLE NAME	DOB Or Approx Age	RESIDENCE ( )
ADDRESS		CITY	STATE	ZIP CODE	BUSINESS ( )
EMPLOYER / SCHOOL		RACE	SEX	HAIR	EYES	HGT	WGT	DRIVER'S LIC / ID CARD / SOCIAL SEC / ALIEN ID	STATE	OTHER # or EMAIL

OFFICER WITNESS	OFFICER #1	OFFICER #2	OFFICER #3	☐ MORE WITNESSES ON PAGE # ____

Case_p2_0602

I HEREBY CERTIFY OR DECLARE UNDER PENALTY OF PERJURY UNDER THE LAWS OF THE STATE OF WASHINGTON THAT THE FOREGOING IS TRUE AND CORRECT

SIGNATURE _____ DATE ____ PLACE ____

Figure 3.11
Sample False Alarm Report Form, St. Paul Police Department

ST. PAUL POLICE DEPARTMENT
FALSE ALARM REPORT

Page _____ of _____

Day	Month	Date	Year	Time:	Squad:	Team:	Residential ☐ Commercial ☐	Class:

Location of Call:	Location of Crime Scene:	Date & Time Occurred or Between Hours:

Residential Owner:	Address:	Home Phone:	Work Phone:

Business Name/Owner:	Address:	Home Phone:	Work Phone:

Complainant/Witness (Who Called Police):	Address:	Home Phone:	Work Phone:

Type of Alarm: ☐ Burglary ☐ Audible ☐ Robbery ☐ Silent   Alarm Reported By: ☐ Alarm Co. ☐ Citizen ☐ Auto Dialer ☐ On Tour   Varda Unit: ☐ Yes ☐ No

Alarm Company:	Address	Phone:

Reason for False Alarm: ☐ Equipment Malfunction ☐ Human Error   ☐ Report Other Crime ☐ Weather   Keyholder Response: ☐ Yes ☐ No   Audible Alarm Ennunciation: ☐ N/A ☐ Over 20 Min. ☐ 3 Per Hour

Permit Displayed: ☐ Yes ☐ No   Permit Number: Permit Color:

NARRATIVE

C.N.

Assisting Officer:	Emp. No.:	Reporting Officer:	Emp. No.:

Report Reviewed By:	Emp. No.:	O.T. ☐ Yes ☐ No	Typist:	R.O.:	Code:	Name Entry:

☐ CHF ☐ Hom ☐ Rob ☐ Juv ☐ Coord ☐ ID ☐ Lab ☐ Rec ☐ Team ☐ Sex ☐ Rptr ☐ Other _____
☐ D/C ☐ Burg ☐ Theft ☐ Prop ☐ CAU ☐ F&F ☐ Auto ☐ DAO ☐ CO ☐ HumServ ☐ CPU

PM 557-92R

Figure 3.12
Sample Pursuit Report, Arizona Department of Public Safety

ARIZONA DEPARTMENT OF PUBLIC SAFETY
PURSUIT REPORT

PAGE 1 OF 4
IAS USE ONLY

Answer all questions. Use "UNK" for "unknown" and "N/A" for "not applicable".

PURSUIT SUMMARY   TO BE COMPLETED BY ALL OFFICERS PARTICIPATING IN THE PURSUIT INCLUDING THE PURSUIT COMMANDER.

OFFENSE / INCIDENT DR NUMBER   P-

REPORT DATE   MONTH   DAY   YEAR   OTHER AGENCY DR NUMBER

ACCIDENT DR NUMBER

PURSUIT COMMANDER NAME (LAST, FIRST, MI)

ID NUMBER   CALL SIGN

REASON FOR INITIATING CONTACT *(Check all that apply)*

☐ TRAFFIC VIOLATION   ☐ POSSIBLE DUI   ☐ ATL BROADCAST
☐ CRIMINAL VIOLATION (NON TRAFFIC)   ☐ VEHICLE REPORTED STOLEN
☐ UNKNOWN   ☐ OTHER:

✱ ☐ YES ☐ NO Did the pursuit begin after stop?

PURSUIT COMMANDER WAS:
☐ PRIMARY UNIT OFFICER   ☐ ON SCENE SUPERVISOR / COMMANDER   ☐ OFF SCENE SUPERVISOR / COMMANDER

PURSUIT INITIATED BY:
☐ DPS   ☐ OTHER AGENCY (DPS ASSIST):

DATE PURSUIT BEGAN   MONTH   DAY   YEAR
TIME PURSUIT BEGAN (USE 24 HOUR CLOCK)
DATE PURSUIT ENDED   MONTH   DAY   YEAR
TIME PURSUIT ENDED (USE 24 HOUR CLOCK)

LOCATION(S) OF PURSUIT

	STREET ADDRESS, HIGHWAY, INTERSTATE, STATE ROUTE, ROAD/STREET NAME	MILE POST	CROSS ROAD/STREET	DIRECTION OF TRAVEL	COUNTY	H.P. DIST.
BEGAN				☐ NORTH ☐ EAST ☐ SOUTH ☐ WEST		
ENDED				☐ NORTH ☐ EAST ☐ SOUTH ☐ WEST		

PURSUIT DESCRIPTION

<u>PURSUIT COMMANDER:</u> Provide a brief summary of the pursuit, including reason initiated, how it progressed and ended (note injuries). Describe unusual occurrences, equipment, operational or communication problems; recommendations for change to procedures, etc. **Complete all pages of the Pursuit Report form. Include data from page 1 of the pursuit reports received from other officers involved in the pursuit.**

<u>OTHER OFFICERS PARTICIPATING IN THE PURSUIT:</u> 1) Complete the Vehicle data below and 2) briefly <u>describe your participation</u> in the pursuit including topics listed under **PURSUIT COMMANDER**. **Complete page 1 only and forward to the Pursuit Commander for compilation.**

DRIVER NAME: ID. NO.:   CALL SIGN:
☐ PRIMARY UNIT ☐ SECONDARY UNIT ☐ SUPPORT UNIT   YEAR OF LAST DRIVER TRAINING 19
LENGTH OF DPS SERVICE Years: Months: PREVIOUS NUMBER OF PURSUITS (IF NONE, WRITE ZERO)
PASSENGER NAME: ID. NO.:   CALL SIGN:
VEH. YEAR: MAKE: TYPE ☐ A ☐ B   MODEL:

Quantities of the prior version of this form, dated 9/93, may be used until exhausted.

DPS 802-04089 Rev. 8/94

Continued

Figure 3.12—*continued*

PURSUIT ENVIRONMENTAL CONDITIONS

PREDOMINANT TYPE OF ROADWAY
- ☐ INTERSTATE-DIVIDED
- ☐ HIGHWAY-DIVIDED
- ☐ FRONTAGE
- ☐ 2-WAY ROAD/STREET
- ☐ 1-WAY ROAD/STREET
- ☐ OTHER:------------->

PREDOMINANT ROADWAY SETTING
- ☐ URBAN
- ☐ RURAL

ROAD CONDITIONS (CHECK ALL THAT APPLY)
- ☐ DRY   ☐ WET
- ☐ GREASE/OIL
- ☐ LOOSE SAND/GRAVEL
- ☐ CONSTRUCTION ZONE
- ☐ SNOW/ICE
- ☐ OTHER:-->

PREDOMINANT TRAFFIC CONDITIONS
- ☐ LIGHT   ☐ HIGH
- ☐ MODERATE

LIGHT CONDITIONS
- ☐ DAYLIGHT
- ☐ DAWN/DUSK
- ☐ DARKNESS

WEATHER CONDITIONS (CHECK ALL THAT APPLY)
- ☐ CLEAR   ☐ RAIN   ☐ SNOW
- ☐ DUST   ☐ FOG   ☐ STRONG WINDS
- ☐ OTHER:-->

PURSUIT CHARACTERISTICS

DISTANCE OF PURSUIT	MAXIMUM SPEED BY VIOLATOR	NO. OF AGENCIES INVOLVED INCLUDING DPS	ACCIDENT(S) ENCOUNTERED	☐ NONE

MILES   M.P.H.

ACCIDENT(S)	961A / 962A / 963A
DPS:	☐ 961A ☐ 962A ☐ 963A
OTHER AGENCY:	☐ 961 ☐ 962 ☐ 963
SUSPECT:	☐ 961 ☐ 962 ☐ 963
3RD PARTY:	☐ 961 ☐ 962 ☐ 963

NUMBER OF EACH TYPE OF VEHICLE INVOLVED

☐ DPS-->	TYPE A CARS	TYPE B CARS	MOTOR-CYCLES	AIRCRAFT	UNMARKE	OTHER

☐ OTHER AGENCY-------->	CARS	MOTORCYCLES	AIRCRAFT

ASSISTING DPS REGIONAL COMMUNICATIONS CENTER
- ☐ NO CONTACT
- ☐ NORTHERN (FLAGSTAFF)
- ☐ SOUTHERN (TUCSON)
- ☐ CENTRAL (PHOENIX)

Did the pursuit involve a critical incident as defined in GO 22.037   ☐ NO   ☐ YES: TYPE: (shooting, injury, etc.):------>

CRITICAL INCIDENT DR NUMBER

UNITS INVOLVED IN PURSUIT

1/1 PRIMARY UNIT
- ☐ DPS--> -OR-
- NAME: ID. NO.:   CALL SIGN:
- ▲ DRIVER→ YEAR OF LAST DRIVER TRAINING 19 ___ LENGTH OF DPS SERVICE Years: ___ Months: ___ PREVIOUS NUMBER OF PURSUITS (IF NONE, WRITE ZERO) ___
- PASSENGER NAME: ID. NO.:   CALL SIGN:
- VEHICLE YEAR-> ___ MAKE-> ___   TYPE ☐A ☐B   MODEL-> ___
- ☐ OTHER AGENCY NAME:

2/2 SECONDARY UNIT
- ☐ DPS--> -OR-
- NAME: ID. NO.:   CALL SIGN:
- ▲ DRIVER→ YEAR OF LAST DRIVER TRAINING 19 ___ LENGTH OF DPS SERVICE Years: ___ Months: ___ PREVIOUS NUMBER OF PURSUITS (IF NONE, WRITE ZERO) ___
- PASSENGER NAME: ID. NO.:   CALL SIGN:
- VEHICLE YEAR-> ___ MAKE-> ___   TYPE ☐A ☐B   MODEL-> ___
- ☐ OTHER AGENCY NAME:

3/3 SUPPORT UNIT
- ☐ DPS--> -OR-
- NAME: ID. NO.:   CALL SIGN:
- ▲ DRIVER→ YEAR OF LAST DRIVER TRAINING 19 ___ LENGTH OF DPS SERVICE Years: ___ Months: ___ PREVIOUS NUMBER OF PURSUITS (IF NONE, WRITE ZERO) ___
- PASSENGER NAME: ID. NO.:   CALL SIGN:
- VEHICLE YEAR-> ___ MAKE-> ___   TYPE ☐A ☐B   MODEL-> ___
- ☐ OTHER AGENCY NAME:

3/4 SUPPORT UNIT
- ☐ DPS--> -OR-
- NAME: ID. NO.:   CALL SIGN:
- ▲ DRIVER→ YEAR OF LAST DRIVER TRAINING 19 ___ LENGTH OF DPS SERVICE Years: ___ Months: ___ PREVIOUS NUMBER OF PURSUITS (IF NONE, WRITE ZERO) ___
- PASSENGER NAME: ID. NO.:   CALL SIGN:
- VEHICLE YEAR-> ___ MAKE-> ___   TYPE ☐A ☐B   MODEL-> ___
- ☐ OTHER AGENCY NAME:

3/5 SUPPORT UNIT
- ☐ DPS--> -OR-
- NAME: ID. NO.:   CALL SIGN:
- ▲ DRIVER→ YEAR OF LAST DRIVER TRAINING 19 ___ LENGTH OF DPS SERVICE Years: ___ Months: ___ PREVIOUS NUMBER OF PURSUITS (IF NONE, WRITE ZERO) ___
- PASSENGER NAME: ID. NO.:   CALL SIGN:
- VEHICLE YEAR-> ___ MAKE-> ___   TYPE ☐A ☐B   MODEL-> ___
- ☐ OTHER AGENCY NAME:

DPS 802-04089 Rev. 8/94

Figure 3.12—*continued*

SUBJECT OF PURSUIT	PAGE 3 OF 4

VEHICLE TYPE

☐ CAR   ☐ TRUCK   ☐ MOTORCYCLE   ☐ ATC/ATV   ☐ VAN   ☐ OTHER:--->

VEHICLE YEAR:---> [   ]   **MAKE:->** [   ]   **MODEL:->** [   ]   **COLOR:-------->** [   ]

☐ YES   ☐ NO   Was the driver driving the vehicle after dark with the headlights *and* taillights off?

TOTAL NUMBER OF OCCUPANTS:--> [   ]   **DRIVER SEX:-->** ☐ MALE ☐ FEMALE   **RACE / ORIGIN** ☐ WHITE ☐ HISPANIC (MEXICAN)   ☐ BLACK ☐ OTHER: ☐ UKNOWN ☐ NATIVE AMERICAN   **AGE:---->** [   ]

SUSPECT ARMED/ WEAPON AVAILABLE: CHECK ALL THAT APPLY ☐ UNKNOWN   ☐ NONE ☐ HANDGUN ☐ RIFLE ☐ SHOTGUN ☐ KNIFE ☐ OTHER: [   ]

SUSPECT DUI: ☐ NOT DUI ☐ ALCOHOL ☐ DRUGS ☐ UNKNOWN   **FELONY STOP MADE:** ☐ YES ☐ NO   **VEHICLE FOUND TO BE STOLEN:** ☐ YES ☐ NO

PREDOMINANT CONDITION OF CAPTURE	PREDOMINANT CONDITION OF ESCAPE

SELECT ONLY ONE

☐ SUSPECT ESCAPED (COMPLETE CONDITIONS OF ESCAPE) ➡
☐ SUSPECT STOPPED
☐ SUSPECT VEHICLE BROKE DOWN
☐ SUSPECT VEHICLE SPUN OUT
☐ SUSPECT VEHICLE COLLIDED
☐ SUSPECT VEHICLE CHANNELED & STOPPED
☐ SUSPECT VEHICLE BOXED-IN & STOPPED
☐ CLASS B ROADBLOCK USED
☐ CLASS C ROADBLOCK USED
☐ OTHER AGENCY CAPTURED SUSPECT
☐ OTHER:-->

SELECT ONLY ONE

☐ SUSPECT VEHICLE OUTRAN PURSUIT VEHICLE
☐ SUSPECT ABANDONED VEHICLE & FLED
☐ DPS VEHICLE BROKE DOWN
☐ DPS VEHICLE SPUN OUT
☐ DPS VEHICLE INVOLVED IN COLLISION
☐ PURSUIT COMMANDER TERMINATED PURSUIT
☐ DPS SUPERVISOR/COMMANDER
   TERMINATED PURSUIT
☐ OTHER:-->

REASON
- - - - - -
- - - - - -

REASON
- - - - - -
- - - - - -

TYPES OF OFFENSE(S) THE DRIVER WAS CHARGED UPON ARREST

CHECK ALL THAT APPLY

☐ **Assault**   ☐ **Unlawful Flight**

☐ **Criminal Damage**   ☐ **Reckless Driving**

☐ **DUI**   ☐ **Theft**

☐ **Drug / Paraphernalia Possession**   ☐ **Weapon Misconduct**

☐ **Endangerment**

☐ **Other:** [   ]

DPS 802-04089 Rev. 8/94

Continued

Figure 3.12—*continued*

PURSUIT COMMANDER:-->	SIGNATURE	MONTH / DAY / YEAR	▼ COMMENTS ▼

SUPERVISOR:-->	SIGNATURE	MONTH / DAY / YEAR	▼ COMMENTS ▼

DISTRICT COMMANDER:-->	SIGNATURE	MONTH / DAY / YEAR	▼ COMMENTS ▼

☐ NO FURTHER REVIEW REQUIRED

☐ FURTHER HQ REVIEW REQUIRED DUE TO APPARENT DEFICIENCY IN:

☐ POLICY ☐ TRAINING

☐ TACTICS ☐ EQUIPMENT

☐ OTHER-->

REVIEW BEYOND DISTRICT COMMANDER IS REQUIRED ONLY IF FURTHER ACTION IS RECOMMENDED REGARDING THIS PURSUIT.

DIVISION COMMANDER-->	SIGNATURE	MONTH / DAY / YEAR	▼ COMMENTS ▼

ASSISTANT DIRECTOR:-->	SIGNATURE	MONTH / DAY / YEAR	▼ COMMENTS ▼

FOLLOWING REVIEW, FORWARD COMPLETED REPORT TO INFORMATION ANALYSIS FOR PROCESSING.   DPS 802-04089 Rev. 8/94

Figure 3.13
Sample Face Page Report Form, Federal Bureau of Investigation

FD-263 (Rev. 4-30-85)

FEDERAL BUREAU OF INVESTIGATION

REPORTING OFFICE	OFFICE OF ORIGIN	DATE	INVESTIGATIVE PERIOD

TITLE OF CASE	REPORT MADE BY	TYPED BY
	CHARACTER OF CASE	

APPROVED	SPECIAL AGENT IN CHARGE	DO NOT WRITE IN SPACES BELOW
COPIES MADE:		

Dissemination Record of Attached Report				Notations
Agency				
Request Recd.				
Date Fwd.				
How Fwd.				
By				

COVER PAGE

FBI/DOJ

An interesting and confusing thing occasionally happens when an agency has a report writing manual for all criminal reports and there is a mandated state form for particular events with its own manual that requires a different format. State-mandated forms are usually those documenting motor vehicle collisions and events that are in the public or legislative eye, such as domestic abuse. In 1987, using a federal grant, New Mexico developed a statewide reporting system. Since that time the grant has run out and some agencies have amended the reporting process to meet their own needs. Also notice that security report forms are often similar to those used for law enforcement.

Study these forms for similarities and differences. Notice that some of the face page forms have room for the narrative of the report while others have spaces only for filling in information such as names, addresses, descriptions, etc. The FBI's face page form (Figure 3.13) asks for very little information and requires the writer to provide most of the format. Many face page forms require that narrative reports be included on separate forms. Chapter 4 covers the use of such narrative continuation and follow-up reports.

Correct Abbreviation and Capitalization

As noted previously, many directives state, "Do not abbreviate," but the size of blocks on many forms makes abbreviation absolutely necessary. Ask someone in authority rather than guess what abbreviations are proper.

Many forms now use ethnic origin rather than race, because there are only three races: Caucasoid, Negroid, and Mongoloid. Japanese, Chinese, Korean, and Okinawan are, for example, ethnic rather than racial terms and would all be considered to be of the Mongoloid race. Ethnic sensibilities even enter the picture in terms of abbreviations. World War II made *Jap* an offensive term, so the use of *Jap* as an abbreviation is not correct. A few examples of acceptable abbreviations might include: *Jpse.* for Japanese, *Ptgse.* for Portuguese, *Fil.* for Filipino, and *Chi.* for Chinese. If you are not sure of an abbreviation, look it up in a dictionary that contains abbreviations, look in your agency's report writing guide, or write it out.

It is easy to see how this situation can vary. *Chi.* might mean Chicano to some, Chinese to others. Be sure not to offend ethnic sensibilities; wherever you are, check for locally accepted abbreviations. Also find out correct capitalization and nomenclature.

You may think that capitalization was decided by grammar books long ago. Not so. Capitalization varies enormously. Military and police in all services are familiar with a much wider variety of capitalized titles and words than is common in civilian life. Thus, lieutenant may be *Lt.* on a civilian report referring to police, and *LT* with no period on a military report. On the other hand, the FBI capitalizes every letter of a person's entire name, but not his or her title.

Dealing with Names

Capitalization of all or part of a name on a report is a helpful device practiced by most states. As in journalism, "names make the news," and a means of emphasizing the names facilitates the reading and interpretation of a report, whether the names are on the face page or elsewhere. Various agencies have different means of emphasizing last names, whether the name refers to an employee, complainant, victim, witness, or suspect.

Here are some ways of calling attention to and clarifying names:

1. Capitalize the entire name.

2. Capitalize only the last name. This has two advantages: it determines the last name when both names sound like first names, as in James LAWRENCE, and clarifies the last name when there is a two-word last name. This happens sometimes with Asian names and with hyphenated last names. Examples: Samuel KIM HAN, Cindy SMITH-COLLINS.

3. Underline the last name. Example: <u>Jones</u> arrived home and found John <u>Adams</u> there.

After the full name and middle initial have been given, both male and female persons may be identified in the narrative by last name only, except when more than one person in the report has the same last name. Where a person has no middle initial, *NMI* is frequently used. In the rare case of a person with just initials for first and middle names, initials and last name are given with the notation in parentheses (*Full Name*). Be sure to check your agency's guidelines.

Note that *AKA* means *also known as*. This term is used if the person has an alias, a name that has different spellings, or a name that has been changed through marriage or court action. The term AKA is also sometimes used for military rank and serial number.

There are several methods of capitalization and abbreviation, and the formats vary from state to state, and even from agency to agency. In some agencies, the last name is not capitalized in full, and the alias is written in quotation marks following the correct name. In others, the last name is placed in all capital letters whenever written in the report.

Positioning of the name is another concern. In some states, a person's first and last names are reversed only on the face page or the first time that the person's name appears. In other places, the name is reversed when it heads a block of description, even though the block is contained on a continuation page. Such a block is usually indented halfway or even further across the page:

> JONES, John J.
> Caucasian male,
> DOB 11-25-78
> . . . .
> . . . .

The name is never reversed when it is part of a sentence, even in the synopsis on the face page. The following type of narrative writing is unacceptable:

> SMITH, John, awoke to the sound of a crash and found that the car belonging to his son, SMITH, John, Jr., had been hit by a truck.

Should you fill in every blank on the face page? Traditionally, most directives require that every blank should either be filled in or marked *DNA* for "Does Not Apply." However, the use of DNA is no longer recommended because it is now used as an abbreviation for deoxyribonucleic acid, the tongue-twisting name for the material that carries the genetic pattern of each individual. It is now often recommended that a line be drawn through the block to be left without information, showing that you are aware of the block but have no information to be included. Some agencies want the block left empty so that it can be filled in later if the information becomes available. Find out what is required by your agency.

Writing a Good Synopsis

Many agencies have moved away from the use of synopses in recent years. They were originally included so that they could be listed on daily logs to help locate cases. Modern use of computers has eliminated some of the need for a synopsis. If you are required to use a synopsis, the writing of a good synopsis starts with brevity. Law enforcement and security personnel consider the *who, what, when, where,* and *how,* but usually not the *why* in the synopsis. Concentrate on making the synopsis as brief and clear as possible, including crucial information. Write in the first person if your agency allows it. Some agencies allow you to leave out your own name when it is quite obvious that the action is yours. An example of this is:

> Found stolen 2006 white Lincoln Navigator, license XJR800, in the Safeway parking lot, 1400 King Street, and notified owner, Earl F. JONES, 1862 Adams Street.

Keeping Up with Trends

Whether you are an officer or a student, living in a metropolis or a small town, you can learn something by comparing methods and material. A good way to keep up with new methods is to read journals and magazines dealing with your own field, such as *Police Chief, Law and Order, Law Enforcement Technology, Law Enforcement Product News,* and *Security Management.* Magazines like *Time* and *Newsweek,* as well as daily newspapers, often report on innovative techniques being applied in jurisdictions throughout the country. Government and association publications also provide much information.

Summary

1. Both face pages and laws and ordinances vary widely from state to state and in the case of face pages, sometimes within states. The Uniform Crime Reporting Program for the FBI was developed to have a standardized method of defining and collecting crime statistics. NIBRS is planned as a replacement for UCR because it contains more detailed information. It is currently being tested by several states that also continue to report using UCR categories.

2. Face pages may contain considerable detail or may provide only general information.

3. On most face pages, there are blanks to be filled in for who, what, when, where, and how.

4. The method of writing the names of victim(s) and suspect(s) also varies. In some agencies, for example, every letter of all last names is capitalized whenever a name is mentioned. Other agencies require that the last name be underlined whenever mentioned. The names are usually reversed on the face page (except for the officer's signature, which is in normal order) and when set off in indented description format. Names (still with last name fully capitalized) are in normal order in narrative sections. In some agencies, the pronoun "I" is never used. In others, the officer has the option of using first or third person. No matter which person is used, the report writer must be consistent throughout.

5. It is important that you request a usage directive on capitalization and abbreviations from your immediate supervisor, because such usage varies from agency to agency, within states, and across the nation.

6. Synopses must be brief, clear, and contain crucial information. There is a great emphasis on brevity in writing a synopsis. Shortcuts in grammar such as leaving your name out are sometimes allowed. Check with your agency about its requirements.

Chapter 3 — TEST

1. Face pages on police reports _____ widely from state to state and even within states.

2. A department may have a number of different face page reports or only one or two. In law enforcement, the old newspaper questions of _____, _____, _____, _____, and _____ are answered in a report. The _____ of a report must be carefully justified if it is included in a law enforcement report.

3. Important sections of reports may have shaded areas or may be otherwise marked for the purpose of _____.

4. Names are usually reversed on the _____ and on subsequent pages when the name and description are indented and set off in block form. The name is never reversed when it is _____.

5. _____ of every letter in the last name is sometimes used in reports. One variation occurs when the last name is _____.

6. Fill in the meanings for the following abbreviations:

   AKA _____

   NMI _____

   DNA previously meant _____, but is now an abbreviation for deoxyribonucleic acid, which is analyzed in genetic testing.

CHAPTER 4

The Narrative –
The Continuation Page
and Follow-Up Report

It is the writing of the continuation page — the narrative part of your report — that determines where you stand or fall as a writer. On the face page, blanks are provided and the sequence is arranged. Once you have learned the format and correct abbreviations to use, the writing is fairly simple, especially in large agencies that have individualized forms for many procedures. In many agencies, versatility may be required, particularly when one employee handles more than one phase of the work or when a single face page is used for most types of reports. Reports in these agencies sometimes combine the face page and the continuation page (for example, see Figure 4.1).

Agencies have various names for the types of forms on which to record additional information. They are commonly called continuation pages, follow-up reports, or supplementary reports or material.

Whatever the size or type of agency you serve, it is important that you learn the proper sequence of information in your report and how to use the narrative section on the proper form for your agency. Take a look at Figures 4.1 through 4.10. Notice that while these forms may look very different, they are all used to identify the cases that they document and provide a means for the narratives to be written.

DOI: 10.1016/B978-1-4377-5584-8.00011-6

Figure 4.1
Sample Drug Influence Evaluation Form, Arizona Department of Public Safety

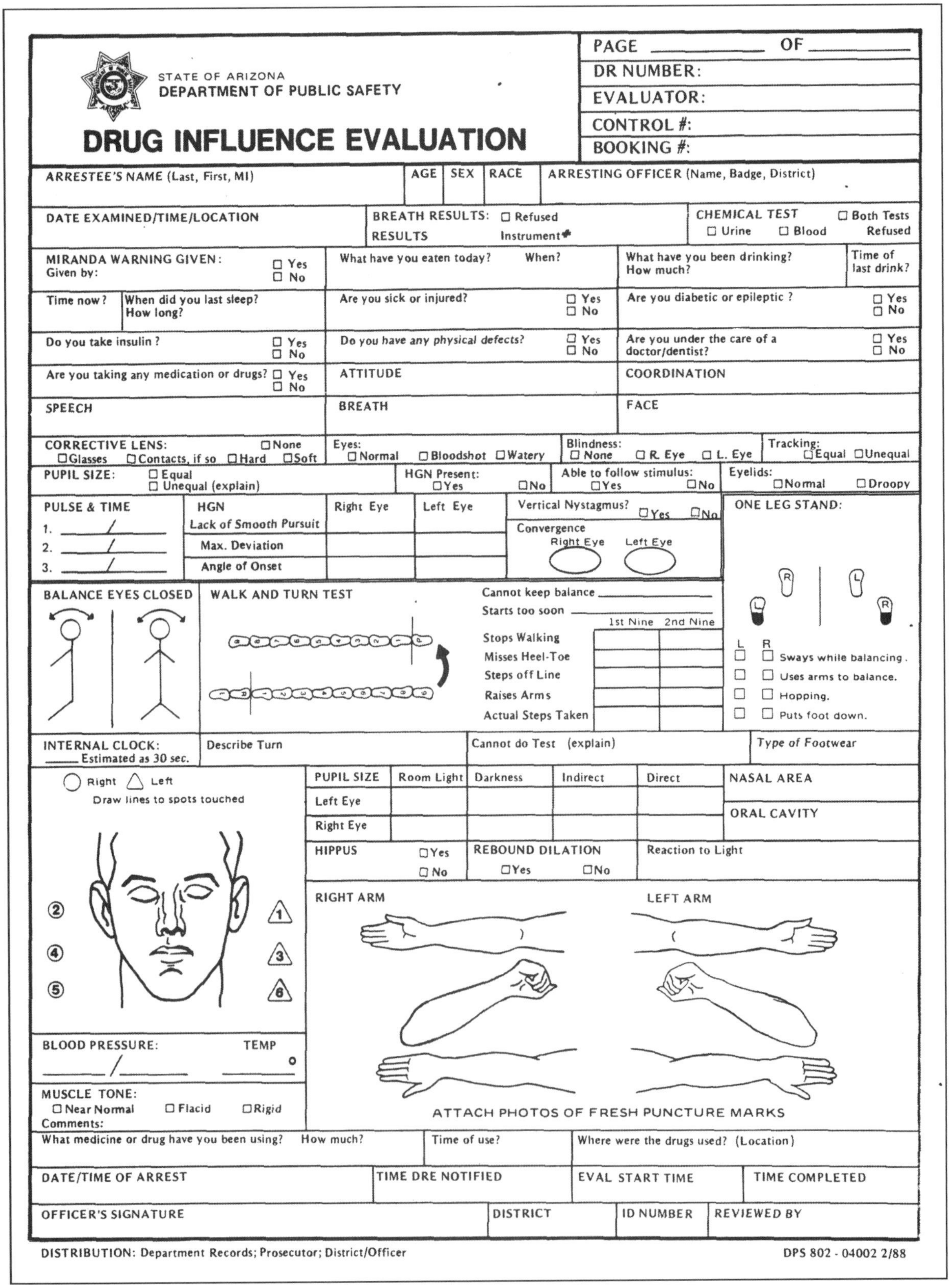

STATE OF ARIZONA
DEPARTMENT OF PUBLIC SAFETY

DRUG INFLUENCE EVALUATION

PAGE ______ OF ______
DR NUMBER:
EVALUATOR:
CONTROL #:
BOOKING #:

ARRESTEE'S NAME (Last, First, MI) | AGE | SEX | RACE | ARRESTING OFFICER (Name, Badge, District)

DATE EXAMINED/TIME/LOCATION | BREATH RESULTS: ☐ Refused RESULTS Instrument# | CHEMICAL TEST ☐ Urine ☐ Blood ☐ Both Tests Refused

MIRANDA WARNING GIVEN: Given by: ☐ Yes ☐ No | What have you eaten today? When? | What have you been drinking? How much? | Time of last drink?

Time now? | When did you last sleep? How long? | Are you sick or injured? ☐ Yes ☐ No | Are you diabetic or epileptic? ☐ Yes ☐ No

Do you take insulin? ☐ Yes ☐ No | Do you have any physical defects? ☐ Yes ☐ No | Are you under the care of a doctor/dentist? ☐ Yes ☐ No

Are you taking any medication or drugs? ☐ Yes ☐ No | ATTITUDE | COORDINATION

SPEECH | BREATH | FACE

CORRECTIVE LENS: ☐ None ☐ Glasses ☐ Contacts, if so ☐ Hard ☐ Soft | Eyes: ☐ Normal ☐ Bloodshot ☐ Watery | Blindness: ☐ None ☐ R. Eye ☐ L. Eye | Tracking: ☐ Equal ☐ Unequal

PUPIL SIZE: ☐ Equal ☐ Unequal (explain) | HGN Present: ☐ Yes ☐ No | Able to follow stimulus: ☐ Yes ☐ No | Eyelids: ☐ Normal ☐ Droopy

PULSE & TIME
1. ___/___
2. ___/___
3. ___/___

HGN	Right Eye	Left Eye
Lack of Smooth Pursuit		
Max. Deviation		
Angle of Onset		

Vertical Nystagmus? ☐ Yes ☐ No
Convergence
Right Eye Left Eye

ONE LEG STAND:
L R
☐ ☐ Sways while balancing.
☐ ☐ Uses arms to balance.
☐ ☐ Hopping.
☐ ☐ Puts foot down.

BALANCE EYES CLOSED

WALK AND TURN TEST

	1st Nine	2nd Nine
Cannot keep balance ______		
Starts too soon ______		
Stops Walking		
Misses Heel-Toe		
Steps off Line		
Raises Arms		
Actual Steps Taken		

INTERNAL CLOCK: ______ Estimated as 30 sec. | Describe Turn | Cannot do Test (explain) | Type of Footwear

○ Right △ Left
Draw lines to spots touched

PUPIL SIZE	Room Light	Darkness	Indirect	Direct
Left Eye				
Right Eye				

NASAL AREA
ORAL CAVITY

HIPPUS ☐ Yes ☐ No | REBOUND DILATION ☐ Yes ☐ No | Reaction to Light

RIGHT ARM LEFT ARM

BLOOD PRESSURE: ___/___ TEMP ___°

MUSCLE TONE: ☐ Near Normal ☐ Flacid ☐ Rigid
Comments:

ATTACH PHOTOS OF FRESH PUNCTURE MARKS

What medicine or drug have you been using? How much? | Time of use? | Where were the drugs used? (Location)

DATE/TIME OF ARREST | TIME DRE NOTIFIED | EVAL START TIME | TIME COMPLETED

OFFICER'S SIGNATURE | DISTRICT | ID NUMBER | REVIEWED BY

DISTRIBUTION: Department Records; Prosecutor; District/Officer
DPS 802 - 04002 2/88

Figure 4.1—*continued*

DRUG INFLUENCE EVALUATION

PAGE _____ OF _____

NARRATIVE:

DR NUMBER

DPS 802-04002 2/88

Figure 4.2
Sample Supplement/Narrative Form, Anne Arundel County Police Department

ANNE ARUNDEL COUNTY POLICE DEPARTMENT, MILLERSVILLE, MD.		Supplement/Narrative	Page 2 of 2

1. OFFENSE/INCIDENT	2 BUSINESS NAME/VICTIM (LAST, FIRST MIDDLE)	3. CASE NUMBER

4. DATE WRITTEN 9/19/2005	5. DISTRICT/POST	6. BUSINESS/VICTIM'S ADDRESS	7. ORIG. DATE	8. MULTIPLE CLEAR-UP YES NO

9. CHECK ONE OR MORE:
☐ ORIGINAL,   ☐ FOLLOW-UP,   ☐ OFFENSE,   ☐ ACCIDENT,   ☐ ARREST,   ☐ PROSECUTION,   ☑ SUPPLEMENT,   ☐ CONTINUATION

10. LIST IN NARRATIVE ALL RELATED CASE NUMBERS IF MULTIPLE CLEAR-UP.

CODE	57. SUSPECT NAME	DOB	SEX	RACE	EYES	HAIR	WEIGHT	HEIGHT
	ADDRESS			PHONE (home)		PHONE (work)		
	IDENTIFIERS							

11. DISPOSITION:
OPEN   CLOSED   SUSPENDED   CLEARED BY EXCEPTION   FALSE REPORT   CLEARED BY ARREST

12. FIRST OFFICER	ID	13. SECOND OFFICER	ID	14. SUPERVISOR	ID	15. REPORTS REVIEW OFFICER ID

Form # 09-13-60-1-B

Figure 4.3
Sample Continuation Page, Camden County Sheriff's Department

OFFICE OF THE SHERIFF CAMDEN COUNTY				CONTINUATION PAGE SO-1A	
1. Unit:	2. Code: N/A	3. Area Code, Phone, Extension:	4. Prosecutor's Case Number: N/A	5. CCSD Case Number: YEAR CASE SUFFIX 05	

74. Rank/Name/Badge:	75. Page 2 of: 2	77. Reviewer/Badge:
78. Signature:	76. Date of Report: 8/15/2005	79. Supervisor Signature/Date:

SO#1A 8/14/03   512

Figure 4.4

Sample Narrative Report, Oakland County Sheriff Department

OAKLAND COUNTY SHERIFF DEPT.
1201 N. Telegraph Rd., Pontiac, MI 48341
Phone: 248-858-5011 ORI # MI6316300

NARRATIVE REPORT

PO # ______

☐ SUPPRESS ☐ PRIMARY ☐ SUPP PAGE ___ OF ___

	DATE	DAY	SHIFT	PLAT	BADGE 1	BADGE 2	INCIDENT STATUS ☐ CLR ARREST ☐ UNF ☐ CLR EXCEPT ☐ INACT	CRIME CLASS	YEAR	INCIDENT #
01										

02
03
04
05
06
07
08
09
10
11
12
13
14
15
16
17
18
19
20
21
22
23
24
25
26
27
28
29

Form 107 4-96	INVESTIGATING OFFICER(S)	REVIEWED BY	ASSIGNED TO / BADGE	ATTENTION TO

Figure 4.5
Sample Supplemental Continuation Report, St. Paul Police Department

Page _____ of _____	ST. PAUL POLICE DEPARTMENT			
☐ SUPPLEMENTAL REPORT	☐ CONTINUATION OF: ☐ ORIGINAL REPORT	☐ SUPPLEMENTAL REPORT		
Date & Time of Report:	Offense/Incident:		Team:	Time of Arrest:

NARRATIVE

Arrest Number	Last Name	First	Middle	Address	DOB	Age	Sex	Race

C.N.

Assisting Officer:		Emp. No.:	Reporting Officer:				Emp. No.:
Report Reviewed By/Unit Commander:		Emp. No.:	O.T.: ☐ Yes ☐ No	Typist:	R.O.:	Code:	Name Entry:

☐ CHF ☐ Hom ☐ Rob ☐ Juv ☐ Coord   ☐ ID ☐ Lab ☐ Rec   ☐ Team ☐ Sex   ☐ Rptr   ☐ Other _____

☐ D/C ☐ Burg ☐ Theft ☐ Prop ☐ CAU   ☐ F&F ☐ Auto ☐ DAO   ☐ CO ☐ HumServ   ☐ Type   PM 622-93R

Figure 4.6
Sample Property List, Anne Arundel County Police Department

ANNE ARUNDEL COUNTY POLICE DEPARTMENT, MILLERSVILLE, MD.				**Property List**		**Page 1 of 1**

1. OFFENSE/INCIDENT	2 BUSINESS NAME/VICTIM (LAST, FIRST MIDDLE)			3. CASE NUMBER	

4. DATE WRITTEN Sep. 19, 2005	5. DISTRICT/POST	6. BUSINESS/VICTIM'S ADDRESS		7. ORIG. DATE	8. MULTIPLE CLEAR-UP YES NO

ITEM	DESCRIPTION (BRAND NAME, ARTICLE)	MODEL	SERIAL #	COLOR(S)	SIZE/ CALIBER	VALUE

	9. TOTAL LOSS VALUE	$ 0.00

10. OWNERS SIGNATURE	11. DATE SIGNED	12. HOME PHONE #	13. OFFICERS WORK PHONE	14. SHIFT
64. FIRST OFFICER ID	65. SECOND OFFICER ID	66. SUPERVISOR ID	67. REVIEW OFFICER ID	

Form # 0224182

Figure 4.7
Sample Statement Form with Waiver of Constitutional Rights, Bellevue Police Department

---

WAIVER / STATEMENT

City of Bellevue POLICE

PAGE_____ OF _____

CONCERNING THE FACTS OF:

CASE NO

DATE	TIME	PLACE

THE FOLLOWING IS A TRUE AND ACCURATE
STATEMENT GIVEN TO:

STATEMENT BY:	LAST NAME	FIRST NAME	MIDDLE NAME	D.O.B.

ADDRESS	CITY	STATE	ZIP	RESIDENCE ( )	BUSINESS / OTHER ( )

EXPLANATION OF MY CONSTITUTIONAL RIGHTS

BEFORE QUESTIONING AND THE MAKING OF ANY STATEMENT, I, _____ , HAVE BEEN

ADVISED BY _____ OF THE FOLLOWING:

(1) I HAVE THE RIGHT TO REMAIN SILENT;

(2) I HAVE THE RIGHT AT THIS TIME TO AN ATTORNEY OF MY OWN CHOOSING AND TO HAVE HIM/HER PRESENT DURING QUESTIONING AND THE MAKING OF ANY STATEMENT.

(3) IF I CANNOT AFFORD AN ATTORNEY, I AM ENTITLED TO HAVE AN ATTORNEY APPOINTED FOR ME AND TO HAVE HIM/HER PRESENT BEFORE AND DURING QUESTIONING AND THE MAKING OF ANY STATEMENT.

(4) I HAVE BEEN ADVISED THAT ANYTHING I SAY CAN BE USED AGAINST ME IN A COURT OF LAW.

(AS A JUVENILE, ANY STATEMENT I MAKE CAN BE USED AGAINST ME IN A CRIMINAL PROSECUTION IN THE EVENT THAT JUVENILE COURT DECLINES JURISDICTION IN MY CASE.)

(5) I UNDERSTAND THAT I HAVE THE RIGHT TO EXERCISE ANY OF THE ABOVE RIGHTS AT ANY TIME DURING QUESTIONING AND THE MAKING OF ANY STATEMENT.

I HAVE READ OR HAVE HAD READ TO ME THE ABOVE EXPLANATION
OF MY CONSTITUTIONAL RIGHTS AND I UNDERSTAND THEM.   SIGNATURE: _____

WAIVER OF MY CONSTITUTIONAL RIGHTS

I, _____ HAVE READ OR HAVE HAD READ TO ME THE ABOVE STATEMENT OF MY CONSTITUTIONAL RIGHTS. I FULLY UNDERSTAND WHAT THEY ARE AND I WISH TO WAIVE THEM. THIS STATEMENT IS FREELY AND VOLUNTARILY GIVEN AND NO PROMISES OR THREATS HAVE BEEN MADE TO ME ABOUT WAIVING THESE RIGHTS.

DATE_____   TIME_____   SIGNATURE: _____

SIGNATURE: _____

BPD_S-Waiver_05-97

Continued

Figure 4.7—*continued*

WITNESS STATEMENT

City of Bellevue
POLICE

CONCERNING THE FACTS OF:

DISCLOSE INFO ☐

PAGE_____ OF _____

CASE NO

DATE	TIME	PLACE

THE FOLLOWING IS A TRUE AND ACCURATE STATEMENT GIVEN TO:

STATEMENT BY:	LAST NAME	FIRST NAME	MIDDLE NAME	D.O.B.

ADDRESS	CITY	STATE	ZIP	RESIDENCE ( )	BUSINESS ( )

AGE	RACE	SEX	HAIR	EYES	HGT	WGT	EMPLOYER / SCHOOL

EMPLOYER / SCHOOL ADDRESS	CITY	STATE	ZIP

*** DOES THE WITNESS NEED TO SIGN A MEDICAL RELEASE? SEE BACK PAGE**

I CERTIFY UNDER PENALTY OF PERJURY UNDER THE LAWS OF THE STATE OF WASHINGTON THAT MY STATEMENT IS TRUE AND CORRECT AND MAY BE USED IN A COURT OF LAW.

SIGNATURE:_____ DATE:_____ PLACE:_____

STATEMENT TAKEN BY	PERSONNEL NO	DATE	APPROVED BY	DATE

Witness 0902

Figure 4.8
Sample Continuation Page to Incident Report, Louisiana State Penitentiary

★★★ TO BE USED AS ADDITIONAL PAGE FOR INCIDENT REPORTS ONLY WHEN NEEDED ★★★

LOUISIANA STATE PENITENTIARY
INCIDENT REPORT

ADDITIONAL PAGE NO. _____

INMATE'S NAME: _____ NUMBER: _____

DATE: _____ TIME: _____

COPY GIVEN TO INMATE BY: REPORTING OFFICER:

_____   _____

Figure 4.9
Sample Continuation Page, Loss Prevention, Longs Drug Stores, Inc.

LOSS PREVENTION DEPARTMENT - INVESTIGATION NOTES

Investigator: _____ District: _____

Date	Subject:	Location:

Figure 4.10
Sample Report Form, Federal Bureau of Investigation

FD-302 (REV. 3-10-82)

FEDERAL BUREAU OF INVESTIGATION

Date of transcription_____

Investigation on_____ at _____File #_____

by_____Date dictated_____

This document contains neither recommendations nor conclusions of the FBI. It is the property of the FBI and is loaned to your agency;
it and its contents are not to be distributed outside your agency.

Continuation Page, Follow-Up Report, and Supplementary Report or Material

Various terms are used in different agencies, but the following are fairly common:

1. The continuation page, written by the same person who wrote the face page, provides (in narrative form) information for which there was no room allotted on the face page.

2. The follow-up report provides information secured through additional investigation; it is usually written by a person other than the initial writer. However, in some instances, it may be written by the person who wrote the original report.

3. Supplementary report or material refers to the attachments that may be added to the face, continuation, or follow-up pages. These attachments include the waiver, receipt, release, test results, laboratory analysis, or other forms or reports connected with a specific situation. Newly developed techniques constantly increase the possibility that there will be more documents to attach. Some agencies do not use forms, but only plain paper for any follow-up material; this paper and these reports are commonly referred to as "supplementary."

In Figures 4.1 through 4.10, you saw samples of the various types of continuation pages, follow-up report forms, and supplementary report forms.

Reports may range from only a few pages for a simple incident to more than 100 pages for an involved homicide or any incident that may lead to liability for you and your employer. Essentially, the format is the same for law enforcement and security officers. Reports that are accurate, brief, and complete are prepared using headings and subheadings, providing ease of reading with strong visual impact. Personnel in corrections, probation, and parole may use a different format, but also take advantage of headings and subheadings for organization purposes and to provide visual impact in accurate, brief, and complete reports.

In this chapter, the continuation page, follow-up report, and supplementary report or material are discussed as one because they have in common a need for narrative style. The writing in this part of the report emphasizes organization. The use of headings and subheadings helps to organize the information to be recorded, increasing visual impact and ease of reading. Before you start, you must know your purpose and your readers.

What Is Your Purpose?

In law enforcement, your purpose is to be completely impartial in recording facts so that the peculiarities of each situation may be objectively interpreted by your readers. Never withhold even the smallest fact, despite your belief that it does not seem to "fit the picture." You are not really "painting" the picture if you withhold such facts.

It is natural for you to believe that your suspect is guilty and to "forget" — actually or intentionally — to record points that apparently favor the suspect's defense. It is also human to try to present yourself, your fellow employees, and your employer in the best possible light. However, your work will be more credible and hold up better in court if your facts are obviously unbiased. You must keep in mind that your suspect is only a *suspect* and may not be the *actual criminal*. If the suspect is eventually found to be the guilty party, your work will gain credibility from your attempts to be fair. If the suspect is not the criminal, failing to record information may hinder the search for the real criminal. The same is true when recording incidents in security, probation and parole, and corrections. Your purpose is to be accurate, brief, complete, and *objective*. Avoid value judgments in your reports.

Who Are Your Readers?

To be a writer means that you will have readers. Civil servants rarely think of themselves as writers, even though a large percentage of their time is spent writing reports. Yet later, they are dismayed when someone who writes "great reports" gets the first advancement. No matter how good an investigator you are — whether in law enforcement, corrections, probation, parole, or security — you have to be a good writer as well. People above you in the chain of command see your reports, while they do not always see you in action. Supervisors, employers, lawyers, judges, and jurors will evaluate not only you but your agency by the caliber of your reports. If justice is not done, the blame may fall on you and on your agency.

Too many writers think of readers as part of a faceless public. You will improve your writing if you realize that no matter how many people see the report, it is read by only one person at a time. *Who will be the first person to read it? The typical person? The most important person?* Analyze all possible readers of your report. Figure 4.11 lists possible readers of a law enforcement report.

Answer the above questions in your mind and characterize your readers, their levels of knowledge, reasons for reading, biases to consider, and axes to grind. The process varies according to the size and function of your agency and your own position in it.

You may write, check, and read your own writing if you are a one-person agency in a small town. In a large city or office, there is a good chance that there will be several readers. If you are the beat officer, your immediate superior usually is the first one to check your face page and continuation report. The same is true in any agency where reports are submitted to a boss. If your supervisor doesn't like it, it is likely that no one else will see it.

At this point you may need to cater to the peculiarities of your immediate supervisor. If your supervisor is "old school," he or she may insist that you write in a way that you consider outdated, that is, require you to use pseudo-legal terms, cumbersome sentences, and a wide variety of synonyms for "said." Because your supervisor is your supervisor, you may have to go along with the required form temporarily, but in the event that you become the supervisor, be sure that you do not perpetuate earlier errors.

Figure 4.11
Possible Readers of a Police Report

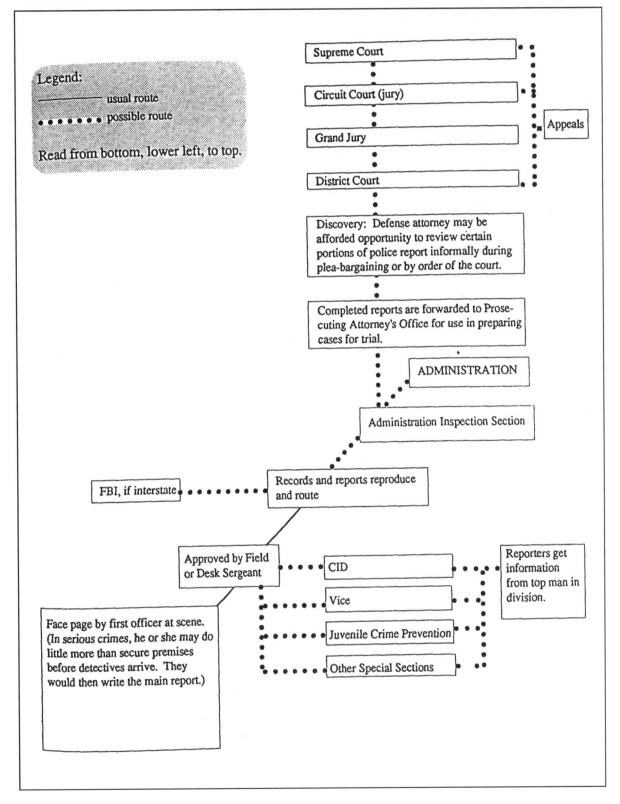

Security officers' reports may go through supervisory personnel, directly to the employer, and/or be shared with law enforcement. Corrections reports vary and may go through a process similar to those done by law enforcement officers. The Presentence Investigation Reports (PSIRs) of probation and reports of parole officers may go directly to judges, prosecutors, and defense attorneys.

Whatever the size of your agency, your report will go on file in some system of records and reports. If you have determined that more investigation is necessary, and you mark the report "Pending further investigation by Narcotics Division" or "Pending follow-up, by Officer Doe," a copy of your report will go to the proper person or office, depending on your recommendation. Be clear about and boldly indicate the need for follow-up, such as laboratory work, so that your report can be quickly routed. If your report is not precise, you may be called to explain your request.

A term that you should know is "tickler file." This is used by many agencies, including the FBI and many police departments. In a tickler system, cards, often $3 \times 5''$ and color-coded, are attached to folders or sent individually to officers to alert them that there is an omission, that a discrepancy exists, or that something must be done by a specific time about a certain report. With the advent of computerized records management systems, many tickler files have become automated.

Welcome all such reminders and act promptly. Keep in mind that anything you write, however simple, may wind up as part of a more complex project. As such, it may go to your boss, the head of your agency, or to the highest court in the land. Stopping someone for a simple traffic violation, for example, may uncover evidence of the transportation of drugs. This may bring in other agencies to follow up on your report. Wherever your writing goes, be sure that it is a credit to you and your agency.

Chronological Organization

This is one advantage that you have going for you in writing criminal justice-related reports. Most occurrences in the criminal justice system are recorded in sequence of time and in the past tense, since they have already occurred. Exceptions are letters, memoranda, meeting minutes, and administrative, departmental, and research reports (discussed in Chapter 6).

Consider time in two ways: sequential and exact. Your report will be written in the sequence of what happened first and what happened next. The exact time needs to be given only for the highlights of these events. Many beginning writers fall into the trap of trying to put an exact time on each action, no matter how small. The reader gets the impression that consulting a watch does not leave time for much else.

For law enforcement, save the exact-minute timing for the most important points: when you received the assignment, arrived on the scene, administered appropriate warnings, arrested a suspect, and transported the suspect to the station. These are times that warrant notation of exact times, but be careful to coordinate the recording of such times with others who are submitting reports, and most authorities recommend writing all times with the caveat "at approximately."

The following experiment will confirm that attempting to record exact times can lead to confusion. When you are with a number of persons, ask them all to look at their watches and tell you the time. It would not be unusual for there to be a 5- to 10-minute variation in the times announced. Consider what this could do to a report involving several persons in a single incident. The person that arrives first at an incident may record a time of arrival several minutes after persons that arrive later. Again, be as accurate as possible, but include the word "approximately" when using times.

Using Military Time

Many criminal justice system agencies use the military style of time to avoid confusion between a.m. and p.m. In this method, 12 hours are added to the afternoon times: 1:00 a.m. is 0100, and 1:00 p.m. is 1300. One should make an exception to this when quoting a victim or witness exactly and something like this is said: "I always get to work at exactly 7:45 in the morning, but this morning I was delayed. When I got there at about 8:00, I saw someone run from the office and into the alley."

Use the past tense and write in sequence or logical order. Give the time for the highlights of the action, noting that it is an approximate time only.

Headings and Subheadings as a Way of Organizing

Almost any report submitted in the criminal justice system, a school or class, personal correspondence, or private industry can be organized under a few main headings, and these, in turn, may be divided into subheadings. You should remember how headings and subheadings were used in Chapter 2. They are used for the same reasons in the writing of continuation reports. Many reports that you have to write are common ones that you will have to write over and over again, often using the same headings.

While examples in this section apply primarily to law enforcement personnel, they also can be appropriate for use in corrections, probation, parole, and security report writing.

Unless you have an extraordinary case or unusual information to be added to a routine case report, you probably will not have to go through the first few steps of the shopping list method shown in Chapter 2. You will know the headings and will need only to provide the information to go with them. Sections that have a lot of information may need to be divided into two or more subheadings. You can use the shopping list method to help you make the subdivisions.

Common Law Enforcement Report Writing Headings
(Check your agency's format)

MISCELLANEOUS CASES
Assignment/Arrival
Officer's Observations
Victim's or Reporting Person's Statement
Witnesses' Statements
Investigation
Evidence
Latent Prints
Check for Witnesses
Arrests
Notification
Other Actions of Officer(s)
Disposition

BURGLARY CASES
Assignment/Arrival
Officer's Observations
Victim's or Reporting Person's Statement
Witnesses' Statements
Investigation
   Description of Scene (include sketch)
   Entry/Exit
   Culprit's Activity
   Check for Latent Prints
   Evidence
   Check for Witnesses
   Other Actions of Officer(s)
Disposition

THEFT CASES
Assignment/Arrival
Officer's Observations
Victim's or Reporting Person's Statement
Witnesses' Statements
Property Taken (if not listed on face page)
Investigation
   Description of Scene (include sketch)
   Culprit's Activity
   Check for Latent Prints
   Evidence
   Check for Witnesses
   Other Actions of Officer(s)
Disposition

ASSAULT CASES
Assignment/Arrival
Officer's Observations
Scene
Weapons or Method of Assault
Victim's Injuries
Victim's or Reporting Person's Statement
Witnesses' Statements
Investigation
   Check for Latent Prints
   Evidence
   Check for Witnesses
   Other Actions of Officer(s)
Disposition

AUTO THEFT CASES
Assignment/Arrival
Observations of Officer on Arrival
Scene
Vehicle Condition
Last Driver of Vehicle
   Owner's or Driver's Statement
   Registered Owner Check
Vehicle Keys/Others with Permission
Witnesses' Statements
Investigation
   Evidence
   Latent Prints
   Check for Witnesses
   Other Actions of Officer
Disposition

ROBBERY CASES
Assignment/Arrival
Observations of Officer on Arrival
Property Taken (if not listed on face page)
Victim's Statement
Witnesses' Statements
Weapons Used
Suspect's Demand
Investigation
   Evidence
   Latent Prints
   Other Actions of Officer
Disposition

The following items may or may not be included as headings and subheadings. Other headings may be required as situations arise. Some may not be needed if the subject is properly covered on the face page of the report.

Synopsis
Scene Description or Diagram
Others Called to or Arriving at Scene
Others Notified/Time/Date
Entry/Exit
Damage to Property
Weapons Used
Injuries
Description of Suspect(s)
    Words Used by Suspect(s)
    MO or Trademarks of Suspect(s)
Vehicle(s) Involved
Suspect(s) Arrested
    Identification of Suspect(s)
    Time/Date/Location of Arrest
    Warning of *Miranda* Rights
    Intoxication (including BAC results)
    Injuries/Treatment of Injuries
    Suspect(s) Statement(s)

Letters in all words of the main headings are usually set off in capital letters and are sometimes underlined as well. In the subheadings, the main words have the first letter capitalized, as in the title of a book. If you skip a space between paragraphs it is not necessary to indent under headings. Subheadings are usually indented and may be underlined. Again, this may depend on your agency's policy. Additional levels of organization may be needed in a long report, such as for a homicide or a complicated drug case.

In addition, a different form of indentation may be employed to set off descriptions of a person. Such a description is often set off about one-half or two-thirds of the way across the page, headed by the name (capitalized and in reverse order) and followed by all of the lines in block form.

The indentations make for easier reading because the eye is automatically directed to the important parts. If you were to take the above headings and subheadings and adapt them to a burglary, both police and security reports would look something like this:

ASSIGNMENT/ARRIVAL
   xxxxxxxxxxxxxxxxxxxxxxxxxxxxxxxxxxxxxxxxxxxxxxxxxxxxxxxxxx
xxxxxxxxxxxxxxx

Description of Complainant
                  DOE, JOHN xxxxxxxxxxxxxxxxxxx
                  xxxxxxxxxxxxxxxxxxxxxxxxxxxx
                  xxxxxxxxxxxxxxxxxxx
                  xxxxxxxxxxxxxxxxxxxxxxxxxx

COMPLAINANT'S STATEMENT
   xxxxxxxxxxxxxxxxxxxxxxxxxxxxxxxxxxxxxxxxxxxxxxxxxxxxxxxxxxx
xxxxxxxxxxxxxxxxxxxxxxxxxxxxxxxxxxxxxxxxxxxxxxxxxxxxxxxxxxx
xxxxxxxxxxxxxxxxxxxxxxxxxxxxxxxxxxxxxxxxxxxxxxxxxxxxxxxxxxx
xxxxxxxxxxxxxxxxxxxxxxxxxxxxxxxxxxxxxxxxxxxxxxxxxxxxxxxxxxx
xxxxxxxxxxxxxxxxxxxxxxxxxxxxxxxxxxxxxxxxxxxxxxxxxxxxxxxxxxx
xxxxxxxxxxxxxxxxxxxxxxxxxxxxxxxxxxxxxxxxxxxxxxxxxxxxxxxxxxx
xxxxxxxxxxxxxxxxxxxxxxxxxxxxxxxxxxx

   Missing Property
      xxxxxxxxxxxxxxxxxxxxxxxxxxxxxxxxxxxxxxxxxxxxxxxxxxxxxxxx
xxxxxxxxxxxxxxxxxxxxxxxxxxxxxxxxxxxxxxxxxxxxxxxxxxxxxxxxx
xxxxxxxxxxxxxxxxxxxxxxxxxxxxxxxxxxxxxxxxxxxxxxxxxxxxxxxxx
xxxxxxxxxxxxxxxxxxxxxxxxxxxxxxxxxxxxxxxxxxxxxxxxxxxxxxxxx
xxxxxxxxxxxxxxxxxxxxxxxxxx

INVESTIGATION

   Scene
      xxxxxxxxxxxxxxxxxxxxxxxxxxxxxxxxxxxxxxxxxxxxxxxxxxxxxxx
xxxxxxxxxxxxxxxxxxxxxxxxxxxxxxxxxxxxxxxxxxxxxxxxxxxxxxxx
xxxxxxxxxxxxxxxxxxxxxxxxxxxxxxxxxxxxxxxxxxxxxxxx

   Entry/Exit
      xxxxxxxxxxxxxxxxxxxxxxxxxxxxxxxxxxxxxxxxxxxxxxxxxxxxxxx
xxxxxxxxxxxxxxxxxxxxxxxxxxxxxxxxxxxxxxxxxxxxxxxxxxxxxxxx
xxxxxxxxxxxxxxxxxxxxxxxxxxxxxxxxx

   Suspect's Activity
      xxxxxxxxxxxxxxxxxxxxxxxxxxxxxxxxxxxxxxxxxxxxxxxxxxxxxxx
xxxxxxxxxxxxxxxxxxxxxxxxxxxxxxxxxxxxxxxxxxxxxxxxxxxxxxxx
xxxxxxxxxxxxxxxxxxxxxxxxxxxxxxxxxxxxxxxxxxxxxxxxxxxxxxxx
xxxxxxxxxxxxxxxxxxxxxxxxxxxxxxxxxxxxxxxxxxxxxxxxxx

Latent Prints
    xxxxxxxxxxxxxxxxxxxxxxxxxxxxxxxxxxxxxxxxxxxxxxxxxxxxx
xxxxxxxxxxxxxxxxxxxxxxxxxxxxxxxxxxxxxxxxxxxxxxxxxxxxxxx
xxxxxxxxxxxxxxxxxxxxxxxxxxxxxxxxxxxxxxx

Witnesses Interviewed
                        Witness #1
                        ROE, Sally R., 26 yrs., DOB: xx/xx/xx
                        xxxxxxxxxxxxxxxxxxxxxx
                        xxxxxxxxxxxxxxxxxxx
                        xxxxxxxxxxxxxxxxxxx

Statement of Witness #1
    xxxxxxxxxxxxxxxxxxxxxxxxxxxxxxxxxxxxxxxxxxxxxxxxxxxxxx
xxxxxxxxxxxxxxxxxxxxxxxxxxxxxxxxxxxxxxxxxxxxxxxxxxxxxxxx
xxxxxxxxxxxxxxxxxxxxxxxxxxxxxxxxxxxxxxxxxxxxxxxxxxxxxxxx
xxxxxxxxxxxxxxxxxxxxxxxxxxxxxxxxxxxxxxxxxxxxxxxxxxxxxxxx
xxxxxxxxxxxxxxxxxxxxxxxxxxxxxxxxxxxxxxxxxxxxxxx

                        Witness #2
                        BLOW, Joseph R., 37 yrs., DOB: xx/xx/xx
                        xxxxxxxxxxxxxxxxxxxx
                        xxxxxxxxxxxxxxxxxxx
                        xxxxxxxxxxxxxxxxxxx

Statement of Witness #2
    xxxxxxxxxxxxxxxxxxxxxxxxxxxxxxxxxxxxxxxxxxxxxxxxxxxxxx
xxxxxxxxxxxxxxxxxxxxxxxxxxxxxxxxxxxxxxxxxxxxxxxxxxxxxxxx
xxxxxxxxxxxxxxxxxxxxxxxxxxxxxxxxxxxxxxxxxxxxxxxxxxxxxxxx
xxxxxxxxxxxxxxxxxxxxxxxxxxxxxxxxxxxxxxxxxxxxxxxxxxxxxxxx
xxxxxxxxxxxxxxxxxxxxxxxxxxxxxxxxxxxxxx

DISPOSITION
    xxxxxxxxxxxxxxxxxxxxxxxxxxxxxxxxxxxxxxxxxxxxxxxxxxxxxx
xxxxxxxxxxxxxxxxxxxxx

Security personnel follow much the same format on incident reports for crimes such as burglary or theft, both of which often occur in hotels, businesses, museums, and other establishments for which security personnel are responsible.

Creating Visual Impact and Ease of Reading

The advertising world has long known the advantage of leaving white space to emphasize material. Indentation alerts the eye to matters of consequence, while at the same time places secondary facts in the lesser position. This system aids the reader in understanding the facts of the report. From a mere glance at the graphically presented report above, the reader knows that the writer has taken the time to organize. Compare the graphic presentation of the form below to the form with categories above.

REPORT # 123456-10
```
    xxxxxxxxxxxxxxxxxxxxxxxxxxxxxxxxxxxxxxxxxxxxxxxxxxxxxx
xxxxxxxxxxxxxxxxxxxxxxxxxxxxxxxxxxxxxxxxxxxxxxxxxxxxxxxxxx
xxxxxxxxxxxxxxxxxxxxxxxxxxxxxxxxxxxxxxxxxxxxxxxxxxxxxxxxxx
xxxxxxxxxxxxxxxxxxxxxxxxxxxxxxxxxxxxxxxxxxxxxxxxxxxxxxxxxx
xxxxxxxxxxxxxxxxxxxxxxxxxxxxxxxxxxxxxxxxxxxxxxxxxxxxxxxxxx
xxxxxxxxxxxxxxxxxxxxxxxxxxxxxxxxxxxxxxxxxxxxxxxxxxxxxxxxxx
xxxxxxxxxxxxxxxxxxxxxxxxxxxxxxxxxxxxxxxxxxxxxxxxxxxxxxxxxx
xxxxxxxxxxxxxxxxxxxxxxxxxxxxxxxxxxxxxxxxxxxxxxxxxxxxxxxxxx
xxxxxxxxxxxxxxxxxxxxxxxxxxxxxxxxxxxxxxxxxxxxxxxxxxxxxxxxxx
xxxxxxxxxxxx
    xxxxxxxxxxxxxxxxxxxxxxxxxxxxxxxxxxxxxxxxxxxxxxxxxxxxxx
xxxxxxxxxxxxxxxxxxxxxxxxxxxxxxxxxxxxxxxxxxxxxxxxxxxxxxxxxx
xxxxxxxxxxxxxxxxxxxxxxxxxxxxxxxxxxxxxxxxxxxxxxxxxxxxxxxxxx
xxxxxxxxxxxxxxxxxxxxxxxxxxxxxxxxxxxxxxxxxxxxxxxxxxxxxxxxxx
xxxxxxxxxxxxxxxxxxxxxxxxxxxxxxxxxxxxxxxxxxxxxxxxxxxxxxxxxx
xxxxxxxxxxxxxxxxxxxxxxxxxxxxxxxxxxxxxxxxxxxxxxxxxxxxxxxxxx
xxxxxxxxxxxxxxxxxxxxxxxxxxxxxxxxxxxxxxxxxxxxxxxxxxxxxxxxxx
xxxxxxxxxxx
    xxxxxxxxxxxxxxxxxxxxxxxxxxxxxxxxxxxxxxxxxxxxxxxxxxxxxx
xxxxxxxxxxxxxxxxxxxxxxxxxxxxxxxxxxxxxxxxxxxxxxxxxxxxxxxxxx
xxxxxxxxxxxxxxxxxxxxxxxxxxxxxxxxxxxxxxxxxxxxxxxxxxxxxxxxxx
xxxxxxxxxxxxxxxxxxxxxxxxxxxxxxxxxxxxxxxxxxxxxxxxxxxxxxxxxx
xxxxxxxxxxxxxxxxxxxxxxxxxxxxxxxxxxxxxxxxxxxxxxxxxxxxxxxxxx
xxxxxxxxxxxxxxxxxxxxxxxxxxxxxxxxxxxxxxxxxxxxxxxxxxxxxxxxxx
xxxxxxxxxxxxxxxxxxxxxxxxxxxxxxxxxxxxxxxxxxxxxxxxxxxxxxxxxx
xxxxxxxxxxxxxxxxxxxxxxxxxxxxxxxxxxxxxxxxxxxxxxxxxxxxxxxxxx
xxxxxxxxxxxxxxxxxxxxxxxxxxxxxxxxxxxxxxxxxxxxxxxxxxxxxxxxxx
xxxxxxxxxxxxxxxxxxxxxxxxxxxxxxxxxxxxxxxxxxxxxxxxxxxxxxxxxx
xxxxxxxxxxxx
    xxxxxxxxxxxxxxxxxxxxxxxxxxxxxxxxxxxxxxxxxxxxxxxxxxxxxx
xxxxxxxxxxxxxxxxxxxxxxxxxxxxxxxxxxxxxxxxxxxxxxxxxxxxxxxxxx
xxxxxxxxxxxxxxxxxxxxxxxxxxxxxxxxxxxxxxxxxxxxxxxxxxxxxxxxxx
xxxxxxxxxxxxxxxxxxxxxxxxxxxxxxxxxxxxxxxxxxxxxxxxxxxxxxxxxx
xxxxxxxxxxxx
```

Which of the two versions of the sample report from Chapter 2 shown below would you want to read? In which would you be able to find key facts quickly? Imagine yourself as a prosecutor in court needing to quickly find facts to clarify an issue.

The March 4, 2010, edition of *The Mooseville Reporter* reported on the death of a male held in the Mooseville Police Department cell block in an article titled "Drinking, Littering Suspect Hangs Himself in Cell Block." The article was read to AJ138, Police Reporting Class by the class instructor Mr. Foley at about 5:35 p.m. on March 5, 2010, and we were instructed to write a report on the article using the shopping list method of report writing.

On March 3, 2010, at about 5:00 p.m., a male was arrested for the offenses of criminal littering and public drinking at the corner of First and Elm Streets. Both of the offenses are misdemeanors. The male suspect was reported to be a 45-year-old truck driver who lived in the Pine Street area. Police will not release the man's name pending notification of his next of kin.

The suspect was placed in a disorderly cell due to his extremely violent behavior and his inability to post bail. As officers were just about to strip the suspect and place him in a padded cell, an officer found him hanging by his jacket from the bars in the cell block. The officer who found the suspect took him down from the bars and began an unsuccessful attempt at resuscitation. The man had been checked 10 minutes prior to 7:35 p.m. when he was discovered hanging. Police said the video camera monitors of the cell block area where the hanging occurred do not show the interior of the cell.

A 45-year-old truck driver arrested for public drinking and criminal littering hung himself in the Mooseville Police Department cell block on March 3, 2010. Police declined to identify him until his family is notified.

Or would you rather read:

INTRODUCTION

The March 4, 2010, edition of *The Mooseville Reporter* reported on the death of a male held in the cell block of the Mooseville Police Department in an article titled "Drinking, Littering Suspect Hangs Himself in Cell Block." The article was read to AJ138, Police Reporting Class by the class instructor Mr. Foley at about 5:35 p.m. on March 5, 2010, and we were instructed to write a report on the article using the shopping list method of report writing.

SUSPECT ARRESTED

On March 3, 2010, at about 5:00 p.m., a male was arrested for the offenses of criminal littering and public drinking at the corner of First and Elm Streets. Both of the offenses are misdemeanors.

MALE IDENTIFIED
   The male suspect was reported to be a 45-year-old truck driver who lived in the Pine Street area. Police will not release the man's name pending notification of his next of kin.

SUSPECT HELD IN CELL BLOCK
   The suspect was placed in a disorderly cell due to his extremely violent behavior and his inability to post bail.

SUSPECT FOUND HANGING
   As officers were just about to strip the suspect and place him in a padded cell, an officer found him hanging by his jacket from the bars in the cell block. The officer who found the suspect took him down from the bars and began an unsuccessful attempt at resuscitation.

PRIOR CHECKS
   The man had been checked 10 minutes prior to 7:35 p.m. when he was discovered hanging. Police said the video camera monitors of the cell block area where the hanging occurred do not show the interior of the cell.

CONCLUSION
   A 45-year-old truck driver arrested for public drinking and criminal littering hung himself in the Mooseville Police Department cell block on March 3, 2010. Police declined to identify him until his family is notified.

Which of the above would you rather read? Imagine that you have to find specific information quickly. With which report could you go right to the facts you need? Which report would appear to you to be the most professional — the one with selected headings or the one without headings?

Remember, your headings and subheadings may be selected to suit the elements of the particular crime. In a gambling case, for example, law enforcement officers may include these subheadings: *Vantage Point Taken*, *Observations Made/ Violations Committed*, *Raid Effected*, *Warnings Given*, *Evidence Confiscated*, or *Supervisor Notified*. Such material, carefully spaced on the page, is easy to read. It becomes very easy to find a specific piece of information without having to read the entire report. Think how important this is to your supervisor answering a complaint or providing information in response to a citizen's request. Also think about how important this could be to the prosecutor during the course of a trial.

When you have an extremely involved report, such as for a homicide, you will probably select subheadings that fit only that particular case. Routine headings such as those previously mentioned may not be enough to alert the reader's eyes to the various ramifications of the case.

An example is a portion of a report of a valuable witness who has seen animosity building up between two men until one kills the other:

STATEMENT OF WITNESS #1
xxxxxxxxxxxxxxxxxxxxxxxxxxxxxxxxxxxxxxxxxxxxxxxxxxxxxxxxx
xxxxxxxxxxxxxxxxxxxxxxxxxxxxxxxxxxxxxxxxxxxxxxxxxxxxxxxxx
xxxxxxxxxxxxxxxxxxxxxxxxxxx

First Incident at Kelly's Bar
xxxxxxxxxxxxxxxxxxxxxxxxxxxxxxxxxxxxxxxxxxxxxxxxxxxxxxx
xxxxxxxxxxxxxxxxxxxxxxxxxxxxxxxxxxxxxxxxxxxxxxxxxxxxxxxxx
xxxxxxxxxxxxxxxxxxxxxxxxxxxxxxxxxxxxxxxxxxxxxxxxxxxxxxxxx
xxxxxxxxxxxxxxxxxxxxxxxxxx

Second Incident at Kelly's Bar
xxxxxxxxxxxxxxxxxxxxxxxxxxxxxxxxxxxxxxxxxxxxxxxxxxxxxxx
xxxxxxxxxxxxxxxxxxxxxxxxxxxxxxxxxxxxxxxxxxxxxxxxxxxxxxxx
xxxxxxxxxxxxxxxxxxxxxxxxxxxxxxxxxxxxxxxxxxxxxxxxxxxxxxxx
xxxxxxxxxxxxxxxxxxxxxxxxxx

Shooting at the Ace Carnival
xxxxxxxxxxxxxxxxxxxxxxxxxxxxxxxxxxxxxxxxxxxxxxxxxxxxxxx
xxxxxxxxxxxxxxxxxxxxxxxxxxxxxxxxxxxxxxxxxxxxxxxxxxxxxxx
xxxxxxxxxxxxxxxxxxxxxxxxxxxxxxxxxxxxxxxxxxxxxxxxxxxxxxx
xxxxxxxxxxxxxxxxxxxxxxxxxx

Suspect's Statement
The suspect Joe Black said, "Okay, so I shot him! Who wouldn't?"
xxxxxxxxxxxxxxxxxxxxxxxxxxxxxxxxxxxxxxxxxxxxxxxxxxxxxxxxx
xxxxxxxxxxxxxxxxxxxxxxxxxxxxxxxxxxxxxxxxxxxxxxxxxxxxxxxxx
xxxxxxxxxxxxxxxxxxxxxxxxxxxxxxxxxxxxxxxxxxxxxxxxxxxxxxxxx
xxxxxxxxxxxxxxxxxxxxxxxxxxxxxxxxxxxxxxxxxxxxxxxxxxxxxxxxx
xxxxxxxxxxxxxxxxxxxxxxxxxxxxxxxxxxxxxxxxxxxxxx

Note that quotation marks are reserved only for key words. Other material is paraphrased because usually a witness cannot remember all the exact words. If a dictating machine or tape recorder is used for a confession, all words can then be in quotations, or the fact that the statement is verbatim can be mentioned at the beginning of the statement. Corrections and security personnel often attach a statement written by persons involved or paraphrased by the officer.

Avoiding Repetition and Meaningless Material

Headings also can help to eliminate the repetition that is so often found in reports, especially those submitted by law enforcement or security officers. An example of this is: "The victim stated that he … He also related … He further indicated that on the night of . . . He also stated that . . . He related that at this time . . . He concluded by saying . . . ."

In this case, the use of *stated*, *related*, and *indicated* weakens what might have been a good report. To make matters worse, *stated*, *related*, and *indicated* become meaningless variations of *said*. Consider the connotations as well as denotations of the words that you use. Connotations are the suggested, associated, or secondary meanings, and denotations are the specific or exact meanings. Very few words are exact synonyms. This is true especially for "said." The overused words previously mentioned may also have these meanings:

State: to declare or to set forth in a precise and authoritative manner.
Relate: to bring into or establish a relationship, association, or connection.
Indicate: to be a sign of; to imply sometimes with a gesture rather than a word, e.g., to point to; to state or express briefly in a general way.

Of these three words, *state* is the most positive, implying a willingness to stand behind what was said and to authorize a specific quotation. *Relate* gives the feeling of a possible chance connection, e.g., a grandfather relates from memory the deeds of his youth, sometimes making very tenuous relationships. *Indicate* can be either very weak or very strong, depending on whether it is used as a predicate after persons or things:

Weak:
"He indicated that he would buy a kilo."

How did he indicate? Did he nod? Was he possibly the victim of entrapment? What did he say? What did the officer say? Exactly how was an agreement of sale reached?

Strong:
"The L-shaped cut in the screen, the removal of three louvers left neatly stacked to the right of the door, the neat search resulting in the taking only of paper currency — all of the evidence *indicates* that the same person is responsible for the burglaries that occurred on the same night and in the same block."

Note how weak the words *He indicated* . . . are. Think about how a witness testifying before a congressional inquiry could use these words when not wanting to be pinned down. *He indicated* . . . is hard to prove. *Evidence indicated* . . . is hard to deny.

Material can also be meaningless when it is introduced in the wrong place. If you are writing under the heading of VICTIM'S STATEMENT, be sure that you do not introduce any observations of your own without setting them apart in brackets, or, better still, put them in a separate place. Some investigators, for example, add the word *sober* to a victim's statement. Because the word is not part of the statement, it casts doubt on the truth of the rest of the report. If you must add a comment, use brackets to indicate that the words added are those of the writer, not the speaker. [Sober.] It should be noted that brackets are very rarely used for this purpose. It would be preferable to introduce added comments earlier in your report.

Getting Rid of Stereotyped Fillers

By clearing up the confusion regarding *stated*, *related*, and *indicated*, you will dispose of much meaningless filler. It will then be beneficial for you to consider other terms that you have been adding automatically and unnecessarily. Although you have probably noticed that some people have a tendency to add unnecessary words, it is likely that you have remained unaware of a similar habit of your own.

A very common mistake is overuse of the word *area*. One man wrote, "While on patrol in the Bar Harbor area, I heard a fight going on near the old dock area ... His assailant hit him in the facial area on the back of the neck." Here, *area* is much overused, and the result sounds absurd.

You surely have noticed the use of many other unnecessary words, such as:
"Submitted for your information ..." (Isn't everything?)
"Pursuant to orders ..." (How else?)
"Please be advised that ..." (Just tell him.)
"The question as to whether ..." ("Whether" is enough.)

Look over your own work objectively. Use only the words you need. Arrange them carefully. Quit.

Summary

1. In writing for law enforcement and security matters, the continuation page, written by the same person that wrote the face page, provides additional information in narrative form. The follow-up report, usually written by another employee of the agency, is prepared after additional investigation. Supplementary material can include many attachments, such as waivers, receipts, releases, test results, and laboratory analysis.

2. In both law enforcement and security matters, before you write you should know your purpose, which is to give an accurate, brief, and complete report in an objective manner. Your reader may be only your immediate superior, but there is a possibility that any report may go to the highest court in the land. Write to bring credit to yourself and your agency.

3. Most reports are organized in sequence of time and written in the past tense. Past tense is used for everything except direct quotations. Time is given only for significant events and even then is qualified with "approximately." Quotation marks are reserved for key statements and should not be overused.

4. Headings, written completely in capital letters and underlined, divide the report into the most important parts. Subheadings are capitalized (as in book titles), sometimes underlined, and indented. Subheadings give specifics and may be chosen to suit the case. A very long report may have further subdivisions.

5. Visual impact and ease of reading are enhanced by the use of space and headings that help the reader skim the facts.

6. PSIRs and reports by parole officers are also organized for visual impact as well as being accurate, brief, and complete.

Chapter 4 — TEST

1. The continuation page usually is written by the _____ who wrote the face page. It provides _____ in _____ form. The _____ report contains additional information and usually is written by someone other than the person who wrote the original report. Supplementary material attached to a report may include such things as a _____, _____, _____, _____, and _____.

2. The subjective report is not usually used in criminal justice writing. The writer should avoid making value judgments and should always maintain a(n) _____ attitude. The report should keep to the ABCs of writing: _____, _____, and _____.

3. _____ is used in criminal justice reports, meaning that the sequence of time is observed.

4. Quotation marks often are overused. Use quotation marks for _____ _____ only.

5. _____, in all capital letters and underlined, divide the report into its most important parts. Such organization methods increase the _____ impact by cutting down on words and supplying space for emphasis and easy reading.

6. The following words are frequently and often incorrectly used; give the connotation:

   stated _____

   related _____

   indicated _____

7. Terms that are overused unnecessarily are referred to as ___ _____ and should be avoided.

CHAPTER 5

Habits that Make for Speedy Writing

Whatever your task, you must develop a style of writing with which you are comfortable and then stay within the framework that you have chosen. Too many people waste time by reacting to each situation as if it were new. The more things that you can make habitual — to the point of not having to think which comes first — the better writer you will be. The checklists in Figures 1.1 through 1.3 can become automatic. You will gain in both speed and accuracy: speed, because you follow a predetermined format, and accuracy, because with such a format you are less likely to leave things out.

What habits can you develop? You can form habits regarding your method of referring to yourself, your method of describing others, your system for listing and describing items, and your method of checking and describing places, MOs, and trademarks. A clear-cut plan for doing these things will make your reports easier to write, faster to read, and less likely to contain errors or omissions.

Writing about People

How should you refer to yourself? How should you refer to others? Your agency may have decided this for you. As mentioned in Chapter 2, it is recommended that you use the first person. Some agencies still insist on the use of the third person, but the trend in recent years has been moving toward using the first person. If you have the choice, use the first person and stick with it throughout your writing. Otherwise, you will have a mishmash of pronouns and a report that is sometimes confusing when it comes to who did what. The use of first person in reports is recommended because it simplifies both the writing of the report and

123

DOI: 10.1016/B978-1-4377-5584-8.00012-8

the understanding of the report by readers. Remember and apply the "KISS rule": Keep it short and simple.

You and Your Fellow Employees

As previously stated, some agencies do not give you a choice about what person to use when writing. If the third person is the rule in an agency, the following examples would be appropriate:

> Corrections Officer Brown first made checks of Area One before *she* found the prisoner in Yard Two.

> Officers Jones and Gilbert looked under the automobile where *they* found the victim unconscious.

On a face page, there may be little opportunity to use anything other than the third person, except perhaps in the synopsis. Even there, it may be avoided by use of the past tense with the subject understood:

> Arrested persons listed below for violation of Gambling Ordinance Section 13-312 at 1400 hours on 3-26-10 at 1801 East 12th Street.

Some persons writing in the third person make frequent use of *this officer, the writer, the undersigned*, or even *the undersigned security officer*. Infrequent use of these terms may be acceptable, but when they occur often in a report, a labored, artificial effect results:

> *This officer* started to present his credentials when the suspect yelled, "Cops!" and ran. *The undersigned* chased him to the corner of First and Main Streets, where *this writer* had to use reasonable force to subdue the suspect.

Imagine several paragraphs of this type of writing. If read in court, it sounds especially ludicrous. One officer had "the undersigned" so deeply ingrained in his style that when he was asked in court, "Did you observe the money being handed over for the drugs?" he replied, "Yes, the undersigned observed this with my own eyes!"

It is important not to mix the use of first, second, and third persons. The result can be very confusing and even ridiculous as Officer Jones writes about an incident: "Officers Jones and Gilbert saw the suspect coming toward us. Officer Jones reached for my gun."

Describing Other People

There is a great deal of material to consider when describing people. Remember three basic things:

1. Always describe people in the same way, in a preset order.

2. Be exact; do not guess or add vague recollections later.

3. Do not press someone too hard for a description; a frightened victim may not recollect much and, if pressured, may not be accurate.

Most agencies have forms for this. In general, describe a person from top to bottom (see Figure 5.1).
Typical checklists should include:

General: Name, gender, age, height, weight, build, address, phone, occupation, business address, business phone, skin color and/or ethnic origin, marital status, and peculiarities.

Clothing: Hat, shirt, coat, dress, trousers, stockings or socks, shoes, accessories, jewelry, general state of clothing, and peculiarities.

Facial: Shape, hair, forehead, eyes and brows, nose, ears, cheeks, mouth, chin, neck, age lines, scars, general expression, and peculiarities.

The general description occurs briefly on the face page and sometimes in much more detail on the continuation or follow-up page, where it is usually set off in block form halfway or further across the page (see Chapter 4). Scrupulously check all possible details. A street address may not be enough. Is there an apartment or room number? Is there a phone number for home and for work? Mentioning that a person is self-employed is not enough. Find out how he or she is self-employed. If you are not thorough, the result may be that much valuable information is irretrievably lost.

Race is a term not used much on forms, as *race* technically means three major groups: Mongoloid, Negroid, and Caucasoid. *Ethnic origin* is the preferred term. In describing skin color, wording needs to be exact — for example, *tan* refers to natural color; *tanned* refers to the temporary effect of sunning. Mixtures of ethnic origins may be listed with a slash between, with the dominant type coming first. Some groups look quite similar. For example, if you think that a person might be Spanish, Portuguese, Mexican, or of a similar group, it would be proper to list Latin.

Speech and accent are often omitted when they could be of value. Is the voice shrill, harsh, soft, or slurred? Is the language accented and, if so, what kind of accent is it? Are the terms used those of an educated person? Is the slang of a particular subculture used? Do certain key words recur?

Be careful not to leave out peculiarities. Wigs, tattoos, deformities, scars, and artificial limbs are all important to note. An unusual type of walk should be listed; for example, as very fast, jerky, slow, stumbling, limping on right foot, etc.

Clothing peculiarities might include clothes that are very large or very small, combinations of new and old, or sloppy or neat. Just listing the color and kind of clothes from top to bottom may leave out valuable bits of information.

Facial characteristics deserve special attention because the face is the most important feature and sometimes the only one that a witness or victim sees. In

Figure 5.1
Face Description Sheet

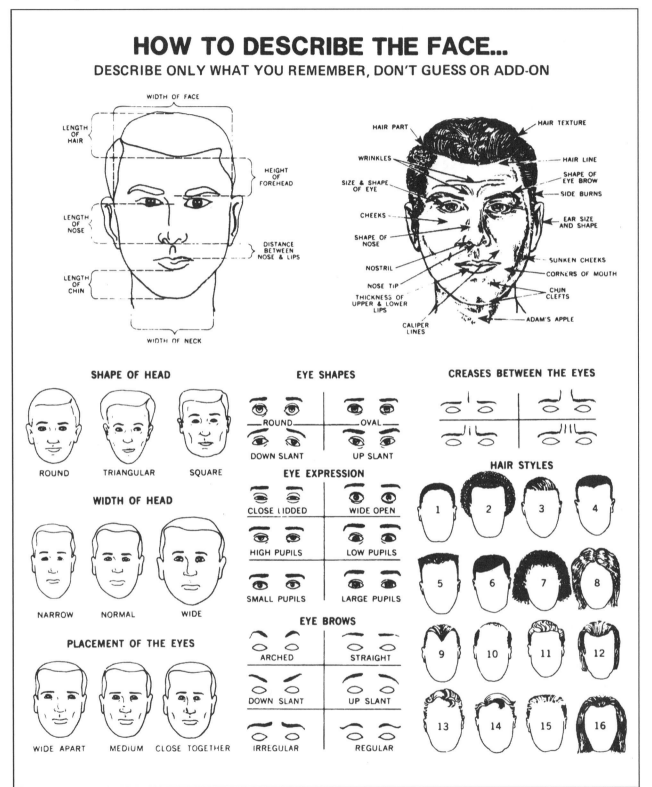

questioning a victim, it is best to ask only, "What do you remember?" or other general questions rather than to press too hard for each feature of the perpetrator. You may get a description, but an inaccurate one, if a victim tries too hard, or if your questions suggest a certain answer. Witnesses are very susceptible to suggestion, so it is important not to put ideas into their minds.

If you see the suspect yourself, you can be much more specific. Train yourself to observe features that many neglect. Begin with the overall shape of the face: oval, triangular, round, or square. Hairstyles and hairlines should be noted. Eyes can be of various colors and shades, possibly even eyes of two different colors. Consider placement of the eyes: wide apart, medium, or close to each other. Some slant up or down. Lids can be heavy, thin, half shut, or wide open. Pupils may be small, large, dilated, or uneven; all of these conditions should be considered for signs of injury or drug use. Perhaps there are unusual eyebrows, such as exceptionally thin or bushy ones, and there may be frown lines or creases. Noses vary tremendously in size, shape, type of bridge, and flare of nostril.

Some criminal justice employees specialize in noting a certain feature. One Ohio inspector, for example, said that he always checked ears for the overall form, amount of protrusion, and size of lobes. "It is getting pretty common to wear wigs," he said, "and contacts change eye color, but ears most people leave alone."

Maybe you will specialize, as this inspector does, in a hard-to-change feature. The thickness of the lips or the bracket lines around the mouth may be considered, as well as the size of the mouth. Teeth that are even and white, jagged or stained, or unusually far apart take effort to disguise.

Despite a great number of variations in human features, too many writers routinely fill in a vague description, such as:

> Unknown male, about 30, white, about 5'9", medium build and weight, brown hair, unknown color eyes, average features, white shirt, dark pants and shoes, seen running east on Adams Street.

How would you like to look for a person like that, especially if he stopped running?

Naturally, you will not describe with equal care the person involved in a minor incident and the one suspected of homicide or burglary. You should have the ability to describe in great detail when necessary.

Composite descriptions, received from several people, are sometimes compared and put together by a staff artist to put on a bulletin for circulation among law enforcement personnel (see Figure 5.2). In some cases, the artist pools the information from officers, victims, and witnesses to come up with a single composite. The information contributed by each person is used; however, each person is interviewed individually. The resulting sketch by the artist often looks amazingly like the suspect when he or she is apprehended.

Writing about Property

Vehicles represent a big investment and are fairly easy to steal or are used as part of a crime or in fleeing from a crime. A good sequence for listing items in the description of a vehicle is in the line of recognition: license, make, model or

Figure 5.2
Sample Crime Information Bulletin

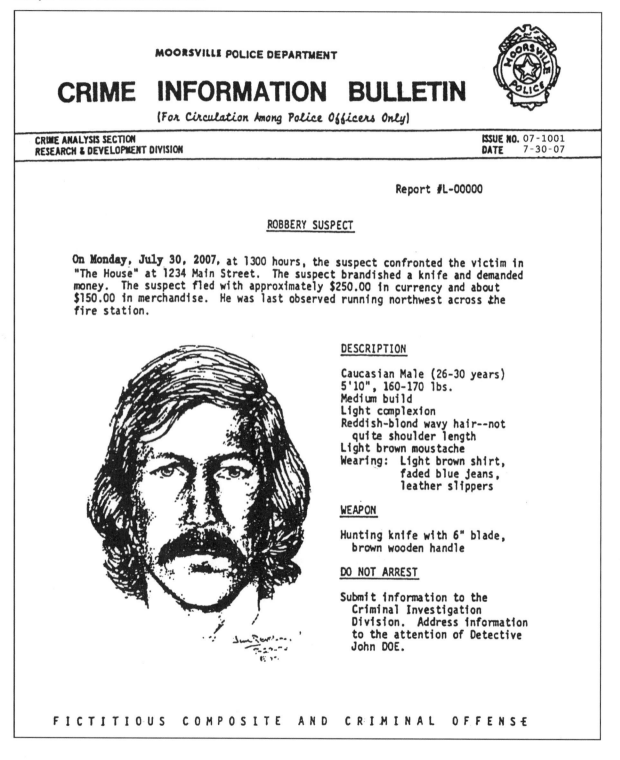

MOORSVILLE POLICE DEPARTMENT

CRIME INFORMATION BULLETIN

(For Circulation Among Police Officers Only)

CRIME ANALYSIS SECTION
RESEARCH & DEVELOPMENT DIVISION

ISSUE NO. 07-1001
DATE   7-30-07

Report #L-00000

ROBBERY SUSPECT

On Monday, July 30, 2007, at 1300 hours, the suspect confronted the victim in "The House" at 1234 Main Street. The suspect brandished a knife and demanded money. The suspect fled with approximately $250.00 in currency and about $150.00 in merchandise. He was last observed running northwest across the fire station.

DESCRIPTION

Caucasian Male (26-30 years)
5'10", 160-170 lbs.
Medium build
Light complexion
Reddish-blond wavy hair--not
  quite shoulder length
Light brown moustache
Wearing: Light brown shirt,
          faded blue jeans,
          leather slippers

WEAPON

Hunting knife with 6" blade,
  brown wooden handle

DO NOT ARREST

Submit information to the
  Criminal Investigation
  Division. Address information
  to the attention of Detective
  John DOE.

FICTITIOUS COMPOSITE AND CRIMINAL OFFENSE

type, year, color, and peculiarities. With the exception of year, most of these characteristics are easily discernible. Color, however, is sometimes deceptive, depending upon the lighting. In a brightly lit parking lot at night, a yellow vehicle may appear white, and a blue vehicle may appear gray. Peculiarities such as dents and other damage, loud muffler, bumper stickers, and customized work are often obvious and should be listed.

When a vehicle has occupants, describe them. No one wants to look for "a white Volkswagen with a blurred yellow license driven by an unknown male." There would be a much better chance of finding "a white Volkswagen with a muddy yellow license plate, first digits possibly 543, dented left rear fender, driven by a short man in a baseball cap and dark overcoat."

If you are unfamiliar with certain types of property, consult catalogs that sell such items. Owner's manuals often have pictures or drawings of the items. Ask victims for them. These will help you identify sizes, shapes, and proper listings for a huge variety of things, from baguette diamonds to casting rods. The Miami-Dade Police Department in Florida includes drawings of gem cuts in their standard operating procedures for report writing and in their property loss report completed by victims (see Figure 5.3). Hospital and hotel security personnel must often deal with lost or misplaced items, such as jewelry and watches. A report of the incident should be made even if the objects are later recovered. An up-to-date collection of catalogs is a valuable addition to your personal library. Such a collection can be put together at little or no expense.

Writing about Places

Few people are specific enough in describing places. Do not assume that recording the street address of a place is enough. Many law enforcement personnel have experienced cases in which the room numbers or apartment numbers were missing. The current tendency not to post identifying numbers or names on doors or entrances often causes valuable time to be wasted in trying to find the addresses later. It is, therefore, sometimes just as important to include a description of how to find a location as it is to give a legal address. Examples: "The dirt road leading to the location is approximately 2/10 of a mile east of mile post 23 on the north side of the road." "While the address is 2001 Walsh Lane, the parking lot and entrance to the building fronts Foley Street, just west of Broome Pie Shop." By including such details you eliminate the need for follow-up personnel, including those serving court orders, from having to struggle to find the location.

If a fight occurred outside a place, state whether it happened on the sidewalk, in the street, in an alley, etc. What is the intersection nearest the activity? Vague street directions are not enough. Light conditions and accompanying sounds should also be noted. What was the visibility? Was there a noisy party or a loud TV program going on at the same time? If so, where was this in relation to the place stated?

In a prison fight, the Corrections Officer (CO) often has a particularly hard time deciding what actually happened. Reliable accounts from witnesses are difficult to obtain. The specific location, time, and general activity will at least give a basis for further investigation.

Figure 5.3
Sample Property Loss Report, Miami-Dade Police Department

PROPERTY LOSS REPORT

BURGLARY VICTIM INSTRUCTIONS

General - We at the Miami-Dade Police Department regret that you have been the victim of a burglary and we will make every effort to solve the case and recover any property that was taken from you. So that you will understand the general procedures for investigating burglaries, the following information is provided:

1. **Preliminary Report -** The first officer or Public Service Aide (PSA) who comes to the scene of your burglary will prepare a preliminary case report. He will also examine the crime scene to determine if certain factors are present which indicate a need to perform specialized evidence processing procedures. If any such factors are present, the officer or PSA will initiate a request for crime scene processing.

2. **Crime Scene Processing** - The officer or PSA who prepares the preliminary report of your burglary will advise you if he has initiated a request for crime scene processing. If he has, please follow any instructions he has given you to preserve evidence for processing. You will be contacted by telephone, usually the next day, by a member of our Crime Scene Section who will arrange to come and process the scene. If he cannot contact you by telephone, he will attempt to make personal contact at the location where the burglary was reported. If he cannot make contact at that location, he will leave a card providing a telephone number so you can contact him to arrange processing.

3. **Property Taken** - It is necessary for the police to have a complete list of all property taken in your burglary as soon as possible. For this reason, we request that you thoroughly check the premises that were burglarized and complete the attached Property Loss Report. The more detail you can provide, such as serial numbers and identifying marks, etc., the easier it will be to recover the items. Next, mail the report to the Miami-Dade Police Station listed at the top of the Property Loss Report as soon as possible.

4. **Follow-up Investigation** - All burglary cases are assigned to a detective for investigation. This detective will contact you by telephone or in person, usually within 72 hours after receiving the case for follow-up. The detective is the one most qualified to advise you concerning the solvability factors of your case.

5. **Case Disposition** - In the event your case is closed, offender (s) arrested, or any of your property is recovered, you will be notified.

6. **Additional Information** - If you have any further information about this case or have any questions, please call the detective assigned to your case at the telephone number indicated at the top of the Property Loss Report. If you do not know the name of the detective assigned to your case, provide the Agency Report Number (case number) when calling.

VICTIM (ALSO TAKE COMPLETED GREEN COPY)

32.02.09-17 Rev. 1/05 MIAMI-DADE POLICE DEPARTMENT

Figure 5.3—*continued*

PROPERTY LOSS REPORT   Page _____ of _____

THIS AREA MUST BE COMPLETED BY THE REPORTING OFFICER

Date of Supplement	**MIAMI-DADE POLICE DEPARTMENT**	Agency Report Number

Original Date Reported	Original Primary Offense Description	Victim #1 Name

Incident Location (Street, Apt. Number)	City	Zip

Owner of property on this form is [Person Code #] _____ on original report.
(V=Victim, P=Proprietor)

Residence Telephone ( )	Business Telephone ( )

Mail this report to: _____   Status Code: [ ] (1=Stolen, 5=Lost)   Damage Code [0]

(Give complete address of unit to do follow-up investigation).

City	Unit Name / Street / FL State / 33 ZIP	Telephone Number / Supervisor / Assigned To:

THIS AREA MUST BE COMPLETED BY THE VICTIM.   SEE INSTRUCTIONS ON REVERSE SIDE.

Property Type   USE TYPEWRITER OR PRINT FIRMLY WITH A BALL POINT PEN. YOU ARE MAKING 5 COPIES.

CODES

A. Auto Accessory/Parts	F. Food/Liquor/Consumable	K. Clothing/Fur	P. Art/Collection	U. Currency/Negotiable	Z. Miscellaneous
B. Bicycle	G. Gun	L. Livestock	Q. Computer Equipment	V. Credit Card/Non-Negotiable	
C. Camera/Photo Equipment	H. Household Appliance/Goods	M. Musical Instrument	R. Radio/Stereo	W. Boat Motor	
D. Drug	I. Plant/Citrus	N. Construction Machinery	S. Sports Equipment	X. Structure	
E. Equipment/Tool	J. Jewelry/Precious Metal	O. Office Equipment	T. TV/Video/VCR	Y. Farm Equipment	

PROPERTY	Person Code #	Item #	Status	Damage ○	Property Type	Quantity	Name	Brand	Model Name/Number
	Serial Number			Owner Applied Number				Description (Size, Color, Caliber, Barrel Length, Etc.)	
	Value $					Additional Information			

PROPERTY	Person Code #	Item #	Status	Damage ○	Property Type	Quantity	Name	Brand	Model Name/Number
	Serial Number			Owner Applied Number				Description (Size, Color, Caliber, Barrel Length, Etc.)	
	Value $					Additional Information			

PROPERTY	Person Code #	Item #	Status	Damage ○	Property Type	Quantity	Name	Brand	Model Name/Number
	Serial Number			Owner Applied Number				Description (Size, Color, Caliber, Barrel Length, Etc.)	
	Value $					Additional Information			

PROPERTY	Person Code #	Item #	Status	Damage ○	Property Type	Quantity	Name	Brand	Model Name/Number
	Serial Number			Owner Applied Number				Description (Size, Color, Caliber, Barrel Length, Etc.)	
	Value $					Additional Information			

PROPERTY	Person Code #	Item #	Status	Damage ○	Property Type	Quantity	Name	Brand	Model Name/Number
	Serial Number			Owner Applied Number				Description (Size, Color, Caliber, Barrel Length, Etc.)	
	Value $					Additional Information			

PROPERTY	Person Code #	Item #	Status	Damage ○	Property Type	Quantity	Name	Brand	Model Name/Number
	Serial Number			Owner Applied Number				Description (Size, Color, Caliber, Barrel Length, Etc.)	
	Value $					Additional Information			

PROPERTY	Person Code #	Item #	Status	Damage ○	Property Type	Quantity	Name	Brand	Model Name/Number
	Serial Number			Owner Applied Number				Description (Size, Color, Caliber, Barrel Length, Etc.)	
	Value $					Additional Information			

TOTAL	Property Stolen	Total, this Page	$	Total for entire report, if last page	$

NOTICE: To assist in the rapid recovery of your property, it is extremely important for you to complete this form and return it within 48 hours.

Under penalties of perjury, I declare that I have read the foregoing and that the facts stated in it are true.

Victim's Signature _____   Date: _____

(PLEASE NOTE: A person who knowingly makes a false declaration is guilty of the crime of perjury by false written declaration, a felony of the third degree, punishable as provided in Florida Statutes, s.775.082, s.775.083, or s.775.084.)

32.02.09-17 Rev. 1/05 MIAMI-DADE POLICE DEPARTMENT   RECORDS BUREAU

Continued

Figure 5.3—*continued*

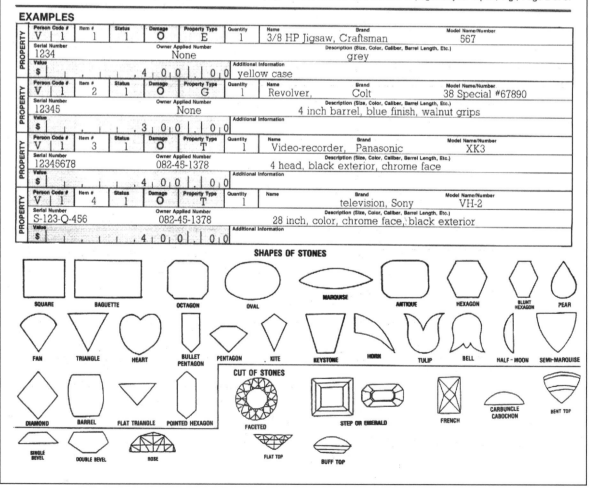

PROPERTY LOSS REPORT — MIAMI-DADE POLICE DEPARTMENT

MAIL THE COMPLETED FORM(S) TO THE ADDRESS RECORDED BY THE OFFICER. KEEP THE GREEN COPY FOR YOUR RECORDS.

INSTRUCTIONS: USE TYPEWRITER OR PRINT FIRMLY WITH A BALL POINT PEN. YOU ARE MAKING 5 COPIES.

Person Code #:   Fill in this block exactly as shown in the section completed by the officer.

Item #:   Number first item as 1, second item as 2, etc.

Status Code: Fill in this block exactly as shown in the Status Code block completed by the officer.

Property Type: Fill in the appropriate property type code from the code section located before the property item blocks. For example, if you are listing a television, print a "T" in the property type block. Should the item you want to list not appear as a choice in the code section, print a "Z" for Miscellaneous.

Owner Applied Number: Numbers that have been applied by the owner to the property. Some typical numbers used are driver's license number or social security number.

Remaining blocks: These blocks are self-explanatory. Examples of how the form can be completed are below.

Additional Instructions: Appliance/Electronic Equipment: List maker or brand name, serial and model numbers, size, color, physical description, and identification marks added after purchase of item. **Jewelry:** Indicate if engraved, and type and color of metal, size, weight, shape, and number of stones. **Furs:** Indicate type, color, style, size, and manufacturer of item. **Firearms:** Indicate manufacturer; model and serial numbers; caliber or gauge; barrel length; color of metal and stock; and whether revolver, automatic, semi-automatic, pistol, shotgun, rifle, or other.   **Currency:** Indicate U.S. or foreign currency and denomination. **Bank checks, traveler's checks, credit cards:** Indicate name of issuer or bank and serial and account numbers. **Value:** Report items at fair market value, subject to depreciation. Merchants should enter wholesale cost.

Additional Pages: If your report requires additional pages, copy the information that the officer recorded in the top part of the form in the shaded blocks onto the subsequent pages. Also fill in the page number and the total number of pages in your report, e.g., Page 2 of 5.

In security, any event that is not routine requires mention in the log, and an incident report with the exact location noted is a definite requirement. Did a parade go by the hospital when a patient became violent in the psychiatric ward? Through what entrance was an internationally known celebrity spirited at a world-class hotel? In what precise location of the men's department was the register that was found short? In what room in Apartment B of the condominium was the body found in a case of unattended death? Where did the body lie in relation not only to furniture but to fixed points of reference, such as doors and walls?

Specific Parts of a Location

Some crimes, including burglary and homicide, call for extreme precision in the description of a room and the location of the exact part of the room that was affected. The exact location of the point of entry is important. The location of the place in question should be noted in connection with fixed objects, such as a door or wall. Movable objects, such as furniture or the body of the victim, also need to be noted in relation to fixed objects. If you customarily survey a room from left to right, describe it in the same way. Keep in mind the use of photographs and diagrams to help document the scene.

> The beginner usually has to learn not to do things hastily. Stop. Think. Secure the crime scene. Then record evidence with extreme care.

Describing MOs and Trademarks

Of everything you record, the *modus operandi* (MO) is one of the most important because a criminal's method of operation becomes habitual in many cases. If a burglar found a certain technique effective the first time he or she used it, the technique will, in all likelihood, be repeated. A perpetrator works more efficiently from habit, just as you work more efficiently when you have fewer things to consider consciously. The criminal's habits are what most often assists in locating him or her. Comparing the type of force used to make an entry in burglaries in a neighborhood can indicate that the same person or group is responsible for all of the burglaries.

Definitions of MO and Trademark

Some agencies treat the MO and the trademark as the same thing, while others differentiate.

1. The MO is a method of operation used to achieve an end.

2. The trademark is any action by the person committing a crime other than the MO. It can be an act necessary to the successful accomplishment of the

crime, including preparations for the crime and the methods used to avoid apprehension. Usually, however, trademarks involve unnecessary acts such as eating food or drinking items from the refrigerator, changing clothes, leaving items, or using the bathroom. These acts often delay the perpetrator or make the perpetrator more vulnerable, as in the case of a superstition or a compulsion. There have been many reports of persons defecating at the crime scene (marking their territory, in a sense). Sometimes the trademark is an unconscious gesture, a tic, or a method of speaking.

The important thing to remember is to document very carefully the MO and trademarks used in the commission of a crime. Such evidence is often crucial in identifying suspects and linking similar crimes and series of crimes.

Examples of an MO

The following were taken from actual reports.

Methods of entry: Cutting screen in an L shape. Removing louvers near lock. Using passkey for hotels.

Actions during burglary: Taking only money, never televisions or other valuables. Using delivery truck to transport.

Actions during holdup: Using same words ("Put 'em here.") Wearing stocking mask. Taking victim's money and car. Working only certain parts of town.

Examples of a Trademark

Method of entry: Removing bottom three louvers, no matter where the culprit enters.

Actions during burglary: Stopping to eat and drink. Neatly replacing items in drawers. Removing his own clothing, raping woman victim after robbery. Defecating or urinating in particular place, e.g., bedspread in master bedroom. Turning furniture upside down, burning holes in rug, smashing dishes. Scrawling obscenities on bathroom mirror with lipstick.

Actions during holdup: Taking gum and candy as well as valuables.

Some examples of MOs and trademarks are quite common. Others can be bizarre. The more accurate and complete your report is, the more likely it is to assist you in apprehending the suspect.

Avoid Being Called on Your Time Off

Be specific. That is the best way to ensure that your off-duty hours (and your sleep) remain uninterrupted. Being vague or general makes it difficult for the person who follows up and increases the risk that you will be called. Many persons writing reports, tired at the end of a watch, slack off and write a perfunctory report. Sometimes it is read by an equally tired supervisor, who may just give it a glance and send it on its way, with the notation, "Pending further investigation." If follow-up investigators find large gaps, what you thought was time saving will turn into a loss of time. You will do yourself and others a big favor if you submit accurate, brief, and complete reports so that there will be no need to question you during your time off.

Summary

1. Always refer to yourself in the same person. Some agencies require personnel to use third person. If you do use a third-person format, stick to it throughout your report so you do not confuse your readers by switching back and forth. The use of first person in reports is recommended because it simplifies both the writing of the report and the understanding of the report by readers. Remember the "KISS rule": Keep it short and simple.

2. Systematize your method of description of persons, property, and places so that your descriptions are always in the same sequence. For example, describe persons from top to bottom and places from left to right.

3. Give special attention to studying hard-to-change features.

4. Get copies of catalogs to help you describe things you are not familiar with. Keep an up-to-date library or file of these.

5. Exercise special care in recording the MO and trademarks because they are often crucial in solving series of crimes.

6. Make your writing habitually specific, so you won't be called on your time off.

Chapter 5 — TEST

1. Habits work for report writers as well as for criminals. List five habits that will help you:

    (a) _____

    (b) _____

    (c) _____

    (d) _____

    (e) _____

2. Some of the characteristics of people that are least commonly described are:

    (a) _____

    (b) _____

    (c) _____

    (d) _____

    Be careful not to leave out _____

3. If you are having trouble describing certain types of property, get copies of _____ to keep on file.

4. Define:

    MO _____

    Trademark _____

    Give three examples of each:

    MO:

    (a) _____

    (b) _____

    (c) _____

Trademark:

(a) _____

(b) _____

(c) _____

5. The best way to avoid being called on your time off is to be _____ when writing your report.

CHAPTER 6

Other Types of Writing

Most report writing in the criminal justice system is organized chronologically. Care is taken not to give an opinion or evaluation; one gives "just the facts." The exceptions are the Presentence Investigation Report (PSIR) in probation departments and the monthly reports on parolees in parole departments; these may address the *why* of a situation.

However, the further you climb up the ladder, the more you will be called upon to write memoranda (commonly called *memos* or *To/Froms*), letters, meeting minutes, administrative reports, or research reports. These reports may or may not call for chronological organization. How then, do you get started if your subject is something other than a sequence of events?

First, check to see if your agency has a form or format model that covers the situation. If it does, use the form. Do not, however, pull just any material from the file to use as a sample. Remember what was covered in Chapter 1 about choosing a good sample. If you do not choose a good sample, you may end up with a model of how *not* to write.

Many criminal justice agencies have writings on file that do not read well. Most personnel in law enforcement are interested in the action end of things and have paid little attention to writing, other than what was learned about how to fill in a face page in their basic recruit class or other training courses. Sometimes criminal justice professionals copy lawyers' expressions (e.g., "The aforementioned party, one John Jones did knowingly and willfully on said night . . .") or use official sounding jargon (e.g., "The undersigned officer is cognizant of the fact that . . .").

Don't pattern your report on the legal profession's formalities and sentence structure. Even lawyers are trying to cease the use of stilted terms. Official jargon is even more meaningless. Neither of these antiquated forms will serve your purposes well. Learn the modern way.

139

DOI: 10.1016/B978-1-4377-5584-8.00013-X

In this chapter you will find a speedy method of organizing material, hints on writing evaluations and comparisons, and ideas for clearer visual presentation. All of these will combine to make your work forceful.

Learning from the Short Memo

Before dealing with the longer, nonchronological material, you will probably be faced with the short *To/From* memorandum — the memo used for interoffice communication. It is a good means by which to develop your skills. The format of the *To/From* memorandum is as follows:

```
TO:
FROM:
DATE:
SUBJECT:
```

Some agencies require the date as a heading at the top of the page, while others have you date the memo near the signature block. Also, many agencies require a signature or initials on the *FROM* line rather than having a signature block.

> The format of the memo emphasizes the two-pronged approach that should be followed in almost any writing: To whom are you writing, and why?

People often write as if addressing a faceless public or a large, unidentifiable group of people. Aim and fire your words — do not just fire shots off in all directions. A memo is read by an individual; even if several hundred people read it, each of them reads it individually. Keep this fact in mind. Your writing will automatically improve when you analyze the reader's level of competence, relationship to the subject, and reason for reading what you write.

Consider the tone, and keep it from being either too formal or too folksy. Your tone should be determined by the audience (the person addressed in the *TO* portion of the memo). Is the reader your supervisor? A fellow officer? Naturally, your tone will vary a bit with each audience that you address. Is your supervisor a traditionalist? If so, do not use a style that is too familiar. Is your supervisor a vigorous person-on-the-go? Then do not waste valuable time. If you are addressing a group, try to single out a representative person in your mind's eye and write directly to that person, even though you are not putting any individual names after the *TO*. Picturing someone will keep your writing from sounding wooden and insincere. School yourself in a simple, active style. Know your reader, your reason for writing, and the reader's reason for reading. Above all, focus sharply on your subject.

Stating your subject briefly, as you must in a memo, will force you to select an important emphasis. In this way, the short memo virtually organizes itself. It should not include too much material. State specifics and then stop. Because the memo is usually distributed within the department, you do not usually need to define terms or explain in detail as you would to outsiders. You might even use a modified outline form with numbered items. The memo is not always signed at the bottom as with a letter. A memo may be signed or initialed beside or above your name after the *FROM*. How and where to sign the memo is often dictated by the policy of your agency.

Writing the short memo will give you practice and confidence in attacking other nonchronological material, such as longer memos, meeting minutes, letters, administrative reports, or research reports.

Writing a Letter

Techniques for the memo are adaptable to letter writing. Because letters are often addressed to parties outside the agency, there are additional points to consider.

1. *Know the competence of the person addressed.* Are you writing the sheriff of a nearby county or the president of the garden club? When addressing a layperson, explain criminal justice terms the first time you use them. A word or abbreviation that is very familiar to you may have an entirely different meaning to the uninitiated. An example of such a term is *Mal Con*, which in this case means "malicious conversion of a car to another's use." Three women were given this term and were told that it was used in connection with police work. All guessed that it meant "malcontent," meaning a person not happy about prevailing conditions. Such a person, they reasoned, might protest or react in a violent manner. This illustrates how everyday language or jargon in one field or agency can be most confusing to people outside of that field or agency.

2. *Know your own place in the procedure.* This means being definite about what you have to do. Has the letter been passed on to you, are you going to answer it, or are you passing it on to someone else? If you are answering the letter, is it being prepared for someone else's signature?

    In many agencies, important outgoing mail is signed by the agency head as a matter of policy. Letters may be assigned to the most knowledgeable person in a specific field for the drafting of a letter of reply. It is important that the letter be drafted with the appropriate style and tone of the person who will sign it. The reply then goes through channels until it reaches the top again. An exception to this is the minor letter and answer of inquiry exchanged between persons on similar levels in familiar agencies. Another exception is the all-purpose, usually computerized form letter in answer to frequent requests of the same nature. This type of letter is often sent out with a department name and phone number given in case the recipient needs more information. Before you use your agency's letterhead in any way, check the routine and procedures of the agency.

3. *Do not hide behind meaningless but high-sounding words.* Get your point across to the lowest common denominator of your readership. Too often, people try for high-sounding sentences that avoid responsibility: "We are turning your letter over to the _____ division for appropriate action." This sounds official to some people but means nothing. Who is "we"? What is "appropriate action"? Is it a suit for libel or a recommendation for a commendation? Write specifics. If you do not know, ask. If the subject isn't your business, say so, and do not fake it with formalities that infuriate rather than impress your reader.

4. *Use the shopping list approach.* Even with short material it helps to brainstorm for ideas. Use a topic sentence and develop your points, numbering them if you find it helpful. Illustrate with specifics, and write a good conclusion. A letter is usually an attempt to get someone to do something, even if it is only to acknowledge shared information. Be definite in the conclusion. What action do you want? Never leave your reader wondering, "This is all very well, but why send it to me?"

5. *Use the accepted format for typing the letter.* Your agency probably has an accepted format for letters and a secretary to type them. Such formats are normally found in a procedural guide or secretary's manual. If you find that you need to select your own format, you may want to choose a style that lines up all material from the left margin (block style). This may seem a bit lopsided to you, but it is a simple form that avoids a lot of space-setting problems. Another popular format is the modified block style shown below. Note that business letters are single-spaced with a double space between paragraphs.

The modified block style format is found in Figure 6.1.

Faxing and Other Technological Advances

Faxing has some obvious advantages over writing a letter but also has one disadvantage. Anything that is supposed to be confidential really is not. If material is very sensitive, either do not fax it or call to make sure the intended person is near the machine to receive it immediately. In that way you will be able to convey a lengthy message in writing and include graphics.

Figure 6.1
Letter in Modified Block Format

Sender's address (if there is no letterhead)

¶

¶ *(3 lines)*

¶

Date

¶

¶ *(4 lines)*

¶

¶

Name and rank of person addressed
Person's address

¶

¶ *(2 lines)*

Dear Dr. _____:

¶

¶ *(2 lines)*

xxxxxxxxxxxxxxxxxxxxxxxxxxxxxxxxxxxxxxxxxxxxxxxxxxxxxxxxxxxxxx
xxxxxxxxxxxxxxxxxxxxxxxxxxxxxxxxxxxxxxxxxxxxxxxxxxxxxxxxxxxxxx
xxxxxxxxxxxxxxxxxxxxxxxxxxxxxxxxxxxxxxxxxxxxxxxxxxxxxxxxxxxxxx
xxxxxxxxxxxx

¶

¶ *(2 lines between paragraphs, no indentation needed)*

xxxxxxxxxxxxxxxxxxxxxxxxxxxxxxxxxxxxxxxxxxxxxxxxxxxxxxxxxxxxxx
xxxxxxxxxxxxxxxxxxxxxxxxxxxxxxxxxxxxxxxxxxxxxxxxxxxxxxxxxxxxxx
xxxxxxxx

¶

¶ *(2 lines between body copy and closing)*

Sincerely,

¶

¶ *(4 lines to allow for handwritten signature)*

¶

¶

Typed name of sender
Rank or title in capital letters

In the bottom left corner of the letter, indicate any additional notations. For example:

c: (Give name or names of recipients if copies are being sent to others and if
       the person addressed is to know that fact.)

bc: (Give name or names on copies only. This form means "blind copy" and is
       used where the first person addressed is not to know that copies are being
       sent to others.)

Enc: (This tells the reader that there are enclosed items.)

xc: (extra copy)

The fax cover sheet is similar to a memo and includes the following:

DATE:
TO:
FAX NUMBER:
FROM:
FAX NUMBER:
NUMBER OF PAGES INCLUDING THIS SHEET:
MESSAGE:

To be sure your fax is received as sent, you may add: "If any part of this fax is missing or is not clear, please call or fax."

Whether you are using computers, fax machines, databases, word processors, or any other of the ever-growing list of technological devices, it is more important than ever that your writing be precise. Remember the adage: "Garbage in, garbage out." Technological devices will help you in many ways, but can only work with what you have given them. You must keep the ABCs of writing in mind.

Recording Minutes of a Meeting

There are some rewards to being the recorder of a meeting. You will remember the facts better, others may be impressed by your expertise, and you will contribute to the smooth functioning of your agency or office. The important point is to know your responsibilities. Never remain silent and bewildered if you find yourself in a bind. If information is unclear during the meeting, it will be much muddier when you are alone at your typewriter, trying to make sense of your notes. Check your approach against these suggestions:

1. *Record names of all persons present, their ranks, and (in some cases) their reasons for being at the meeting.* Names of uniformed persons with rank and name visible are easy to record, of course, but people in plain clothes complicate the task. The easiest way around this is to circulate a sign-in page with these headings:

   Name   Rank   Representing   Telephone #

   Be sure that you do not miss latecomers; just quietly pass the sign-in page to them. Through this device, people get credit for attendance at the meeting, and those who should have been there but weren't can be identified, so that information can be channeled to them. If the same group meets regularly, only the absentees need to be noted.

2. *Give the date and purpose of the meeting.* If an agenda has been sent out, keep it handy and refer to it to see that all points are covered. State if it is a regular or special meeting.

3. *Give a brief summary of a previous meeting if background material is needed to understand the present one.*

4. *Record significant points either in the order given or grouped under appropriate topics.* The expertise of the meeting chairperson counts here. Some chairpersons are informal or disorganized in approach, so you will have to sort things out. A more organized meeting chairperson can be counted upon to produce an agenda and follow that in sequence. You cannot, however, always count on getting an organized agenda, or, for that matter, any agenda in advance.

5. *Stop and ask for clarification, if necessary.* It is always appropriate to ask for clarification or restatement. Explain briefly that what the speaker is saying is important and that you wish to be sure that you have it right, and then read back what you have and ask for correction or acceptance.

6. *Request permission to quote a person directly on any controversial statement.* Read the statement back to the person to ensure you have it right. You need not interrupt the person or the proceedings; catch the person before he or she leaves the meeting.

7. *Do not, however, go to the other extreme of trying to pin a name to everything said at an informal meeting.* If an agreement was reached, it doesn't matter how it happened. If one was not reached, perhaps those speaking for or against it wish to be identified. Ask them after the meeting whether they want their positions noted. In a formal meeting, the persons making and seconding motions should be identified. In an informal meeting, the main facts should be briefly noted.

8. *Request a summary if time is running out, and there seems to be no closure to the meeting.* Agreement may not have been reached, but points of agreement or disagreement may have been ironed out, and suggested action stated. In any case, you have the right to request a summary or final statement from the chairperson. Do so. Often, the chairperson and everyone else will benefit.

   Be as professional about recording the meeting as possible. Headings, numbering, and underlining may be used in your minutes to set points apart and call attention to certain facts. See that your minutes are easy to read and visually forceful. Corrections should be made before the final copy is produced. When you are asked to take minutes, whether at work or in other organizations to which you belong outside of work, take the challenge. Preparing minutes of meetings is good practice.

The Presentence Investigation Report

The person who completes the Presentence Investigation Report (PSIR) carries a heavy responsibility in report writing. The purpose of informing the judge and recommending treatment and/or a sentence is made difficult by the fact that there are many possibilities to choose from, including about two dozen probation conditions. Most often, the selection is a combination of possibilities, ranging from imprisonment to volunteer work in the community.

Reports are usually double-spaced and sometimes numbered by line on the left margin. This makes it easier to correct errors made in typing and for the readers to refer to lines that need further questioning. Considering the load under which both the probation officers and the court labor; questions may be minimal and recommendations very often followed.

Standards vary, but traditionally such reports were written without the use of first person by the officer. Quotes from the offender help to strengthen the justification for recommendations and should be recorded in the first person. Both long and short forms may be used. While headings may vary from one probation department to another, the long form usually includes the following information, complete with names of all involved:

Location of court, judge, probation officer, and lawyers.

Identification facts as used in police reports (e.g., name, date of birth, Social Security number, gender, physical description, identifying marks).

Personal data (e.g., time spent in the county, birthplace, nationality, education, occupation, marital status).

Family (e.g., parents' names and birthplaces, closest living relative, including address).

Instant offense (e.g., type, docket number, prosecutor, defense attorney, address, decision convicted by).

The PSIR itself repeats the location of sentencing and gives the sentencing date with a listing of offenses.

Official version, attached.

Defendant's version, in offender's own words.

Victim Impact Statement, including costs and receipts.

Previous jail time, including type of offense and any other prior trouble, given in order from oldest to most recent.

Social history, including parents' and siblings' backgrounds and attitudes, along with quotes, if possible, from the defendant and others involved as to how they see the situation. Education, marital status, employment histories, current economic situation, religious affiliation, outside interests, health, and present attitude of defendant are also included. Plea agreement, fiscal impact, and psychiatric insights may all be included if applicable.

Statement of probation officer, providing opinions based on specifics and explanation of the recommendation that follows.

Recommendation, usually including a selection of the possibilities of conditions — alone or in connection with each other.

Probation plan, with reports and conditions.

Appendix A contains a model Presentence Report. Appendix B contains a Worksheet for Presentence Report that is used in the Federal Probation System to help probation officers gather the appropriate information for the Presentence Report. Appendix B also contains a State of Tennessee Monthly Reporting Form. The probationer fills in information every time he or she reports and the probation officer checks off certain items (such as verification of restitution and/or employment) and then adds narrative comments on the back.

Research and Other Reports

Even if you can you write a good incident report quickly using a "what happened next" approach, you may find yourself hesitating over other forms of writing. The problem lies in organizing your thoughts and breaking that white expanse of paper or blank computer screen. When necessary, use the shopping list method discussed in Chapter 2 to help you organize your thoughts for your report. This method will get you started on any subject, be it a justification of a past action, a suggestion for a future program or purchase, an evaluation or comparison, an annual report, legislative testimony, or a term paper for school.

A good step-by-step approach to organizing a report includes the following:

1. *Make your shopping list by simply listing any words that come into your head concerning the topic.*

    This should be done on a piece of scratch paper with no more thought of organization than you would give in preparing any shopping list. This might include information such as names and places involved, actions, ideas, costs, quotations, etc. No one but you is going to see this part, so work your mind for every thought on the subject and put each one down in the shortest form possible. Stop only when you can't possibly think of another idea.

    The method should work like this: Suppose that you have to write a long memorandum regarding a proposal that your squad go on a 10-hour, four-day work week rather than the conventional eight-hour, five-day week. This plan, of course, involves complex planning in logistics, but all you have been asked for is your own reaction. Jotted down, your list might look like this:

Four days	Better beat coverage?
Go fishing	Extra men needed?
Time with Joan	Sick leave?

Drive to L.A.	Too tired first day off?
Take in the games?	Extra reports?
Lots of advantages?	Time overlap?
Some problems?	Work partners?
What about college class?	Moonlight extra days?

You might think of more ideas in addition to these. You should list everything in any order, with no criticism allowed. When you criticize yourself too early, you place a block in your idea gathering. Quit writing in "shopping list" style only when your ideas cease. Then and only then should you allow self-criticism.

2. *Go through the list, then decide which are the main points, which are the subtopics, and which ones do not belong. Put things in order of importance.*

You will almost always find that your mind takes some time to get started. Many times your first ideas are too obvious, too personal, or even irrelevant. If you start writing without organizing, you will risk putting down minor points first. Look for a pattern. Everything should fall under two or three points. In the situation of the 10/4 (10-hour, 4-day) plan, as opposed to the 8/5 (8-hour, 5-day) plan, you will be listing advantages and disadvantages of the new proposal as compared to the status quo. Select your major points and mark out those that are irrelevant or too personal. If you are given time, check data on points you marked with a question.

Some reports just list each idea with a number, including up to two dozen ideas with no attempt to categorize. Do the organizing on your time, not the reader's time. Follow this method.

The organization of your list might look like this:

10/4 Plan   **8/5 Plan**

Advantages   Advantages

_____   _____
_____   _____
_____   _____

Disadvantages   Disadvantages

_____   _____
_____   _____
_____   _____

CONCLUSION

_____
_____
_____
_____
_____

Do not swing back and forth from one point to the other in a series:
... However ... nevertheless ... on the one hand ... but on the other ... some may say ... but others ...

By the time you get to the conclusion, your reader will be dizzy. You can use such words for one or two comparisons, but do not use them in a series as above. Instead, list all the points on one side under a single heading or subheading and all the points for the other side under a single heading or subheading.

As you organize your material, it may fall into several major points. Perhaps you will find that your first two notations are utterly irrelevant and should be taken out. Maybe your fifth idea listed is really your third point, your eighth is your first, and your tenth is your second. Other points may fall under these as examples and illustrations while others should be left out.

3. *Write a topic sentence that includes, in parallel construction, the two or three main points in the reports.*

Write a good topic sentence that says what is at the heart of the paper. Incorporate this information into your introduction so that the reader knows what will follow. It pays to be direct in your writing. If you express your first point in a phrase or clause, use the same style for your subsequent points.

4. *Develop each point in the order given in the introduction.*

If it is a long report, each point may be shown as a separate topic. Headings should be in all capital letters and underlined for emphasis. A particularly long report may have subheadings, as on the continuation page of a criminal justice report. Back up your topics by using specific examples and definite illustrations, including information such as time, place, and cost, as well as other factors. Always remember that generalizations are extremely weak. Taking pains to be exact is always the mark of a professional.

5. *Write a good summary, question, evaluation, justification, request for action, or other form of conclusion to round out the writing.*

The first and last sections are the most important in any nonchronological material. The experienced reader looks for facts and conclusions in these positions. If the reader finds generalities or pleasantries, he or she may not read the middle points at all. However, if your work is well organized, visually appealing, and easy to read, you should be able to convince the reader to read the report. Use the conclusion to summarize the information contained in the report. As a result, you may secure the desired reaction, such as moral or financial backing, or any other goal. Use this outline to check your organization:

Topic Sentence
Include two or three main points in parallel construction.
1. _____
2. _____
3. _____

Develop in sequence presented, allowing equal space and including examples.
1. _____
2. _____
3. _____

Conclusion

---

6. *Start writing immediately, so you have time to revise.*

It is only human to wait until the last minute, draft the report hurriedly, and then badger some poor secretary to type it after hours. Do not fight yourself as well as the problem. Use this method to get going immediately: write, relax, reread, revise, and then fire it off.

7. *If you are documenting material taken from someone else or even your own previous writings, do not forget to use references such as footnotes, endnotes, and reference pages.*

Pick a standard documentation style such as Turabian, Modern Language Association of America (MLA), or the American Psychological Association (APA) and then consult the appropriate reference guide (see Selected Readings).

Summary

Learning from the Short Memo

1. Use your agency's format, if there is one.
2. Aim your communication at the appropriate audience.
3. Analyze your reader's level of competence, relationship to the subject, and reason for reading your communication.
4. Limit your subject carefully; state specifics and then stop.

Writing the Letter

1. Know the competence of the person addressed.
2. Know your own place in the procedure.

3. Use the shopping list approach: prepare a topic sentence, carefully develop headings, finish with a forceful conclusion defining what results you expect.
4. Use accepted format for typing the letter.

Recording the Meeting

1. Record the date as well as the names and ranks of those present; if the same group meets regularly, also list the absentees.
2. Give the purpose of the meeting.
3. Give background information if needed.
4. Record significant points.
5. Ask for clarification when necessary.
6. Verify important quotes.
7. Request a summary if time is running out.

Presentence Investigation Report

1. The purpose of the PSIR is to give the judge information and to provide sentencing recommendations.
2. Is often double-spaced with lines numbered in the left margin.
3. Provides information about all parties to the case.
4. Includes the official version and the defendant's version of the incident.
5. Provides information on the impact of the incident on the victim.
6. Includes the criminal and social histories of the defendant.
7. Includes a statement of the probation officer's evaluation, along with recommendations for sentencing and/or a probation plan.

Research and Other Reports

1. Use a shopping list approach. Write any words that come into your head on the subject.
2. Go through the list, and decide which are the main points, which are the subpoints, and which points do not belong. Organize the points you have.
3. Write an introduction to the report that includes the main points in the report in parallel construction.
4. Develop each point in the order given in the introduction. If comparisons are given, state them separately; do not swing back and forth.
5. Write a good summary, question, evaluation, justification, request for action, or other form of conclusion to round out the writing.
6. Start writing immediately, so that you have time to revise.

Chapter 6 — TEST

1. Chronological material is written in a _____ sequence. Non-chronological material should be organized in order of importance, with a _____ sentence, documentation, or development of points and a _____.

2. Examples of nonchronological writing are _____, _____, and _____.

3. Tone of writing is important; it should be determined by the _____.

4. The shopping list approach to writing is a method of organizing material that is easier to follow than the old, stilted style. It involves these steps:

   (a) Make a _____.

   (b) Go through the list, and decide on the _____ points, the _____, and those ideas that do not belong in the list at all. Look for a pattern, especially in the case of comparison, so that the writing does not become confusing.

   (c) Write a _____ sentence that includes only two or three separate points expressed in parallel constructions. Develop each point in order, allowing roughly the same amount of space for each.

   (d) Write a good conclusion in the form of a _____, _____, _____, _____, or _____.

   (e) Start work immediately so you have a chance to _____.

5. When recording a meeting, be sure to get the names of all persons, their _____ and whom they _____. The simplest device to get this information is the _____.

6. Be sure to include in your meeting report the _____, _____, and _____ listed under appropriate topics.

7. The PSIR is used by the judge in determining the defendant's _____. It provides information about both the official version and the _____ version of the incident. The PSIR also includes the probation officer's _____.

CHAPTER 7

Reading and Correcting Reports

Many people in the early stages of their careers in the criminal justice system believe that they do not have to worry about reading and correcting reports. After all, they won't be eligible for promotional examinations for some time. The truth of the matter is that by the time one has an opportunity to be promoted, one should have a great deal of experience reading and correcting reports. You should start reading and correcting reports now. An important rule to remember is not to submit any report — even a simple, straightforward one — without first having proofread it. Your first experiences in reading and correcting reports should be in reading and correcting your own reports. It is true that after having just finished writing a report the last thing you may feel like doing is reading your report. However, doing so will make a tremendous difference in the quality of reports you submit.

Even if you are a new employee and not a supervisor, there will be times when you have to read and correct other people's reports. Almost from day one, brand new law enforcement officers are sent to shoplifting arrest cases and find themselves reading reports written by store clerks, managers, or security officers. They also find themselves taking handwritten statements from witnesses and victims. Reading and correcting the reports of others takes more expertise than many people realize. It is one thing to write and proofread something concerning your own investigations, but it is quite another to be responsible for accepting and approving the writings of others. Your signature indicates that you endorse the writing as being correct to the best of your knowledge. Are you sure that it is? If it is not, you — as well as the original writer — may be called on to explain.

So while the responsibility of reading and correcting reports of others is usually thought of as only belonging to supervisors, most people within the criminal justice system are also given this responsibility. More and more agencies are developing

155

DOI: 10.1016/B978-1-4377-5584-8.00014-1

forms to be filled out by the public. For example, by Nebraska law, any operator of a motor vehicle involved in an accident resulting in injury or death to any person, or in property damage in excess of $500 to the property of any one person, including the operator of the vehicle, must submit a report (see Figure 7.1). Persons having difficulty filling out the report are referred to their insurance agent or to the nearest police authority. Many agencies have specific forms to be completed by the civilian who makes a citizen's arrest for minor offenses such as shoplifting or trespassing. In addition, almost all agencies have some sort of victim or witness statement form that is completed by those involved in a criminal case.

You will notice in Figures 7.2 and 7.3 two samples of witness statement forms used to record, in the witnesses' own handwriting where possible, statements that may be used in court later. Such forms have been found to be very effective in clearly documenting in the witnesses' own words their observations and experiences. It is also very difficult for the witnesses to change their recollections of the events at a later date when such a document written in their own handwriting is available. At the very least, such a document protects law enforcement officers from false charges resulting from the events. Figure 7.4 is an example of a shoplifting report, which is completed by civilians who make citizen's arrests for shoplifting.

The Denver Police Department has a special Follow-Up Offense Report that folds into a self-addressed, postage-paid envelope. It is used by citizens to provide additional lost or stolen property listings for cases in which an initial report has already been written (see Figure 7.5).

Be prepared to lend assistance if your agency has forms to be completed by citizens. The forms do not always take the place of incident reports prepared by officers; sometimes they are an additional source of information. Sometimes they are designed to let the public report on a matter of great concern, thereby increasing service to the public and saving time for the law enforcement or security officer.

Do not just hand a citizen a report form and expect it to be completed properly. You help the person by interviewing him or her as you would any witness, listening to the person's own presentation first, then asking questions to obtain additional needed information, and finally by having the person write a statement. If the statement or information required is complex, help the person by making a list of questions that need to be answered or providing headings and subheadings for use in the report. Failure to do so may result in a statement such as: "I saw him. He had a gun. I gave him my money." The statement is all true but doesn't give the reader much information and will be of little help in preparing the witness for court.

One of the authors of this text once handled an offense of leaving the scene of a traffic collision in which the passenger in the automobile that was hit was a well-known television actor. He was handed a witness statement form and was asked to complete it. His report of the incident was: "He hit our car. He ran. I tackled him. The rest is history." While this was amusing it is not very helpful for either investigative or court purposes.

Another example is with the shoplifting problem. Retail stores are grateful to have pads of forms that aid in the gathering of facts needed for a successful prosecution, and the individual officer may be called upon to work with store managers and employees to assist them in completing reports.

Figure 7.1

Sample Driver's Motor Vehicle Accident Report Form, Nebraska Department of Roads

Use Black Ink State of Nebraska **Driver's Motor Vehicle Accident Report** Questions? 1-402-479-4645

Mail within 10 days of accident to: Highway Safety, Nebraska Department of Roads, P.O. Box 94669, Lincoln, NE 68509-4669

DATE OF ACCIDENT M M / D D / Y Y Y Y 2 0 — S M T W TH F S — TIME OF ACCIDENT *(In Military Time)* — FOR STATE USE ONLY

LOCATION OF ACCIDENT

COUNTY | CITY | Total Number of Vehicles Involved

ROAD ON WHICH ACCIDENT OCCURRED STREET/HIGHWAY NO. *(If no Hwy. No., identify by name)* | Posted Speed Limit on the Street You Were Traveling

DISTANCE FROM MILEPOST FEET | N S E W | OF MILEPOST NO. | HIGHWAY NO. | PRIVATE PROPERTY? YES NO | ONE-WAY STREET? YES NO

IF AT INTERSECTION — NAME OF INTERSECTING ROADWAY

IF NOT AT INTERSECTION — FEET MILES | N S E W | OF NEAREST STREET, BRIDGE, RAILROAD CROSSING

IF ACCIDENT WAS OUTSIDE CITY LIMITS, INDICATE DISTANCE FROM NEAREST TOWN | MILES | N S E W | AND MILES | N S E W | OF NEAREST CITY OR TOWN

YOUR VEHICLE (VEHICLE NUMBER - 1)

DRIVER | PHONE ( ) –

DRIVER ADDRESS | CITY, STATE, ZIP | SEX FEMALE MALE

DRIVER LICENSE STATE | NUMBER | DATE OF BIRTH (MM/DD/YYYY) / /

VEHICLE

LICENSE PLATE YEAR (Plate expires) | STATE | NUMBER | ESTIMATED DAMAGE $

YEAR | MAKE | MODEL | BODY STYLE | COLOR

VEHICLE ID NO. *(VIN)*

OWNER NAME | PHONE ( ) –

OWNER ADDRESS | CITY, STATE, ZIP

OTHER VEHICLE (VEHICLE NUMBER - 2)

DRIVER | PHONE ( ) –

DRIVER ADDRESS | CITY, STATE, ZIP | SEX FEMALE MALE

DRIVER LICENSE STATE | NUMBER | DATE OF BIRTH (MM/DD/YYYY) / /

VEHICLE

LICENSE PLATE YEAR (Plate expires) | STATE | NUMBER | ESTIMATED DAMAGE $

YEAR | MAKE | MODEL | BODY STYLE | COLOR

VEHICLE ID NO. *(VIN)*

OWNER NAME | PHONE ( ) –

OWNER ADDRESS | CITY, STATE, ZIP

VEHICLE MOVEMENT BEFORE COLLISION

VEH NO.	N	S	E	W	ROAD OR HIGHWAY NAME
1					
2					

Vehicle 1 2

01 ☐ ☐ Essentially straight ahead
02 ☐ ☐ Backing
03 ☐ ☐ Changing lanes
04 ☐ ☐ Overtaking/Passing
05 ☐ ☐ Turning right
06 ☐ ☐ Turning left
07 ☐ ☐ Making U-turn
08 ☐ ☐ Entering traffic lane
09 ☐ ☐ Leaving traffic lane
10 ☐ ☐ Parked
11 ☐ ☐ Slowing or stopped in traffic
12 ☐ ☐ Other
13 ☐ ☐ Unknown

POINT OF IMPACT AND MOST DAMAGED AREA

(Enter numbers for each vehicle)

	YOUR VEHICLE NO. 1	OTHER VEHICLE NO. 2
POINT OF IMPACT		
MOST DAMAGED AREA		

00 None
09 Top & windows
10 Undercarriage
11 Total (all areas)
12 Other

02 03 04 / 01 Front 05 / 08 07 06

TRAFFIC CONTROL DEVICE

(Check one for each vehicle)

Vehicle 1 2

1 ☐ ☐ No controls
2 ☐ ☐ Traffic control signal
3 ☐ ☐ Flashing traffic control signal
4 ☐ ☐ School zone signal
5 ☐ ☐ Stop sign
6 ☐ ☐ Yield sign
7 ☐ ☐ Warning sign
8 ☐ ☐ Railroad crossing device
9 ☐ ☐ Unknown

DISPOSITION OF VEHICLE

(Check one for each vehicle)

Vehicle 1 2

1 ☐ ☐ Towed – due to damages
2 ☐ ☐ Towed – other reasons
3 ☐ ☐ Left at scene
4 ☐ ☐ Driven away
5 ☐ ☐ Unknown

Total number of persons in your vehicle

AIRBAG DEPLOYED

For each person in your vehicle, enter an Airbag Deployed code for their seating position

Front

1 Deployed – front
2 Deployed – side
3 Deployed – both front/side
4 Not deployed
5 Not applicable/ No airbag available
6 Unknown

RESTRAINT USE

For each person in your vehicle, enter a Restraint Use code for their seating position

Front

1 None used
2 Lap & shoulder belt used
3 Shoulder belt only used
4 Lap belt only used
5 Child safety seat used
6 Child booster seat used
7 Helmet used
8 Restraint use unknown

Complete this section for all injured persons in your vehicle, also any bicyclists, pedestrians or fatalities involved in the accident. Enter the code number which best answers questions 1- 5 in the appropriate box located at the lower right.

1. Seating Position *(Enter one)*

10. Other enclosed passenger/cargo area
11. Other unenclosed passenger/cargo area
12. Riding on vehicle exterior
13. Sleeper section of truck cab
14. Trailing unit
15. Moped
16. Motorcycle operator
17. Motorcycle passenger
18. Pedestrian
19. Bicycle *(pedalcycle)*
20. Unknown

Front		
01	02	03
04	05	06
07	08	09

2. Ejected/Trapped *(Enter one)*

1. Not ejected or trapped
2. Partially ejected
3. Totally ejected
4. Trapped - Occupant removed without use of equipment
5. Trapped - Equipment used in extrication
6. Unknown

3. Body Region with Most Severe Injury *(Enter one)*

01. Head
02. Face
03. Neck
04. Chest
05. Back/spine
06. Shoulder/upper arm
07. Elbow/lower arm/hand
08. Abdomen/pelvis
09. Hip/upper leg
10. Knee/lower leg/foot
11. Entire body
12. Unknown
13. None

4. Injury Severity *(Enter one)*

1. **Killed**
2. **Disabling** - cannot leave scene without assistance *(broken bones, severe cuts, prolonged unconsciousness, etc.)*
3. **Visible** but not disabling *(minor cuts, swelling, etc.)*
4. **Possible** but not visible *(complaint of pain, etc.)*
5. None

5. Transported to Medical Facility *(Enter one)*

If the individual was transported from the crash site to a medical facility for treatment of injuries received in the crash:

Source of Transport:

1. Not transported
2. EMS *(Ambulance)*
3. Police
4. Other
5. Unknown

NAME	ADDRESS	DATE OF BIRTH (MM / DD / YYYY)	1 Seat Position	2 Eject	3 Body Region	4 Injury Sev.	5 Trans.	SEX M F
		/ /						
		/ /						
		/ /						
		/ /						

DR 41, Aug 03 — Return all three completed pages to the address above. — Page 1

Continued

Figure 7.1—*continued*

Driver Contributing Circumstances
(Check one per driver)

Vehicle
1 2

- 01 ☐ ☐ No improper driving
- 02 ☐ ☐ Failed to yield right of way
- 03 ☐ ☐ Disregarded traffic signs, signals, road markings
- 04 ☐ ☐ Exceeded authorized speed limit
- 05 ☐ ☐ Driving too fast for conditions
- 06 ☐ ☐ Made improper turn
- 07 ☐ ☐ Wrong side or wrong way
- 08 ☐ ☐ Followed too closely
- 09 ☐ ☐ Failure to keep in proper lane or running off road
- 10 ☐ ☐ Operating vehicle in erratic, reckless, careless, negligent, or aggressive manner
- 11 ☐ ☐ Swerving or avoiding due to wind, slippery surface, vehicle, object, non-motorist in roadway, etc.
- 12 ☐ ☐ Over-correcting/over-steering
- 13 ☐ ☐ Visibility obstructed
- 14 ☐ ☐ Inattention
- 15 ☐ ☐ Mobile phone distraction
- 16 ☐ ☐ Distracted - other
- 17 ☐ ☐ Fatigued/asleep
- 18 ☐ ☐ Operating defective equipment
- 19 ☐ ☐ Other improper action
- 20 ☐ ☐ Unknown

Driver Condition *(Check one per driver)*

Vehicle
1 2

- 1 ☐ ☐ Apparently normal
- 2 ☐ ☐ Physical impairment
- 3 ☐ ☐ Emotional (depressed, angry, disturbed, etc.)
- 4 ☐ ☐ Illness
- 5 ☐ ☐ Fell asleep, fainted, fatigued, etc.
- 6 ☐ ☐ Under the influence of medications/drugs/alcohol
- 7 ☐ ☐ Other *(specify)*
- 8 ☐ ☐ Unknown

Road Contributing Circumstances
(Check one)

- 01 ☐ None
- 02 ☐ Road surface condition (wet, icy, snow, slush, etc.)
- 03 ☐ Debris
- 04 ☐ Rut, holes, bumps
- 05 ☐ Work zone (construction/maintenance/utility)
- 06 ☐ Worn, travel-polished surface
- 07 ☐ Obstruction in roadway
- 08 ☐ Traffic control device inoperative, missing or obscured
- 09 ☐ Shoulders (none, low, soft, high)
- 10 ☐ Non-highway work
- 11 ☐ Other (specify)
- 12 ☐ Unknown

Road Character *(Check one)*
- 1 ☐ Straight and level
- 2 ☐ Straight and on slope
- 3 ☐ Straight and on hilltop
- 4 ☐ Curved and level
- 5 ☐ Curved and on slope
- 6 ☐ Curved and on hilltop

Environment Contributing Circumstances *(Check one)*
- 1 ☐ None
- 2 ☐ Weather conditions
- 3 ☐ Vision obstruction
- 4 ☐ Glare
- 5 ☐ Animal in roadway
- 6 ☐ Other *(specify)*
- 7 ☐ Unknown

Light Condition *(Check one)*
- 1 ☐ Daylight
- 2 ☐ Dawn
- 3 ☐ Dusk
- 4 ☐ Dark–lighted roadway
- 5 ☐ Dark–roadway not lighted
- 6 ☐ Dark–unknown roadway lighting
- 7 ☐ Other *(specify)*
- 8 ☐ Unknown

Road Surface *(Check one)*
- 1 ☐ Concrete
- 2 ☐ Asphalt
- 3 ☐ Brick
- 4 ☐ Gravel
- 5 ☐ Dirt
- 6 ☐ Other *(specify)*

Total Number of Through Lanes *(Check one)*
- 1 ☐ One lane
- 2 ☐ Two lanes
- 3 ☐ Three lanes
- 4 ☐ Four lanes
- 5 ☐ Five lanes
- 6 ☐ Six or more lanes

Weather Condition *(Check up to two)*
- 01 ☐ None
- 02 ☐ Cloudy
- 03 ☐ Fog, smog, smoke
- 04 ☐ Rain
- 05 ☐ Sleet, hail, freezing rain/drizzle
- 06 ☐ Snow
- 07 ☐ Severe crosswinds
- 08 ☐ Blowing sand, soil, dirt, snow
- 09 ☐ Other *(specify)*
- 10 ☐ Unknown

Road Surface Condition *(Check one)*
- 1 ☐ Dry
- 2 ☐ Wet
- 3 ☐ Snow
- 4 ☐ Ice
- 5 ☐ Sand, mud, dirt, oil, gravel
- 6 ☐ Water *(standing, moving)*
- 7 ☐ Slush
- 8 ☐ Other *(specify)*
- 9 ☐ Unknown

Median Type *(Check one)*
- 1 ☐ Median barrier
- 2 ☐ Raised median *(curbed)*
- 3 ☐ Grass median *(no curb)*
- 4 ☐ Painted *(no curb)*
- 5 ☐ None

Was the crash in or near a construction maintenance or utility work zone? *(Check one)*
- 1 ☐ No   2 ☐ Unknown   3 ☐ Yes

INDICATE BY DIAGRAM WHAT HAPPENED

Indicate North by Arrow

DESCRIBE WHAT HAPPENED (Refer to your vehicle as No. 1, any others as No. 2, No. 3, etc.)

PROPERTY

| NON-VEHICLE OBJECT DAMAGED | OWNER NAME | ADDRESS | PHONE ( ) – | APPROX. COST OF DAMAGE $ |
| NON-VEHICLE OBJECT DAMAGED | OWNER NAME | ADDRESS | PHONE ( ) – | APPROX. COST OF DAMAGE $ |

Was a Police Officer Contacted? ○ YES ○ NO   OFFICER NAME OR BADGE NUMBER   DEPARTMENT *(Name of City, County, etc.)*

I certify, to the best of my knowledge, that this report is true and accurate.   OPERATOR SIGNATURE *(Required if physically able)* X   DATE

DR 41, Aug 03   Return all three completed pages of Accident Report to address located on top of page 1.   Page 2

Figure 7.1—*continued*

State of Nebraska — Driver's Motor Vehicle Accident Report — Questions? 1-402-479-4645

Every operator of a motor vehicle involved in an accident resulting in either injury, death or damages over $1,000.00 to the property of any one person (including the operator) must complete and return this confidential report within 10 days following the accident.

If the driver is physically unable to fill out the report, the owner of the motor vehicle is required to do so. If you have difficulty filling out the report, consult your insurance agent or nearest police authority. Failure to report an accident as required is a misdemeanor, punishable by a fine of $50.00.

Report Form Instructions *(print in ink or type)*

Accident location:

After entering the date, county and city information, describe where the accident occurred. If the crash happened on a numbered rural highway, give the direction and number of feet from the nearest milepost. If your accident occurred on an urban highway, skip the "distance from milepost" section.

If the accident occurred at an intersection, enter the name of the intersecting roadway. For those accidents not located at an intersection, enter the approximate distance in feet from the nearest landmark (intersection, city limit, bridge name, etc.).

Vehicle and driver involvement:

Answer the questions asked about your vehicle and any other vehicle involved in the accident to the best of your ability. If more than two vehicles were involved, complete an additional form(s). Refer to your vehicle as vehicle number 1 throughout the report. Information on bicycles may be entered in the "other vehicle" section.

Be careful when listing the estimated damage to your vehicle. Use a garage estimate whenever possible.

Airbag deployment coding:

For every occupant in your vehicle, including yourself, enter the correct airbag deployed code according to each person's seating position. For help in marking the car graph see the following example.

Example: There are a total of three occupants in the vehicle, with the driver and one occupant in front, and the third person in the back seat behind the driver. Both the driver and the front passenger seats are equipped with front air bags. The driver's air bag does not deploy during the crash, the front seat passenger's air bag does deploy. The passenger in the backseat does not have an airbag available. The car graph would be marked as shown.

1 Deployed – front
2 Deployed – side
3 Deployed – both front/side
4 Not deployed
5 Not applicable/ No airbag available
6 Unknown

Restraint use coding:

For every occupant in your vehicle, including yourself, enter the correct restraint code according to each person's seating position. For help in marking the car graph, see the following example.

Example: If there were three occupants in the vehicle, with the driver and one occupant in front, both using lap and shoulder belts, and the third occupant in the back seat behind the driver not using any restraint, the car graph would be marked as shown.

1 None used – vehicle occupant
2 Lap & shoulder belt used
3 Shoulder belt only used
4 Lap belt only used
5 Child safety seat used
6 Child booster seat used
7 Helmet used
8 Restraint use unknown

How to enter information about injured persons:

Carefully complete this section for each person injured in **your vehicle** and any **pedestrians** or **bicyclists** injured in the accident. After providing the name, address, date of birth, and sex of each injured person, answer questions 1-5 by writing your response in the appropriate box. If you need to provide injury information for more than four persons, complete another report form.

Example: Assume the car you were driving collided with a bicycle. The bicycle operator was seriously injured and rushed to the hospital. Although you bruised your shoulder and one of your passengers complained of neck pain, no one riding in your vehicle received immediate medical treatment.

NAME / ADDRESS			DATE OF BIRTH (MM / DD / YYYY)	1 Seat Position	2 Eject	3 Body Region	4 Injury Sev.	5 Trans.	SEX M F
Sam Public	123 Elm St.	Lincoln, NE 68502	10 / 17 / 1993	1 9		0 5	2	2	M
Jan Doe	3456 Vermont Ave.	Lincoln, NE 68503	07 / 31 / 1964	0 1	1	0 6	3	1	F
Mary Doe	3456 Vermont Ave.	Lincoln, NE 68503	12 / 30 / 1989	0 3	1	0 3	4	1	F
			/ /						

Instruction Page for Page 1 of the Accident Report.
Discard this sheet after use.

Continued

Figure 7.1—*continued*

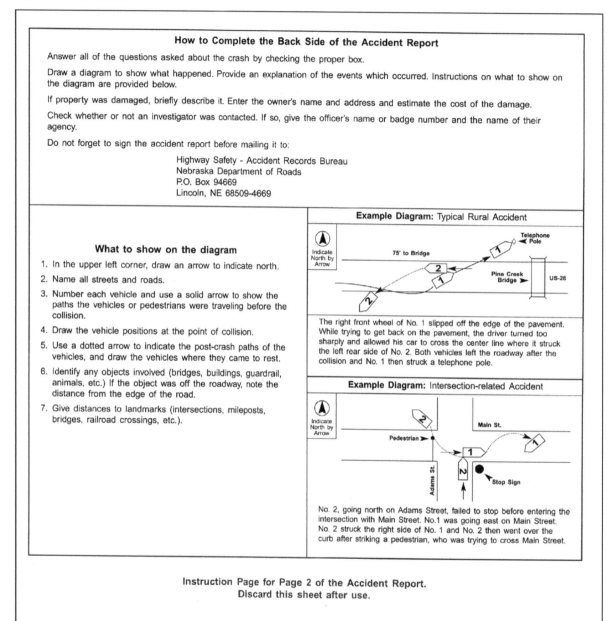

How to Complete the Back Side of the Accident Report

Answer all of the questions asked about the crash by checking the proper box.

Draw a diagram to show what happened. Provide an explanation of the events which occurred. Instructions on what to show on the diagram are provided below.

If property was damaged, briefly describe it. Enter the owner's name and address and estimate the cost of the damage.

Check whether or not an investigator was contacted. If so, give the officer's name or badge number and the name of their agency.

Do not forget to sign the accident report before mailing it to:

Highway Safety - Accident Records Bureau
Nebraska Department of Roads
P.O. Box 94669
Lincoln, NE 68509-4669

What to show on the diagram

1. In the upper left corner, draw an arrow to indicate north.
2. Name all streets and roads.
3. Number each vehicle and use a solid arrow to show the paths the vehicles or pedestrians were traveling before the collision.
4. Draw the vehicle positions at the point of collision.
5. Use a dotted arrow to indicate the post-crash paths of the vehicles, and draw the vehicles where they came to rest.
6. Identify any objects involved (bridges, buildings, guardrail, animals, etc.) If the object was off the roadway, note the distance from the edge of the road.
7. Give distances to landmarks (intersections, mileposts, bridges, railroad crossings, etc.).

Example Diagram: Typical Rural Accident

The right front wheel of No. 1 slipped off the edge of the pavement. While trying to get back on the pavement, the driver turned too sharply and allowed his car to cross the center line where it struck the left rear side of No. 2. Both vehicles left the roadway after the collision and No. 1 then struck a telephone pole.

Example Diagram: Intersection-related Accident

No. 2, going north on Adams Street, failed to stop before entering the intersection with Main Street. No.1 was going east on Main Street. No. 2 struck the right side of No. 1 and No. 2 then went over the curb after striking a pedestrian, who was trying to cross Main Street.

Instruction Page for Page 2 of the Accident Report.
Discard this sheet after use.

Figure 7.1—*continued*

ON-LINE VERSION	DRIVER MUST COMPLETE IN FULL	

You, the driver, must provide information about the liability insurance covering the motor vehicle you were driving. Please complete the following.

Name of Insurance Company Affording
Liability Coverage on Date of Accident _____

Address _____

Vehicle Information: VIN No._____ Year _____ Make _____ Model _____

Name of Agent
Who Sold Policy _____ Address _____

Policy No. _____ Date of Accident _____ In or near _____ , Nebraska
                                                            (Month)   (Day)   (Year)

Driver _____ Address _____

Owner _____ Address _____

Name of Policyholder _____

SR-21L

ON-LINE VERSION	THIS SIDE FOR INSURANCE COMPANY USE ONLY	

TO: **Department of Motor Vehicles**
     Financial Responsibility Section
     301 Centennial Mall South
     PO Box 94877
     LINCOLN NE 68509-4877

Please return this form immediately if policy was not in effect as described by motorist.

Do not return form if policy was in effect.

The undersigned company advises that the insurance policy, as described on the reverse side, does not afford liability coverage to both the driver and owner in the limits of $25,000 – $50,000 bodily injury and $25,000 property damage for this accident **because of the following reasons:**

_____
(please complete)

_____   _____   _____
Name of Insurance Company   *Authorized Representative*   *Date*

INSURANCE INFORMATION

Please read instructions carefully.
Return this entire page with the completed Accident Report.

Figure 7.2
Sample Witness Statement Form, Oakland County Sheriff's Office

COUNTY OF OAKLAND
OFFICE OF THE SHERIFF
JOHN F. NICHOLS

THOMAS QUISENBERRY
Major

HENRY BUFFA
Undersheriff

WITNESS STATEMENT   COMPLAINT # _____

NAME _____

ADDRESS _____

DATE OF BIRTH_____   TELEPHONE _____ HOME

DATE & TIME _____   _____ WORK

STATEMENT _____

_____

_____

_____

_____

_____

_____

_____

_____

_____

_____

_____

_____

_____

_____

_____

_____

_____

_____

_____

SIGNATURE_____   OFFICER'S SIGNATURE_____

92-982-AS (6-97)   45576

BLDG 10 EAST   ★   1201 N TELEGRAPH RD   ★   PONTIAC MI 48341-1044   ★   248/858-5008

Figure 7.3
Sample Statement Form, Honolulu Police Department

HONOLULU POLICE DEPARTMENT STATEMENT FORM   Report No.

Statement of:	Classification:
Address:	Date of Occurrence:
Age: Date of Birth: SSN:	Occupation:
Res. Ph.: Bus. Ph.:	Employer:
Location of Interview:	

Please give a detailed statement answering all of the following questions:

1. What **DATE** and **TIME** did it happen?
2. **WHERE** did it happen?
3. **WHO** was involved?
4. What **WITNESSES** do you know of?
5. **WHAT** happened?
6. **HOW** did it happen?
7. **WHY** did it happen (prior events/causes)?
8. **ANY OTHER** relevant information?
9. **DID YOU IDENTIFY** any suspects? Explain.
10. **DID YOU IDENTIFY** any weapons? Explain.
11. . . . any property? Explain.
12. . . . any vehicles? Explain.

The undersigned freely and voluntarily provides the following statement:

_____

_____

_____

_____

_____

_____

_____

_____

_____

_____

_____

_____

_____

_____

_____

_____

_____

_____

I have read this statement prepared by _____ which consists of this typed/handwritten page and _____ continuation page(s), and have been given the opportunity to make corrections thereon. I attest that this statement is true and correct to the best of my knowledge, and that I gave this statement freely and voluntarily without coercion or promise of reward.

_____   _____
            Signature   Investigator's Signature

Date: _____   Time: _____   Date: _____   Time: _____

HPD-252 (R-12/96)

Continued

Figure 7.3—*continued*

STATEMENT FORM CONTINUATION PAGE

Page _____ of _____ pages

Statement of:

Rpt. No.:

Signature

Investigator's Signature

Date: _____   Time: _____   Date: _____   Time: _____

HPD-252A (R-12/96)

Figure 7.4
Sample Shoplifting Report Form, Honolulu Police Department

HONOLULU POLICE DEPARTMENT

SHOPLIFTING REPORT

1 REPORT NO.
2 DISTRICT	3 CENSUS	4 BEAT	5 WATCH

6 FIRM'S NAME	7 ADDRESS	PHONE

| 8 DEFENDANT'S NAME | 9 SEX RACE AGE | 10 DOB | 11 OCCUPATION | 12 SOCIAL SEC. NO. |

| 13 ADDRESS | 14 PLACE EMP / SCHOOL ATT | RES. PHONE | BUS. PHONE |

| 15 PLACE OF OFFENSE/CLOSEST INTERSECTING STREET | 16 DATE/TIME/DAY | 17 NO. ARRESTED | 18 INJURIES ☐ YES ☐ NO |

| 19 PLACE OF ARREST | 20 DATE/TIME/DAY | 21 ARRESTING PERSON |

| 22 FATHER'S NAME | EMPLOYED BY | BUS. PHONE |

| 23 MOTHER'S NAME | EMPLOYED BY | BUS. PHONE |

CODE   W - Witness   R - Arresting Person   S - Additional Suspects   (Fill in Composite Descriptions)

24 NAME	AGE SEX	CODE	ADDRESS	RES. PHONE	BUS. PHONE

25 SEX	RACE	AGE	HEIGHT	WEIGHT	BUILD	HAIR	EYES	COMP	CLOTHES/ID CHARACTERISTICS

26 DEPT. NO.	27 QUANTITY	28 DESCRIPTION OF MERCHANDISE	29 VALUE

| 30 EVIDENCE RETAINED AT | 31 IN CUSTODY OF | 32 TOT. VAL. |

33 STATEMENT OF CIRCUMSTANCES. (1) ACTIONS PRIOR TO AND AFTER SHOPLIFTING (2) METHOD OF OPERATION (3) WHERE THE ARTICLES WERE CONCEALED (4) LIST ANY PURCHASES MADE (5) IDENTIFY ADDITIONAL SUSPECTS OR WITNESSES AND ANY STATEMENTS TAKEN (6) DESCRIBE ARREST (7) DESCRIBE INJURIES IN DETAIL IF APPLICABLE (8) USE REVERSE SIDE FOR ADDITIONAL FACTS.

34 THE UNDERSIGNED BEING A PERSON PRESENT DURING THE COMMISSION OF A CRIME AND HAVING WITNESSED THE TAKING OF MERCHANDISE DID PLACE THE DEFENDANT(S) UNDER CITIZEN'S ARREST.

35 REPORT WRITTEN BY	BADGE NO.	36 POSITION	DATE/TIME

| 37 RELEASED TO ☐ POLICE ☐ GUARDIAN ☐ PARENT ☐ OTHER | 38 SIGNATURE OF PERSON TAKING CUSTODY | DATE/TIME |

HPD-317 (REV. 5/78)

Figure 7.5
Sample Follow-Up Offense Report Form, Denver Police Department

PRINT CLEARLY - USE BLACK INK
INSTRUCTIONS FOR CITIZENS

In order for your report to be properly processed, it is necessary for all information to be clearly printed, complete and correct. These easy instructions will help you with the report.

- Fill in the information about your vehicle **ONLY** if the offense involved damage to your vehicle or theft from your vehicle. Here is an example:

VICTIM'S VEHICLE	YEAR	MAKE	MODEL	LIC. NO.	YEAR	STATE	VIN
	1979	Olds	Cutlass	ZZZ-123	96	CO	ABCD123456789012F88

- It is **VERY IMPORTANT** to describe all lost, stolen or damaged property as completely as possible. Use more than one line if necessary. Here are some examples:

#	QTY.	ARTICLE TYPE AND BRAND NAME	MODEL (#)	COLOR	SERIAL NUMBER	EST. VALUE
1	1	Anybrand VCR	Easy Touch #369	black/silver	XYZ 1234567	$450.00
2	1	18K Gold necklace, heavy serpentine design	n/a	Gold	None	$200.00

TOTAL VALUE ⟳	CURRENCY	JEWELRY 200.00	FURS	CLOTHING	MISC. 450.00	A L L	TOTAL $650.00

If you are reporting the theft of a cellular telephone, please include the name and telephone number of the cellular telephone service company **and** the telephone number of the stolen cellular telephone.

- The **NARRATIVE** tells the Police Department what happened. Be brief, but include all information you may believe will be helpful. These are examples of brief, informative narratives:

I put my purse in my desk drawer when I got to work at 8:30 A.M. At noon, I opened the drawer to get my purse and discovered it was missing. The drawer was not locked. I did not notice any unfamiliar people in the office during the morning.

OR

I parked my car on the street in front of my house at 10:00 P.M. on Monday. The car was locked. When I went out at 7:30 A.M. on Tuesday, I discovered that somebody had broken the front window on the driver's side with a rock. The rock was on the front seat of the car. The inside of the car had been ransacked and my radio and tape deck were gone.

- If you need more space to complete your report, use a separate sheet of paper. Make sure you include your name, the location of the offense, the date of the offense and your signature on each page.

- When you have completed the report, mail it to:
  . DENVER POLICE DEPARTMENT, Records Section
  . 1331 Cherokee Street, Room 420
  . Denver, CO 80204-2787

- A copy of your report showing the Denver Police Department case number will be mailed to you if you include a check or money order for $5.00 and a long, stamped, self-addressed envelope with the report. You can also get the case number for your report by waiting 72 hours and then calling the Police Department Records Section at 640-3920 any weekday between 10:00 A.M. and 4:00 P.M.

- An investigator will contact you **ONLY** when new information has been developed or property has been recovered.

- If additional information becomes available to you after this report has been mailed, contact the Criminal Investigation Division. If the crime involves your vehicle, call 640-3591. If the crime involves any other property, call 640-3681. **CALL IF:**

  1. There was a witness to the crime, or

  2. A suspect in the crime can be named, identified or described, or

  3. A suspect vehicle can be identified, especially if a license plate number has been identified.

Figure 7.5—*continued*

PRINT ALL INFORMATION - USE BLACK INK

OFFENSE REPORT • DENVER POLICE DEPARTMENT

☐ COUNTER REPORT   ☐ TELEPHONE REPORT   Page _____ of _____ Pages
☐ RADIO ROOM MAIL-IN REPORT
☐ NO WITNESS TO OR SUSPECTS IN THIS OFFENSE NOR ANY   ☐ ORIGINAL REPORT
　 SIGNIFICANT PHYSICAL EVIDENCE PRESENT   ☐ ADDITIONAL REPORT
☐ ADDITIONAL LOST/STOLEN PROPERTY BEING REPORTED BY
　 THE VICTIM AND MAILED TO THE DPD   OFFENSE REPORT NO. _____

OFNS

| TYPE OF OFFENSE | | OFFENSE OCCURRED BETWEEN | DATE | 24 HR. TIME | DAY | A N D | DATE | 24 HR. TIME | DAY |
| LOCATION OF OFFENSE | | APT. NO. | PRECINCT | TYPE OF PREMISES | | | WEAPON/TOOL USED | | |

VICTIM

| NAME (Last,First, MI) | | | DOB | | RACE | SEX | HGT. | WGT. | SOCIAL SECURITY NO. |
| ADDRESS WHERE BEST CONTACTED | | CITY | | COUNTY | | STATE | ZIP CODE | | HOME PHONE |

| VICTIM'S VEHICLE | YEAR | MAKE | MODEL | LIC. NO. | | YEAR | STATE | VIN | |

| OFFENSE REPORTED BY ☐ VICTIM ☐ OFFICER ☐ OTHER | | DOB | RACE | SEX | REL. TO VICTIM | SOCIAL SECURITY NO. |
| ADDRESS WHERE BEST CONTACTED | | CITY, STATE, ZIP CODE | | | | BUS. PHONE |

LIST LOST / STOLEN / DAMAGED PROPERTY, THEN BEGIN NARRATIVE NEEDED

#	QTY.	ARTICLE TYPE AND BRAND NAME	MODEL (#)	COLOR	SERIAL NUMBER	EST. VALUE

Print the list of your lost, stolen or damaged property, then tell what happened.
See Instructions on Back Side.

☐ COMPLETED BY VICTIM

| | TOTAL VALUE ○ ○ ○ | CURRENCY | JEWELRY | FURS | CLOTHING | MISC. | A L L | TOTAL |

ADM

OFFICER TAKING REPORT / SER. NO	DATE OF REPORT / /	I AFFIRM THIS INFORMATION IS TRUE AND CORRECT
☐ CASE INACTIVE, NO FURTHER INVESTIGATION	TIME REPORT INITIATED	SIGNED_____
INVESTIGATOR ASSIGNED	_____ HRS.	☐ NO FURTHER INVESTIGATION RECOMMENDED	READ AND APPROVED BY:

DPD 250SR (Rev. 1/97)

0250

It is also important to keep in mind that the average person in the United States reads at a seventh- or eighth-grade level and may, in fact, write at a level lower than that. In such cases you may have to help the person by writing or typing out the person's statement and then having the person sign it after agreeing that it is an accurate account.

If you are working with someone involved in a motor vehicle collision, it will probably be a one-time experience for the person. The owner or manager of any store that is a frequent site of shoplifting, however, may appreciate help in writing reports more effectively, so that you can better assist him or her with the recurring problem.

The same general principles for writing reports can be used in reading and correcting reports, so they can be considered for anyone who is under your direction. Is all the information needed in the report — the who, what, when, where, and how? Is the report accurate, brief, and complete?

Of course, you will deal slightly differently with the public than with an officer under your direction, but some of the same points would be considered in both situations. Whether you are dealing with a new recruit to whom everything is new and difficult or an employee transferred from another section, your help may be needed for completing reports.

Common Problem Areas

Many problems with reports involve misinterpretations or omissions, usually on the face page. Other problems involve grammatical errors, usually on the continuation or follow-up report. These are often difficult for the supervising officer to identify and help correct.

Misinterpretation often results from difficulty in reading the form. This is almost always true of the outsider, such as a chain store manager, who may know a lot about the habits of shoplifters but not much about security or law enforcement terminology. Officers need to take time to help. Most people are reluctant to read directions; as one store manager put it, "Now go over it all with me. I listen better than I read." Even though he had been given an instruction manual for each form, he still got mixed up on the term *Comp*, thinking it referred to *composite*, when it was asking for information about *complexion*. More than one officer has had the occasion when a civilian wrote "yes" in the block labeled "Sex." Be sure that people under your direction not only have read the instructions, but also understand what is required of them in order to complete the report.

Omission is the easiest mistake to check. It isn't difficult to say, "You forgot to put in the color of the stolen bicycle," but it may require that the next investigator make another trip or phone call to find out this information. Sometimes material omitted during the first interview is lost when a witness cannot be found, a wrong address is given, or a person forgets or has second thoughts about cooperating. Train people under your supervision to be thorough. Some agencies require that *UNKNOWN, DOES NOT APPLY, NONE,* or a straight line be inserted rather than leaving an entry blank. An example is the witness's phone number, which is a very important piece of information. Some witnesses do not write anything in the blank for phone number if they do not have a phone, rather than writing in *none*. As mentioned in Chapter 3, DNA (Does Not Apply) was formerly used to indicate that there was no information to put in that blank. However, because DNA in modern usage is an abbreviation for deoxyribonucleic acid, it should not be used for *Does Not Apply*. Some agencies require that the blank be left blank if there is no information available, allowing the information to be inserted at some future time if it becomes available. It is important that you find out the policy of the agency you are working for and follow it.

A fast way to make sure sufficient information is included in a report is to use the charts in Chapter 1 (Figures 1.1, 1.2, and 1.3) that are labeled for Law Enforcement, PSIR, and Security. (Permission is given by the authors to photocopy these charts only.) When dealing with the same people over and over you can suggest they keep such a checklist. The point is to be able to use the checklist again and again.

Is it possible that you are overcorrecting and insisting on a duplicate of your own style even though another is correct? For example, one probation officer may use an inductive method for giving the recommendation required, while another prefers a deductive method. A supervisor should always make the format clear. However, corrections should not be made merely for the purpose of wielding authority.

Grammatical errors may be the most difficult for you to correct. You did not join your agency to become an English teacher; however, you need to understand some of the basic concepts and their applications in order to help yourself and others. Chapters 8 through 13 are devoted in detail to these concepts.

What are the most common grammatical errors? How do they affect the value of reports? First, consider the fact that word meanings and styles of grammar do change. Second, there are exceptions to rules and styles. As pointed out previously, FBI and military writing varies from other writing in the use of capitalization and punctuation. However, there are certain basic points that should be discussed. In order of importance, the following are some key areas of concern:

1. *Lack of organization* is shown in margin-to-margin writing with no headings (or too few headings) and no paragraphing. This kind of report may contain good information from a careful investigation, but it is presented in a way that forces the reader to search for the facts. One police major remarked, "When I get a report like that, I won't even look at it. Back it goes. What a waste of time!" It is the writer's responsibility to organize the report and the facts contained within it, not the reader's.

2. *Run-on sentences* are often part of a poorly organized report, but they can occur in any report, even those that are arranged well under good headings and subheadings. The run-on sentence is the "grandfather" of all mistakes. You cannot correctly punctuate a sentence that isn't correct at the start. Usually, a run-on sentence includes a variety of misplaced modifiers, dangling participles, changes in person, and incorrect pronoun usage. It is hard to correct the writing of others containing such errors because it is often difficult to determine exactly what the writer was trying to say and any correction may change the meaning, focus, or intent of the report.

3. *Misspellings* often cause ludicrous mistakes, even if the intended meaning is clear. At best, such errors cause embarrassment; at worst, they may lose a case.

4. *Punctuation* can entirely change the meaning of a sentence. Note placement of commas: (1) "Put the heat on Joe" (meaning to pressure or coerce someone named Joe), and (2) "Put the heat on, Joe" (telling Joe to turn up the thermostat).

5. *Capitalization errors* occur most often in reports written by people who handprint rather than type or use cursive writing in their reports. Some people emphasize certain words in speech, so they put these in upper case in a report, but at the same time, they may write a proper noun in lower case. For example, "His english was Poor and he spoke with a slight Stutter."

6. *Word choices* rarely are made with enough care. Choosing the precise word and the right place for it requires vocabulary study and correction. Everyone errs occasionally, but there is little excuse for confusion in words that are commonly used, such as *apprised* and *appraised*. Many officers, in referring to the *Miranda* warning, say, "He was appraised of his rights," rather than "He was *apprised* of his rights." In fact, a sergeant in a large municipal station, when informed that appraised meant "to ascertain the value of" rather than "to inform," insisted, "In my office, the word is appraised!" You must be sure of your facts; repeating mistakes learned from previously uninformed people does not make it correct.

As you can see, grammatical and spelling errors can reduce the professional appearance of your work, your subordinate's work, and even the work of citizens who fill out forms and reports, and may even give a defense attorney a much-desired loophole. In most professions, an occasional error is overlooked. It is assumed that the person intended the logical meaning. In law, however, such errors may be used to throw out a case — even if the actual meaning is obvious. Few writers face the scrutiny that criminal justice professionals face. Every report submitted has the potential to be a key element in a high-profile case. Make sure that every report you prepare or are responsible for is accurate, brief, and complete.

Many forensic reports may contain errors in addition to those mentioned above. Some common errors in forensic reports include:

1. Poor differentiation among methods, results, and opinions

2. Errors in critical judgment/logic

3. Presenting conflicting opinions

4. Use of unsubstantiated or unsupported tests

5. Performing irrelevant or unnecessary tests

6. Misleading results and/or failure to state limitations of testing

7. Erroneous conclusions based on incorrect interpretation of results

8. Recommending unnecessary testing

Use of Word Processors

The use of word processors has allowed people who are poor typists to complete professional-looking reports. Word processors have also allowed professional typists to speed up their work and be able to complete many "original" documents, rather than photocopied documents, when sending out mass mailings. The use of word processors has speeded up the completion of booking reports, as well as common arrest or incident reports. Word processors also allow the typists to cut and paste sentences, paragraphs, and sections of one report into another. In addition, word processors have grammar and spelling checkers. While all of these things are good and help the writer produce professional-looking documents, they also lend themselves to the production of common errors. As was mentioned earlier in this text, spelling checkers will only reject words that do not exist and cannot differentiate words when there is improper usage. (Some state-of-the-art spelling-checker programs flag commonly made errors, then ask the user to double-check the usage. Each new generation of programs is likely to make further advances.) Grammar-check programs often flag common grammatical problems, but leave it up to the user to determine the final edit. The writer must then know the grammar rules in order to determine whether to make the change. Added to these concerns are the problems that occur when the typist cuts and pastes. This process lends itself to subject-verb, noun-pronoun, and gender disagreements. The bottom line is that the use of word processing does not eliminate the need for proofreading, but in many cases requires more careful proofreading to avoid these problems.

Improving the Agency by Helping the Individual

Just as your reading public is made up of one person reading at one time, your department is made up of the effectiveness of one person's action at one time. In a computerized world, the importance of the individual is easily lost. It is worth it to make the effort to help each person.

In many agencies, the "tough guy" attitude prevails: "If he can't cut it, kick him out!" If the individual is already a member of the agency, the reaction might be: "Rewrite this! Get a dictionary and carry it at all times. That's an order." This really doesn't do anything to help the individual or the agency who has already invested much time and money in hiring and training the individual. Wouldn't a little help in the area of report writing be a better response?

Keep in mind that a correction should never be considered a one-time thing. If you correct an error in an employee, you have corrected it once. If you make the person understand the error, you will keep that person from repeating it. Some people may need a course in writing, not just your casual assistance. You should familiarize yourself with sources of help and means of meeting any costs of such help. Investigate the educational opportunities available in your area. Classes may be offered in four-year colleges, universities, or community colleges. Also look for Adult Education Centers or Continuing Education listings, as well as night-school classes offered in local high schools. Check your local educational television listing for programs that may be helpful, or explore the use of computer programs or the Internet for methods that are available for self-instruction. Looking up these sources of help will take time, but not as much time as it would take to fire one person and hire and train another.

Poor spelling is so frequent in today's society that people merely make excuses for their inability: "Oh, you know me, I never could spell!" Poor spelling skills should not be dismissed as some sort of genetic problem that cannot be changed. Unfortunately, many schools and employers do not insist upon good spelling and writing skills. It is important to stress the need for accurate spelling. People who are poor spellers need to learn the rules that apply to spelling (see Chapter 11) and should learn to use references to find correct spellings.

You can do a lot for your agency by making sure your own training and that of the people you supervise is adequate for the requirement of the job. If formal training is not available, use self-education, roll call training, and make it a habit to use references, including this text. Each time you correct your own or someone else's reports, you are helping yourself, the report writer, and your agency. The second section of this text is designed to help the reader improve his or her grammar and can be used as either a workbook or a classroom text.

Summary

1. When you read and pass on the reports of others, your signature should never be a perfunctory "rubber stamp," because signing a report means that you accept it as being correct to the best of your knowledge.

2. You may be called upon to help three kinds of writers: new recruits, individuals transferred from other departments, and members of the general public.

3. Assisting the public, such as store managers working with shoplifting forms, may make law enforcement more effective.

4. Misinterpretation and omission are common errors in recording information.

5. Common grammatical errors involve the following: lack of organization, run-on sentences, and problems in spelling, punctuation, capitalization,

and word choice. Run-on sentences often include misplaced modifiers, dangling participles, changes in person, and incorrect pronoun usage.

6. As a supervisor, you should know how to correct other people's errors. You should inform the person needing help that there are available resources such as adult education, community colleges, and other programs in your vicinity.

7. By taking time to help a person under your supervision, you may salvage a valuable individual, keep yourself from having to train a new employee, and save your agency time and money.

Chapter 7 — TEST

1. When you are a supervisor reading the reports of subordinates, your signature should not be a _____. Signing the report means that you accept it as _____ to the best of your knowledge.

2. You may be called on to help these kinds of writers: (a) _____, (b) _____, and (c) _____.

3. Common problem areas in report writing include: _____, _____, and _____ _____.

4. The most common grammatical errors include:

   (a) _____

   (b) _____

   (c) _____

   (d) _____

   (e) _____

   (f) _____

5. Give two examples of incidents when the public fills out forms:

   _____ and _____.

6. Taking time to help someone under your direction can help in the following ways:

   (a) It could salvage a _____.

   (b) You might save yourself time that would be necessary to _____ _____.

   (c) You may save your agency _____ and _____.

The Mechanics of Report Writing

CHAPTER 8

Simplified Study of Grammar

Many people hate grammatical terms, but the fact remains that you need to know the terms in order to deal with them. Even if you do not have trouble with grammar, you may be supervising someone who does. As stated in the previous chapter, strong-arm tactics are not very effective, but assistance is.

There is no need to go to the other extreme, however, and study too many fine points in grammar. You need only to learn enough points to allow you to put together a well-written sentence.

To determine what makes up a correct sentence, you need to investigate the parts of speech and their varying uses, the subject-verb-direct object pattern, and the different types of clauses and phrases.

Correct sentence structure is basic. Most grammar books tell you much more than you want to know. Some books use new terms for things that already had a name, and some try new methods of analysis. There may be merit in new ideas, but to save time it is easier to learn the most common terms and methods well, and then review them briefly.

Identifying Parts of Speech

You probably remember the basic parts of speech: noun, pronoun, verb, adjective, adverb, preposition, and conjunction. The interjection is sometimes listed as the eighth part of speech, but it is rarely used by criminal justice personnel.

A noun is the name of a person, place, thing, idea, or quality.
Examples: officer, England, book, loyalty

A pronoun stands in place of a noun.
Examples: he, she, it, they, them, their, you, your

DOI: 10.1016/B978-1-4377-5584-8.00015-3

A verb expresses action or state of being.
Examples: ride, run, hide, be, seem

An adjective modifies or limits a noun or pronoun.
Examples: red, curly, dark, smart, quick

An adverb modifies or limits a verb, adjective, or another adverb. It is sometimes an intensifier.
Examples: carefully, quickly, very, too

A preposition shows the relationship, often of space or time, between a noun or pronoun and some other word in the sentence.
Examples: to, in, on, between, among, with, of, after, under

A conjunction joins or connects words, phrases, or clauses; it is either coordinating or subordinating.
Examples: and, but, for, or, nor, so, yet, after, because, until

Interjections are independent words used to express strong feeling or emotion and should be used only in a direct quotation.
Example: "Hell! That's the price of a kilo. Take it or leave it!"

Using One Word in Several Ways

Few people seem to realize that a word may become a different part of speech, depending on its use in a sentence. It is entirely possible for the same word to be used as three or more different parts of speech.

Example:
This fax (noun) just came in. Fax (verb) him an answer right away. The fax (adjective) business is growing rapidly along with other technology.

How does it help you to know these points? It can help you analyze your own mistakes and the mistakes of others.

Using Verbs in the Past Tense

In most reports, the verb is usually in the past tense, recording what has already happened. In your own reports and those of others, check for violations to this rule. Many reports incorrectly use the present tense for the past tense verb, often because the present tense sounds very similar to the past tense. No one pronounces walked as walk-*ed*. Because the *ed* is not pronounced as a separate syllable, it is often left out, leading to a misused or misspelled word in the written report.

Example:
I walk down the hall and saw the pharmacy door was open.

It should read:
I walked down the hall and saw the pharmacy door was open.

When you are writing a report, remember that the events you are writing about took place in the past. Some past forms of verbs pronounce the *-ed*, such as, "I hand*ed* him the ticket." You rarely leave out that *-ed*. Watch for the *-ed* that does not require another syllable. (See Chapter 11)

There are, of course, a few times when you will correctly use past and present verb forms together. The present is often used in direct quotations: He *said* (past), "This *is* (present) a holdup!" The future is used in some cases: "This report *will be* (future) ready tomorrow."

The Sentence

Words (parts of speech) are used to form sentences. A sentence is a complete thought that consists of a **subject** and a **predicate**. Although it is possible to express a complete thought in one word (for example, "Help!" expresses the same thing as "Come here and help me!"), most sentences require more than one word to express a complete thought. The complete subject is the word or group of words that tells us about what or whom the writer is talking. The complete predicate is the part of the sentence that makes a statement about the subject, telling what the subject is doing or what is happening to the subject.

Examples:

Complete Subject	Complete Predicate
The *suspect*	*waved* a gun and *fled*.
He	*lives* at 123 Main Street.
The *officer* on duty	*was* John Doe.
A 2010 white *Toyota* with Ohio license plates	*hit* the pedestrian.
Snow and *ice*	*covered* the street.

The *simple subject* is the particular word (or words, in the case of a compound subject) in the complete subject about which something is said. The *simple predicate* consists of the key word (or words, if it is a compound predicate) in the complete predicate. The simple subject is a noun and the simple predicate is a verb. The simple subjects and simple predicates are italicized in the examples above.

Direct Objects versus Indirect Objects: Learning the Patterns

You can investigate grammar the same way that you investigate a case. *The basic pattern is WHO DID WHAT and TO WHOM, WHEN, WHERE, and HOW.* Be careful about *WHY* because this becomes a value judgment. The *why* is used mainly by probation and parole officers, who are required to give opinions and recommendations to the court or corrections administrators. Law enforcement and security professionals rarely use the *why* unless it is carefully documented with statements and evidence.

Consider first the *subject*, *verb*, and *direct object* (S, V, and DO):

WHO	DID	WHAT
S	V	DO
He	gave	an order.

Adding an *indirect object* (IO) to the above, you might have this:

WHO	DID	TO WHOM	WHAT
S	V	IO	DO
He	gave	the sergeant	an order.

The indirect object can be changed into a *prepositional phrase* that would follow rather than precede the direct object:

WHO	DID	WHAT	TO WHOM
S	V	DO	prepositional phrase
He	gave	an order	*to the sergeant.*

Some verbs do not need objects: for example, *Birds fly*. However, even that same verb may take an object in another situation: for example, *He flies a kite.*

Sometimes a verb takes a predicate noun or predicate adjective, which is related to the subject rather than acting as an object of the verb.

Examples:

She	is	a detective.
	(linking verb)	*(predicate noun)*
He	appeared	sober.
	(linking verb)	*(predicate adjective)*

Such verbs are called linking verbs. The most common linking verb is *be* in its many forms, such as *is, are, was, were, will be,* and *has been.* Some other linking verbs are *seem, appear, smell, taste, sound, act,* and *look.*

Identifying Active and Passive Verbs

An active verb shows the action that the subject took. The subject does the action: He wrote the report. (4 words)

In the passive form, the subject is acted upon. The passive form also requires a form of the verb "to be." The passive verb requires more words: The report *was written* by him. (6 words)

Whenever you can, use active verbs rather than passive verbs. Your reports will be briefer and often clearer.

Many mistakes in report writing result from the overuse of the passive verb. Often this use is an attempt to avoid two problems:

1. *You may be uncertain of how to refer to yourself:* "Sergeant Jones," "this writer," "the undersigned," "I," etc., are all possibilities. As pointed out in Chapters 1 and 5, you should decide and stay with your choice of the first

person or third person. The first person (*I, me, my, mine, we, us, our, ours*) is allowed in many departments; if not allowed on the face page, it is often allowed on the continuation or follow-up pages. If first person is allowed, use it.

2. *You may wish to avoid being the subject of the sentence too often, no matter how you refer to yourself.* You can avoid this pitfall by using headings and starting out with a past tense verb in each sentence for which the subject is understood to be you. This form is allowed by some agencies or departments but is forbidden by others.

    Example:

    INVESTIGATION
    Dusted for latents. Lifted prints from dresser top and mirror. Asked the complainant if anyone else had used the room since morning, and he said that no one had. Checked adjoining bathroom.

If you make full use of headings and subheadings, your reports can be briefer because you can use this past tense, active form, in which the subject is understood. It may be somewhat terse, but it is easily understood. Remember that the use of passive verbs often results in ridiculous sentences.

    Examples:

    The car was stolen while in the restroom.

    While patrolling on a motorcycle, the burglar was apprehended by this officer.

In both of these examples, the problem of the passive form was intensified by modifiers that appear to modify the wrong word. Was the car in the restroom? Was the burglar patrolling, or were you? Any defense attorney would have a field day bringing such an inaccuracy to the attention of the judge or jury. If one sentence cannot be trusted, why should the jury trust your other statements? You may become an unintentional witness for the defense. To avoid misunderstandings, use active verbs whenever possible. Your reports will take fewer words, be clearer, and be more forceful.

Identifying Independent and Dependent Clauses

An *independent clause* contains a subject and predicate and is able to stand alone. Even two words are enough.

    Example:

    He fled.

A *dependent clause* contains a subject and predicate but is not able to stand alone. It is introduced by a subordinating conjunction that makes it depend on — literally hang from — another grammatical form. If you proofread aloud, your voice will go up at the end of a dependent and down at the end of an independent clause.

A small child may often speak in short independent clauses (e.g., "I like candy." "I want the dog.") In adult conversation and writing, one thing often depends upon another. Something happens *when, if, because, since,* or *although* something else occurs. To analyze a sentence, you must understand these two kinds of clauses. The dependent clause may also be introduced by *who, that,* or *which.* It is usually used as an adjective describing a noun or pronoun in the independent clause.

Depending on its use in the sentence, the dependent clause is used as an adverb, an adjective, or a noun.

Example:

S	V		S	V
			(adverbial clause)	
He	fled	when	the officer	came.

In this example, the subordinating conjunction *when* introduces a dependent clause that modifies the verb fled. This dependent clause is used as an adverb.

S	V	O	V	
	(predicate noun)			
The man	who is wearing	the red coat	is	the suspect.

In this example, the subordinating word *who* is a relative pronoun as well and acts as subject of the dependent clause. Obviously, the dependent clause describes the subject of the independent clause (*man*) and is used as an adjective.

S	V	N
(predicate adjective)		
That he is guilty	is	evident.

In this example, the entire dependent clause is the subject of the independent clause and is thus used as a noun.

For the purpose of visualizing independent clauses, try marking in the margin a larger square for an independent clause and a smaller square for a dependent clause.

Example:

☐ = independent clause

☐ = dependent clause

You will use this method to determine sentence structure, which is dealt with in more detail in Chapter 9.

Recognizing Prepositional, Participial, and Infinitive Phrases

The prepositional phrase consists of a preposition plus its object and may include modifiers of this object. The preposition itself is never modified. There are many common prepositions: *about, after, among, around, at, between, before, down, for, from, in, on, of, to, through, upon, up, with, by,* and others (as shown by the list of prepositions later in this chapter).

Sometimes, the same word will be used as a preposition in one sentence and as a subordinating conjunction in another.

Examples:
After the game, they had a snack.
(This is a prepositional phrase, as *game* is the object of *after.*)

After they left, it began to snow.
(Here *after* is a subordinating conjunction because it introduces a dependent clause containing a subject and predicate.)

The *participial phrase* consists of a participle plus its object and/or modifiers. A participle is a verb form that is used as an adjective — it is the *-ing* or *-ed* form of a verb that is not used as the main verb in the sentence. Both the participle and its object may be modified.

Examples:
The reports were *discouraging.*
(Here, *discouraging* is a participle; it is an adjective modifying *reports.*)

Quickly using wire cutters, he cut the screen.
(In this participial phrase, both the participle and object are modified by the word *quickly.*)

Dressed conservatively, he went unnoticed.

Wearing black, she appeared to be in mourning.

An irregular verb is one for which the past form does not end in *-ed* (e.g., *caught*).

Example:
Caught (past participle) *while trying to escape,* the prisoner was placed in maximum security.
(In this participial phrase, the irregular past participle *caught* is modified by the adverb and is used as an adjective to modify *prisoner.*)

The infinitive phrase consists of an infinitive (the verb form that begins with *to*, e.g., *to be*, *to go*) plus its object and/or modifier. Both infinitive and object can be modified.

Example:
To start the engine motor quickly is difficult.
(Infinitive phrase used as a noun.)

Using Phrases as Adverbs, Adjectives, and Nouns

Like dependent clauses, phrases cannot stand alone and are used instead as adverbs, adjectives, and nouns.

Prepositional phrases:

Examples:
Adv.   He left home *at 0800 hours*.
            (Adverb tells when.)

Adj.   One *of the men* shot him.
            (Adjective tells who.)

Noun   *Of Human Bondage* is the book.
            (Noun is used as subject.)

Participial phrases:

Examples:
Adv.   *Working swiftly*, he finished the job.
            (Adverb tells how he finished.)

Adj.   The girl *wearing the red coat* is the suspect.
            (Adjective describes the person.)

Noun   *Working overtime* causes fatigue.
            (Participial phrase is the subject.)

Infinitive phrases:

Examples:
Adv.   The man obviously came *to make trouble*.
            (Adverb, showing why, modifies the verb came.)

Adj.   He had plenty of reasons *to be afraid*.
            (Adjective describes the kind of reasons.)

Noun   The witness refused *to discuss the shooting*.
            (Noun is used as object of the verb.)

The participial phrase sometimes becomes dangling, by apparently modifying something that it should not.

Example:
Driving down the street on a motorcycle, a dog was hit by this officer.

Overuse of passive form often causes this type of error. Was the dog driving? Dog is the closest noun for the phrase to modify.

I hit a dog is clearer and uses fewer words.

Using Prepositions in Your Report

Currently, there are growing numbers of people in law enforcement circles for whom English is a second language. Many who teach English as a second language find that students have difficulty using prepositions and their objects with the terms that are usually found in report writing. The following list provides some common examples of preposition use in report writing.

Prepositions commonly used with certain verbs:

account for his time
apologize to the victim
appear at the hearing
approve of the sentence
argued with his neighbor
arrested for reckless endangering
attend to details
borrow from the loan shark
check for latents
confer with his lawyer
consent to the change of venue
convince the judge of his innocence
decide on the sentence
depend on the evidence
get in the car
get off the plane
get on the bus
look at the facts
mark up the furniture
match with previous evidence
meet at the office
meet at 10 o'clock
meet on time
meet with the plaintiff
object to the accusation
petition for another hearing

provide him with incentives
provide me with information
query for the records
radio to the station for help
read rights to the suspect
record in the file
recover for evidence
restrain by leg irons
save for evidence
serve for years
serve in the army
serve to the customer
slip in the mud
slip on the wet floor
sort out the conflicting reports
state for the record
state in response
switch on the light
talk about the plans
talk to the child
talk with the opposition
tell her from her sister
tell on her neighbor
tell to the security guard
track down the marijuana growers
trade in the car

place her on the docket
turn on the light
turn out for the best
turn to a friend
use for his own purpose
vault over the fence
veer to the left
volunteer for the assignment
vouch for his alibi
wait for the next one
wait on the customers
watch for signs of trouble
wire for funds

turn in his neighbor
work at the station
work in the office
work on the report
work out at the gym
work up the crowd to hysteria
wrap around the body
wrap up the kilo
X out the names
X-ray for broken bones
yield to his demand
yield under pressure
zero in on the problem

Prepositions commonly used after certain expressions:

according to the witness
angry at the accusation
angry with his neighbor
appear at the trial
assist at the scene of the accident
aware of the problem
based on the information
capable of the duties involved
check for latents
composed of prior reports
contact by noon today
dependent on
description of the suspect
details on how it happened
disappointed in the results
discharged on Tuesday

due to conflicting information
followed by other complaints
in accordance with the proceedings
in regard to the memo
independent of the others
involved in the drug ring
limited by his handicap
limited to those requirements
married to the defendant
pursuant to reviewing the facts
recovery of evidence
related to the survivor
resulting from the collision
sample of his handwriting
with respect to the judge's ruling

Summary

1. The basic parts of speech include the noun, pronoun, verb, adjective, adverb, preposition, conjunction, and interjection. Words may become different parts of speech based on usage.

2. In most reports the verb is used in the past tense documenting what has already happened.

3. Words (parts of speech) form sentences. A sentence is a complete thought that consists of a subject and a predicate.

4. There are patterns in sentence structure and grammar. The basic pattern is WHO DID WHAT and TO WHOM, WHEN, WHERE, and HOW. Be careful about the use of WHY because it may involve a value judgment.

5. In reporting, active verbs are preferred over passive verbs. The active form of writing is clearer and uses fewer words. With the use of headings and subheadings, the subject may be left out in some cases (because it is understood). Check with your own agency to determine if this is an acceptable format.

6. Independent clauses contain a subject and predicate and are able to stand alone. Dependent clauses contain a subject and predicate but are not able to stand alone.

7. Prepositional phrases consist of a preposition and object and may include modifiers of the object. Participial phrases consist of a participle and its object and/or modifiers. Infinitive phrases consist of an infinitive (the verb form that begins with *to*, e.g., *to be*, *to go*) plus its object and/or modifier.

8. Like dependent clauses, phrases cannot stand alone and are used instead as adverbs, adjectives, and nouns.

9. Many people, especially those for whom English is a second language, have difficulty using prepositions and their objects with terms that are found in report writing. Proper usage comes with practice and review of such usage.

10. Remember to investigate grammar just as you would a case (see Figure 8.1).

Figure 8.1
The "Whodunit" Approach to Grammar

Investigate grammar just as you would a case:

subject	predicate	object	preposition	object	(may vary)	conjunction	(may vary)
WHO	DID	WHAT	TO	WHOM	WHEN, WHERE, HOW	AND	WHY

Possibilities:

The subject is usually a noun or pronoun, but it can be a dependent clause, a phrase, or even an infinitive or participle. The simple predicate is a verb. The object has the same options as the subject.

An independent clause has a subject and predicate and can stand alone. A dependent clause also has a subject and predicate, but it cannot stand alone; it usually is introduced by a subordinating conjunction and is used as an adverb, adjective, or noun. Phrases—prepositional, participial, or infinitive—are used like dependent clauses. The same word, phrase, or dependent clause may vary according to use in the sentence.

Parts of speech:

noun:	name of person, place, thing, idea, or quality
pronoun:	word used in place of noun
verb:	expresses action or state of being; may or may not take an object
preposition:	used with an object to show relationship to some other word in sentence
conjunction:	connecting word, either coordinate or subordinate
adjective:	modifies nouns or pronouns
adverb:	modifies verbs, adjectives, or other adverbs

Variations of *when, where, how,* and *why*

		example:
when:	preposition + object	in the morning
	dependent clause	when she left
	adverb	suddenly
how:	preposition + object	with a crowbar
	participle + object	using a revolver
	adverb	angrily
why:	dependent clause	because he was angry
	infinitive phrase	to open the door
where:	preposition + object	at the door
	dependent clause	where he had gone

Variations on description of subject or object:

	example:
adjective:	a *Caucasian* male
participial phrase:	the woman *wearing a red shirt*
dependent clause:	the man *who left first*
prepositional phrase:	one *of the bags*

Chapter 8 — TEST

1. In the space provided, write definitions:

    (a) Noun _____
         _____

    (b) Pronoun _____
         _____

    (c) Verb _____
         _____

    (d) Adjective _____
         _____

    (e) Adverb _____
         _____

    (f) Preposition _____
         _____

    (g) Conjunction _____
         _____

    (h) Interjection _____
         _____

2. (a) In what tense are most verbs in reports? _____

    (b) What is the most frequent use of the present tense? _____

    (c) What often causes misspelling of verbs in the past tense? _____
         _____

3. A sentence is a complete thought that consists of a _____ and a
    _____.

4. A(n) _____ shows the action that the subject took.
    Many mistakes in report writing result from overuse of the
    _____.

5. Define independent clause: _____

    _____

    Define the dependent clause, and explain how it is used.

    _____
    _____
    _____

6. Define the three types of phrases, and explain how each type is used:

    (a) _____

        _____
        _____

    (b) _____

        _____
        _____

    (c) _____

        _____
        _____

Avoiding Errors in Sentence Structure

Have you ever had a report or paper returned to you with instructions to rewrite it? Worse still, have you ever had to instruct someone else to rewrite a report or paper without a clear idea of how it should be done?

There is one outstanding suspect in most cases of mixed-up writing: the run-on sentence. What is it? What makes it different from a long but correctly written sentence? How can the supervisor locate and explain the errors? How can the writer correct them?

The Run-On Sentence — Source of Many Errors

The run-on sentence, the "grandfather of all mistakes," usually goes on too long without having any clear connection between its many clauses and phrases. Because it is so involved, it begets many errors:

1. How can you punctuate a sentence that is incorrect in the first place?

2. How can you be sure that the subject-verb relationship is clear when so many words come between the subject and verb?

3. How can a pronoun refer to a definite noun when there are too many possible references?

4. How can you tell which word is being modified by a participial phrase when more than one word appears possible?

193

DOI: 10.1016/B978-1-4377-5584-8.00016-5

With all these possibilities for mistakes in a very long sentence, can long sentences ever really be correct? They surely can. Legal papers abound in which sentences go on, not only for a paragraph but sometimes for pages. (This may even contribute to the time that it takes for cases to get through court.) Military writing used to rival legal writing in confusing structure, though this is no longer true. Military manuals are now succinct and explicit. A reform in legal writing is occurring in New York and California, states that often prove to be models in the area of law. Some banks and insurance companies are now writing documents — or at least providing an explanation — in "plain English." At any rate, the law enforcement officer who uses "legalese" as a model will confuse rather than clarify. Corrections, probation, and parole personnel should not use complicated structure, even in writing directed to a judge.

If you are not trying to imitate long legal forms, why are you likely to write run-on sentences? Often you are working under pressure, trying to get a report out in a hurry. You are tired and want to go home. Instead of putting a period at the end of a complete thought, you put a *comma*, a *dash*, an *and*, or *an ellipsis*, and then you keep on going. The more tired you are, the longer you may go on before you remember to complete a thought, put in a period, and start a new sentence.

Another reason for the overlong sentence is wordiness. In Chapter 12 you will find out how to replace old-fashioned rambling with modern brevity.

It will help you as a writer, or supervisor of other writers, to know the types of sentences and how to use them. In Chapter 8, you had a review of the two kinds of clauses and the three kinds of phrases, as well as the ways in which they may be used. The independent clause was visualized as a larger block, and the dependent clause as a smaller block. This may sound like game-playing, but it will help you overcome the difficulty you may have in visualizing what is discussed regarding grammar. You can then follow through by visualizing sentences in block form.

How will it help you to mark blocks in the margin to identify clauses? It will enable you to find your own pattern of writing. Perhaps you use too many overly long compound-complex sentences. Just as a criminal has a particular *modus operandi*, every writer develops individual patterns and habits. Blocking out sentences will quickly show you what mistakes you may be making, which usually are either run-on or incomplete sentences. It is also a tool to sort out problems in sentence structure for those whose reports you are expected to sign.

☐   An **independent clause** contains a subject and predicate and *is able to stand alone as a complete thought.*

☐   A **dependent clause** also contains a subject and predicate but is *unable to stand alone.* It is usually introduced by such words as *after, although, as, because, before, how, if, since, so, that, though, unless, until, what, when, where, whether, which, while, who, whom, why,* and combinations of these, such as *so that, in order that, whoever,* and *whichever.* The preceding words do not always introduce a dependent clause. Sometimes words such as *before* and *after* can introduce a prepositional phrase, e.g., before the game. A clause, even a dependent clause, must have a subject and predicate. Sometimes words such as *who, what,* and *that* can act as relative pronouns and be part of an independent clause.

Example:
Who came?
(Independent clause. Simple sentence.)
Joe is the man who came early.
(*Who* in this case introduces a dependent clause used as an adjective to modify *man.* Complex sentence.)

Block Method of Visualizing Sentence Structure

☐.   A **simple sentence** contains one independent clause.

.   A **complex sentence** contains one and only one independent clause plus one or more dependent clauses.

☐, ☐ ☐.   The dependent clause may come first, in which case a comma usually sets it off from the independent clause.

.   A **compound sentence** contains two or more independent clauses joined by a coordinating conjunction and a comma, by a semicolon alone, or by an adverbial conjunction and a semicolon. Parentheses indicate that more of the same type of clause may be included with the sentence still coming under the same category.

☐; ☐ ☐.   A **compound-complex sentence** contains two independent clauses and one dependent clause as a basic structure. More dependent and independent clauses can be added.

Note these special points:

1. Phrases — prepositional, participial, and infinitive — do not affect the sentence structure defined above. Often, however, too many phrases may make even a simple sentence much too long. The prepositional phrase is a frequent offender, but other types of phrases cause problems as well.

    Example:
    To convince the judge (infinitive phrase) of his innocence (prepositional phrase) at the time (prepositional phrase) of the crime (prepositional phrase), he claimed (subject and predicate) to have been (infinitive

phrase) at church (prepositional phrase) having found God (participial phrase) changing his whole life (participial phrase) into one (prepositional phrase) of conventional morality (prepositional phrase) with a sincere desire (prepositional phrase) to help, not harm, others and to pay his debt (infinitive phrases) to society (prepositional phrase) in a way (prepositional phrase) to convince anyone (infinitive phrase) of his innocence (prepositional phrase) of this particular crime (prepositional phrase) at this specific time (prepositional phrase).

Actually, this particular sentence is grammatically correct if you can stay with it long enough to sort it out. The average reader understands sentences much better if the word count stays around 20 words instead of 65 words as in the example above.

2. "Subject-less" sentences are those in which the subject is understood. These are allowed by some agencies but frowned on by others. *Check your agency's preferred style.* Usually such sentences occur under headings, and the subject of the action is evident.

    Example:
    VICTIM'S STATEMENT
    Returned home early. Found door standing open and could see furniture scattered around the front room. Ran next door and called police.
    Victim is the assumed subject in each of the above sentences. Two of the sentences contain compound predicates: *found* and *could see* in the second and *ran* and *called* in the third. The above sentences would be blocked off as three simple sentences because a simple sentence can have a compound or double subject or predicate:

$$\square . \square . \square .$$

How would the same information be given in sentences?

    Example:
    VICTIM'S STATEMENT
    I returned home early. I found the door standing open, and I could see furniture scattered around the front room. I ran next door and called the police.

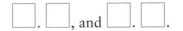

The same information can also be given in a complex sentence followed by a simple sentence:

Example:
When I returned home early (dependent clause introduced by *when*), I could see furniture overturned and things spilled on the floor. I ran next door to call the police.

Note that a comma follows the introductory dependent clause.

How would the same sort of information be expressed in a compound sentence?

Example :
I returned home early; I found the door unlocked, and I could see furniture overturned and things spilled on the floor. I ran next door to call the police.

Not much improved, is it? Here you have three independent clauses forming a compound sentence, followed by a simple sentence:

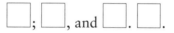

(In this case, *and* is a coordinating conjunction.)

The information can also be given in a compound-complex sentence:

Example :
When I returned home early, I found the door unlocked, and I could see furniture overturned and things spilled on the floor. I ran next door to call the police.

By using the subordinating word *when*, the first clause becomes dependent, as it cannot stand alone. Because the dependent clause is followed by two independent clauses, the sentence is compound-complex, followed by a simple sentence:

Example of wall-to-wall writing with run-on sentences:

VICTIM'S STATEMENT
He indicated that he came home early that day because he felt sick and business wasn't too good anyhow so the boss let him have time off and he stated that when he went to unlock the door he saw that the door was open and someone else must have done it. He further related that when he looked into his front room some of the furniture was upside down and things were spilled all over the floor so he figured that a burglar must have done it and ran next door and called the police.

Do you think that this example sounds exaggerated? Most supervisors can tell you of their experiences with writing similar to this. There are plenty of errors in the above paragraph. Block it off and see what you get (although even expert grammarians might not come out with the same number of clauses because of different interpretations of meaning).

Note that the use of the words *indicated*, *stated*, and *related* entice one to use longer and longer sentences. Once you start using these words, which many think sound professional, it is almost impossible for you to quit repeating them in the same sentence or paragraph. A simple paraphrase of what the person said is easier to read and will stand up better in court.

Next time you are faced with a run-on sentence — your own or someone else's — block off the clauses. It should become clear that there are too many clauses. If you are a supervisor, show a subordinate who is guilty of run-on sentences how the sentences look in blocked-off form. Then cut the sentences down to the bare bones. This will take you a little time at first, but it should save both of you time in the long run.

Punctuation Problems

In an actual report, you would probably find commas strewn throughout. Some people tend to use punctuation like pepper on soup — without careful placement. Commas are not the only punctuation abused. Often the writer will incorrectly use the dash (—) or the ellipsis (. . .) as well. Actually, the ellipsis indicates that words have been deleted, because they are unimportant. The dash and the ellipsis habits are contagious. The solution is simple: write short sentences, and you won't need much punctuation. Punctuation will be dealt with in more detail in Chapter 10.

Subject-Verb Agreement

In a run-on sentence, confusion often exists as to which subject goes with which verb.

> Example:
> . . . he figured that a burglar must have done it and ran next door and called the police.

It was helpful of the burglar to call the police, wasn't it? Or was it the victim who called, not the burglar? Court is no place for explanations that begin: "What I meant was ..."

People in the criminal justice system are not given the benefit of the doubt. Writing stands as it was written, not as it was intended. The defense attorney will be happy to pounce on any such mistake and point it out in court. He or she will then suggest that if a writer wasn't reliable in one such instance, perhaps the writer should not be believed on other points. The result is a lot of ammunition for the defense and humiliation for the report writer.

Noun-Pronoun Agreement

Look at the same incorrect example:

> ... he figured that a burglar must have done it and ran next door and called the police.

As this statement had the heading <u>VICTIM'S STATEMENT</u>, *he* refers to the noun, *victim*, and is the subject of the verb. It is better to repeat names rather than to overuse personal pronouns. In this way you will avoid the awkward use of names in parentheses, as in the following example.

> Example:
> Then he (JONES) went to the neighbor's house to report that the suspect (WILSON) had burglarized his (JONES'S) house.

Dangling Participles

No dangling participles are shown in the example given for the run-on sentence. However, participles alone and participial phrases often appear to attach themselves to the wrong noun or pronoun.

> Example :
> Running down the street he saw the man he suspected of the burglary.

If you try to analyze the previous example, it immediately becomes a problem to determine whether it was the victim or the burglar running down the street. Watch out for similar dangling participles and for participial phrases that can modify more than one word.

Sentence Fragments

Most people think of the sentence fragment as the sentence that is too short. However, a very long group of words introduced by a subordinating word like *when*, *although*, *since*, or *because* may still be a sentence fragment. It is possible for report writers to create such a fragment by inserting periods merely because they have been typing a long time and not because they are at a place that indicates the conclusion of a *complete thought*.

Note that even though it is long, the following is a fragment.

> Example:
> When the bell started ringing, the one recently installed by Emergency Warning System, in the Workman's Hardware Store at the intersection of Fifth and Marshall Streets and the people were shoving and pushing to see what was happening and getting in the way of Unit 410 which answered the call.

The subordinating word *when* introduces a dependent clause that contains 50 words and includes within it two other dependent clauses. The word *and* connects *the people* with the original *when*. Without that *and, the people* would be the subject of an independent clause. Reread the paragraph carefully for analysis.

One way to test for the sentence fragment is to read it aloud. Does your voice go up at the end, even though the words do not constitute a question? If so, you are probably dealing with a dependent clause:

> After I left.
> If he is on probation.
> When Sergeant Jones heard the All Points Bulletin.
> Because the cash register was locked.

If initiating an idea, these four clauses are dependent (literally meaning "hanging from"). While reading these, your voice goes up. However, each of the above examples could be a complete thought if given in response to a related question:

When did he come?   *After I left.*
When did he begin pursuit? *When Sergeant Jones heard the All Points Bulletin.*

Most people correctly use many shortcuts and fragments when speaking. In certain situations, even a dependent clause or a group of related words without a full subject-predicate structure can be an acceptable sentence. However, to be on the safe side, it is best to abide by the rules with which you are familiar.

Summary

1. The run-on sentence is the "grandfather of all mistakes," as it may include errors in (a) punctuation, (b) subject-verb agreement, (c) noun-pronoun agreement, and (d) dangling participle or other modifiers.

2. Long legal sentences that go on for several pages may be correct in form if written by experts. Because it is risky and may be confusing to write that

way, it is best for personnel in the criminal justice system not to imitate the so-called legalese style of writing.

3. Visualize sentence structure by marking off a large square for each independent clause and a small square for each dependent clause.

4. A simple sentence contains one independent clause. A complex sentence contains one independent clause and one or more dependent clauses. A compound sentence contains two or more independent clauses joined by a coordinating conjunction and a comma, by a semicolon alone, or by an adverbial conjunction and a semicolon. A compound-complex sentence has a basic structure of two independent clauses and one dependent clause, although more of each type may be added.

5. Phrases are not considered in determining whether a sentence is simple, complex, compound, or compound-complex. However, too many phrases added to even a simple sentence can make it confusing.

6. In cases in which the subject is identified with a heading such as VICTIM'S STATEMENT, the subject may be omitted if it is understood. (Check with your agency on this.)

7. Use short sentences followed by periods. Do not use a comma, dash, or ellipsis when you should use a period.

8. Learn to analyze sentences — your own, and, if you are a supervisor, those of your subordinates — to see if any are run-on sentences or sentence fragments.

9. Testing sentences by reading them aloud will help locate errors. Overly long and confusing sentences will be more obvious. Sentence fragments may be revealed by the way that the voice goes up rather than down.

10. To be on the safe side, be brief and abide by your agency's rules.

Chapter 9 — TEST

1. The source of most errors in sentence structure is the _____.

2. Name the sentence structure shown in the block forms.

   ☐. _____

   ☐☐☐☐. _____

   ☐, and ☐. _____

   ☐, ☐; ☐ ☐. _____

3. The convoluted language used in long, legal-type sentences is commonly called _____. It is unwise for the report writer to imitate legal models.

4. Use a period at the end of a sentence. Avoid using these three other forms of punctuation in place of a period:

   (a) _____

   (b) _____

   (c) _____

5. When a heading is used, the subject may be _____ if it is clearly understood who is doing the action.

6. In the space provided, put a large or small block for each type of clause. Then identify the type of sentence.

   (a) She had already been missing for two days before her absence was reported.

       (Blocks) _____ (Type) _____

   (b) Wearing a bright red rayon dress with matching patent-leather pumps and carrying a red-and-white patent leather clutch handbag, she left the house at about 0550 hours on March 10, 1998.

       (Blocks) _____ (Type) _____

   (c) No one has seen her since that date.

       (Blocks) _____ (Type) _____

(d) Numerous tips have been followed up, but no reliable information has been received.

(Blocks) _____ (Type) _____

(e) Although questions have been asked about her recent contacts, her friendship with a known gambler is now being investigated, and his whereabouts are being sought.

(Blocks) _____ (Type) _____

CHAPTER 10

Making Punctuation Work

Punctuation is one of the more logical and helpful aspects of grammar. Learn enough about it so that it will work for you.

Few people realize that there are two kinds of punctuation: open and closed. Open refers to using the fewest possible punctuation marks, e.g., omitting the comma before the final *and* in a series or leaving off the period at the end of a line when listing points on separate lines. Open was the more popular form in the 1970s and 1980s, but more and more references are mandating the use of a comma before the final conjunction in a series. Periods are omitted at the ends of items in a vertical list or enumeration, unless the items are complete sentences.

Overpunctuation is the bane of many reports. The solution is simple: when in doubt, leave it out. This is particularly true in the case of the comma. Many people use far too many commas. One old rule says, for example, to use a period when there is a long pause and a comma when there is a short pause. This may work sometimes, but what about the times when you are interrupted by the phone, a fellow officer, or the need for a cup of coffee while typing? Many people hit the comma key compulsively if they so much as exhale. Overpunctuation in the case of colons and ellipses is also rampant in many agencies. Learn how to use punctuation and use it sparingly.

As introduced in Chapter 8 of this text, the block method of identifying independent and dependent clauses will help you to understand punctuation.

□ = independent clause

□ = dependent clause

DOI: 10.1016/B978-1-4377-5584-8.00017-7

The Comma

Commas are used between independent clauses when they are joined by *and, or, so, nor, for, but,* or *yet.* If no coordinating conjunction is used to join independent clauses, then the comma is incorrect. In the absence of the coordinating conjunction, the semicolon is properly used.

☐ , *and, or, so, nor, for, but,* or *yet* ☐ . This is correct.

☐ ; ☐ This is correct.

☐ , ☐ . This is a comma splice and is incorrect if no coordinating conjunction is used.

Correct examples:
The neighbor knocked on the door, but she received no reply.
The neighbor knocked on the door; no one answered.

In both of these cases there are two independent clauses. They could have made separate sentences, but they were so closely related that a compound sentence seemed best. It would be incorrect to use a comma in the second sentence, because there is no coordinating conjunction.

When a long dependent clause precedes an independent clause, a comma follows the dependent clause. However, when the independent clause comes first, usually no comma is used.

☐ , ☐ . *When he realized the seriousness of the charge, he requested an attorney.*

☐ ☐ . *He requested an attorney when he realized the seriousness of the charge.*

Note how the words flow without pause in the second sentence. In the first sentence, there is a pause between the words *charge* and *he.* This pause does not naturally exist between *attorney* and *when* in the second sentence. On occasion, it is possible to omit the comma after a short dependent clause that precedes the independent one. However, because it is never incorrect to do so, it is best to always include the comma in this instance.

Example:
Before he left, he signed out at the desk.

There are other common uses for the comma in report writing:

1. In addresses, commas are used to set off towns, counties, and states, but are not used before the zip code.

   Example:
   He lived at 1210 Adams Street, Williamstown, NE 69042.

2. In correspondence, commas are used after the close of a letter (e.g., "Yours truly," "Sincerely yours,") When a letter is formal, a colon is used after the salutation (e.g., "Dear Ms. Jones:").

3. In dates, commas are needed to separate the day of the week, day, month, and year.

   Example:
   The accident occurred on Wednesday, January 16, 2010.

   On many forms, dates are used in numerical form and are set off by dashes or slashes. Use the form that is accepted at your agency. Alternate forms may be these: 1-16-10 or 1/16/10. Military and European usage may reverse the order and omit the commas: 16 January 2010 or 16 Jan 10.

4. Commas may separate the words in a series before the final conjunction *and*, *or*, or *nor*. As previously mentioned, the more modern form of punctuation includes the comma immediately before the final conjunction.

   Examples:
   The refugee begged for food, clothing, and a place to stay.
   The officer submitted a burglary, theft, and assault report.

   Where a series of adjectives are parallel (modifying the subject in equal proportion, as opposed to modifying an idea expressed by the combination of an adjective and a noun), commas are needed.

   Example:
   It was a cold, stormy, dark night.
   However, when adjectives are not parallel, omit the comma.

   Example:
   He wore heavy logging boots.
   A test for parallelism is to try to reverse the adjectives. *Logging heavy boots* would not make sense.

5. Commas set off direct quotations. Where the word referring to the speaker and *said* (or a similar word) interrupt the quotation, commas appear both before and after those words.

   Examples:
   The suspect said, "Let me out of here."
   "No one," he said, "could pin me to the crime." (This interrupted form of quotation is rarely used in reports.)

   Very short quotations that are structurally a part of the sentence are not set off with commas.

   Example:
   The prisoner in the adjoining cell, G-345, described the fight in G-347 as a "bad scene."

6. When titles or degrees are used, commas set off information.

   Examples: John JONES, Jr.
   Walter ADAMS, M.A., Ph.D.

7. A comma is used to separate the last name when a name is inverted.

   Example: JAMES, Edward

8. Commas may be used in cases where confusion would result if they were omitted.

   Example:
   He could not interpret the handwriting, expert though he was.
   (Omitting the comma would make it appear that *handwriting* modifies *expert*.)

9. In showing the person addressed, the comma sets off the name by coming either before or after it, depending on the position of the name in the sentence.

   Examples:
   Officer Brown, please take the stand.
   The client said, "Come here, Mary."

   If the name is in the middle of the sentence, the comma precedes and follows it as well.

   Example:
   Isn't it true, Lieutenant Malcolm, that you did not see the oncoming car?

10. With nonrestrictive modifiers (those that are not required for a sentence to make sense), the voice naturally pauses in the reading. This indicates that the comma is needed.

> Examples:
> While in the office, he often complained of an overload.
> The prisoner, Jack JONES, then threw the plate at the guard.

Sometimes the meaning is completely changed with the addition or omission of commas with modifiers.

> Examples:
> Prisoners who do not respond to treatment should be transferred to this facility.
> Prisoners, who do not respond to treatment, should be transferred to this facility.

In the second case, all prisoners would be grouped together as people who do not respond to treatment — indicating that prisoners, in general, should be transferred. In the first case, a distinction is made, indicating that only those prisoners who do not respond to treatment should be transferred. Use a comma to clarify. If you think your reader(s) will still have a difficult time understanding your point, rewrite the sentence.

11. Dashes and parentheses may take the place of commas and are sometimes used interchangeably. Frequently, a nonrestrictive clause or phrase is added as an additional bit of information or an aside. Dashes and parentheses interrupt the flow of thought more than commas and call attention to the words. Dashes are used to emphasize, while parentheses tend to de-emphasize. A common use of parentheses is to confirm a specific amount such as ($500) in a burglary.

The Semicolon

The semicolon is rarely needed in crisp writing in criminal justice. One exception might be the writings of probation officers. Because these officers are attached to the courts, they are sometimes required or expected to follow legal style. They also tend to qualify statements more often than others in the criminal justice field.

> Example:
> The client has committed a felony; however, he has made restitution, has a job, and appears to be a candidate for probation.

On the other hand, corrections officers working in a prison should follow the law enforcement format in stating facts, not opinions. Incidents such as thefts or fights should be noted in logs with references made to incident reports for more complete descriptions.

1. As indicated in the section on commas, the semicolon separates independent clauses when they are not joined by a comma and a coordinating conjunction, such as *and, or, nor, for, but, so,* or, *yet.* This style is useful when the independent clauses are very closely related.

     Suspect 1 refused to talk; Suspect 2 complied.

Both punctuation styles may be used in one sentence.

   ☐ ; ☐ , or ☐ . Nothing further could be done; the officer had to maintain surveillance, or the careful planning would have no results.

Transitional words such as *however, hence, consequently, therefore, moreover,* and *in fact,* called adverbial conjunctions, require a semicolon preceding and a comma after the word when they are used to join two independent clauses. These are not coordinating conjunctions.

> Example:
> Sergeant Jane Ross had already worked eight hours; however, in the emergency, she offered to continue at the receiving desk.

2. The semicolon also may be used to separate long or possibly confusing items in a series, especially when these items already include commas.

    > Example:
    > The following were elected: Captain Walter White, president; Captain Mary Stanton, vice-president; Lieutenant Wilfred Walker, secretary; Captain John Marshall, treasurer.

3. Semicolons may be used to group items in a series when the individual items are set off by commas.

    > Example:
    > For the Wilderness Survival workshop, the officers took the following: dehydrated food, coffee, eggs; ponchos, tarps, Coleman stoves; rifles, ammunition, knives.

Note that similar items are put together and set off by commas; the semicolon acts as a "super comma" to set off each series.

Rather than using a semicolon to separate a series of clauses in which there are commas, create a heading and put the series in list or outline form under that heading. It will be easier to read because the reader won't have to sort out what belongs to what.

Example:
For the Wilderness Survival workshop, the officers took the following:

<u>FOOD</u>
dehydrated food
coffee
eggs

<u>GEAR</u>
ponchos
tarps
Coleman stoves

<u>WEAPONS</u>
rifles
ammunition
knives

The Colon

The colon usually means that something will follow. It is a form of punctuation often overused in police communications. For example, the heading need not have a colon following it, because it usually stands alone on the line and is distinguished by all capital letters and underlining.

Example:
<u>VICTIM'S STATEMENT</u>
xxxxxxxxxxxxxxxxxxxxxxxxxxxxxxxxxxxxxxxxxxxxxxxxxxxxxxxxx
xxxxxxxxxxxxxxxxxxxxxxxxxxxxxxxxxxxxxxxxxxxxxxxxxxxxxxxxx

A colon is not needed after the heading unless space is at such a premium that the statement continues on the same line.

<u>VICTIM'S STATEMENT</u>: xxxxxxxxxxxxxxxxxxxxxxxxxxxxxxxxxxx
xxxxxxxxxxxxxxxxxxxxxxxxxxxxxxxxxxxxxxxxxxxxxxxxxxxxxxxxx

Interoffice communications use the colon following the words *TO, FROM, DATE,* and *SUBJECT.* The placement is also important. Most offices have forms, but sometimes you need to make out your own. The colon should not go farther across the page than the end of the longest word, which is *SUBJECT.*

Example:
TO: TO:
FROM: or   FROM:
DATE: DATE:
SUBJECT: SUBJECT:

The colon is used after words introducing a series.

Example:
You are required to bring the following items: pick, shovel, bucket, and marking stick.

The salutation of a formal letter is followed by a colon. An informal letter can use a comma.

Example:
Dear Ms. Brown:

You may use a colon to introduce material that explains, supplements, restates, or amplifies the preceding clause.

Example:
The report to the mayor must be very carefully written: it will explain the "high incidence of crime" times and places, and it will document the need for personnel.

The colon is also sometimes used to introduce a quotation.

The Apostrophe

The most frequent use of the apostrophe is to show possession. It can also show that something has been omitted.

1. As a general rule, use an apostrophe followed by an *s* to show possession. To form the possessive of a plural noun ending in *s*, add only an apostrophe. To form the possessive of a plural noun or a plural proper noun, add an apostrophe to the accepted plural form.

   Examples:
   one officer's work   witness's statement
   the officers' assignments   witnesses' statements
   man's time   The Vanderbilts' estate

   Do not use an apostrophe before the final *s* to form a plural instead of a possessive. In the case of an irregular plural, add an apostrophe to the accepted plural form followed by an *s*.

   Example:
   children's clothes

2. The apostrophe follows the final word in a compound noun.

   Example:
   the mother-in-law's house

3. To show joint possession, add the apostrophe and *s* to the last noun. However, when the compound nouns are considered separately, add the apostrophe and *s* to each.

> Examples:
> The incident occurred at Tom and Jerry's Bar.
> No one asked Tom's or Jerry's opinions.

4. Pronouns such as *my, mine, our, ours, your, yours, his, hers, its, their, theirs,* and *whose* have possession already built in without an additional apostrophe or s. Note that *its* is a possessive pronoun that is gender-neutral. (*It's* is a contraction meaning 'it is.')

> Examples:
> This is his beat.   Whose gun is this?
> The dog chased its tail.   The responsibility is yours.

Some indefinite pronouns need an apostrophe and *s* to form the possessive.

> Examples:
> anybody's opinion   another's complaint
> someone's job   no one's work
> someone else's testimony

The apostrophe may also show omission of one or more letters.

> Examples:
> I've (I have)   can't (cannot)

The Ellipsis

Like the apostrophe, the ellipsis indicates missing material, but the ellipsis shows that one or more words rather than letters are missing. In its correct usage, the ellipsis is formed by three periods with spaces between them (. . .) indicating that a word, words, or sentences have been left out, usually because they are irrelevant. By its nature, the criminal justice professional's report very rarely requires an ellipsis. It is expected that only relevant material is included. The problem is that many report writers use the ellipsis in one of its forms as a substitute for some other punctuation, such as a period:

> Example:
> Left Joe's Bar at 2400 hrs . . . Interviewed Suspect 1 . . . He could not explain actions prior to incident . . . Radioed his description to Dispatch . . . Pending further investigation by CID . . .

Note that this is a common but incorrect usage. Avoid the usage of the ellipsis and explain this reasoning to those whose work you must correct.

Parentheses

Parentheses are sometimes used to set off nonrestrictive material, that is, words that interrupt sentences and may add accuracy but do not alter the main meaning, although they tend to de-emphasize whatever they enclose. A common use in law enforcement is to restate the cost of an item in numeric form.

> Examples:
> The patient claimed that the watch missing from the nightstand had cost forty dollars ($40.00).
> The suspect (who had previously eluded his captors) was located in Kansas City.

Note that short parenthetical material within a sentence needs no internal punctuation. However, a complete sentence set off by parentheses should have punctuation that is within the parentheses.

> Example:
> The prisoner in C 242 is a repeater. (Note: He was charged with theft three times in 2010.)

When lists are in numerical or alphabetical order, the assumption might be made that the event or material listed under (1) came before that listed under (2) in order of time or importance. This is not the case when items in a list are set off with a bullet, which seems now to be gaining in usage and is represented by the bold circle or square.

> Example:
> Agenda for the June meeting:
> * Vote on committee chairperson
> * Discuss budget considerations for the next fiscal year
> * Distribute pension plan proposal for discussion and review

Brackets [ ] are similar to parentheses, but are used mainly in academic writing. Brackets enclose material added by someone other than the writer. They also are used around the Latin term *sic* in order to call attention to the retyping of an error made on an original report or when there is a grammatical error in a direct quote.

> Examples:
> The victim [Ann Doe] was found next to the car.
> The too [*sic*] victims then called for help.

Quotation Marks

There are four basic uses for quotation marks: to set off a direct quotation, to draw attention to a different use of a word, to set off some types of writing, and to indicate titles of news and journal articles, essays, and short stories contained in a larger volume with other similar works. You are probably most familiar with the direct quotation.

Example of a direct quotation:
He said, "I have just arrived."

Example of an indirect quotation:
He said that he had just arrived.

Note the placement of the quotation marks before the first word in the quotation and after the final punctuation. This is correct in about 99 percent of quotations. An exception may be the following:

Do you think that the suspect told the truth when he yelled, "I swear I didn't shoot him!"?

Here you are guided by the obvious actual meaning. However, when in doubt, put the quotation mark on the outside of the other punctuation.

Each part of an interrupted quote begins and ends with a quotation mark.

Example:
"If I have to stay," he said, "I will draw overtime."
(Note: This interrupted form of quotation is rarely used on reports.)

A quotation within a quotation is indicated by single quotation marks.

Example:
Officer Owens testified, "The suspect kept referring to his 'connection' during the buy."

When you have a long transcript of testimony, such as that taped and recorded in a serious case, you may have several paragraphs of quoted material. One style of punctuation for lengthy quotes is to indent the left margin and single space without using quotation marks.

If the report is written in the form of question and answer, quotation marks need not be used.

Example:
Question: When did you leave the house?

Answer: At about 12:30. I went to get lunch.
Q: Is this your regular time to leave?
A: No, I generally go an hour earlier.

Sometimes only one, two, or three words are quoted. This can be used to show that specific words in a paraphrased statement are quoted directly. Another purpose of this type of quoting is to show irony.

Examples:
The victim said that the suspect in this case is his neighbor David Smith, who is an "idiot."

He said that the budget would be given "careful consideration," at least, "to some extent."
(This implies that the writer does not believe that the consideration is careful. The second quotation shows the absurdity of the situation.)

Guard against overuse of the quotation mark; it can imply opposite meaning.

Example:
The captain issued "special" orders.
(A number of writers use the quotation mark to imply importance and call attention. Here, the mark calls attention, but in the wrong way. The implication might be that the orders are called special but that the writer doesn't agree.)

The quotation mark is correctly used to set off short literary works, such as poems, essays, and short stories contained within a larger volume of work. Underline or italicize the name of a book, magazine, journal, or newspaper from which the shorter material is taken. Old-fashioned usage was to quote all literary works, short or long. The newer method makes a distinction.

Example:
"Three Arrested on Murder Charge" is an article on p. A-9 of *The Washington Post*, May 12, 2010.

The Dash

On a typewriter, a dash is two hyphens typed together, with no space placed before, between, or after the hyphens. On a computer or word processor, there is usually a key for an em dash (named such because it is the width of an *m* in typeset print). Dashes can be substituted for commas, colons, semicolons, and parentheses to interrupt a thought or add further information.
Dashes can also be used to set off nonrestrictive material.

Example:
The prisoner — incarcerated January 7, 2006 — is up for parole in 2010.

Avoid overusing dashes.

Dashes are sometimes used to make obscenities publishable, such as with s— or f—. In such cases, a single dash is used for each letter omitted with no space between. In a criminal justice system report obscenities should be spelled out exactly.

A direct quotation from a witness showing a change of mind is an acceptable use of dashes:

Example:
"Tuesday was the last time I saw him alive — or maybe it was Wednesday — last week, anyhow."

Underlines

Underlining is often used for emphasis. It is also used to show titles of books, magazines, newspapers, films, or other such works. Words underlined in a manuscript are changed to italics when the material appears in print. Most word processing programs have the capability of italicizing, eliminating the need for such underlining.

Summary

1. Overpunctuation is a common problem. When in doubt, leave it out.

2. The block system of visualizing points out basic sentence punctuation. A semicolon is used between independent clauses not joined by a conjunction. When clauses are joined by *and, or, nor, for, but, so,* or *yet,* a comma is used before the coordinating conjunction. When a dependent clause precedes the independent clause, it is set off with a comma. When the dependent clause follows the independent one, usually no comma is needed.

3. The comma has many uses:
   to set off parts of an address (except the zip code)
   to set off the day of the week, the day, month, and year
   to set off words in a series
   to set off quoted material from the rest of the sentence
   to set off titles or degrees
   to avoid confusion in interpretation
   to indicate the person being addressed
   to set off parenthetical or nonrestrictive material
   to separate the last name when a name is reversed

4. The semicolon separates long or possibly confusing items in a series, especially when such items also include commas. The semicolon separates independent clauses when no coordinating conjunction is used. Adverbial conjunctions like *however, hence, consequently,* and *in fact* are not coordinating conjunctions. They are followed by commas when used to introduce a new clause. Where such a word connects two or more independent clauses in a sentence, a semicolon is used to set off the independent clause preceding this transitional word.

5. The colon usually means that something will follow. It may be used to introduce words in a series, a long formal statement, or even a quotation. It is used following the salutation in a formal letter and after words such as *TO, FROM, DATE,* and *SUBJECT* in interoffice communications.

6. The apostrophe most frequently is used to show possession. The apostrophe also may show omission of a letter or letters, as in *can't* for *cannot.*

7. The ellipsis, shown as three dots, means that something has been omitted, usually because it is irrelevant. It sometimes looks like four dots if it is at the end of a sentence ending with a period. It is overused by many report writers, who substitute it for correct punctuation between sentences.

8. Parentheses may be used to set off words that add accuracy to, but do not alter, the main meaning of a sentence. They can also be used to enclose numbers or letters in an outline.

9. Quotation marks set off direct quotations and set off short literary works such as poems, essays, short stories, or other selections from a larger volume of work. (The publication title is underlined or italicized.) When quotation marks set off a word or just a few words in a sentence, they call attention to these words, sometimes implying irony. One format for lengthy quotes is to indent the left margin and single space, omitting quotation marks. Like other forms of punctuation, quotation marks often are overused.

Chapter 10 — TEST

1. The most common problem in punctuation is _____.

2. Using the block method of visualizing, supply the missing punctuation in the following sentences:

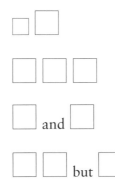

3. The comma has many uses:

    (a) to set off parts of a(n) _____, except for the _____;

    (b) to set off time elements, such as _____, _____, and _____;

    (c) to set off _____ material from the rest of the sentence;

    (d) to set off words in a _____;

    (e) to avoid confusion in _____;

    (f) to show the person _____; and

    (g) to set off parenthetical or _____ material.

4. The semicolon separates _____ clauses when they are not joined with a conjunction.

5. The colon means that something will _____. It may be used following a _____ in a letter. In interoffice communication it is used following such words as _____, _____, _____, and _____.

6. The apostrophe is most frequently used to show _____.

    The apostrophe may also indicate _____.

7. The ellipsis usually means _____.

8. Quotation marks are used most often to set off _____.

CHAPTER 11

Breaking the Spelling Jinx

How many people enter the criminal justice professions because they enjoy writing? It is doubtful that many would say, "I love to write! I was always the English teacher's favorite, and I was the state champion in spelling when I was in junior high."

Spelling is only one area of consideration in writing a report, but it is an area in which mistakes are easily made that can be highlighted by the defense to make you look like a fool in court. The term for this is "impeaching your credibility," which is a way of asking the judge or jury, "How can you trust this person?" Errors such as the following crop up frequently:

1. *Spelling the defendant's name incorrectly* or in more ways than one in the same report is a common occurrence. (This often can require reappearance to establish that the right person is on trial — a costly delaying tactic.)

2. *Misspelling words so commonly used* in the criminal justice field that they should have become automatic.

3. *Making gross errors in everyday words.*

4. *Using a word that sounds similar but means something totally different.*

Even if everyone in court knows what was meant, the words as actually written must stand. If your report is reprinted to become part of a large document, the erroneous words will be reproduced exactly as you wrote them, followed by the Latin term *sic*. *Sic* is defined in the *Merriam Webster's Collegiate Dictionary*, 10th ed., as: "Latin; so, thus: intentionally so written — used after a printed word or passage to indicate that it is intended exactly as printed or to indicate that it exactly reproduces an original." Picture a page of one of your reports reproduced with *sic* appearing

221

DOI: 10.1016/B978-1-4377-5584-8.00018-9

several times. You have declared open season on yourself. Your court opponent is thinking, "Yes! We can sink this officer's credibility right there."

Is this fair? Perhaps not. Your favorite sportscaster can make some terrible bloopers and be considered colorful. *The New Yorker* and *Reader's Digest* feature stories that make fun of erroneous material printed in newspapers or magazines. However, you and your reports will not be given the benefit of the doubt and you and your bosses will not find the results humorous. Others may be able to get by with mistakes, but the criminal justice report writer cannot.

This chapter contains some common spelling problems and ways to avoid them in your professional writing.

Take Special Care with Names

Get the name right on the very first encounter. Ask for the person's middle name and for any nicknames. If you do not get the name from a license or other form of identification, even if the name is *Mary Jane Smith*, ask, "And how do you spell that?" It could be *Mari Jayne Smythe*. Do not make assumptions when it comes to spelling names. If there is no middle name or initial, write *NMI*, which means "no middle initial." If the subject has aliases, nicknames, or pseudonyms, write *AKA* (also known as), followed by the name or names. *LNU* can be used to indicate "last name unknown."

Ask to ensure correct spelling, even though you might think that asking makes you sound stupid. It is better to ask at the time of the interview rather than risk embarrassment in court. Leslie or Lesley can be masculine or feminine, as can Marion or Marian (although the former is more often the masculine form). Jean and Jeanne can both be feminine, but the former is often the male spelling for one of French descent. Francis is generally masculine and Frances feminine, but it would be a mistake to count on anything. Kim, Pat, Tony, Kelly, and Chris are just a few examples of names that are commonly spelled the same way by both men and women. Check the full name when a shortened version is used. Jerry, Jerri, Jeri, Gerri, Geri, or Gerry (masculine or feminine) can be short for Jerrold, Jerald, Gerald, Gerard, Jerilyn, or Geraldine. Never assume the spelling of a name.

Be particularly careful when a last name is the same as a commonly known first name. This is where the system of placing the last name in all capital letters is practical as well as visually easy to locate on the page. There are many first names that also appear often as last names, such as John, Martin, Franklin, Allen, Frederick, James, Lawrence, Norman, and Lloyd. If you capitalize the last name in full, you will eliminate confusion: John Martin FRANKLIN, Allen Frederick JAMES, and Lawrence Norman LLOYD will make it clear.

This system of capitalization is particularly useful with foreign names. Many cities have many people that have Latin or Asian names; these cities in particular tend also to recruit male and female officers of varied ethnic backgrounds. From Florida to New York and from San Diego to Seattle, you can pass through blocks of non-English-speaking people. Likewise, some universities have found that their student body is becoming largely comprised of people who speak English as a second language. Names such as KIM, WONG, TANAKA, or VALDEZ are encountered more frequently than they were in the past, and many report forms in large cities are now written in more than one language. To avoid confusion, use all capital letters to help distinguish last names from first names, if your agency allows it.

Check every name carefully. Witnesses' names deserve the same care as the principal people in the case, that is, victims, suspects, and officers.

Learn Words Commonly Used in Report Writing

Why do most people quit criminal justice professions? Fear of shootings? Strange hours? Guess again. The director of a criminal justice program to which many agencies send their recruits said:

> A number one reason — or at least right close — is worry about reports, the time they take, the chance of being made a fool of in court. You'd think it was danger, right? Wrong! Many reports are thrown out by the prosecutor as impossible to handle — that doesn't enhance an officer's record, either.

From the other side of the fence, a public defender said this:

> A poorly written investigation is the best defense I have to defend the virtually nondefensible. You have a mass murderer who has said right off, "She deserved it, the bitch, and all her family, too." And how do I get the guy off? A glitch in the report. Even poor spelling — and how often do I see a report that has none? — can help me impeach the credibility of the writer. One officer had to keep coming back to court to prove he was talking about the right person since he had the name spelled two different ways. Do not blame me when someone you worked long at getting presumably to justice walks out free. You did my job for me when your report had more holes than a sieve and even the spelling and word use favored dismissing the case. Wise up. Quit doing my work for me!

It may be that you or someone you supervise is a problem speller. Poor spelling has never been proven to indicate poor intelligence, but misuse of words — sometimes connected with poor spelling — is an indication of poor vocabulary skills.

Anyone can improve spelling and vocabulary skills in a specific work area. Although spelling and word use are separate areas of concern when writing, the two come together when words sound alike but are spelled differently. Criminal justice professionals are notorious for confusing words and for using words that sound the same but mean something different. When people mutter and do not pronounce words carefully, the problem increases.

You will cut down on writing time by learning how to spell key words in your field. If you fail to do so, whenever you come to a problem word you will slow down, guess that something is wrong, stop and look it up, then forget it again before the next usage. Another time-wasting device is to try to think of an alternate word or a synonym for the one that you can't spell. The second gambit may result not only in wasted effort but also in distorted meaning.

> Remember — you do not make thousands of mistakes; you make a few basic mistakes a thousand times. If you learn how to correct one mistake beyond a shadow of a doubt, you can correct an endless number. If you are not sure, look it up and take the time to learn it so it won't be a problem in the future. Be absolutely sure of the words that you use daily in your work.

Consider this simple way to improve your spelling and word use: the 3 × 5″ card trick used with both spelling and word use. Every time you come across a word that you keep forgetting how to spell, put it on the card. Write no more than five words on each card, and keep them on hand to memorize, one card at a time. Tack the card on which you are working on your bathroom mirror, put it in your pocket, or consult it when you are going up in the elevator. The point is to make the card an automatic form of study, and remember to study no more than 10 words at a time.

Try associating the words with something that triggers the memory — something that involves the senses or even something silly. Any means of fixing key words in your mind is referred to as a mnemonic device (and if you can spell mnemonic, you can spell almost anything). Use mnemonic devices to get over your spelling problems. For example, take *tattoo*, an often misspelled word used in identification. Visualize the strangest tattoo that you have ever seen. Think of the repeated taps with the needle that puncture the skin, repeat the word in syllables (*tat • too*), hear the double t as you say it, and write it on the card. Consult the card at any time that you can throughout the day or night. Learn each word on your list by visualizing it, saying it, and writing it.

By involving your senses and by keeping the card with you to consult in your free time, you will be surprised at how many difficult words you can fix in your memory. Keep your cards and review them; they work for vocabulary as well as for spelling. The following is a list of words commonly spelled incorrectly in law enforcement, corrections, probation, parole, and security reports:

Commonly Misspelled Words

a lot	abscond	accomplish	acquitted
abandon	abstinent	accosted	across
abate	abutment	account	adamant
abdomen	accelerant	accumulate	adapt
abduction	accelerator	accurate	addict
aberration	accept	accused	additional
abetting	access lane	accustomed	address
abhor	accessible	achievement	adjacent
abortion	accessories	acknowledged	adjoining
abrasion	accompanied	acquaintance	adjust
abrogate	accomplice	acquired	admission

admit	apoplexy	basically	cardiac
admonition	apparently	battery	careful
adultery	appearance	bayonet	carnally
advantageous	application	bazaar	carrying
adversary	appoint	beginning	cartridge
advertisement	appraise	behavior	cashier
affidavit	apprehended	beige	cassette
affiliated	apprise	believe	casualty
affirmative	approached	belligerent	catastrophe
affront	approximate	berserk	Caucasian
again	argument	biceps	ceiling
aggravated	arraignment	bicycle	cemetery
aggressive	arrangement	bigamy	certificate
airplane	arrest	billiard	character
alcohol	arson	binoculars	chauffeur
alias	artery	bizarre	cheat
alibi	article	blackmail	chief
all right	artificial	bolster	choose
allegations	ascertain	bona fide	chose
alleged	asked	bookkeeper	chronological
alleviate	assault	boundary	circle
allotment	assignment	boutique	circuit
allusion	assistance	brake	circumference
alongside	assistants	break	circumstantial
already	associate	brevity	citing
altered	assortment	bribery	citizen
alternate	assumed	brief	clarify
although	asthma	brother-in-law	client
always	athletics	bruises	coarse
amateur	attached	build	cocaine
ambulance	attacked	built	coerce
ammunition	attendance	bulletin	cognizant
amnesia	attorney	bunco	cohabitation
among	attribute	bureau	coherent
amount	audacity	burglary	collaborate
amputation	auditory	business	collar
amusement	authoritative	bystander	collateral
analysis	automatic		collision
analyze	autopsy	cache	collusion
animosity	available	cafeteria	colonel
announce	avert	cajole	coma
annoyance		calendar	comatose
annual		caliber	combination
anonymous	backpack	campaign	combustible
answer	backward	candid	comfortable
antenna	bail	candidate	commercial
antipathy	bail bond	canister	commission
anxiety	bale	capricious	committed
apartment	ballistics	captain	committee
apathy	bandage	carburetor	communicate
	barricade		

compel
compensate
competition
complacent
complainant
complement
compliance
compliant
complying
compulsory
concealed
conciliatory
concur
concurrent
condone
conductive
confession
confined
connive
conscience
conscious
consent
conspiracy
construction
construe
consult
contempt
contents
contusion
convenience
converge
conviction
cooperate
copulation
corner
coroner
corporal
corporation
corps
corpse
correction
correlate
correspondence
corroborate
corrugated
cough
council
counselor
counterfeit
county

coupon
court
courteous
credibility
creditor
criminal
critical
criticism
crotch
cruelty
cruising
culminated
curfew
curly
currency
current
cursory
custody
customary
cylinder

damage
damaging
dangerous
debris
debt
deceased
decedent
deceptive
decision
decomposed
defamation
default
defecated
defective
defendant
defensive
definite
defraud
deleterious
delinquent
demeanor
demented
demonstration
denied
denomination
dependent
deployed
deposition
derogatory

derringer
descending
description
desecrate
desperate
despondent
destination
detainer
detective
developed
diabetes
diagnosis
diagonal
diaphragm
diarrhea
didn't
diesel
different
dilapidated
dining
disappearance
disastrous
discipline
discotheque
discreet
discrepancy
discrete
discrimination
disease
disguise
disinfectant
disinterested
dislocation
dispatched
dispensary
dispersed
disposition
disqualify
disseminate
dissipated
distinction
divergent
diversion
divide
divorcee
divulge
docket
documentary
doesn't
domestic

dormitory
drawer
driveway
drowsy
drunkard
drunkenness
dual
dubious
duffle bag
duplex
duplicate
duress
during
dynamite

earring
eccentric
eclectic
eighth
electricity
elevator
elicit
eligible
eliminate
embarrassed
embedded
embezzlement
embracing
emergency
emphysema
employee
employment
encounter
endemic
enemy
enforcement
ensuing
entice
entrance
entrust
environment
epileptic
equipment
equivalent
erection
erotic
err
erratic
especially
establishment

estimate
eviction
evidence
except
exception
excite
excused
executed
exercise
exhaust
exigent
existence
exonerate
expedite
experience
expire
explanation
explicit
explosion
expression
extinguish
extortion
extradition
extremely
extremities
exuberant
ex-wife

facetious
facility
facsimile
familiar
fascinating
father-in-law
fatigue
fax
February
feces
federal
fellatio
felony
feminine
fictitious
Filipino
filthy
finally
financial
fisticuffs
flammable
flashlight

flippant
fondling
forcibly
forearm
foreign
forfeit
formally
formerly
fornication
forth
fortitude
forty
fourteen
fourth
fracture
fraudulent
friend
frightened
fugitive
fulfill
furlough
furniture
futile

gagged
gambling
garage
garbage
gassed
gauge
generally
genuine
ghetto
government
gradually
graffiti
graffito
gratification
graveled
grease
grenade
grievance
guarantee
guard
guidance
guilty
guitar

habitually
half

Halloween
hallucinogen
handkerchief
harassment
Hare Krishna
hazard
hazardous
headache
heard
height
hemorrhage
heroin
herself
hiccup
hijacked
hindered
Hispanic
hitchhiked
homicide
hone
hoping
horizontal
humane
humiliate
hunted
hurrying
hydrant
hypodermic
hysterical

ideal
identified
idiosyncrasy
ignorance
illicit
illiterate
imaginary
imitation
impatient
impeccable
imperfect
impervious
implicit
impossible
impression
impromptu
impugn
inadequate
incapacitation
incest

inchoate
incidentally
incineration
incoherent
incompetent
inconsistent
incorrigible
incredible
indecent
indefinite
independent
indicating
indict
indifference
indigent
indignant
indiscriminate
individual
induce
inept
inevitable
inflammable
informant
infringe
ingenious
ingredient
inhibition
initial
injured
in-laws
inmate
innocent
inquiry
inquisitive
inscribed
insinuate
insolence
instead
instigate
instinct
insufficient
insurance
intelligent
intercept
intercourse
interest
interfering
interior
interpret
interrogate

interrupted
intersect
interstate
interview
intimidate
intoxicated
intractable
intruder
invasion
investigation
irrelevant
irresistible
isolate
issuance
it's
its

jalousies
janitor
jealousies
jealousy
jeopardize
jurisdiction
justifiable
juvenile

kerosene
khaki
kidnapping
kleptomaniac
knowledge
knuckles

label
laboratory
laceration
larceny
lascivious
latent
later
latter
lattice
Laundromat
lawyer
legal
legible
legitimate
leisure
length
lessee

lessor
lewd
liable
liaison
libel
license
lien
lieutenant
lightning
likely
liquor
litigate
lividity
loiter
longer
loose
lose

losing
louvers
Luger
luggage

machete
magazine
maintain
maintenance
majority
malicious
malign
management
mandatory
maneuver
manual
margin
marijuana
marital
marriage
martial
matinee
maturity
mayhem
meant
medal
medevac
medical
memorandum
memorize
menace
menstrual
merely

metal
microphone
midriff
mileage
minimum
minor
minute
miscellaneous
mischievous
misdemeanor
misspelled
mitigate
moccasin
moisture
molest
monogrammed
moped
moral
morale
morgue
morphine
motorcycle
mountainous
multiple
municipal
murdered
murmur
muscle
museum
mustache
mutilated

naive
narcotics
narrow
natural
necessary
necklace
nefarious
negative
neglect
neighborhood
nephew
nervous
neutral
niece
ninety
noisy
nonpayment
noticeable

notify
nuisance
numerous
nunchaku

obedience
obligation
obnoxious
obscene
obscure
obsolete
obstacle
obstinate
occasion
occurred
occurrence
odor
offender
offense
official
often
operator
opinion
opium
opponent
opportunity
opposite
ordinance
ordnance
oscillate
overt

painful
pandering
panicked
parallel
paramedic
paraphernalia
parole
partial
participate
particular
passed
passenger
pastime
pathology
patience
patients
peace
pedestrian

penalty	presence	realize	ruptured
penchant	presentence	really	ruse
pendants	pretrial	receding	
penis	previous	receive	sacrifice
perform	prime	recidivism	salary
perhaps	principal	reciprocal	salient
perishable	principle	reckless	satisfactory
perjury	prior	recognizance	Saturday
permanent	prisoner	recognize	sawed-off
permeate	pristine	recollect	scarcely
permissible	privilege	recommend	scatter
permittee	probably	recreation	scene
perpetrator	probation	rectify	schedule
persecute	procedure	reddish	scheme
perseverance	proceeds	redness	scissors
personal	procuring	redo	scraped
personnel	profane	reference	scrutinize
perspiration	progress	referred	scuffle
persuade	prohibit	refuse	secluded
petulant	projectile	release	secretary
Philippines	promiscuous	relevant	sedative
physical	pronounce	religious	seen
picketing	pronunciation	remanded	semiautomatic
picnicking	proposition	remedial	semiconscious
placate	prosecute	remember	sense
placid	prostitution	renewal	sentence
planning	protective	repeat	separation
plausible	provocation	repetition	sergeant
plea	psychologist	representation	sexual
pleasant	publicity	reprieve	sheriff
pneumatic	Puerto Rican	reprisal	shining
poisonous	pulse	repugnant	shone
polygamy	punctured	reputation	shotgun
Portuguese	pungent	residence	shoulder
possession	pursuit	resident	shrubbery
posture		resistance	sidewalk
practically	qualification	resolution	signature
practice	quality	respiration	silhouette
preceding	quantity	responsible	similar
precipitate	quarrel	restaurant	simultaneous
precise	quiet	restitution	since
predicament	quite	resuscitated	sincerely
predication	quota	revived	site
pregnancy		revoke	skeleton
prejudice	racial	revolver	skeptical
preliminary	raid	ridiculous	slapped
premeditation	railing	rigor mortis	sleight
premises	rally	robbery	slight
prerogative	readily	roommate	snub-nosed
prescription	reality	rummaging	sodomy

solicitation
son-in-law
specimen
spherical
spontaneous
sprain
squalid
statement
statistics
statue
statute
stomach
strangulation
strictly
striped
stripped
subduing
subject
subjugate
submitting
subpoena
substantial
substantive
subterfuge
subtle
subversive
succeed
successful
suede
suffocation
sullen
summons
sundry
superintendent
supersede
supervisor
supplement
supplies
surely
surprise
surrender
surreptitious
surveillance
suspect
suspended
suspicion
swerve

sympathy
symptom

tacit
tamper
tattoo
taut
technical
telephone
temperament
temperamental
temperature
tendency
testimony
tetanus
theater
their
there
they're
thieves
thorough
thought
throat
through
to
together
tongue
too
topless
towel
toxic
tractor
traffic
trafficking
tranquil
transferred
traverse
treacherous
trespassing
tries
trouble
truancy
T-shirt
Tuesday
turbulent
turpitude
turquoise

two
typewriter
typical

umbrella
unconscious
undoubtedly
uniform
union
unnatural
unnecessary
unregistered
unsanitary
until
unusually
unwilling
urgent
using
utility

vacancy
vaccination
vacuum
vagina
vagrant
valid
validity
valuable
variety
vehement
vehicle
velocity
vendor
venereal
venue
veracity
verify
versatile
version
vertical
vicinity
vicious
victim
Vietnamese
village
vindictive
violation

viscous
visible
vitamin
vivid
volume
volunteer

wagon
waist
waitress
wanton
warehouse
warrant
waste
wealth
weapon
wear
weather
Wednesday
weight
weighty
weird
welfare
where
whether
whole
whore
wily
wiry
witnessed
women
wounded
wreck
writing
written

yield
you're
young
your
youthful

zealous
zero
zigzag
zone

Study Common Problem Areas

Clearing Up the "-ing" Confusion

The rule for adding *-ing* is when the final letter is a consonant, double it if: (1) its last two letters are a vowel followed by a consonant, and (2) it has one syllable or is accented on the last syllable. If the word ends with *e*, drop the final *e* unless doing so would cause confusion. If you have trouble following this rule, you might try the following exercise:

When you end a word with *-ing*, do you know when to double the letter that precedes it? Try these:

slope   1.   He fell on the (slopping, sloping) roof.
win   2.   She has been (winning, wining) the games.
rape   3.   The suspect was accused of (raping, rapping) the victim.
write   4.   He was (writing, writting) his report.
bid   5.   I was (bidding, biding) on the auction item.

Correct answers: sloping, winning, raping, writing, bidding

What shortcut rule can you develop from considering these words? When a word has a long vowel (a vowel that is pronounced like the letter itself), drop the *e* and add *-ing*; do not double the consonant. When a word has a short vowel, double the consonant before adding *-ing*. The long *o* in sloping comes from *slope*, which ends in *e*, and the long *a* in raping comes from *rape*, which ends in e. Sound a word out. You can tell if it is a long vowel or a short one.

Vowels are *a, e, i, o, u*, and sometimes *y* (as in *system*). Consonants are the other letters. Remember that long vowels are vowels that are pronounced the same as the letter itself is pronounced — short vowels are pronounced differently. *Rape* is a good word to remember for the above rule. If you write *rapping* (which has a short *a*, as in *apple*), the meaning is not the same at all. Remember, *rape* has a long sound, so you drop the *e* and add *-ing* to get *raping*.

The phrase *The sloping roof* would look silly if you wrote *slopping*. Similarly, a security report that referred to a janitor moping in the hall sounds like the janitor was depressed. His mood might have changed when a patient slipped on water left from someone mopping the halls. A person that has been wining and dining the night before may not be winning the marathon the next day. One can be gripping a hammer and griping about low pay. How many examples of this can you think of? List them and be sure that the spelling is right. Are any of them exceptions?

The following are five exceptions to the sound rule, but not exceptions to the rule about dropping the e before adding *-ing*:

Giving, having, living, coming, and *loving* all are pronounced with the short vowel sound. *Giving* does not have a long vowel sound like *jiving*. If you have a tendency to misspell these words by doubling the consonants, it means that you are more logical than the English language. It also means that your work is going to look bad if you spell them wrong. They are very common words. Write them on a card and learn each one. All except *loving* are very common on reports, and even that word shows up sometimes.

A few words can be written either with single or double consonants, for example *kidnapping* (or *kidnaping*) and *traveling* (or *travelling*). Newspapers tend to use the single consonant. In any case, do not vary the spelling of such words in the same report.

What do you do when the word ends in two consonants, as with *dust* and *knock*? Even though the sounds are short, you just add -ing without doubling the consonant: *dusting* for latents and *knocking* at the door.

Learning Words with Tricky Letter Combinations

It is difficult to make many general spelling rules because of the many exceptions in the English language. However, learn the rules, apply them when you can, and memorize the words that are tricky.

Remember your rules from grammar school:

> Use *i* before *e* except after *c* or when pronounced *ay* as in *weigh* or *neighbor.*

That rule holds true most of the time:

> Examples:
> bel*ie*ve, rel*ie*ve, gr*ie*ve, ch*ie*f, p*ie*ce, w*ie*ld, y*ie*ld, n*ie*ce, f*ie*ld
> rec*ei*ve, rec*ei*pt, dec*ei*ve, conc*ei*ve, perc*ei*ve
> *ei*ght, r*ei*gn, sl*ei*gh, d*ei*gn, v*ei*n, f*ei*gn

Unfortunately, English is full of exceptions:

> h*ei*ght, for*ei*gn, st*ei*n, h*ei*r, *ei*ther, n*ei*ther, l*ei*sure, s*ei*ze, counterf*ei*t, forf*ei*t, sl*ei*ght, w*ei*rd, consc*ie*nce, financ*ie*r, sc*ie*nce

Some words are spelled differently in England, Canada, or other countries that have been under British influence. Pronunciation may be the same, but a letter may be added or reversed. *Honor* in the United States becomes *honour* in the United Kingdom; *favor* becomes *favour* and *behavior* becomes *behaviour*. *Theater* is spelled *theatre* and *center* is spelled *centre*. Use locally accepted forms in your own writing, but leave the spelling as it is on reports that come from other countries.

Another source of confusion is words ending in *-er* or *-or*. These endings are often used to develop verbs into nouns that indicate people or things that perform some act. Many such words are common on law enforcement reports. However, there is no rule that covers these examples, so one must go back to the 3 × 5″ memory cards to learn problem words.

Many add -er to the verb form.

Examples ending in -er:
advertis*er*, consum*er*, kill*er*, manufactur*er*, peddl*er*, promot*er*, propell*er*

Some of the words ending in -or are developed from verbs, but some are not.

Examples ending in -or:
accelerat*or*, administrat*or*, advis*or*, carburet*or*, competit*or*, conduct*or*, distribut*or*, govern*or*, inspect*or*, legislat*or*, mot*or*, object*or*, propriet*or*, spectat*or*, spons*or*, supervis*or*, ventilat*or*

To make things thoroughly confusing, there are a few words ending in -ar: e.g., begg*ar*, burgl*ar*, li*ar*.

Forming Plurals

The plurals for nouns are formed in a number of ways. There are exceptions to almost every rule for pluralizing words; however, the following lists should prove helpful in most instances.

Most plural forms are made by merely adding an *s*.

Singular	Plural
drug	drugs
table	tables
vehicle	vehicles
street	streets

Nouns ending in *s*, *sh*, *ch*, *x*, or *z* form the plural by adding -es.

Singular	Plural
bus	buses
stash	stashes
church	churches
ax	axes
waltz	waltzes

For nouns ending in *o* preceded by a vowel, add *s*.
(For musical terms ending in *o* preceded by a consonant, add *s*.)

Singular	Plural
patio	patios
rodeo	rodeos
piano	pianos
cello	cellos

For some nouns ending in *o* preceded by consonant, add *s*; for others, add *-es*. (Some can be formed either way.)

Singular	Plural
dynamo	dynamos
kimono	kimonos
hero	heroes
potato	potatoes
veto	vetoes
tornado	tornadoes or tornados
cargo	cargoes or cargos
volcano	volcanoes or volcanos
zero	zeros or zeroes

For nouns ending in *y* preceded by a consonant, change the *y* to *i* and add *-es*.

Singular	Plural
city	cities
sky	skies
duty	duties
body	bodies

Nouns ending in *y* preceded by a vowel usually add *s*. (In many cases, the vowel before the final *y* is *e*.)

Singular	Plural
alley	alleys
key	keys
day	days

Some nouns ending in *f* or *fe* change the f or fe to *v* and add *-es*. Some simply end in *s*. (Some can be made plural either way.)

Singular	Plural
wife	wives
thief	thieves
half	halves
life	lives
wharf	wharves or wharfs
chief	chiefs
staff	staffs

Some nouns form the plural by changing the vowel.

Singular	Plural
man	men
woman	women
foot	feet

Some nouns form the plural by changing form completely.

Singular	Plural
child	children

Some nouns have the same form for both singular and plural.

Singular	Plural
fish	fish
gross	gross
series	series
rice	rice

The plural form of compound nouns is generally formed by adding *s* to the main word of the compound noun.

Singular	Plural
mother-in-law	mothers-in-law
attorney general	attorneys general or attorney generals
court-martial	courts-martial

However, compound nouns ending in *-ful* are made plural by adding *s* to the end of the compound noun.

Singular	Plural
handful	handfuls
spoonful	spoonfuls

Occasionally, both parts of the compound noun are made plural.

Singular	Plural
manservant	menservants
woman doctor	women doctors

Some foreign words incorporated into the English language form plurals according to their original language. In a few cases there are English versions of the plural form.

Foreign Singular	Plural
analysis	analyses
appendix	appendices or appendixes
axis	axes
bacterium	bacteria
basis	bases
cactus	cacti or cactuses
candelabrum	candelabra or candelabrums

crisis	crises
criterion	criteria or criterions
curriculum	curricula or curriculums
datum	data
focus	foci or focuses
formula	formulae or formulas
gymnasium	gymnasia or gymnasiums
hypothesis	hypotheses
index	indices or indexes
medium	media or mediums
memorandum	memoranda or memorandums
phenomenon	phenomena or phenomenons
synopsis	synopses
thesis	theses

The following are some examples of nouns that are used only in the plural.

billiards	pants	shears
clothes	pliers	suds
forceps	remains	
gallows	scissors	

Dealing with Other Complexities of the English Language

Spelling difficulties may arise due to other complexities in the English language:

1. Incorrect pronunciation of verbs in the past tense.

2. Confusion over past tense and past participles of irregular verbs.

3. Confusion in homonyms, which sound alike but mean something different and are spelled differently (see Chapter 12).

4. Slang and dialect.

The worst offender is the *-ed* on a verb in the past tense. Reports refer to incidents that happened in the past, so this problem comes up all the time. On a security log at the hospital, one is likely to find:

> I *past* the door at 0830 and it was locked, but at 0930 it was open and there was no one in where the drugs are kept.

Passed is the correct form, but it is often spelled incorrectly because of its pronunciation. The same thing happens to words like *walked* and *talked*, which are correctly pronounced as if they end in a *t*. Rarely would anyone make such a mistake with the common example "I *handed* him a ticket," as *handed* has a clear sound of the *-ed*. To make matters worse, there are a few irregular verbs.

A regular verb is a verb that forms the past tense and the past participle by adding *-ed* or *-d* to the form of the present tense. (Sometimes the *-ed* or *-d* changes to *-t.*)

Present Tense	Past Tense	Past Participle
(present time)	(past time)	(with *have, has, had*)
call	called	called
join	joined	joined
build	built	built

An irregular verb is a verb that does not form the past tense and the past participle in the regular way. The past tense and past participle for irregular verbs may be formed in various ways. The most common way is by changing a vowel (e.g., *sing, sang, sung*); however, for a few verbs the same form is used for all three verb tenses (e.g., *hurt, hurt, hurt*).

Present Tense	Past Tense	Past Participle
(present time)	(past time)	(with *have, has, had*)
drive	drove	driven
go	went	gone

The regular verbs cause little trouble in writing. It is the irregular verbs that are responsible for most verb errors. Refer to the following list of troublesome verbs when in doubt about verb forms.

Present Tense	Past Tense	Past Participle
(present time)	(past time)	(with *have, has, had*)
be	was, were	been
beat	beat	beaten
become	became	become
begin	began	begun
bid (offer to buy)	bid	bid
bid (command)	bade	bidden, bid
blow	blew	blown
break	broke	broken
bring	brought	brought
broadcast	broadcast	broadcast
burst	burst	burst
catch	caught	caught
choose	chose	chosen
climb	climbed	climbed
come	came	come
cut	cut	cut
dive	dived, dove	dived
do	did	done
drag	dragged	dragged
draw	drew	drawn
drink	drank	drunk

drive	drove	driven
drown	drowned	drowned
eat	ate	eaten
fall	fell	fallen
flow	flowed	flowed
fly	flew	flown
forget	forgot	forgotten
freeze	froze	frozen
get	got	got, gotten
give	gave	given
go	went	gone
hang (a picture)	hung	hung
hang (a criminal)	hanged	hanged
hurt	hurt	hurt
know	knew	known
lay (to place, to put)	laid	laid
lead	led	led
leave	left	left
lend	lent	lent
let	let	let
lie (to recline)	lay (not laid)	lain (not laid)
lie (tell a falsehood)	lied	lied
lose	lost	lost
prove	proved	proven, proved
ride	rode	ridden
ring	rang	rung
rise	rose	risen
run	ran	run
say	said	said
see	saw	seen
send	sent	sent
set	set	set
shake	shook	shaken
shine (give light)	shone	shone
shine (polish)	shined	shined
show	showed	shown, showed
shrink	shrank, shrunk	shrunk, shrunken
sing	sang, sung	sung
sink	sank, sunk	sunk
sit	sat	sat
spring	sprang, sprung	sprung
steal	stole	stolen
swear	swore	sworn
swim	swam	swum
swing	swung	swung
take	took	taken

teach	taught	taught
tear	tore	torn
tell	told	told
think	thought	thought
throw	threw	thrown
try	tried	tried
understand	understood	understood
wake	woke	woken
wear	wore	worn
weave	wove	woven
weep	wept	wept
wind	wound	wound
wring	wrung	wrung
write	wrote	written

Another area of possible confusion is in writing slang words. The rule of thumb for the writing of slang words is: Use slang only in the case of direct quotes and do not attempt it unless it is simple and easily understood (e.g., "Stick 'em up!"). Note the use of the apostrophe for missing letters. Even prominent literary authors find it difficult to write using slang or dialect. Unless it is a significant statement, do not try to write in this manner. When it is necessary to do so, be sure to write an explanation for the slang word so that your reader(s) will understand the usage. Write out obscenities in full when they are part of a significant statement.

Strengthen Your Overall Writing Ability

The more you read — not just in your own field — the better you will write. Good writing is good writing in any field. Investigative reports of any kind, however, have the potential to affect a great number of people and should never be done carelessly. Poor spelling can make a mishmash of even a good factual report. Your goal should be to meet the standard required by your field of work.

Developing Proofreading Techniques

Most of us see only what we expect to see. If you are reading your own work, you must be especially alert. Proofread twice — once for the meaning and then for grammar and spelling. Reading your writing out loud will help you discover some errors more easily. If you do not have a place to read your writing out loud, pick a quiet place to read it to yourself so that you can hear the words in your head as you read it. Sensitive reports should be read by more than one person — possibly with one reading aloud and one or more people checking copies. This is an example of how important it is to have several proofreaders: A city group was submitting a report to the legislature, complete with pictures and captions. Six people read the report before anyone noticed that in a caption, the state *c*apitol was referred to as the state *s*apitol. These types of errors are easily overlooked because the reader *expects* the word to be capitol.

Summary

1. Double check the spelling of every name in the report. Never take names for granted: SMITH can also be SMYTH or SMYTHE. An incorrect letter can delay a case or even cause a case to be dismissed.

2. Spelling is the most common problem on reports. You may not leap from being a problem speller to being a perfect speller, but you can learn how to spell the most commonly misspelled words. Check the list in this chapter, and work on it until you become sure of every word. Keep your own list of commonly misspelled words and misused vocabulary, and be sure to write them in the proper form. Use 3 × 5″ cards as study aids.

3. Do not keep looking up the same word or keep avoiding it by searching for synonyms — substitute words may not be exactly accurate. If you correct words firmly in your mind, you will save time and confusion. Use mnemonic devices to help you remember words. Involve as many of your senses as you can in remembering, and use a play on words if that helps. Note hard and soft sounds and silent letters.

4. The sound rule for words ending in -ing is that after a long vowel sound (as in *rape/raping*) you drop the e, use a single consonant, and add -*ing*. Double the consonant before adding -*ing* when the vowel in the preceding syllable is short: *rap/rapping*. The common exceptions to this rule are: *giving*, *having*, *living*, *coming*, and *loving*. If you pronounce words correctly, you will be more likely to spell them correctly.

5. Learn some common spelling rules and their exceptions. Use *i* before *e* except after *c* or when pronounced *ay* as in *neighbor*. Memorize key nouns ending in *er*, *or*, and *ar* so that you do not misspell them.

6. Plural nouns are formed in a number of ways. Most plural forms are made by adding *s*. Review the rules for other plural forms, and memorize the most common exceptions.

7. Spelling problems may arise due to complexities in the English language, such as incorrect pronunciation of verbs in the past tense, confusion over past tense and past participles of irregular verbs, misuse of homonyms or synonyms, and writing using slang or dialect.

8. Develop proofreading techniques, including reading your work twice, once for meaning and the second time for grammar and spelling. If at all possible, read your writing out loud.

Chapter 11 — TEST

1. The general rule for ending a word in *-ing* is to use a single consonant after a _____ vowel sound in the preceding syllable and a double consonant after a _____ vowel sound. List three examples of each type:

   (a) _____, _____, _____

   (b) _____, _____, _____

   List five common exceptions to the rule:

   (c) _____, _____, _____, _____,
   _____

2. Pronunciation — or mispronunciation — can affect your spelling. Give two examples of past tense verbs that are frequently misspelled because the final *-ed* is not pronounced as a separate syllable:

   _____ and _____

3. Complete the old rule: Use *i* before *e*_____

   _____

   Give three examples of when *i* appears before *e*:

   (a) _____

   (b) _____

   (c) _____

   Give three examples of when *e* appears before *i*:

   (a) _____

   (b) _____

   (c) _____

4. List three ways of improving your spelling:

   (a) _____

   (b) _____

   (c) _____

CHAPTER 12

Using or Abusing Words

Words define you as much as you define them. Your spoken language can place you within a certain group. Your written language can help determine how clearly you think, how logically you act, and how far you will go professionally.

You may think of yourself primarily as a person of action. Action obviously counts in a crisis situation, but it is a short-term measure. You also need knowledge and sensitivity about words, so that your report conveys exactly what you mean, nothing more or less. Administration of justice depends on people acting on behalf of the public good. However, it also depends on the documentation of all action, whether by client, criminal, victim, witness, or officer, as accurately as possible. To do this, you need to become a word detective. Learn as much as you can about words — how they change, what they can and cannot do, and what they reveal about yourself and others.

How well do you think? Your mental processes are dependent upon words. True, you can have a feeling, a premonition, or even a "gut-level" reaction. But how do these turn into thought processes? A vague stirring in the subconscious does not have much substance until it surfaces in the form of words. Thinking, reading, writing, talking with another to test your idea — all of these are part of your thought processes. If your vocabulary is limited, so will be your ideas and your ability to report.

Vocabulary plays a big part on civil service and intelligence tests because a good vocabulary is considered an indicator of intelligence. This does not mean that the person who uses a lot of big words is necessarily the smartest. Using words to impress rather than to express is childish; however, having a large vocabulary and being sensitive to shades of meaning and different uses in different situations are important.

How logically do you act? You act in response to an outside stimulus, e.g., hearing a bulletin, checking on a parolee, noticing a dangerous situation, or witnessing a crime. Much of the time, however, you react to words and their meanings.

DOI: 10.1016/B978-1-4377-5584-8.00019-0

If you misinterpret the words, you misinterpret the person's thoughts. Your actions then become illogical and inappropriate. In hearing the words of another person, you think that you understand what the person intended, but this may not necessarily be true.

Do not skip this chapter because you feel secure for either of these two reasons:

1. You understand and can use plain language, which is the best style for reports.

2. Whatever mistakes you make in spelling, vocabulary, and grammar can be corrected by computer software.

Courtrooms are littered with the remains of careers of people who thought they knew English. David Mellinkoff, author of the classic reference, *The Language of the Law*, said, "Plain language is a very ambiguous term. What is plain to you and what is plain to me are often not the same thing." Mellinkoff pioneered in simplifying legal language; his landmark book came out in 1963 and stayed in print for decades. Even now, the points he made are news to some people.

What you consider simple may not be simple to others. Both you and the reader may have biases you are not aware of. Include antonyms, synonyms, homonyms, homophones, jargon, dialects, and street talk, and you may not be speaking the same language. Add nonverbal communication and you can see how confusion can set in.

Biases

Your word choice may depend on your feelings about the person with whom you are dealing. Use specific, everyday language as often as you can, taking care to avoid prejudice, euphemisms, and stereotypes. "Nerd" and "computer specialist" may refer to the same person. Perhaps neither is accurate. One is prejudiced, the other euphemistic. Both are stereotypes.

1. *Prejudice* refers to prejudgment of a person or idea before collecting accurate data. "Never expect a fair deal from a _____." (You can fill in this blank with almost any racial, ethnic, religious, gender, sexual orientation, or slang name.)

2. *Euphemism* is the substitution of a vague or polite term, often mild or indirect, for what might be a harsh or offensive term. "The senator is ethically challenged."

3. *Stereotype* is a standardized concept of members of a group. It involves tacking on a label rather than considering an individual as an individual. Stereotyping often concerns the age, race, religion, and/or gender of an individual. "Of course the sarge lost her cool. It's probably that time of the month."

Everyone is guilty of such biases at one time or another. The trick is to be able to reduce prejudice, euphemism, and stereotyping as much as you can. The worst situation is when a person knowingly and maliciously uses such terms to sway another's opinion. In high-level statesmanship, the exact word at the exact time can be excruciatingly important. The same thing is true about report writing.

Slang and Dialects

Be a word detective: look up a word's meaning and find out how the word has changed. Slang, dialects, and street language change faster than formal English and are worthy of close scrutiny. Think about the change in the meaning of words in your lifetime. If you are middle-aged, you can probably remember when the meaning of the word "gay" was "happy." Now it is used mostly as a synonym for "homosexual." California psychologist Dr. Eugene E. Landy found that he could understand the language of addicts that he was treating, but they could not always understand or express themselves in standard English. He wrote *The Underground Dictionary* as a result of dealing with a woman addict who could not define the language that she used. Published in 1971, the book has already become dated, in addition to being limited because some of the language is typical in California but not elsewhere.

In recent years a number of slang languages have been developed, including those of street gangs or other groups. The personal computer, the Internet, and cell phone texting started a whole new language of their own.

Do Not Use Legalese

Some people protest that simple language doesn't sound professional. These people may favor "legalese."

> Examples:
> The above-mentioned client did willfully and knowingly ...
> (The client's name would be simpler here, and the adverbs here are a value judgment.)
>
> One John JONES.
> (The word *one* is not necessary. How many John Joneses are there in this incident?)
>
> *Person of the first part, hereby, whereas,* and *perpetrator* are all examples of unnecessary legalese.

There is a move among some in the legal profession toward the use of everyday language. In September 1989, the State Bar of California, Office of Communication and Public Affairs, reported that the Board of Governors

unanimously adopted a resolution that not only calls for lawyers and
legal organizations to simplify forms, documents and language used
in the practice of law, but also commits the bar to developing guidelines for attorneys and bar staff members to follow as the battle is
waged against "legalese."

Have you noticed that when you apply for an automobile loan, a homeowner's
loan, or a mortgage, in addition to receiving a copy of the loan or mortgage document, you also receive a sheet of paper or a pamphlet explaining what the larger
document means? This is because both federal and state laws and because juries
have sometimes been hesitant to enforce long contracts written in legalese.

How far will you go professionally? You won't go very far on glib word use
alone. Neither will you go very far if you have to search for the right word when
speaking or slow down for the exact word to document action. When two people
of similar ability and seniority are competing for advancement, word power counts.
In today's sophisticated criminal justice system, professionalism and the ability to
handle a variety of tasks are important.

Again, good language skills include accuracy, brevity, and clarity in speaking
and writing. It is not modern to fall back to the jargon that was sometimes accepted
in the past. Avoid long sentences, words of many syllables, passive rather than
active verbs, overworked terminology, high-flown but vague language, and referring
to a place rather than a person so that no one is responsible (e.g., This office is cognizant of the fact that ...).

Tax manuals and appliance instructions may seem unbelievably complicated,
but the trend is toward simplification. Military and legal papers used to almost defy
reading, but they are changing. Overworked comparisons, "doublespeak," euphemisms, and meaningless language occur nightly on television; however, such language is used for a time and then is gone. The writings of criminal justice officials
must stand and be judged.

Following is an example of a recommendation written by a police officer:

Example:	Comment:
It has been my honored	How can a privilege be honored?
privilege to have been	Why not "worked with"?
intimately associated with	"Intimate" means what?
Lt. Mary Jones since this	
program was first initiated	Why not "began" instead of
at its inception.	six words meaning the same thing?
Although on the	
distaff side, she has	Do you even know what the
conducted herself in	word distaff means?
the proud tradition that	
has always characterized	But what has she done?
the Blanksville Police	What does all this verbiage
Department. I can with	mean?
impunity recommend her	"Impunity" is the wrong word.
for any position for	
which her particular	You still haven't said what
talents qualify her.	her qualifications are.

If you haven't read — or written — this sort of recommendation letter, you are more fortunate than most people. It might have been acceptable in the past, but in today's fast-moving criminal justice system, this type of writing will not help you to advance. Always use simple, direct language.

Old style:	Modern:
in view of the fact that	as
until such time as	until
the question as to whether	whether
he is a man who	he
this is a subject that	this subject
in the event of	when
initiate	start
finalize	finish, end
at your earliest convenience	soon
facilitate	arrange for
at the present time	now
for the reason that	because
in spite of the fact that	although
for sanitary purposes	for cleanliness
make inquiry regarding	ask
a great deal of the time	often
with reference to	about
it is believed	I (or a definite name) believe(s)
for the purpose of	for
in connection with	with
utilize, utilization	use
in the near future	soon (or definite date)
due to the fact that	because

There are many more such examples. Length is not strength. Some officers believe that if they can parlay five words into 25, the result will be more impressive. It will not. Cut out the fat.

Avoid Using Words or Phrases that Draw Conclusions

Many people use words or phrases in their reports that are really drawing conclusions or making assumptions. They often confuse this with documentation of factual information. Many of these conclusions that are inappropriately drawn by criminal justice personnel are legal conclusions that are properly determined by a judge, based on testimony. Criminal justice personnel are notorious for writing, "The defendant gave a spontaneous statement to me stating . . . ." There will probably be a major battle in court over whether the statement is admissible and was in fact a spontaneous statement. A much better report would include the facts that led the officer to conclude that it was a spontaneous statement.

Examples:

"As I approached the group of 10 people on the sidewalk fronting 123 Main Street, the defendant in the case later identified as Ian Trouble stepped forward from the crowd and stated, 'I punched him because he scratched my car.'" (The reader of the report will then be able to come to his or her own conclusion that this was in fact a spontaneous statement.)

"The suspect drove in a heedless and reckless manner." It would be much better to write, "The red Ford that Mr. Trouble was driving was clocked in excess of 55 mph in the 25-mph-posted zone, crossed the center line as he approached Main Street, swerved back to the right hand lane after crossing Main Street, and then swerved back to the second lane to avoid hitting a parked automobile before hitting a mailbox fronting 1234 Smith Street."

"The driver of the automobile made an excited utterance to me." This statement really doesn't tell us much. A better statement would be "When I pulled over Mr. Trouble's automobile at the corner of First and Main, I approached the automobile from the driver's side door. Before I could say anything, Trouble stated in a loud voice, 'I didn't see the little girl before I hit her. I didn't do it on purpose, it was an accident. I was scared so I kept going.' Trouble was wringing his hands, moving his head from side to side, and his voice was trembling as he said this, appearing to be distraught."

The last part of the sentence may be considered a conclusion but is really an inference based on the factual information that was presented. There are a number of other common areas in which criminal justice personnel confuse conclusions with facts. They include but are certainly not limited to:

> Plain view
> Suspicious behavior
> Probable cause
> Hindering prosecution
> Resisted arrest
> Suspect was nervous
> Suspect made a furtive gesture

Sometimes persons providing statements will draw conclusions in their statements. Example: "The automobile was traveling at a high rate of speed." The investigator needs to report the statement as given and then ask follow-up questions such as, "What led you to that conclusion?" The person may answer with facts such as the noise the vehicle was making, the fact that it was moving much faster than other vehicles, or other information that allows a reasonable person to infer that the vehicle was traveling at a high rate of speed. Of course, information that the person timed, clocked, or used a radar or laser gun to substantiate the speed is even more useful. The bottom line is to ask witnesses to provide you with the facts that led them to their inferences or conclusions.

Improve Your Vocabulary

Why improve your vocabulary if you are going to use only the simplest terms? Your knowledge of words is like an iceberg: very little of it shows on the surface, but others will assume that there is much more to it below. Every writer should consciously work on increasing his or her vocabulary.

There are three forums for vocabulary: speaking, writing, and reading. You need to master all three.

In speaking, you need to know the language of the streets, that is, local dialect and current slang. On most occasions, you will speak in simple, standard English, but the ability to blend in with others is invaluable at times.

In writing, you need to use the precise word. If a three- or four-syllable word is the only one that would be appropriate for a certain spot, use it — but explain it if any of your potential readers may not understand. In any case, always select the simplest word possible if a choice exists.

In reading, you need to be familiar with vast resources of vocabulary to draw upon. The act of reading itself will furnish much of this depth. Some words have many meanings, depending upon the situation. Seeing a word in context is the best way to understand its meaning or meanings.

Even if you are taking a classroom course and the text has a glossary of meanings, make your own list of words, and add to it each time a new word surfaces.

The dictionary habit is a good one, but it can also be abused:

1. A small dictionary is good only for a spelling and pronunciation guide. Because it is oversimplified, it will sometimes lead you astray on words.

2. Try to figure out the word first from associations in the sentence and from the breakdown of the word itself. Learn certain word roots, prefixes, and suffixes. Latin and Greek words and parts of words are commonly represented. Use the dictionary section on word roots, prefixes, and suffixes and you can then mix and match them to arrive at meanings. Examples of prefixes include *a-* (meaning less, not, or without), *ab-* (meaning from, away, or off), *ad-* (meaning motion or direction), *bi-* (meaning two), *bio-* (meaning life), *ex-* (meaning out of or off), *gyn-* (referring to woman), *poly-* (meaning many), or *uni-* (meaning one). Examples of suffixes include *-al* (denotes belonging to or pertaining to), *-ee* (denotes object of an action), *-ese* (to denote of or pertaining to a place or country), and *-ous* (meaning full of, abounding in, or having).

3. After you have done your preliminary detective work, check the dictionary to confirm your finds and to learn other possible uses. Use the dictionary as a tool. Try to memorize what you find out.

Why go to all this trouble if you already know most of the words used in criminal justice? It can help in terms of promotion as well as satisfaction. One analysis of civil service exams found that about one-fourth of the questions were based on vocabulary — and not just work-related terminology. A keen eye and ear for words add to professionalism.

The meaning is the most important thing about a word, but develop an ear for the sound of words as well. It can be important in your work if you can identify a certain intonation as coming from a certain part of the country. You may find people prominent in academic and political circles saying "kin" for "can" or using other regionalisms. In fact, politicians sometimes deliberately speak colloquially in order to seem as if they are "just one of the folks." Others do it because they were raised in a particular region. Training yourself to pick up on and identify slang and dialects can prove very useful.

Synonyms, Antonyms, and Homonyms

Understanding synonyms, antonyms, and homonyms will aid your writing and may even help you to pass civil service tests. Be sure that you know the meaning of each.

1. Synonyms are words with similar meanings. Note that exact synonyms are rare because there are gradations in meaning.

   Examples: fearful, afraid, frightened, scared, terrified

2. Antonyms are words having opposite meanings. Again, note that not many words are exactly opposites.

   Examples: confident — insecure; good — bad; hot — cold

3. True homonyms are words that are spelled and sound alike but have different meanings.

   Examples: pole, roll, and head

   Closely related to homonyms are homophones, which are words pronounced alike but are different in meaning.

   Examples: to, two, too; lean, lien; fair, fare; there, their

Common usage combines both homonyms and homophones into the term homonyms. As you can imagine, *homonyms* cause trouble in spelling and word choice. Law enforcement officers are notorious for using homonyms in reports that cause considerable laughter in court. These incorrect terms are sometimes called "policese." The following examples show how a misused word in a report could cause the writer much embarrassment in court.

Examples:

At the time of the raid, the nightclub was filled with *miners*.
(*Miners* refers to those who dig for ore; *minors* refers to those under the age of majority.)

The building was *raised* by the explosion.
(*Raised* means lifted, but *razed* means demolished.)

The *kernel* returned to the barracks at 0800.
(Corn has *kernels*; the army has *colonels*.)

We confiscated the *heroine*.
(*Heroine* refers to a female hero; *heroin* is a narcotic.)

The accident victim was *pail* and shivering.
(A *pail* is a container; *pale* means pallid.)

The splintered door *jam* was evidence of the forced entry.
(*Jam* is a form of jelly; *jamb* refers to the upright surface surrounding a door.)

If you have written or approved a report without correcting its errors, then the report may be submitted with the Latin term *sic* in brackets after such obvious errors. The following list of homonyms and other words that are often confused with one another may help you avoid the pitfalls of poor report writing. The definitions given below are far from complete; they provide only a sense of how far apart the meanings are. Because a computer recognizes any word that is correctly spelled, this can lead to ridiculous results. Keep in mind that some regional differences in pronunciation may mean that some words that are homonyms to one person may not be pronounced exactly the same by someone else, or a speaker may (mis)pronounce them in the same way. All of these words were gleaned from actual reports with incorrect usage:

a bet (wager)
abet (encourage or support, usually in
   wrongdoing)

accept (receive willingly; believe)
except (excluding, only)

adapt (adjust to the situation)
adopt (choose; take as one's own)

all ready (prepared)
already (previously)

all together (everyone or everything in one
   place)
altogether (thoroughly)

allusion (implied or indirect reference)
illusion (action of deceiving; misleading
   image)

all ways (every way possible)
always (invariably; forever)

altar (an elevated place where religious rites are performed)
alter (change; make different)

appraise (set a value on; evaluate)
apprise (tell; inform)

are (plural form of verb to be)
hour (sixty minutes)
our (plural form of my)

ascent (act of rising or climbing)
assent (consent)

assistance (help)
assistants (helpers)

bail (security given for release from imprisonment pending due appearance; to clear water by dipping and throwing)
bale (large, closely pressed package or bundle)

bare (nude; unadorned)
bear (to carry; a large mammal)

bazaar (a fair for the sale of goods)
bizarre (odd, strange; fantastic)

beat (to win; to hit)
beet (vegetable)

bite (grip or hold with the teeth)
byte (8 bits form a byte in computer language)

boar (male swine)
bore (pierce with turning movement; tiresome person; uninteresting)

board (piece of wood)
bored (uninterested)

boarder (person who pays for daily meals and lodging)
border (edge of an area; separating line)

brake (stop; something used to slow down)
break (separate into parts with force; exceed)

bread (baked and leavened food)
bred (produced by hatching or gestation)

bridal (relating to a wedding)
bridle (gear for a horse)

but (yet; on the other hand)
butt (slang for buttocks; person that is an object of derision; to strike)

buy (purchase)
by (next to; through the agency of)
bye (side; incidental; used to express farewell)

cache (a hiding place)
cash (money)

capital (punishable by death; assets; upper-case letter)
capitol (building in which legislature meets)

ceiling (the surface overhead in a room)
sealing (closing)

cent (monetary unit)
sent (caused to go; caused to happen)
scent (smell)

cereal (relating to grain)
serial (a work appearing in parts at intervals)

chord (three or more musical tones sounded simultaneously)
cord (unit of wood cut for fuel)

cite (name in a citation; summons to appear in court; call to someone's attention)
sight (vision)
site (place; location; scene)

coarse (rough)
course (path of movement; class)

colonel (military rank)
kernel (seed or part of a seed)

core (center)
corps (organized military subdivision; group of persons under common direction)

corner (angle; where converging lines, edges, or sides meet)

coroner (public officer who handles deaths that may not be due to natural causes)

council (assembly; administrative body)

counsel (advise)

currant (fruit)

current (recent; flow)

dear (someone close)

deer (an animal)

disburse (to pay out from a fund)

disperse (scatter; disseminate)

decent (modestly clothed; marked by moral integrity)

descent (derivation from an ancestor; process of lowering)

dual (two; double)

duel (combat between two persons)

elicit (draw out, derive)

illicit (unlawful)

fair (just, unbiased; fine; blond; exhibition)

fare (payment; get along; diet)

formally (in a formal manner)

formerly (previously)

forward (toward; ahead)

foreword (preface; introductory statement)

gamble (stake; risk money)

gambol (skip; frisk about)

gorilla (animal)

guerrilla (irregular warfare)

great (unusually or comparatively large, notable)

grate (a guard or framework; to irritate; to grind by rubbing on something rough)

groan (a low mournful sound uttered in pain or grief)

grown (the past tense of grow or an adjective indicating such action)

heard (perceived by ear)

herd (a group of animals together)

heroin (narcotic)

heroine (female hero)

hoarse (husky, raucous)

horse (large, hoofed animal)

hole (perforation; gap opening)

whole (complete, total, entire)

idle (inactive)

idol (object of worship)

insure (buy or give insurance)

ensure (guarantee; protect)

its (possessive pronoun)

it's (contraction of it is)

jam (obstruct; force into; fruit substance)

jamb (upright surface forming the side of an opening, such as a door or window)

key (used to lock or unlock; fundamental)

quay (landing place for ships)

knew (was aware of the truth of)

new (recent; modern)

knot (problem; bond of union; one nautical mile per hour)

not (word used to make a word or group of words negative)

know (to have understanding of)

no (denial; hardly any)

lead (metallic element)

led (directed; past tense of lead)

leak (escape through an opening)

leek (bulbous garden herb)

lean (incline; lack of fat)
lien (charge upon property for debt)

lessen (to reduce in size, extent, or degree)
lesson (a piece of instruction)

liable (responsible; subject to)
libel (a defamatory statement that conveys an unjustly unfavorable impression)

loan (money lent at interest; grant of temporary use)
lone (solitary; only; isolated)

loose (not tight)
lose (suffer loss; not win—supposed to be pronounced "looz")

made (cause to happen)
maid (unmarried girl or woman; female servant)

main (important; chief; pipe or duct for water)
mane (long hair growing on the back)

marital (of or relating to marriage)
marshal/marshall (officer of a judicial district)
martial (war-like; martial law: law administered by government in emergency)

meat (flesh of an animal)
meet (to come upon; athletic competition)

medal (commemorative award)
meddle (interfere without right or propriety)
metal (natural ore material)

miner (digger of ore or metal)
minor (comparatively unimportant; under the age of majority)

muscle (body tissue; brawn)
mussel (marine animal)

naval (having to do with ships)
navel (umbilicus)

oar (paddle)
or (conjunction)
ore (dug from ground)

offal (parts of butchered animal not considered edible by humans; carrion)
awful (inspiring fear; dreadful; terrible)

ordinance (order; a municipal regulation)
ordnance (military supplies including weapons and ammunition)

pail (bucket)
pale (dim; pallid)

pain (punishment; grief; hurt)
pane (piece, section, or side of something)

pair (two similar or associated things)
pare (to trim off)
pear (fruit)

pause (temporary stop)
paws (feet of an animal)

peace (tranquility)
piece (part; slang for firearm)

peal (loud ringing of church bells)
peel (skin of a fruit; to remove by stripping)

pedal (lever pressed by the foot)
peddle (sell or offer for sale)

peer (equal; gaze)
pier (landing place in a harbor)

personal (relating to the person or body; private)
personnel (persons)

plain (to be simple; ordinary)
plane (airplane; level surface; wood working instrument)

pore (a minute opening as in the skin; read or study carefully)
pour (to flow from a container)

pray (address God or a god)
prey (attack)

presence (being present)
presents (gifts)

pride (inordinate self-esteem; group of
    lions)
pried (nosily inquired; raised or moved
    with a lever)

principal (school official; main)
principle (theory)

quiet (not noisy; calm)
quite (completely; positively)

rain (water drops)
reign (to rule)
rein (to guide a horse)

raise (lift; an increase in paycheck)
rays (light given off by the sun)
raze (tear down; demolish)

read (past tense of read)
red (color)

real (genuine)
reel (turn round and round; lively dance)

right (correct; opposite of left)
rite (ritual)
write (to put words to paper)

ring (circular band as in wedding ring;
    to cause a sound as a doorbell; an athletic
    enclosure)
wring (twist forcibly)

road (path)
rode (past tense of to ride)
rowed (propelled a boat)

role (part played by an actor or singer;
    function)
roll (list of names; to put a wrapping
    around)

sail (to travel on water in a boat)
sale (transfer of ownership for a price; sell-
    ing at a reduced price)

scene (locale, place)
seen (past participle of see)

seam (junction)
seem (appear)

shone (illuminated-past tense of shine)
shown (past participle of show)

shoot (to propel; to effect by blasting)
chute (a quick descent; a passage through
    which things must pass)

shutter (solid or louvered cover for a
    window; a means of opening and closing
    a camera lens)
shudder (to tremble convulsively)

stake (keep under observation as in a
    stakeout; cash to use for a wager;
    provide money for; pointed object
    driven into the ground or a vampire's
    heart)
steak (a piece of meat)

stale (tasteless from age; tedious from
    familiarity)
steal (wrongfully taking property of
    another)
steel (a form of iron)

stationary (not moving)
stationery (paper supplies)

straight (unbending)
strait (a water passageway)

tail (to follow; rear end)
tale (account; story; falsehood)

taught (instruction in)
taut (pulled tightly)

team (persons together in work or
    activity)
teem (abound)

their (possessive pronoun)
there (that place)
they're (contraction of they are)

through (finished; into and out of)
threw (past tense of to throw)

to (preposition, indicator of infinitive)
too (also; excessively)
two (the number 2)

track (trail; detectable evidence of passage)
tract (an indefinite stretch or defined area of land; religious pamphlet)

udder (mammary gland, particularly of cows)
utter (speak; absolute, as in utter desperation)

vain (excessively proud)
vein (tube conveying blood; mass of igneous rock; mood, as in a serious vein)
vane (device for showing the direction of the wind)

vary (change; diversify)
very (exceedingly)

vial (container for liquids)
vile (despicable)

waist (middle of the body above the hips)
waste (squander; trash)

wait (stay in place in expectation of)
weight (something heavy; burden)

waive (relinquish; release)
wave (move to and fro)

ware (goods, merchandise)
wear (have on one's person)
where (in which place)

weakly (feebly)
weekly (happening every seven days)

weather (climatic conditions)
whether (if)

whose (possessive form of who)
who's (contraction of who is)

wood (hard substance making up stems and branches of trees)
would (past tense of will)

wrap (cover or enclose in material)
rap (sharp knock; slang for talk; type of music)

your (possessive form of you)
you're (contraction of you are)

This, though far from complete, may be the most important list in this book. All too often similar words are used in place of the word you really want, resulting in misspelling of the intended word. Because dialects vary from region to region, words can also be spelled incorrectly because of regional pronunciations. The result is often amusing, but not to the person whose credibility is impeached.

The misuse of the word must stand as given with *sic* (meaning *thus*), calling attention to the error. This information is never erased from the record or the minds of the jury.

It is obvious that misusing a homonym or similar word would completely change the intended meaning. Be very careful to use the correct word. If you have any doubts about a word, look it up in the dictionary. Dependence on a computer to check your spelling or grammar is playing reporting roulette. The computer will alert you to transposed letters and spellings of words that do not exist. But if the word is an actual word, however ridiculous it is in the context, your computer will accept it. New generations of spell-checking programs are making progress in alerting the user to the misuse of homonyms but they are still far from perfect. It pays to develop a sensitivity to words and their meanings. People outside of the criminal justice field often confuse words such as interview and interrogate, even robbery and burglary. It can be a fascinating hobby as well as a means of advancement in your field to strengthen your ability to use words.

Jargon

Jargon refers to

> a hybrid language or dialect simplified in vocabulary and grammar used for communication between peoples of different speech; the technical terminology or characteristic idiom of a special activity or group; obscure and often pretentious language marked by circumlocutions and long words.

It is to your advantage to know the jargon in your own field, whether it is corrections, probation, parole, law enforcement, security, or one of the many government agencies.

1. Latin terms are common in medical and legal fields. Foreign terms are usually underlined or italicized, but some are so common that this is not always done. A few Latin terms used in criminal justice follow:

   Examples:

   ad hoc: "for this"; an ad hoc committee addresses one specific issue.

   bona fide: "in good faith"; no deception.

   habeas corpus: "you may have the body." Protects an accused by requiring that a person arrested be formally charged before a court.

   mandamus: "we command"; higher court orders lower court to enforce legal duty.

   per annum: "by the year."

   per diem: "by the day."

   per capita: "by the head"; individually.

   prima facie: "at first sight." Evidence appears valid but has not been proved; it is considered unless disproved.

   quasi: "seeming"; but not actual.

   sic: "thus." Appears in brackets or parentheses after words improperly used on reports, which are always transcribed as they appear in the original.

status quo ante: "as things were"; prior existing state.

subpoena: "under penalty." Writ often used to summon a witness.

subpoena duces tecum: a type of subpoena to request evidence or documents used in court.

Two abbreviations from the Latin are often used and abused:

i.e. "*id est*"; that is

e.g. "*exempli gratia*"; for example

Note that these two abbreviations do not mean the same thing. Do not substitute one for the other.

2. Police jargon simplifies communications in memo writing, but it should be avoided when reports might reach people that are not in the field (e.g., a jury):

    Examples:

    watch: time period

    CADS: computer-aided dispatch system

    latents: fingerprints scarcely discernible but developed for study

    RMS: records management system

    stakeout: surveillance of an area or person suspected of criminal activity

    perpetrator or perp: person committing a crime

    wagon: tow wagon or police van

3. Corrections, probation, and parole jargon differs from law enforcement jargon.

    Examples:

    active listening: Necessary while interviewing, not only to ask questions and record replies, but to be sure that answers are completely understood and to ask more, if needed.

    aging out: Point reached when offenders begin to realize that they do not want to repeat criminal activity.

    caseload: Number of cases handled by an officer.

client: Term used to refer to probationers or parolees.

confidentiality: Where PSIR is available to the public, this indicates the existence of sensitive issues that may involve safety of individuals.

electronic monitoring: Use of various devices that monitor an offender without incarceration (thus reducing prison overload and cost).

equity: Fairness; not discriminating against certain groups or against public interest.

MIS: Management Information Systems for databases.

OBCM: Objectives-Based Case Management, by which supervising officer sets behavioral objectives. After a set time, a review takes place.

PSIR: Presentence investigation report by the probation officer to provide information for the court.

4. Security jargon varies with the type of employer — airport, business, hotel, hospital, etc. Here are a few examples:

Examples:

ASIS: American Society for Industrial Security (includes many fields).

foreseeable problem: Basis for many suits due to lack of correction of situation that a person "should have seen coming."

IAHS: International Association for Hospital Security.

incident report: Includes any event out of the ordinary (the event reported does not necessarily have to be illegal); sometimes called case reports, and, in illegal situations, offense reports.

internal shrinkage: Most often used in department stores and other businesses; refers to losses caused by an employee's taking of money and/or merchandise. Defalcation is the term used by some businesses.

key control: Exchange of keys from one officer to another (should always be referred to in logs).

parking reminder: Usually a first-offense note.

party line: Bound or loose-leaf notebooks used to record incidents and keep officers up-to-date. (Should be required reading on entering duty.)

security discrepancy notice: Notice of dangers left by guard (e.g., failure to lock up).

shoplifting: Removing goods from a business without paying for them.

shorts and overs: Shortage or overage of monies from the amount shown on cash register total.

slip-and-falls: Customer or employee accidents. (May result in large suits against the company or organization.)

unit: One-person guard, sometimes referred to as Unit #____.

unattended death: Death that occurs without a doctor being in attendance — a serious concern in hotels, hospitals, etc.

5. Subculture slang is perhaps the most difficult type of jargon to record because it not only changes rapidly over time but also varies from coast to coast. It can also be exported from one geographic area to another. It includes slang used by gangs, street people, police, drug users, and other groups who use expressions not common to society in general. Actually, terms once used by gangs may show up and be understood by people not in the subculture. An example would be the use of "dis," first used by gangs, later used by television commentators.

   Example:

   "He *dissed* me." This was an excuse for a gang shooting because the victim showed disrespect for the person who considered himself superior.

   Recording of slang is a risky business because it changes not only from one class of people to another, but also from place to place and time to time. The following were used in various parts of the country fairly recently:

   Examples:

   bazuko: cocaine paste

   beeper boy: young drug dealer who uses a beeper to make contact with his customers

   bloom: marijuana; also *skunk*, and *blunt* which refers to a joint

   creep defense: if a person is already known as the type to take advantage, a date should have expected sex as part of the evening

   Dirty Harriet: a woman officer who overreacts

   glading: sniffing household products such as glue or Freon to get high; also known as *huffing* and *bagging*

   HIV roulette: unprotected sexual contact

roid rage: unusual irritability, a reaction to use of steroids, also known as gorilla juice

TLB: tough little broad

3 7 77: code formerly used by vigilantes in the nineteenth century, which some claim is now used by militia to threaten death, referring to dimensions of a grave, 3′ by 7′ by 77″

Gang slang is often used for two reasons: to identify members of the same group by language that excludes others, and to express contempt or even suggest bodily harm for those who do not belong. On the other hand, language that is sexist, racist, or ageist (language that is prejudice against an age group, particularly the elderly) may be unintended by the writer, but resented by those described.

Older Examples:

187: usually in graffiti, means to kill, relating to the California Penal Code section for homicide (a slash across a rival gang name can mean the same thing)

20 cents: $20.00 worth of cocaine

bo: marijuana

crack: rock cocaine

cuz or cuzz: what gang members call each other

doin' a rambo: armed attack on a person

dusted: under the influence of PCP (also called angel dust)

head hunter: a female who performs sexual acts for cocaine (in the business world, this is a term for a person who finds people for legitimate executive jobs)

Jim Jones: marijuana that is laced with cocaine or PCP

kibbles and bits: crumbs of cocaine

rock house: place where rock cocaine is sold

You can connect current events with many of the above terms in use in the late 1980s and early 1990s. What's next? Gang members usually are in the 14–24 age range. Young people of the same age often understand gang graffiti that older people take to be meaningless gibberish. In any criminal justice position, it is beneficial to know local slang, as slang terms vary from coast to coast and are influenced by the dominant ethnic groups of the region.

Avoiding Sexism

Only a few decades ago, *he* was accepted as a generic term referring to a man or a woman. At that time very few women were law enforcement, security, corrections, probation, or parole officers. The general public had not had its consciousness raised to see the need to protest, much less to write carefully.

Now, you can't afford to be careless and risk a suit, or at least a condemnation of your attitude. It's not very difficult to supply alternate and more acceptable terms.

In place of this:	Use this:
fireman	firefighter
mail man	mail carrier
man hours	worker hours
manpower	workforce
steward/stewardess	flight attendant
workmen's compensation	workers' compensation

Sometimes changing material into the plural gets around the problem:

A probation officer should justify *his* or *her* recommendations. Everyone has *his* or *her* job description.	Probation officers should justify *their* recommendations. Staff members should have *their* job description.

Avoiding Racism

Sensitivity has grown in this area so much that even well-meaning people may find themselves in trouble. What was acceptable last year may not be acceptable this year, and something previously frowned upon can return to favor.

The writer should be sensitive to how racial or ethnic groups wish to be named. Clearly, in this, the second decade of the twenty-first century, there is no place for names that individuals believe are demeaning. For example, Native Americans now prefer that specific descriptive name to terms that were used 25 or 50 years ago.

Considering Ageism

Many older people object to the euphemism, *senior citizen,* despite its frequent use. "As opposed to what?" a white-haired woman said. "I do not know any junior citizens! I do not mind being called old. When you are 85, you know you aren't in your salad days. And when I die, I expect to die, not 'pass away'!" She objected strongly to the patronizing attitude some people take. She said, "One officer said to me when I hesitated which direction to take, 'May I help you, young lady?' That's just too silly, but you would be amazed how many people call you that."

Often older people are proud of their precise age, but most of them object to *old man* or *old woman*. Very few resent being called *elderly*, which suggests a tendency toward being old and connotes a deserving of respect.

Semantics

This is the study of how people change words and how words change people. Politicians and advertisers often search for emotionally laden words that will persuade the public to buy their program or product. Scrutinize words for changes in meaning. Read or listen carefully for terms that are used to sway your opinion, and try not to slant your own words.

Nonverbal Communication

Law enforcement, security, probation, parole, and corrections officers also need to study the body language people cannot avoid in interpersonal communication. Words may lie, but signals sent out involuntarily by the body are likely to tell the truth.

Dr. Richard L. Weaver II, author of several books and articles on interpersonal communication, states that in a normal conversation, words carry less than 35 percent of social meaning. In an interview or interrogation, it is especially important to look for behaviors that do not agree with words.

A probation officer interviewing a client may find a man using words that will put him in a good light. He may profess eagerness to get a job, but his slouching position and untidy clothes show a lack of effort. Both spoken and unspoken communication should be noted. Actions often do speak louder than words.

Developing Your Vocabulary

It is important to study vocabulary words in order to interpret more clearly what you read and hear. The following list of study suggestions should help you master vocabulary skills:

1. Find a book that helps build relationships between words (several are listed in Appendix C).

2. Keep lists of words, roots of words, prefixes, and suffixes. Write them in sentences. Use the 3 × 5″ card method discussed earlier in this text.

3. Look for key words in newspaper and magazine articles. *Police Chief, Time, Reader's Digest,* and *Wall Street Journal* will provide you with a

variety of words used in different fields. Read frequently. Do not just let it wash over you — think about what you read.

4. Say the words aloud. Get someone involved with you; study with your spouse or partner, using bits of time such as while driving to work.

5. Use a good dictionary, and do not be satisfied with learning just the first meaning listed for a word.

6. Hunt down the source of words to help you remember. (This can be so interesting that it may become a fascinating hobby. For example, the word *assassin* comes from the Arabic *hashshashin*, or eaters of hashish).

7. Develop a feeling for nouns and verbs. Adjectives and adverbs give value judgments. Do not write: "He seemed very nervous." Giving more concrete details, the observation might look like this: "He kept looking over his shoulder as he talked. His left eye twitched, and his lips trembled."

8. Listen carefully to people from all walks of life and from various countries and regions. Try to distinguish words and ways that set these people apart.

9. Do not get word-happy. Keep your word bank to draw on, but do not show off your wealth. Being able to put the exact word in the precise place is your goal.

It is important to remember that in face-to-face conversation you receive information from nonverbal sources as well as from verbal communications. If the person you are talking with does not understand something, he or she can ask you for clarification. If the person "makes a face" or uses some other gesture or expression, you can clarify your point on your own. You can also determine whether the person is understanding your point by the direction of the conversation. With written communications you are not privy to such helpful cues. What you write will be interpreted from the reader's own point of view. It is therefore crucial that you write in a manner that is as clear as possible.

Summary

1. Your written language can help determine how clearly you think, how logically you act, and how far you will go professionally.

2. Administration of justice depends on every person not only acting on behalf of the public good, but also documenting all action.

3. Because mental processes are dependent upon words, a vocabulary test is often used as a quick method of determining a person's level of intelligence.

4. If your word choice reflects prejudice or involves euphemisms or stereotypes, your thinking and writing will not be clear or accurate.

5. Communication depends on who says what to whom and with what effect, depending on tone, semantics, body language, active listening, biases, and the situation.

6. Unclear writing is composed of many things: very long sentences, words of many syllables, passive rather than active words, jargon and overworked terminology, and sometimes even unrelated and illogical writing. While sometimes correct grammatically, unclear writing has no place in reports.

7. Get a good dictionary. From it you can learn word roots, various word meanings, and pronunciation.

8. Try to understand a word from its context, then confirm your ideas and look for additional meanings in the dictionary. Study synonyms, antonyms, and homonyms (including homophones).

9. Words change over a period of time, depending on where the word is used (for example, *discipline* means one thing in military circles and another in academic circles).

10. Train your ear to distinguish regional pronunciation. Learn the language of the streets, current slang, and terms used by various cultures and subcultures.

11. Involve all the senses in learning. Study vocabulary, preferably with another person. Learn by reading frequently and studying relationships between words.

12. Use words only to express, never to impress.

Chapter 12 — TEST

1. Criminal justice depends not only on every person acting on behalf of the public good, but also on the _____ of such action, whether that action is by a _____, _____, _____, _____, or _____.

2. If you misinterpret the words of another, your own action may become _____ and _____.

3. The term "damn hippie" is an example of _____, and "young transient" is an example of a(n) _____.

4. Stereotyping is holding a _____
_____.

5. Communication involves who says what to whom and with what effect, depending on:

    (a) _____, (b) _____, (c) _____, (d) _____,
    (e) _____, and (f) _____.

6. Give a more direct form for the following:

    (a) in view of the fact that _____

    (b) until such time as _____

    (c) at your earliest convenience _____

    (d) in the event that _____

    (e) at the present time _____

    (f) on the occasion of _____

    (g) initiate _____

7. Semantics is the study of _____
_____.

Abbreviating and Capitalizing

Abbreviating and capitalizing are treated together here because sometimes words are both abbreviated and capitalized. In fact, this is the case with most nationally accepted abbreviations. Both abbreviation and capitalization are also treated briefly in Chapter 3.

There is no substitute for checking all information available in your own field and agency. Abbreviation and capitalization vary widely from agency to agency, state to state, and service to service. The main point is to use the locally accepted form. If none is available, the cardinal rule is to be consistent in usage and explain the meaning of abbreviations whenever possible.

While many agencies have a prohibition in their report-writing manuals against using abbreviations, most people do use abbreviations. The important thing is not to use homemade abbreviations that are understood only by yourself or only in a limited region. Your private shorthand has no place in a report that must be read by others and may appear in court. It is also useful to point out the difference between abbreviations and acronyms. An *abbreviation* is a shortened form of a written word or phrase used in place of the whole (e.g., *Mon.* for Monday, *Lt.* for Lieutenant, *FBI* for Federal Bureau of Investigation). *Acronyms* are abbreviations that are pronounced as words and consist of initials or syllable components of other words (e.g., *AIDS* for *a*cquired *i*mmuno*d*eficiency *s*yndrome, *snafu* for *s*ituation *n*ormal, *a*ll "*f*ouled" *u*p).

Abbreviating to Save Time and Space

Ironically, while many agencies and departments have a prohibition against using abbreviations, they produce forms that do not have room for anything more than abbreviations. There are many standard abbreviations. You should make sure

DOI: 10.1016/B978-1-4377-5584-8.00020-7

that you use only standard abbreviations that will be understood by your readers. Avoid using your own made-up abbreviations or ones that are limited to your agency. The following are some commonly used abbreviations; variations are noted. Keep in mind that your agency may have different requirements and uses:

A&B	assault and battery	E/B	eastbound
AIDS	acquired immunodeficiency syndrome	EOW	end of watch
		F	female
AKA	also known as	FAX	facsimile
A/O	arresting officer	FBI	Federal Bureau of Investigation
APB	All Points Bulletin	FI	field interview
ASIS	American Society of Industrial Security	FIL	Filipino
		FU	follow-up
ATT	attempt or attempted	GOA	gone on arrival
B/A	breathalyzer	GRN	green
BAC	blood alcohol content	GSW	gunshot wound
B/C	broadcast	HAW	Hawaiian
BFV	burglary from vehicle	HZL	hazel
BLK	black (also BK)	HBD	had been drinking
BLU	blue (also BL)	HISP	Hispanic
BMV	bureau of motor vehicles	H&R	hit and run
BRN	brown (also BR)	IBR	incident-based report
CADS	computer-aided dispatch system	ID	identification
CAPT	captain	IND	Indian
CAUC	Caucasian	INJ	injury
CFBD	cared for by driver	IQ	intelligence quotient
CHI	Chicano (sometimes used for Chinese)	I/S	intersection
		JPN	Japanese (also JPSE)
CHIN	Chinese	JUV	juvenile
CHPA	Certified Healthcare Protection Administrator	KOR	Korean
		L/F	left front
CPO	Certified Protection Officer	LIC	license
CPP	Certified Protection Professional	LNU	last name unknown
		L/R	left rear
CTS	credit for time served	L/T	left turn
DEFT	defendant	LT	lieutenant
DEL	delivery	M	male
DET	detective	MAJ	major
DMV	Department of Motor Vehicles	MAN	manufacturer
DNA	deoxyribonucleic acid (formerly referred to as "does not apply")	MC	motorcycle
		M/J	missing juvenile
		MO	*modus operandi*, method of working
DOA	dead on arrival		
DOB	date of birth	MPH	miles per hour
DP	data processing	MS	motor scooter
DUI	driving while under the influence (of alcohol or drugs)	N/A	not applicable
		NARC	narcotics
		N/B	northbound
DWI	driving while intoxicated	NCIC	National Crime Information Center
E	east		

NMI	no middle initial	RPO	report by probation or parole officer
OBTS	offender-based tracking system	R/R	right rear
OIC	officer-in-charge	R/T	right turn
OPV	official police vehicle	S	south
PC	penal code	SAC	Strategic Air Command or Special Agent-in-Charge
PC	probable cause	S/B	southbound
PED	pedestrian	SGT	sergeant
PI	point of impact	SOR	supervised on own recognizance
PO	parole, police, or probation officer	SUS	suspect (also SUSP)
POLYN	Polynesian	T/A	traffic accident
PSI	Presentence Investigation Report (also PSIR)	TNT	trinitrotoluene
PTGSE	Portuguese	TRO	temporary restraining order
Q&R	questioned and released	T/T	teletype
R/C	radio call	UNK	unknown
R&D	research and development	V	victim
REC	record	V	vehicle (also VEH)
R/F	right front	VIET	Vietnamese
RMS	record management system	VIS	victim's impact statement
RO	records only, repeat offender, reporting officer, or registered owner	W/B	westbound
		W/O	without

Numbers and Codes Used for Abbreviation

Numbers and codes may be used with the supposition that they are understood only by a restricted number of individuals. However, *10-4* is a fairly common response that means a communication has been received and acknowledged. Other codes may vary widely. In one jurisdiction *Code Zero* may mean officer in trouble while in another jurisdiction, *10-15* may mean the same thing.

Hospitals, hotels, museums, airports, and other places sometimes use color codes or codes that sound like a person's name to call for help to avoid alarming the public. *Code blue* could mean a serious emergency, but another code or number could have the same meaning. "Mr. Stanley Pippen, you have a telephone call in the main lobby" may be a code instructing security to report to the main lobby.

Clarify Abbreviations

If you receive a communication from another agency, department, county, or another state, you will realize how often confusion can exist due to abbreviation. Does *V 1* mean *victim 1* or *vehicle 1*? That is usually easily sorted out from the context, but how about *RO*, which can mean *reporting officer, records only, registered owner,* or *repeat offender*?

The codes used in radio communications and over public announcement systems by various agencies are a form of abbreviation that sometimes appears in criminal justice reports. The writer needs to explain the meaning of the abbreviation. For example, "This officer responded to a 10-49 (driving under the influence) on Wilson Street. The 10-49 was observed traveling in a northerly direction in a blue 2001 Mercury Sable ... ." In this way, those who are unfamiliar with your agency's codes will know that to which you are referring. Remember, reports may be read by many others besides people within your own agency.

Many government agencies are known only by their abbreviations, capitalized in writing and used in normal conversation. You surely know the FBI, and you probably have a vague idea what many others mean, but how many of the following can you identify with exact words?

AFIS	Automated Fingerprint Identification System
ATF	Bureau of Alcohol, Tobacco and Firearms
DEA	Drug Enforcement Administration
FBI	Federal Bureau of Investigation
FCC	Federal Communications Commission
INS	Immigration and Naturalization Service
NASA	National Aeronautic and Space Administration
NCIC	National Crime Information Center
NIBRS	National Incident-Based Reporting System
NRC	Nuclear Regulatory Commission
OSHA	Occupational Safety and Health Administration
UCR	Uniform Crime Reports
VCAP (VICAP)	Violent Crime Apprehension Program

Abbreviations of Latin Terms

Examples:
MO, *modus operandi* — the way in which something is done
etc., *et cetera* — and others and so forth
i.e., *id est* — that is
e.g., *exempli gratia* — for example

E.g. and *i.e.* are often incorrectly used for each other. If you are not sure of the usage, either look them up or use the English translation. Latin or any other foreign term is usually underlined or italicized, but abbreviations such as *MO*, *e.g.*, and *etc.* are used so often that they should not be underlined or italicized. *Etc.* should be avoided in most criminal justice reports.

Changing Rules

How can anyone lay down a hard-and-fast rule for abbreviating, capitalizing, or punctuating? The trouble is that the times and rules are always changing. What is accepted in one district or even in one office may not be accepted in the next. Current practice is to simplify, especially in forms, which abound in criminal justice work. Words of more than four letters are often abbreviated. Capital letters emphasize the abbreviation, and periods after capitalization are fast disappearing, but there are exceptions. The key is to consult an up-to-date source, abide by local usage, and be consistent. If you have any doubt of your reader's ability to understand the abbreviation, spell it out.

Here are some points to consider:

1. *Spell it out first.*

   If there is any chance of confusion, you should spell out the word the first time it is used, followed by the abbreviation or acronym in parentheses. Example: The Special Agent-in-Charge (SAC) introduced himself. He reported that the duties of the SAC include preparing the budget.

2. *Personal and military titles.*

   With personal and military titles, follow current use. There seems to be a growing acceptance of names without titles to indicate gender or marital state. If titles are used, Ms. is accepted for females when marital status is not important, is not known, or when the woman has indicated a wish to have that usage. The United States military abbreviates rank titles by fully capitalizing the abbreviation with no period following. Example: LT Smith. Other usage of rank titles may capitalize the first letter followed by the lower case and period: Example: Lt. Smith.

3. *Last name only.*

   Because on the face page you have identified people involved in the incident and listed them as male or female, personal titles are not needed. Some agencies may require the use of the complete name at the beginning of statement and then allow the use of only the last name subsequently. As mentioned in Chapter 3, in some agencies the entire last name is capitalized throughout reports to clarify and make reading easier.

4. *Titles and titles that follow a name.*

   Examples: *Dr., Jr., Sr., M.D., Ph.D.,* and *M.A.*

   When addressing an envelope, most offices still use Mr., Ms., Miss, or Mrs. (Using the title Ms. eliminates the need to investigate marital status for women, and is thus the most expedient way of handling addresses.) Titles such as *Ph.D., Psy.D., M.D.,* or *M.A.* follow the name, as do *Jr.* and *Sr.* In the case of a doctor, *Mary R. Brown, M.D.,* is the most common style with the salutation being *Dear Dr. Brown.* In the body of a report she may be referred to as *Dr. Brown, Doctor Brown,* or just *Brown.* It is never correct to write *Dr. John H. Brown, M.D.*

5. *Terms that describe a business when they are part of the firm's legal name.*

   Examples: Baxter Co.; John David, Ltd.; Charles & Sons; Badges, Inc.

   The abbreviation of *and* to an ampersand (&) is sometimes acceptable in the small blocks on the face page; however, if *and* is part of the legal name, it should not be abbreviated using an ampersand. Ltd. is a common abbreviation and is preceded by a comma.

Be Consistent

If you use the symbol # for *number* in one case and *pounds* in another, confusion is sure to result. Example: Suspect #1 weighed about 185#.

A few abbreviations are so well known and so unique that it would seem ridiculous to write them out. Not many people would write out *trinitrotoluene* for *TNT*.

Postal Abbreviations for States and Territories

Alabama	AL	Montana	MT
Alaska	AK	Nebraska	NE
American Samoa	AS	Nevada	NV
Arizona	AZ	New Hampshire	NH
Arkansas	AR	New Jersey	NJ
California	CA	New Mexico	NM
Colorado	CO	New York	NY
Connecticut	CT	North Carolina	NC
Delaware	DE	North Dakota	ND
District of Columbia	DC	Ohio	OH
Florida	FL	Oklahoma	OK
Georgia	GA	Oregon	OR
Guam	GU	Pennsylvania	PA
Hawaii	HI	Puerto Rico	PR
Idaho	ID	Rhode Island	RI
Illinois	IL	South Carolina	SC
Indiana	IN	South Dakota	SD
Iowa	IA	Tennessee	TN
Kansas	KS	Texas	TX
Kentucky	KY	Utah	UT
Louisiana	LA	Vermont	VT
Maine	ME	Virgin Islands	VI
Maryland	MD	Virginia	VA
Massachusetts	MA	Washington	WA
Michigan	MI	West Virginia	WV
Minnesota	MN	Wisconsin	WI
Mississippi	MS	Wyoming	WY
Missouri	MO		

According to the "Consumer's Guide to Postal Services and Products," the following format should be used for addressing letters and packages:

1. Abbreviate states as shown above. Also capitalize and abbreviate suffixes: AVE (Avenue), ST (Street), DR (Drive), RD (Road), PL (Place), and CIR (Circle).

2. Capitalize everything in the address.

3. Omit all punctuation in the address, except the hyphen between numbers, as in the ZIP + 4 Code.

4. Endorsements for special services should be placed above the delivery address or below the return address.

5. To expedite delivery, be sure to use the ZIP + 4 Code when available.

Two rules to remember:

1. If you are unsure about an abbreviation or if your reader may have a doubt about your use of an abbreviation, write it out. Remember: *When in Doubt, Write it Out.*

2. Check your agency for guidelines and be consistent in your own reports.

Capitalization

Do Not Over-Capitalize

A word of warning should be given here. Some people capitalize the first letter of words at random just as they sprinkle commas about for no reason. This is more likely to happen in handwritten documents such as security logs. Watch for this problem in yourself and in others under your direction.

General Rules for Capitalization

The following are common uses of capitalization:

1. The day of the week, the month, holidays, but not the season.

    Example:
    This fall, Veterans' Day is on Monday, November 10.

2. Proper nouns, initials, and titles when part of a name. A title preceded by *a, an, the, his,* etc. is written in lower case.

    Example:
    This unit is under the command of Captain John James.
    He is a captain, and his son is a sergeant.

3. Names of locations but not general directions.

    Example:
    The suspect turned south on West 33rd St.

4. Names of specific institutions but not general terms.

    Example:
    He attended several colleges before he graduated from Pepperdine University.

5. Names of specific courses but not general fields of study.

    Example:
    He took History 101 and Psychology 240.
    He took history, psychology, and English.
    (English is capitalized because it is from a proper noun.)

6. The principal words in titles of books or articles, but not articles *a*, *an*, or *the*, or short prepositions such *as of*, *on*, *in*, or *to*, or conjunctions such as *and*, *or*, or *if*, unless it is the opening letter in a title. The rule is not to capitalize prepositions and conjunctions of less than five letters. Capitalize even short verbs such as *Is* and *Be*.

    Example:
    Updike wrote *A Month of Sundays*.

7. The pronoun *I*.

    Example:
    Because of the darkness and fog, I could not determine in which direction the perpetrator fled.

Looking over the above points, you can formulate a rule to follow: Capitalize the specific, but not the general, use of a word.

Capitalizing and Indenting for Brevity and Impact

Everyone has seen the margin-to-margin type of report writing and knows how difficult it is to spot important facts. Headings and subheadings help the reader to spot the important points quickly. Review the headings and subheadings in Chapter 3. Capitalizing, indenting, and underlining are all means of emphasis. One good method is to capitalize and underline the main heading. Indent for the subheading; underline and capitalize only the main words. There is no need to put a colon after the headings.

Example:
<u>HEADING</u>
xxxxxxxxxxxxxxxxxxxxxxxxxxxxxxxxxxxxxxxxxxxx
xxxxxxxxxxxxxxxxxxxxxxxxxxxxxxxxxxxxxxxxxxxx
xxxxxxxxxxxxxxxxxxxxxxxxxxxxxxxxxxxxxxxxxxxx

<u>Subheading</u>
xxxxxxxxxxxxxxxxxxxxxxxxxxxxxxxxxxxxx
xxxxxxxxxxxxxxxxxxxxxxxxxxxxxxxxxxxxx

Skip a space between headings and subheadings. The extra space may seem wasteful, but it is not. It adds to the ease in reading and allows the reader to find important information quickly.

Professionalize your work with capitalization, indentation, and the use of headings.

Summary

1. Ask for a directive on locally accepted abbreviation and capitalization. If none exists, use a standard form and be consistent.

2. The following are commonly abbreviated: forms of address; rank and title; and names of states, days of the week, and months.

3. Capitalization of a word can sometimes be used for emphasis if your agency accepts this as a standard form. In some areas, the last name of a person previously identified in a report may be capitalized in full and used by itself in the narrative.

4. The most common uses for capital letters are these: the first letter of the day of the week, month, and holidays, but not the season; proper nouns, initials, and titles when part of a name; names of exact locations but not general directions; names of specific educational institutions but not general terms; names of specific courses but not general fields of study, as well as the main words in titles but not prepositions, conjunctions, or articles of less than five letters.

5. While foreign terms should be underlined or italicized, some abbreviations are so common that they are not underlined. Latin terms commonly used (MO for *modus operandi*, the way in which something is done, and etc., for *et cetera*) should not be underlined or italicized. Avoid the use of *etc.* in criminal justice reports because it is too general and may result in important information being left out.

6. If you are in doubt about your reader's ability to understand an abbreviation, at least spell out the term in full the first time that you use it. Thereafter, you may use the standard abbreviation for the term.

Chapter 13 — TEST

1. The main rule in both abbreviation and capitalization is to use the _____. If none is available, the cardinal rule is to be _____, and when in doubt, _____.

2. Abbreviation is more commonly accepted on the _____ than on the _____ or _____ pages of a law enforcement report.

3. List five standard uses of abbreviation by the general public:

    (a) _____

    (b) _____

    (c) _____

    (d) _____

    (e) _____

4. Capitalization can be used as an organizational tool for _____ and _____.

5. The most common uses for capitalization are:

    (a) _____

    (b) _____

    (c) _____

    (d) _____

    (e) _____

    (f) _____

6. One general rule is you can follow for capitalization is _____.

SECTION THREE

The Modernization of Report Writing

CHAPTER 14

Innovations and Predictions in Criminal Justice

Learning includes keeping up with innovations. At an annual meeting of the Academy of Criminal Justice Sciences several years ago, then director of the FBI, William S. Sessions, gave a preview of things to come. Sessions also paid tribute to the many academicians and practitioners in attendance by saying in part: "It is your research, your teachings and your practical ideas that help move the criminal justice system from perceived needs to working realities." While many of the areas Director Sessions covered as innovations are reality today, all of his points are still valid.

He stressed three specific needs: improving ways of identifying criminals, identifying crime trends, and improving ways of sharing information among law enforcement agencies. Shared information starts with collecting information and documenting it, usually in the form of a report. Thus, every individual in the criminal justice system can have an important impact on information sharing. Ironically, the FBI has faced recent criticism for problems within its crime laboratory, much of which, it turns out, is related to lack of or poor documentation and handling of evidence.

Identifying Criminals

Electronically sending and receiving fingerprint images through a planned automated image-retrieval system, as well as an automated latent system from a 20-million-print database, constitute a huge improvement over mailing inked cards. New laser identification systems allow for a person to place a finger on an electronic "reader" that is tied directly to a database of all fingerprints on file. This provides for immediate identification of persons who may be either suspects or victims.

283

DOI: 10.1016/B978-1-4377-5584-8.00021-9

The FBI, which receives the fingerprints for almost every felony arrest in the United States, is currently proceeding (although behind its original ambitious time line) with a project called NCIC 2000, which will add an automated fingerprint and arrest photograph (mug) capability to the National Crime Information Center (NCIC). The fingerprint system, called IAFIS (Improved Automated Fingerprint Identification System), when completed, will store all of the fingerprints the FBI has collected over the years in a single computerized fingerprint database. It will also store all new fingerprints received by the FBI, and will, for the first time, include prints for misdemeanor arrests. IAFIS is designed to allow law enforcement personnel and other authorized users anywhere in the country to obtain a rapid fingerprint identification and mug-shot photograph of anyone whose arrest has been entered into the NCIC system. As part of NCIC 2000, the FBI has contracted with major defense contractors to design and produce equipment that will allow officers to submit and check fingerprints and mug-shot photographs from any car in the field equipped with mobile data terminals.

Identifying Trends

Sessions, in his speech, observed, "What we really do, essentially, is to collect information. That's what investigation is all about." Previously, preservation of so much information was impossible, as was the exchange of information between so many agencies. Computers make collecting, sorting, and indexing information much more efficient and productive. They also facilitate the linking of agencies, and one investigation can lead to another. As Director Sessions stated, "The more we know, the more we can know." He gave the example of one investigation that linked eight American and nine Italian cities in drug operations. Computers have made the difference.

Computer systems such as the Organized Crime Information System (OCIS), Investigative Support Information System (ISIS), and Terrorist Information System (TIS) assist with the collection and analysis of needed information on inter-jurisdictional offenses. Expected in the future are developments on existing databases of artificial intelligence that will not only sort data, but also will be able to draw conclusions.

Computerized crime analysis is so closely linked to computerized crime-incident tracking that they almost seem to be the same. The most rudimentary type of crime analysis — i.e., "How many of each type of crime happened, where, and when" — flourished almost as soon as the first computer database was completed, replacing painstakingly hand-compiled analysis, which often used pin maps. This type of analysis, now computerized, is still the most commonly used, because it is easy to do and is very useful in determining how to allocate resources. It also can make an effective presentation to funding agencies at budget time.

With advancements in computer hardware and software, crime analysis has become more sophisticated, moving from printouts of statistics to the current practice of integrating crime analysis with Geographical Information Systems (GIS), which can produce easily updated, detailed maps displaying crime information.

Recently, analysis programs have been developed to make connections between a large number of seemingly unrelated facts, which may be spread out over a very large geographical area, helping to coordinate the investigative and enforcement efforts of many agencies.

Improving Ways of Sharing Information

Two important outgrowths of those early efforts are currently the largest law enforcement computer systems in the world, the National Crime Information Center (NCIC) and the National Law Enforcement Telecommunications System (NLETS, pronounced "inlets" by those who use it). These two immense systems are products of the early 1960s that are dedicated to law enforcement. Both NCIC and NLETS maintain computer networks that reach every state and territory in the United States, every federal and state law enforcement agency, and most municipal law enforcement agencies. They are also linked to the Royal Canadian Mounted Police network in Canada and the Interpol network in Lyons, France. Law enforcement agencies in other countries may also obtain limited information from these databases, but usually not directly.

NCIC is a product of the federal government, and is run by the FBI. It is a single large database containing almost all felony arrest information, and some of the misdemeanor arrest information from the entire United States for the last 30 years. It also contains information about stolen property and arrested or wanted persons.

In contrast to NCIC, NLETS has no databases of its own. NLETS functions by the voluntary linking of the computer systems of states and municipalities throughout the country. This permits law enforcement officers in one area of the country to check on criminal histories, drivers licenses, motor vehicle registrations, and other information from any other geographical area, or from the country as a whole. Their website (www.nlets.org) offers ways of contacting NLETS representatives for a given area.

In addition to adding fingerprints and photographs, a planned improvement for NCIC 2000 is to upgrade the Uniform Crime Reporting (UCR) system, a national computerized system, to the National Incident-Based Reporting System (NIBRS). UCR and NIBRS were discussed in Chapter 3. Although NIBRS is having to overcome considerable opposition from some of the reporting law enforcement agencies, it will store and produce far more information, lending itself to useful crime analyses. The NIBRS computer system itself is complete, and gradually more and more state and local agencies will implement NIBRS crime reporting.

Bringing together information from many different areas is a mission of the FBI. One interesting example of this is the Violent Criminal Apprehension Program (VICAP), which is a national clearinghouse for unsolved murders. There are a number of other specialized computer networks, such as the Western States Intelligence Network (WSIN) and the El Paso Information Center (EPIC), but access to these is closely regulated and they are of little interest to those outside their specialized areas.

Innovations

Translated Forms

Some innovations are as simple as the translation of forms into commonly used languages other than English. Figure 14.1 shows the Arizona Department of Public Safety's form documenting consent to search, written in English and Spanish on the front and back of the same form.

Figures 14.2 and 14.3 show the Honolulu Police Department's Suspect, Weapon and Vehicle Description form, HPD-458, in English and Japanese. A non-Japanese-speaking officer can use the forms with Japanese-speaking witnesses and victims to obtain suspect descriptions.

There are many telephone translator systems available to provide translation services in almost all spoken languages. A lot of major cities have 24-hour translation services available. In addition, many computer programs, including small hand-held devices, allow for translation of specific words and phrases. Figure 14.4 is a portion of a Point Talk® card. Point Talk cards contain phrases needed by law enforcement and EMS personnel in dealing with people who do not speak English. Each phrase is written in English and alongside is printed the same phrase in the any one of several languages. To use it, you simply point to the phrase in English and the person reads the question in his or her own language and replies by pointing to the appropriate phrase. A new CD-Rom version of the system is available in 40 languages.

Automation of Report Writing

Over the years there have been attempts to speed up or make easier the task of report writing. In 1972, the state of California attempted to unify a statewide reporting system through the "One-Write" plan. Under this system, the original field report, written or printed by hand by the initial investigating officer, was the only report used. Information taken in the field was recorded directly onto the report form. Information was not placed in the officer's notebook and then transcribed onto the report. After being approved by the officer's supervisor, the report was duplicated and distributed to the units or agencies that needed to follow up. Various agencies throughout the country use similar systems.

Many law enforcement agencies now use automated report form software such as Automated Law Enforcement Incident Report (ALEIR), which allows officers and investigators to enter reports from laptops in the patrol car. Some automated report-generating software programs allow a police officer or probation officer to enter necessary data, such as address, date of birth, names, and so on and then generate a narrative report. The advantages of these programs include efficiency, rapid submissions, and standardization. However, there are disadvantages that may include inaccuracies and wrong vocabulary usage. Care should always be taken when using automated report-generating software programs to be certain the report is accurate.

There have been changes in the face pages of reports. Many law enforcement agencies moved from a single report form for all offenses to a collection of many different forms — one for each major or common offense. As mentioned in the introduction, some agencies became overwhelmed with forms and have since or are now in the process of moving to fewer, more generic forms. The states of New Mexico and West Virginia obtained federal grants that allowed them to develop statewide forms for use by law enforcement agencies, standardizing the collection of crime data and statistics.

Almost all 50 states have moved to a statewide traffic accident report form for the same reasons. Many states also have legislative mandated report forms and reporting systems for use in investigation of crimes of special concern, such as spouse, child, or elder abuse.

Dictation of Reports

Dictations of reports have been used by various agencies with varying degrees of success. Many specialized units within agencies use such systems. Sometimes only taped statements of witnesses, victims, or suspects are transcribed. At present, dictation systems appear to be most successful in smaller agencies or in smaller units within larger agencies.

Arguments against dictation include the:

1. Possible loss or misinterpretation of information on recording media

2. Difficulty of finding and keeping adequate clerical staff to do the transcribing

3. Difficulty in making sure that reports are transcribed in a timely manner

4. Loss of the chain of evidence of the information in the report

5. Difficulty in getting reports signed by the investigator

Arguments in favor of dictation include:

1. Investigators can dictate faster than they can type; therefore, they can investigate more cases or spend time on preventive activities.

2. Professional typists are less expensive and turn out better products than do investigators.

Professional journals and magazines will most likely continue to document the development of agencies starting dictation programs at the same time others are giving it up. Appendix B gives an example of the instructions for dictating a report using a dictation system.

Figure 14.1
Sample Consent to Search Form — English/Spanish Version

ARIZONA DEPARTMENT OF PUBLIC SAFETY

DR No. _____

CONSENT TO SEARCH

I, _____ , have been requested to consent
          (print full name)

to a search of _____
                      (name the personal property item)

located at _____ .
                      (include full address)

I have been duly advised of my constitutional rights (1) to refuse such consent, (2) to require that a

search warrant be obtained prior to any search, (3) that, if I do consent to a search, any evidence found

as a result of such search can and will be used against me in any civil or criminal proceedings, (4) that

I may consult with an attorney of my choice before or during the search and (5) that I may withdraw my

consent to search at any time prior to its conclusion.

After having been advised of my constitutional rights, I hereby knowingly, intelligently and

voluntarily waive my aforementioned rights and consent to the search. I authorize

_____ and _____ ,
   (enter officer's name or badge #)   (enter officer's name or badge #)

officers of the Department of Public Safety, State of Arizona, to conduct the search.

_____   _____
Signature   Date

_____
Location

WITNESSES:

_____   _____   _____
Signature   Title   Date

_____   _____   _____
Signature   Title   Date

* Note: Spanish translation on other side of form.
* Distribution: Attach consent form to related departmental reports.

DPS 802-04042 3/89

Figure 14.1—*continued*

DEPARTAMENTO DE SEGURIDAD PUBLICA DE ARIZONA

DR No.

CONSENTIMIENTO PARA REVISION

Yo, _____ , habiendo recibido
(Escriba nombre completo en letra de molde)

la peticion para consentir a la revision de mi _____
(nombre el articulo)

localizado en _____
(incluya la direccion completa)

y habiendo sido informado de mis derechos constitucionales; 1) de rehusar tal consentimiento, 2) de re-

querir que una orden de cateo (revision) sea obtenida antes de cualquier revision, 3) que, si consiento

a una revision, cualquier evidencia que se encuentre como resultado de tal revision podra y sera usada

en contra de mi en procedimientos civiles o criminales, 4) que puedo consultar con un abogado que yo

escoja antes y durante la revision y 5) que puedo renunciar al consentimiento de revision a cualquier

tiempo antes de su conclusion.

Despues de haber sido informado de mis derechos constitucionales, por este medio, hago constar que

voluntariamente y con inteligencia renuncio a mis derechos mencionados arriba y doy mi consen-

timiento y autorizo a _____ y
(nombre y # de insignia del oficial)

_____ oficiales de Policia del
(nombre y # de insignia del oficial)

Departamento de Seguridad Publica del Estado de Arizona a que conduzcan una revision completa.

_____

FIRMA

_____

LUGAR Y FECHA

TESTIGOS:

_____

FIRMA, TITULO Y FECHA

_____

FIRMA, TITULO Y FECHA

* English translation on other side of form.

*Distribution: Attached consent form to related departamental reports.

Figure 14.2
Suspect, Weapon, and Vehicle Description (English)

HONOLULU POLICE DEPARTMENT

SUSPECT, WEAPON AND VEHICLE DESCRIPTION
(Please circle or fill in appropriate response)

TIME: _____ DATE: _____ POLICE REPORT NO. _____

SEX	Male Female Transvestite
RACE/ETHNICITY	Black/ Caucasian/ Chinese/ Filipino/ Hawaiian/ Japanese/ Polynesian/ Portuguese/ Samoan/ Other
AGE	Under 15/ 15-17/ 18-20/ Early, Late 20's 30's, 40's, 50's, 60's
HEIGHT	Under 5'0", 5'0", 2", 4", 6", 8", 10", 6'0", 2", 4"
WEIGHT	Under 100 lbs., 100, 120, 140, 160, 180, 200, 220, 240
BUILD	Thin Slim Medium Average Heavy Husky Muscular Fat

HAIR: Color
    Style
    Length
	Black Brown Blond Dirty Blond Red Gray White
	Straight Curly Wavy Afro Tied Neat Wig
	Crew Cut Neck Shoulder Length Long

EYES: Color
    Glasses
    Frames
	Black Brown Blue Green Hazel Gray
	Sunglasses Prescription Wire Frame Plastic Frame Rimless
	Clear Brown Black Gold Silver Other _____

COMPLEXION	Pale Fair Medium Ruddy Tanned Brown Black Clear Acne Pock-Marked
FACIAL HAIR **Color**	Mustache Beard Goatee Black Brown Blond Red Gray White
PECULARITIES	Walk Mannerisms Speech Accent Tattoos Scars Injuries Jewelry Other _____

CLOTHING

HAT
    Color
    Designs
	Baseball Cap Lauhala Hat Other _____
	Blue Red Yellow Brown Black Green Other _____
	Patches Feathers Ornamentation

SHIRT/BLOUSE
 	
    Sleeve Length
    Color
	Pullover T-Shirt Aloha Shirt Sport Shirt Dress Shirt Tank Top
	Other _____
	Short Sleeve Long Sleeve Sleeveless
	_____ Markings/Design _____

TROUSERS/SLACKS **Color**	Jeans Shorts Dress Slacks Sport Slacks Knit Pants Corduroy _____ Design _____ Striped __ Plaid __ Other _____
SHOES	Barefoot Slippers Dress Shoes Work Shoes Boots Sandals
DRESS **Color**	Short Dress Short Muumuu Long Muumuu Long Dress _____ Markings/Design _____
WEAPON **Container**	Handgun/ Revolver/ Automatic Pistol Rifle/ Shotgun/ Knife/ Other _____ Bag/ Paper Sack/ Other _____

VEHICLE
    Make
 	
    Color
    License No.
    Other I.D.
	Car/ Van/ Small Pickup/ Truck/ Motorcycle/ Moped/ Bicycle
	AMC/ Buick/ Chevrolet/ Chrysler/ Datsun/ Dodge/ Ford/ Mercury/ Oldsmobile/ Plymouth/ Pontiac/
	Toyota/ Volkswagen/ Other _____
	_____ Type: 2 Dr./ 4 Dr./ Station Wagon/ Hatchback
	_____ State _____ Color of Plate _____
	Describe: Rust/ Tires/ Upholstery/ Sunroof/ Other _____

INFORMATION PROVIDED BY: _____

HPD-458 (R-4/82)

Figure 14.3
Suspect, Weapon, and Vehicle Description (Japanese)

SUSPECT, WEAPON AND VEHICLE DESCRIPTION
HPD-458

ホノルル市警察本部
犯人の人相・着衣、凶器、自動車の種別等
（該当するものを○で囲むか、適当に記載して下さい）

事件発生の時刻 ＿＿＿＿＿日 PM ＿＿＿＿＿分頃
AM ＿＿＿＿＿分頃

__性別__　　　男、女、　　　　　男装、女装

__人種__　　黒人、白人、中国人、フィリピン人、ハワイ人、日本人、ポリネシア人、ポルトガル人、サモア人、その他
＿＿＿＿＿＿＿＿＿＿＿＿＿＿＿＿＿＿＿＿＿＿＿＿＿＿＿＿＿＿

__年齢__　　15歳以下、15～17、18～20、前半、後半 20代、30代、40代、50代、60代、

__身長__　　150cm以下、150cm 155、160、165、170、175、180、185、190

__体重__　　45、3kg以下、45、3kg 54、4 63、5 72、5 81、5 90、6 99、7 108、7

__体格__　　やせ型、細型、中肉、重量、ガッチリ、筋肉質、肥満型

__頭髪：色__ 黒、茶、ブロンド、くすんだブロンド、赤、グレイ、白

　　髪型　　直毛、カール、ウエーブ、チリチリパーマ、結んでいる、整髪、カツラ使用、

　　長さ　　短い角刈り、首まで、肩まで、長髪

__目：色__　黒、茶、青、緑、薄茶、グレー

　　眼鏡　　サングラス、態様、金属フレーム、プラスチック、フレーム、縁無

　フレーム　透明、茶、黒、金、銀、その他＿＿＿＿＿＿＿＿＿＿＿＿＿＿

__顔色__　　青白、通常、中間、赤、黄褐色、茶、黒、血色良、ぶつぶつ、あばた、

__ひげ__　　口ひげ、頬ひげ、やぎひげ、

　　色　　　黒、茶、ブロンド、赤、グレー、白

__特徴__　　歩きぐせ、癖、話し方、アクセント、入れ墨、傷痕、傷、装飾品

　　　　　　その他＿＿＿＿＿＿＿＿＿＿＿＿＿＿＿＿＿＿＿＿＿＿＿

__着衣__

帽子　　野球帽、ハワイ風麦わら帽子、その他＿＿＿＿＿＿＿＿＿＿＿＿

　　色　　青、赤、黄、茶、黒、緑、その他＿＿＿＿＿＿＿＿＿＿＿＿

飾り物　帽章、羽毛、装飾品、

__シャツ／ブラウス__　セーター、Tシャツ、アロハシャツ、スポーツシャツ、長袖正装シャツ、ランニングシャツ

　　　　　その他＿＿＿＿＿＿＿＿＿＿＿＿＿＿＿＿＿＿＿＿＿＿

袖丈　　半袖、長袖、袖なし

　　色　＿＿＿＿＿＿＿＿＿柄／デザイン＿＿＿＿＿＿＿＿＿＿＿＿＿＿

__ズボン／スラックス__　ジーンズ、短パン、背広下ズボン、スポーツスラックス、ニットパンツ、コールテン

　　色　＿＿＿＿＿＿＿デザイン＿＿＿＿＿＿＿ストライプあり＿＿＿格子じま＿＿＿

　　　　その他＿＿＿＿＿＿＿＿＿＿＿＿＿＿＿＿＿＿＿＿＿＿＿＿

__靴__　　はだし、スリッパ、ビジネスシューズ、労働靴、ブーツ、サンダル

__ドレス__　ショートドレス、ショートムームー、ロングムームー、ロングドレス

　　色　＿＿＿＿＿＿＿＿＿柄／デザイン＿＿＿＿＿＿＿＿＿＿＿＿＿

__凶器__　　けん銃、回転式けん銃、自動式けん銃、ライフル、ショットガン、ナイフ

　　　　その他＿＿＿＿＿＿＿＿＿＿＿＿＿＿＿＿＿＿＿＿＿＿＿

入れ物　バッグ、紙袋、その他＿＿＿＿＿＿＿＿＿＿＿＿＿＿＿＿＿

__自動車__　車両、バン、小型ピックアップ、トラック、自動二輪、原付自転車

メーカー　アメリカンモーターズ、ビューイック、シボレー、クライスラー、ダットサン、ダッジ、フォード、マーキュリー、オールズモービル、プリモス、ポンティアック

　　　　トヨタ、フォルクワーゲン、その他＿＿＿＿＿＿＿＿＿＿＿＿＿

　　色　＿＿＿＿＿＿＿＿型式、2ドアー、4ドアー、ステーションワゴン、ハッチバック

ナンバープレート　＿＿＿＿＿＿＿＿＿州＿＿＿＿＿＿＿プレートの色＿＿＿＿＿＿

その他の特徴　さび、タイヤ、車両装飾、サンルーフ、その他＿＿＿＿＿＿＿＿＿

（あなたのお名前）＿＿＿＿＿＿＿＿＿＿＿＿＿

Figure 14.4
Sample of Point Talk® Translation by Points

ENGLISH (INGGRIS)	INDONESIAN (INDONESIA)	ENGLISH (INGLES)	TAGALOG (TAGALOG)	ENGLISH (ENGLISH)	HMONG (HMOOB)	ENGLISH (ENGLISH)	MIEN (MIENH)
Give me your...	Berikan saya...	Give me your...	Ibigay mo ang iyong...	Give me your...	Muab koj...	Give me your...	Bun yie meih nyei...
• Driver's License	• Surat Izin Mengemudi	• Driver's License	• Lisensiya sa pagmamaneho	• Driver's License	• Daim ntawv tsav tsheb rau kuv	• Driver's License	• Niouv cien daan
• Picture I.D	• Kartu Identitas Berfoto	• Picture I.D	• I.D. na may retrato	• Picture I.D	• Daim duab Aisdis rau kuv	• Picture I.D	• Doix Dongh fangx
• Proof of Insurance	• Bukti Asuransi	• Proof of Insurance	• Prueweba ng seguro	• Proof of Insurance	• Povhawj is suslas rau kuv	• Proof of Insurance	• Beu ciouv zorng-zengx
• Registration	• Tanda Nomer Kendaraan	• Registration	• Rehistro ng kotse	• Registration	• Daim ntawv yuav tsheb rau kuv	• Registration	• Faaux mbuox daan
Write down your...	Tuliskan anda punya...	Write down your...	Isulat mo ang iyong...	Write down your...	Sau koj...	Write down your...	Fiev jienv meih nyei
• Name	• Nama	• Name	• Pangalan	• Name	• Npe	• Name	• Mbuox
• Address	• Alamat	• Address	• Tirahan	• Address	• Chaw nyob	• Address	• Deic-zepv
• Date of Birth	• Tanggal lahir	• Date of Birth	• Petsa ng kapanganakan	• Date of Birth	• Hnub yug	• Date of Birth	• Cuotv seix hnoi
• Phone No.	• Nomer telepon	• Phone No.	• Numero ng telepono	• Phone No.	• Xovtooj #	• Phone No.	• Douc Wac Hoc
• Soc. Security No.	• Nomer Pokok Penduduk	• Soc. Security No.	• Numero social security	• Soc. Security No.	• Xaus saus	• Soc. Security No.	• Mbungh Gox Hoc
Your court date is...	Tanggal sidang anda	Your court date is...	Petsa mo sa korte ay...	Your court date is...	Koj lub hnub ntsib xam	Your court date is...	Meih nyei nyaangh muonh hnoi...
Sign here	Tandatangan di sini	Sign here	Pumirma dito	Sign here	Xyeem npe ntawm no	Sign here	Louc mbuox naaiv
Your blood/breath/urine will be checked for alcohol/drugs.	Darah/nafas/air seni anda akan diperiksa untuk alkohol/narkotik.	Your blood/breath/urine will be checked for alcohol/drugs.	Ang iyong dugo/hininga/ihi susurin para sa alkohol/gamot.	Your blood/breath/urine will be checked for alcohol/drugs.	Koj cov ntshav/pa/zis yuav raug ntsuam xyuas caw/tshuaj	Your blood/breath/urine will be checked for alcohol/drugs.	Meih nyei nziaamv/qiex/yiez zuqc diev mangc diuv/domgc leiz ndie
I am towing your vehicle.	Mobil anda akan diderek.	I am towing your vehicle.	Itotow iyong sasakyan.	I am towing your vehicle.	Kuv tab tom cab koj lub tsheb.	I am towing your vehicle.	Yie tor meih nyei cie aqv.
For victim	Untuk korban	For victim	Para sa biktima	For victim	Rau tus raug xwm txheej	For victim	Zuqc hluqv nyei mienh
Did He/She have...	Apakah ia ber-...	Did He/She have...	Siya ba ay mayroong...	Did He/She have...	Nws pua muaj	Did He/She have...	Ninh maaih...
• Weapons	• Senjata	• Weapons	• Sandata	• Weapons	• Riam phom	• Weapons	• Wuoqc ginc
• Car	• Mobil	• Car	• Kotse	• Car	• Tsheb	• Car	• Cie-ndau
• Bicycle	• Sepeda	• Bicycle	• Bisekleta	• Bicycle	• Tsheb tuam	• Bicycle	• Siang-ping cie
Was He/She...	Apakah IA...	Was He/She...	Siya ba ey...	Was He/She...	Nws yog	Was He/She...	Minh se...
Male or Female	Pria atau wanita	Male or Female	Lalake o babae	Male or Female	Txiv neej los poj niam	Male or Female	Mjangc fai sieqv
• White	• Berkulit putih	• White	• Puti	• White	• Neeg dawb	• White	• Baeqc
• Black	• Berkulit hitam	• Black	• Itim	• Black	• Neeg dub	• Black	• Jieqv
• Hispanic	• Orang latin	• Hispanic	• Latino	• Hispanic	• Neeg Mev xis kaus	• Hispanic	• Yangh baeqc
• Asian	• Orang Asia	• Asian	• Asiano	• Asian	• Neeg Es xia	• Asian	• Mngomqv jieqv
For suspect	Untuk yang dicurigai	For suspect	Para sa nahuli	For suspect	Rau tus neeg raug plaub	For suspect	Zuqc laaic nyei mienh
Do you have...	Apakah anda...	Do you have...	Mayroon ka bang...	Do you have....	Koj puas muaj	Do you have....	Meih maaih...
• Weapons	• Bersenjata	• Weapons	• Sandata	• Weapons	• Riam phom	• Weapons	• Wuoqc ginc
• Drugs	• Membawa narkotik	• Drugs	• Gamot	• Drugs	• Tshuaj	• Drugs	• Domgc leiz ndie
• Money	• Membawa uang	• Money	• Kuwarta	• Money	• Nyiaj	• Money	• Nyaanh zeiv
• Tattoos	• Bertato	• Tattoos	• Tatu	• Tattoos	• Sam txhim rau tawv nquji	• Tattoos	• Nziepv sim
Empty your pockets	Kosongkan isi kantong.	Empty your pockets	Basyuhin ang iyong bulsa.	Empty your pockets	Thau khoom hauv koj hnabrris hnabtxhv tawm	Empty your pockets	Lom kungr meih nyei lui-houx mbuoqc
Sit	Duduk	Sit	Umupo	Sit	Zaum	Sit	Zueiz
Stand	Berdiri	Stand	Tumindig	Stand	Sawv	Stand	Souv
Don't move	Jangan bergerak	Don't move	Huwag kikilos	Don't move	Tsis txhob nti	Don't move	Mv duqv dongz
Follow me	Ikuti saya	Follow me	Sumunod ka sa akin	Follow me	Raws kuv qab	Follow me	San yie daaih
Are you injured?	Apakah anda terluka?	Are you injured?	Nasaktan ka ba?	Are you injured?	Koj puas raug mob?	Are you injured?	Meih zuqc mun fai?
Are you sick?	Apakah anda sakit?	Are you sick?	May sakit ka ba?	Are you sick?	Puas yog koj mob?	Are you sick?	Meih maiv longx?
Point to where it hurts.	Tunjukkan dimana sakit.	Point to where it hurts.	Ituro mo ang masakit.	Point to where it hurts.	Taw tes rau qho mob?	Point to where it hurts.	Nuqv mun vuov norm domgx.
I have just arrested you.	Saya baru menahan anda.	I have just arrested you.	Inaresto ko ikaw.	I have just arrested you.	Kuv nyuam qhuav ntes koj	I have just arrested you.	Yie zorqv jienv meih aqv.

Computer-Aided Dispatching Systems and Records Management Systems

With technical advances in computer hardware and programs in the 1970s and 1980s came two major advances to the law enforcement reporting systems: the Computer-Aided Dispatching System (CADS) and the Records Management System (RMS). In CADS, the computer manages the incoming requests for service, monitors the location and status of the available officers, and either dispatches officers directly or recommends the dispatching of officers to a human dispatcher.

In many systems, a Mobile Data Terminal (MDT), a small computer screen and keyboard that allows for direct electronic communications between the law enforcement vehicle and the dispatcher and/or RMS, is installed in each field vehicle. MDTs allow for the transmittal of information without tying up already cluttered radio airways. With MDTs, the transmission by the dispatcher involves coordinating the units involved rather than just passing along and recording voice-transmitted information. This allows a single dispatcher to deal with a larger geographical area, more units, or both. It is usually advantageous to have fewer geographical boundaries because boundaries frequently cause a loss of information passed between units. The MDT "talks" directly to the CAD computer, with the information displayed to the dispatcher on the CAD terminal and to the field officer on the MDT screen. The main flow of information between the officer and dispatcher is conveyed as short spurts of computer data, replacing the long and frequently unclear voice transmissions of the past. This leaves communications channels available for emergency transmissions.

Most CADS also allow officers in the field to access central databases directly to obtain information on arrests, wanted persons, drivers licenses, and vehicle registrations. This speeds the officers' retrieval of needed information, while again reducing the workload of dispatchers, and freeing voice-radio circuits for emergency transmissions. In many of the systems, the CADS also automatically feeds the resulting crime data into the agency's central crime information database, eliminating the reentry of data by hand.

Records Management Systems are used to provide an automated method of entry and retrieval of all information associated with each report generated and investigation initiated. While some RMSs are stand-alone systems, they are often tied into CADS. A combined system allows all information that is obtained by the dispatcher to be recorded within the RMS. The system is then able to keep track of each incident, related incidents, and all information on persons that have provided information on the case.

Some RMSs require input of information by the report writer, some accept information directly from the tape transcriber, and others require input from report reviewers. Departments with laptop computers can have information directly downloaded from the laptops to the RMS.

Because an RMS is a data-based program, specific information can be obtained from the files. This allows a search of all information within the database to develop leads or MO patterns.

Facsimile Machines, E-mail, and the Internet

Other methods of transmitting reports and other information include the use of facsimile (fax) machines, electronic mail (e-mail), and the Internet. Fax machines, e-mail, and the Internet all can be used to transmit information or images across communications lines, such as telephone lines. The transmissions can include photographs, documents, or reports. This technology allows almost instant sharing of information by field offices of the same agency or between agencies. Many agencies pass information about suspected or wanted criminals to other agencies or even to private security agencies via the use of these methods. Many cities with a large tourist industry use these methods as quick ways to provide information to hotels, motels, condominiums, and other facilities that cater to tourists.

Word Processing

Word processing, once thought of as a luxury, is now a common sight in many criminal justice agencies. While it is basically a form of typewriting, word processing has increased the efficiency and productivity of many agencies. There are many word processing software programs in use. Most agencies use IBM (or compatible) personal computers (PCs) or Apple's Macintosh line of computers for word processing. Desktop publishing refers to the process of creating "professional-looking" copy using PCs and software programs with enhanced features. Most computer word processing software programs are user-friendly, which means that the operator does not require a great deal of knowledge about computers to use them. Word processing has many advantages over typewriting, including: the ability to store material on electronic media such as thumb drives, hard drives, or other storage means; the ability to correct mistakes and edit "on screen" rather than on paper; the ability to send and retrieve written correspondence via phone lines connected to the computer (e-mail); the ability to use different type styles (fonts); and the ability to integrate graphics with text. Other word processing features include spelling and grammar checkers, thesauri, table generators, math functions, and graphics. Many criminal justice agencies now use laptop computers in the field to generate reports in a specific format suited to agency needs.

The Crime Lab

One of the most powerful and far-reaching improvements computers have provided law enforcement is also the least visible. The computerization of most crime laboratory instruments has resulted in chemical and forensic analysis techniques that were unthinkable even just 10 years ago. Computerized gas chromatographs and mass spectrometers now accurately and routinely identify and match traces of material so tiny that they are not even visible. By now, almost everyone is aware of the use of DNA testing, allowing for almost foolproof identification of individuals based on their genetic makeup. The use of such technology has led to convictions of persons accused of crimes and also has led to freedom for many persons unjustly accused and incarcerated for crimes they did not commit. Computerized DNA databases and computerized DNA matching have become incredibly powerful tools. The ability of computers to determine the earlier presence of complex organic compounds in human or other tissue from the residual products of their metabolism long after the original compounds have disappeared is having a major impact upon forensic pathology.

Several other computer uses, such as blood spatter analysis and vehicle collision reconstruction, are also having an important, if more limited, effect on the ability of crime labs to aid in investigations.

Automatic Fingerprint Identification System

Automatic Fingerprint Identification Systems (AFISs) compare fingerprints. Although none of these systems are presently precise enough to make the final determination for court purposes that two prints match, they do sort through the millions of prints on file and present a short list of likely candidates for comparison. It is this capability that makes the AFISs so valuable, because they do something that no human being can, that is, find the owner of a single fingerprint from a huge source of fingerprints. AFIS has become so important to law enforcement that a third multi-agency, multi-state computer network has been created to support it: the Western Identification Network (WIN). WIN exists to support the ability of AFISs in the Western United States to search each other's fingerprint databases for suspects. Headquartered in California just outside of Sacramento, the WIN network contains the largest AFIS database in the world (at least until the NCIC IAFIS becomes operational) and has begun to spread beyond just the western states.

Use of Computers and Television

Another new process is the use of computers and television cameras to monitor both traffic flow and the activities of people in public places. In traffic systems, a computer-controlled TV camera monitors the area of interest, looking for drivers speeding, running red lights, or committing other violations. When the computer detects illegal activity, it stores a picture of the offense and the offending vehicle, decodes the vehicle license plate by Optical Character Recognition, obtains the ownership information from a central database, and sends the owner of the offending vehicle a summons.

Cameras are installed in police vehicles and in many public areas, helping law enforcement and security personnel to monitor many locations simultaneously. Because work in the field of facial recognition is already well advanced, it is not unreasonable to conclude that similar systems capable of recognizing individuals may monitor a wide variety of behavior in coming decades. The need for such systems, will, of course, have to be carefully balanced against civil liberties.

Looking Toward the Future

The law enforcement methods in use today are largely the outgrowth of the past 150 years of modern law enforcement experience. For most of that time, the majority of people lived in communities small enough that each officer knew most of the people in the community personally and was aware of all of the crimes that occurred.

Today, most people live in communities so large that most of the occupants are anonymous to each other, and no one officer can possibly know the details of all of the crimes committed there. Because of this, the ability of computers to gather, manage, retrieve, and analyze has become crucial to the law enforcement community. As the sophistication of computer crime analysis grows, so will the importance of computers in tracking crimes and assisting in their solutions.

What this means for the individual officer is that the ability to type, to use a computer, and to formulate queries logically and intelligently will become increasingly important. Computer skills will never replace an officer's ability to meet and interact with people or his or her powers of observation, but they will leverage these abilities so powerfully that it will be impossible for an officer to succeed without them.

The future of computers in law enforcement will include improvements to what is already available as well as a few new things. The improvements will include the growth of databases, as well as better coordination between them. Further improvements will come in how the information gets into the databases, the sophistication and usefulness of crime analysis, the ease of producing it, and the ability of officers on the street to access the information. Cost is a major factor in the deployment of new systems, and the most important cost is not of the computers, but the people that they replace. Thus, the twin driving forces behind increased computerization are the necessity of managing an enormous flood of data and the need to reduce the cost of getting, keeping, and using it. There is usually an initial cost of inputting data to develop a database as well as the cost of personnel necessary to continue the data inputting process.

Currently, most crime reports are handwritten or typed onto paper. A subset of the information contained in them is converted to data and hand-entered into the computerized databases. That is beginning to change, with the goal being single data entry. In a single data-entry system the officer no longer produces a written report from which crime data is extracted by a clerk and entered into the computerized database as a separate operation. Instead, officers carry computers in the field, write their reports directly on the computer, and all of the information in the report is then uploaded into the department's database automatically. The same computer will allow the officer in the field to retrieve data from the central database as needed. It also replaces the MDT, allowing the officer to be assigned to cases automatically, and potentially tracking officers' locations and progress using geographical locating equipment.

Not surprisingly, the leaders in this field are police departments in the Silicon Valley area of California. The Fremont Police Department, which has already deployed its second generation of such a program, is especially notable.

Many police departments have installed computer systems to aid in the processing of arrested persons, and some of them also incorporate photographs and fingerprints into the automated system. This will continue to grow until most agencies are tied into the national systems of NCIC 2000 and IAFIS.

There are daily technological breakthroughs that can and do impact all fields within the criminal justice system. The only limits are those of the imagination and the willingness of people like you in the criminal justice system. Stay abreast of these new developments. Take some risks and devote time to consider possible new applications in your own field.

APPENDIX A

Model Reports

Because no uniformity exists nationwide, the reports that follow are models or samples. Report requirements vary in states and counties, and even from one office to another in the same building. There is the central thought that "writing is writing" wherever you find it and that the who, what, when, where, and how approach is universal. The why is more applicable to Presentence Investigation Reports or other writing by parole or probation officers. Like anything else, there are exceptions. Just remember to be very careful when explaining the why.

THE REPORTS THAT FOLLOW ARE SIMULATIONS WITH FICTIONAL NAMES AND PLACES AND INVOLVE NO ACTUAL PERSONS LIVING OR DEAD.

Sample Burglary Report

"Assignment/Arrival" and "Property Taken" headings may have been covered on the face page of the report, depending on the circumstances of the case and the type of face page used by the agency involved. Some agencies require a short synopsis of the facts of the case. For example:

Residence at 1025 10th Street was burglarized by a white male while the occupant was home. Handguns were taken.

In addition, block headings as shown in Chapter 3 may be required. This will depend on the information provided on the face page of the report and agency policy.

MILES, Connie S. W Female
1025 10th Street
DOB: 4-1-76 34yrs.
SSN: 555-55-5555
Employed: ABC Chemical Co.
Occupation: Chemist
Tele: (h)(555)923-1111, (w)(555)922-1100

S-3839410
BURGLARY
PAGE 2 of 5

ASSIGNMENT/ARRIVAL
On 2-10-2010 at about 1800hrs. I was sent by police dispatch to 1025 10th Street on a burglary that had just occurred. I responded from South Street, arriving at about 1803hrs.

COMPLAINANT'S STATEMENT

Arrives home from work
Upon arrival I met with Connie S. Miles, who was dressed in a bathrobe and whose hair was wet. She stated that at about 1740hrs. on today's date she returned home from work and almost immediately took a shower in the master bathroom. While she was in the shower she heard a noise coming from the master bedroom area. She was not alarmed by the noise because she presumed it was her husband, who she thought might have returned home early from a business trip.

Observes male
When she looked around the shower curtain and called out her husband's name, she saw a male running out of the master bedroom carrying a pillowcase that appeared full. She then screamed for help, rinsed off, put on her robe and ran out of the house. She then ran to her neighbor's house across the street and called the police. She did not see the man who had been in her house after she screamed.

S-3839410
BURGLARY
PAGE 3 of 5

COMPLAINANT'S STATEMENT CONTINUED

Unusual circumstances
Miles stated that she and her husband normally do not arrive home from work until about 2000hrs. They normally ride to work and back together, but her husband took the car on a business trip to Smithville and that she left work early so that she could catch a ride with a co-worker.

Missing items
Miles stated that she did not find anything belonging to her missing from the house, but she did notice that several of her husband's guns were missing. She could not provide any type of description of the guns saying she knows nothing about the guns other than that he keeps them in a case in the bedroom closet. She will have her husband call the police later in the evening when he returns from his one-day business trip.

Suspect description
Miles described the suspect as being a large, white male, in his 20s, about 6', 200 pounds. He had fair hair and was wearing dark pants and a blue jacket. Miles was not able to give any further description but does think that she can recognize the male if he is seen again.

WITNESS'S STATEMENT

Timothy DeLaney was interviewed at his home at 1030 10th Street on 2-10-2010 at about 1815hrs.

Screams heard
DeLaney stated that he was at home and just before 1800hrs. he heard his neighbor Connie Miles screaming that she needed help. As he ran out of his house he saw her running from her house toward him. She told him that she had been robbed and so he took her to his house so they could call the police.

S-3839410
BURGLARY
PAGE 4 of 5

WITNESS' STATEMENT CONTINUED

Vehicle observed
DeLaney stated that at about 1745hrs. he observed a vehicle arrive at the Miles' home. He looked at it closely because he had never seen a vehicle like that in the neighborhood. He then saw Connie Miles get out of the car and go inside her house. Within about 10 minutes he saw another car pull in front of the Miles' home. Since he knew that Miles was at home he thought nothing of it and sat down in his living room to read the newspaper. When he heard a woman screaming he looked out and noticed the same car heading off in the east direction on 10th Street. He did not get a chance to see the driver of the car and does not know if there was anyone else inside the car.

Vehicle described
DeLaney described the vehicle that he saw parked in front of the Miles' home as being a late model Buick, blue, with chrome rims. He thinks it was a 4-door but is not really sure. He could not remember anything else about the vehicle.

INVESTIGATION

Description of the scene
The Miles' residence is located at 1025 10th Street just South of Center Street. The home is on the West side of the street and is a three bedroom, two bath, single-story building. There is a 6' high wood fence around the house except on the side fronting 10th Street.

Diagram

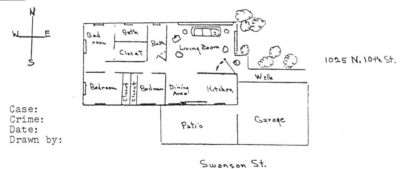

Case:
Crime:
Date:
Drawn by:

Entry/Exit
Entry appears to be made by cutting an L-shaped cut in the screen on the South window of the South/West most bedroom of the home. The cut bordered the bottom and West side frame of the screen and was approximately 6 inches in length in each direction. The pins that hold the screen in place were then removed and the screen was swung up on its hinge allowing the culprit to climb inside through the window that was partway open.

S-3839410
BURGLARY
PAGE 5 of 5

INVESTIGATION CONTINUED

Entry/exit continued
Exit was likely made via the front door. The complainant says that when she ran out of the house the front door was open and she is sure it was closed and locked after she entered the home.

Culprit's activity
After entering the home via the South/West bedroom window the culprit searched the bedroom where entry was made. The closet door was open and things from the shelves were scattered about on the floor.

The master bedroom was also searched. Dresser drawers were opened and items were moved. The suspect also moved items in the master bedroom closet. This is where the complainant's husband kept his guns. The guns were removed from the top shelf of the closet.

There were no signs of a search of other rooms in the house.

Check for latents
I dusted the window frame around the entry point. One set of prints was recovered from the base of the screen on the inside of the frame. The set of prints was submitted into evidence under this report number. No other prints were recovered. Miles stated that she had dusted using Pledge the night before.

Evidence
No other evidence could be found.

Check for other witnesses
Officer James Cotter was assigned to make a neighborhood check for witnesses. He was not able to find any other witnesses. See his follow-up report under this report number for further facts.

Check for firearms registration
I made a check with Firearms Registration for any firearms registered to Michael Miles, the husband of the complainant. According to Wanda Brown of the Firearms Registration, no firearms are listed as being registered to either Michael or Connie Miles.

DISPOSITION
Pending follow-up by the Zone 1 detectives and submission of a list of property taken.

Sample Narcotics Follow-Up Report

V-00079910
PROMOTING A DETRIMENTAL DRUG
PAGE 1 of 6

FOLLOW-UP REPORT

ASSIGNMENT
On 1-26-2010 I was assigned to the Narcotics Detail of the Narcotics/Vice Division as a plainclothes motor patrol officer. My particular assignment on that date was to assist in the execution of a search warrant for the premises of 403 South West 10th, Apartment 201.

SEARCH WARRANT OBTAINED
Based on an affidavit by Officer Clarence ADAMS, a search warrant for 403 South West 10th, Apartment 201, was signed by Judge John WHARTON on 1-20-2010 at about 1630 hours. The search warrant was to be served between 7 a.m. and 10 p.m. and allowed a search for marijuana.

BRIEFING
On 1-26-2010 at about 0700 hours a briefing was held in the offices of the Narcotics Detail. Detective Carl YATES made assignments and provided a raid plan to the Search Warrant execution team.

PERSONNEL INVOLVED

Name	Badge	Assignment
Detective Carl YATES	1020	CASE AGENT
Sergeant Charles HAIG	687	SURVEILLANCE/STOP
Officer Earl WHITE	2422	SURVEILLANCE/STOP
Officer Cliff WILLS	3222	EVIDENCE RECOVERY
Officer Craig YOUNG	3344	PHOTOGRAPHS/DIAGRAM
Chemist Wilfred WATSON	388	EVIDENCE ANALYSIS

V-00079910
PROMOTING DETRIMENTAL DRUGS
PAGE 2 of 6

SUSPECTS DESCRIBED
Detective YATES provided the following descriptions of suspects that have been observed on the premises of 403 South West 10th, Apartment 201. He also provided a vehicle description.

1. NONES, William Walter
    AKA: "Billy Boy"
    DOB: 11-17-87
    White male
    ADD: 403 South West 10th Street, Apt. 201
    SS#: 222-12-8828
    PID: A-88788
    6'1"/186 pounds/brown hair/gray eyes
    Tattoo: Blue bulldog on right wrist

2. SAMSON, Suzanne
    AKA: JONES, Suzanne S.
    DOB: 5-12-93
    White female
    ADD: 403 South West 10th, Apt. 201
    SS#: 222-16-769X
    PID: A-23234
    5'4"/120 pounds/long blond hair w/dark roots/lt. blue eyes/large ears

3. ALLAN, John Henry
    DOB: 11-4-93
    Black male
    ADD: 1022 South Walton, Apt. 403
    SS#: 422-90-7X9X
    PID: A43435
    5'10"/164 pounds/black afro hair/dark eyes slightly crossed/muscular build/jerky walk

VEHICLE
    2009 Nissan Sentra
    White
    AC-2274 (MI)
    RO: SAMSON, Suzanne S.

V-00079910
PROMOTING A DETRIMENTAL DRUG
PAGE 3 of 6

SURVEILLANCE CONDUCTED
At about 1630 hours on 1-26-2010 units took up vantage points to conduct surveillance on apartment 201 of 403 South West 10th. At about 1705 hours Detective YATES reported that the three suspects were leaving the apartment and entering a white Buick station wagon, bearing license plates AC-2274.

SURVEILLANCE CONDUCTED
Units began moving surveillance and followed the Buick east on South West 10th. The operator of the vehicle was identified by Officer WHITE as William Walter JONES.

VEHICLE STOPPED
As the Buick turned east onto West Main Street Detective YATES instructed units to move in. I stopped the Buick as it entered the parking lot of the Golden Glow Amusement Park at 196 West Main Street.

SEARCH WARRANT PRESENTED
Sergeant Charles HAIG informed the suspects that a search warrant had been issued for the premises of 403 South West 10th, apartment 201. Sergeant HAIG then showed a copy of the search warrant to William JONES.

William JONES voluntarily agreed to accompany Sergeant HAIG to apartment 201, 403 South West 10th for the execution of the search warrant.

TRANSPORTATION
William JONES was transported to the apartment by Sergeant HAIG in his police vehicle. Suzanne SAMSON and John ALLAN drove the Buick station wagon and were accompanied by Officer WHITE.

SEARCH WARRANT EXECUTED
At about 1715 hours on 1-26-2010 Officer Clarence ADAMS verified that the tenant of apartment 201, 403 South West 10th was William Walter JONES. William JONES was then presented with a certified copy of the search warrant. The apartment was opened by William JONES and then entered by the search team.

EVIDENCE RECOVERED
At about 1730 hours on 1-26-2010 Officer Cliff WILLS began the recovery of evidence. For further facts and information regarding times and location of evidence recovered refer to attached evidence report submitted by Officer WILLS.

V-00079910
PROMOTING A DETRIMENTAL DRUG
PAGE 4 of 6

CONTRABAND LOCATED
At about 1745 hours a clear plastic packet containing a white powdery substance was found in the jacket of a coat located in the northwest bedroom. The bedroom was established to have been occupied by William JONES and Suzanne JONES. William JONES acknowledged the jacket belonged to him. Other paraphernalia and possible heroin residue were recovered along with the packet.

A greenish vegetable material resembling marijuana was recovered from the refrigerator at about 1750 hours.

ARRESTS EFFECTED
Upon locating the white powdery substance Detective YATES placed William and Suzanne JONES under arrest for Promoting Dangerous Drugs and Unlawful Possession of Drug Paraphernalia.

All three (3) suspects were arrested by Detective YATES for Promoting Detrimental Drugs upon the location of the marijuana in the refrigerator (common area).

SPONTANEOUS STATEMENT
Upon being informed of the arrest for Promoting Dangerous Drugs, William JONES stated, "That's mine. Don't arrest Suzanne. My Stuff. She don't use heroin."

INVENTORY RECEIPT GIVEN
Upon completion of the search of the premises Detective YATES displayed the items seized to William JONES and gave him a copy of an inventory sheet describing these items. William JONES acknowledged receipt of the inventory by signing the inventory sheet in the space provided.

MPD-71 ADMINISTERED
All three suspects, JONES, SAMSON, and ALLAN, were informed of their rights by having MPD-71, WARNING PERSONS BEING INTERROGATED OF THEIR MIRANDA RIGHTS, read verbatim to them. All three exercised their rights and declined to give a statement.

V-00079910
PROMOTING A DETRIMENTAL DRUG
PAGE 5 of 6

EVIDENCE SECURED
The evidence recovered in the search warrant was secured by Officer Cliff WILLS at about 2100 hours on 1-26-2010 in the safe located in the offices of the Narcotics Detail pending the notification of the on-call chemist.

CASES GENERATED
    PROMOTING DETRIMENTAL DRUGS   V-00079910
    PROMOTING DANGEROUS DRUGS   V-00080010
    UNLAWFUL POSSESSION OF DRUG PARAPHERNALIA   V-00080110

EVIDENCE SUBMITTED/ANALYSIS
Police chemist Wilfred WATSON was contacted and the evidence seized in the warrant was turned over at 2210 hours on 1-26-2010 to Officer Cliff WILLS for analysis.

ANALYSIS RESULTS
On 1-27-2010 at about 0245 hours, Police chemist WATSON notified Detective YATES of the results of the analysis as follows:

    V-00079910   173.072 grams containing tetrahydrocannabinol
    V-00080010   .112 grams white powder containing heroin

CONFERRAL WITH LIEUTENANT
On 1-27-2010 at about 0400 hours Lieutenant Stanley McCABE of the Narcotic Detail was informed of the facts and circumstances of this investigation. He instructed Detective YATES to confer with the Office of the Prosecuting Attorney for immediate charges.

CONFERRAL WITH PROSECUTOR/COMPLAINTS SIGNED
On 1-27-2010 at about 0700 hours Detective YATES met with Deputy Prosecuting Attorney Carolyn BROWN and apprised her of the facts and circumstances surrounding this investigation. After conferral Prosecutor BROWN signed complaints against William Walter JONES for Promoting Detrimental Drugs, Promoting Dangerous Drugs, and Unlawful Possession of Drug Paraphernalia.

Charges against Suzanne SAMSON and John Henry ALLAN were declined.

V-00079910
PROMOTING A DETRIMENTAL DRUG
PAGE 6 of 6

COMPLAINTS SERVED
On 1-27-2010 at about 1000 hours the complaints against William Walter
JONES were served at the police cell block.

DISPOSITION
CASE CLOSED. BAIL SET: $5,000.00 AGGREGATE

SUPERVISOR   Clarence ADAMS 011110
                                                 MPO-M Narcotics
                                                 1-28-2010

1625hrs

Sample Security Incident Report

SYNOPSIS: Out-patient fell in the entrance to the restroom in Orthopedics.
INJURY: Banged left knee on tile floor resulting in slight contusion, no fracture.
COMPLAINANT'S/VICTIM'S NAME: John R. ADAMS
DATE OF OCCURRENCE: 1/22/2010
REPORT NO.: F 90 4
CLASSIFICATION: Out Patient Fall
REPORTING PERSON: Mary Sue SMALL, receptionist
ASSIGNMENT/ARRIVAL: 1305, 1/22/2010

PERSON INTERVIEWED: John R. ADAMS, Victim in Room 6 of Emergency Department. At 1405, ADAMS recalled having come from checkup concerning pain in left knee and was going to the restroom when he passed a nurse who was carrying a paper container of water which she had spilled just as he approached. He fell near entrance to restroom further injuring his knee. He got up but a couple of the staff got a gurney and took him to Emergency where he was checked and released. He blames the nurse for spilling the water. Victim's wife, Jane F. ADAMS agrees: "They haven't heard the last of this!"

PERSON INTERVIEWED: Sarah C. BROWN, RN. from Cancer Research next door to Orthopedics. BROWN was taking a paper cup of water from fountain near restroom to relative of patient in waiting room of Cancer Research: "Just after I filled the cup, someone behind me lurched against me causing me to spill the water. I turned to discover the man on the floor supporting himself on his hands and trying to get up. Two men from Orthopedics arrived as he was trying to get up, cautioned him to remain quiet and returned with a gurney and took the patient to Emergency. His wife was complaining and blaming me."

STATEMENT OF WITNESS 1: Martha R. LANE, Receptionist. "It all happened so fast, but I feel sure the water was spilled due to the patient's fall rather than causing it."

STATEMENT OF WITNESS 2: Outpatient, James R. FITZPATRICK: "It's boring waiting and I saw the whole thing. The nurse had the cup in hand and no water was on the floor till that guy bumped her in the back."

INVESTIGATION CONTINUED: I checked with ADAMS's physician, Dr. John H. FREEMAN and he confirmed that the patient was not on medication at the time of the fall, was wearing hard soled shoes and had just left his office after a satisfactory consultation. He phoned Emergency and checked to learn that the checkup and X-rays revealed only a contusion to the left knee, no fracture. The patient was released and sent home at 1525, 1/22/2010.

DISPOSITION: Housekeeping arrived to clean up spill. Security Manager was alerted to possible suit due to the remarks made by Jane F. ADAMS.

Sample Presentence Investigation Report (Short-form PSIR)

RE: CF-80-439
John R. Franklin
Paine County Detention Center, Paine, AL

OFFENSE: Ct. I - Burglary, Class B Felony
                  Ct. II - Theft, Class D Felony
                  Ct. III - Resisting Law Enforcement, Class A Misdemeanor

OFFICIAL VERSION: See attached Information

DEFENDANT'S VERSION: "I was drinking with three friends in the State Park on Labor Day. We saw the Caretaker's home and it looked like it was empty. We broke out a glass in the rear door and went in and took a .410 shotgun, some shells, and food from the refrigerator, and a bowl of change, and a diamond ring, and a VISA card. When we were leaving the park, a police car stopped us and frisked us, and roughed us up, and cussed us out, and told us they were going to throw the book at us."

VICTIM IMPACT: Mr. Gary Ronheim lost $604.82 and VISA lost $319.68.

JAIL TIME: 309 days.

PREVIOUS TROUBLE:

Date	Offense	Disposition
10/10/01	Curfew	Office adjustment
6/16/02	JD Public Intoxication	Informal prob., 6 months
4/19/03	Vandalism	10 days, Detention Center
6/11/03	JD Burglary	State Boys' School, 1 yr.
8/8/04	JD Criminal Conversion	State Boys' School, 180 days
3/3/05	Public Intoxication	Probation, 90 days

— — — — — — — — — —(6/15/05 Eighteenth Birthday)— — — — — — — — — — —

Date	Offense	Disposition
7/5/05	Public Intoxication	$100; 10 days
	Resisting Arrest	
7/30/05	Stop Sign	Warning
8/4/05	Burglary, Class B Felony	Pending
	Burglary, Class B Felony	Pending
8/14/05	Escape	
1/13/06	Theft	Nolle Pros.
3/7/08	Public Intoxication	5 days; $25
5/1/09	Public Intoxication	5 days, $25
5/5/09	Speeding	$25; $31 costs
6/30/10	Burglary	Instant case: CR-80-439
	Theft	
	Resisting Law Enforcement	

RE: CF-80-439
John R. Franklin
Page 2 of 2

SOCIAL SETTING: Home life was turbulent. Both parents were problem drinkers, separating for two years when the defendant was seven years old. The defendant was sent to Boys' School when he was fifteen, repeating the performance of his older brother. Franklin cultivated friends on the edge of criminal culture; his closest associate is currently serving a ten-year sentence for Battery. The father was convicted of Child Molesting and Resisting Arrest. For four years Franklin was in special education classes and still has difficulty reading.

ATTITUDE OF DEFENDANT: Franklin evades responsibility for his own actions, laying the blame on his problem with alcohol. The only time he gets into trouble, he rationalizes, is when he is drunk. He is convinced that the police have a vendetta against him. Psychiatric reports indicate that he has more than his share of emotional problems.

STATEMENT BY PROBATION OFFICER: Franklin is correct when he lays blame for his problems on alcohol, but this is only a small part of the story. He has serious psychiatric problems stemming from his defective parental home environment, exacerbated by an unsatisfactory experience in school. He rarely has a success experience of any kind and nearly all interpersonal relationships are flawed. Incarceration would not improve any of these handicaps, but there is some hope that the relationship he recently established with a therapist at the Comprehensive Mental Health Center, Dr. James Forstead, might turn things around somewhat. Good rapport has been established, and for the first time in his life Franklin has someone whom he accepts and admires. It is suggested that continuation of counseling be a condition of probation and that the supervising Probation Officer work closely with Dr. Forstead.

PLEA AGREEMENT: A signed plea agreement in the file provides that the defendant will plead guilty to all charges and that he will receive six years, suspended, and two years of probation, with special conditions to be set by the court.

RECOMMENDATION:
1. Count I, Burglary, a Class B Felony, sentence to the Department of Correction for six years, 309 days executed and the balance suspended; Count II, Theft, a Class D Felony, sentence to the Department of Correction for two years, suspended and concurrent with Count I; Count III, Resisting Law Enforcement, a Class A Misdemeanor, sentence to the Department of Correction for one year, suspended and concurrent with Count I;
2. Credit for 309 days in jail, with no good time allowed;
3. Probation for two years, with special conditions as listed in the Probation Plan;

RE: CF-80-439
John R. Franklin
Page 3 of 3

4. Restitution to Gary Ronheim in the amount of $604.82 and to VISA in the amount of $319.68;
5. Probation User's Fees (initial fee of $50: monthly fee of $25 for 24 months);
6. Court costs of $75 payable within 30 days.

PROBATION PLAN

1. Formal probation for two years;
2. Semi-monthly reporting for three months; thereafter, monthly unless modified by the PO;
3. Enrollment in a job placement program approved by the Probation Department;
4. Continuation in counseling with Dr. James Forstead or another therapist approved by the Probation Department;
5. Community service of 60 hours, preferably in Oak Hills Park if available.

Source: Clear, Todd C., Val B. Clear, and William D. Burrell (1989). *Offender Assessment and Evaluation: The Presentence Investigation Report*, Append E. Cincinnati, OH: Anderson Publishing Co.

Metro County Probation Department
Pre-Sentence Investigation Report

Court: Metro City Center Court
Judge: Hon. James Knoll
Prosecutor: ADA Robert Nelson
Defense Attorney: Frank P. Balk

Name of Defendant: John Horvath

Address: 505 LaSalle Lane
Metro City, Mountain State 77717

DOB: 10/22/85

Arrest Charge: Petit Larceny, Section 155 Penal Code. Class A Misdemeanor.

Conviction Charge: Petit Larceny, Section 155 Penal Code. Class A Misdemeanor.

[Report will also have additional identifying data such as Social Security number, FBI number, State crime system identification number, weight, height, scars, aliases, etc., Docket Number, Bail/ROR status, etc.]

Prior Record:

7/21/06 Driving While Intoxicated, Section 334 Penal Code
        Arrested by Metro City Police Dept.
10/05/06 Sentenced: Two Years Probation by the Hon. Rosemary O'Donnell, Metro County Court. Discharged with Improvement: 12/31/07.

Official Version of Offense:

On 8/15/09 at 3:35pm Officer Peter Judge of the Metropolitan Police Department responded to a call of Petit Larceny (a violation of Section 155 of the Penal Code) at Carter's Department Store at the Rolling Hills Mall. Security Officer Brenda Kelly informed Officer Judge that she and another Security Officer had detained John Horvath after observing him place three golf shirts valued at $120 ($40.00 each) into a bag and walk out of the store without paying for the items. They approached the suspect in the hallway and asked him about the three shirts. He admitted taking them and proceeded willingly back into the store.

On 10/10/09 the suspect entered a plea of guilty to one count of Petit Larceny before the Honorable James Knoll in Metro City Court. Judge Knoll set sentencing for 11/1/09 and ordered a presentence report.

Defendant's Version:

On 10/16/09 the defendant was interviewed in the probation office by Probation Officer Paul Skipper. The defendant admitted the offense. He stated that he was depressed because he was working at "a dead-end job" and because he was not dating anyone. He also reports few friends. He was in the mall and he liked the shirts and thought that they would "cheer him up."

Victim Impact Statement:

This Officer contacted Amanda Wilson, Head of Security at Carter's Department Store. The shirts were confiscated when the defendant was questioned by store Security so no restitution is requested by the store. However, Ms. Wilson noted that the store takes shoplifting very seriously and requests that the Court impose a sentence that will convey that message to the defendant and to anyone who might be contemplating shoplifting at the store.

Social History:

Education:

The defendant reports being a 2003 graduate of Central High School. The defendant's transcript, obtained by this Officer, verifies that the defendant graduated on May 29, 2003 with a "C" average. IQ testing in the 9th grade indicated an IQ of 102.

Employment:

The defendant has been employed as a server for approximately two years with Jones' Diner in suburban Metro City. Jones' Diner verified that the defendant has been employed from September 14, 2007 to the present. The defendant stated that he worked at the Small Time Café prior to his current employment. This could not be verified as that restaurant is no longer in business. The defendant noted employment at several fast food restaurants prior to that. He produced two old W2 Forms verifying some employment at McDonald's and Burger King in 2006 and 2005.

Family: The defendant is single and has never been married. He is living alone at 505 LaSalle Lane in Metro City. His rent is $375 a month, verified by rental payment slips.

Military Service: The defendant served in the U.S. Army from 2003 to 2005. He was honorably discharged on August 7, 2005. This has been verified by a copy of his discharge papers (copy attached).

Health Status: The defendant reports that he is in good health and does not abuse alcohol or drugs. As noted in the Prior Record Section, however, the defendant has one prior arrest and conviction for Driving While Intoxicated. He was placed on probation for that offense and Discharged with Improvement after serving one year on probation. Probation Officer Harry Zobel noted that the offender seemed to have avoided any alcohol related problems while he was on probation.

The defendant was referred for an evaluation by the County Forensic Psychology Clinic. Clinic Psychologist Dr. Rick Laswell described the defendant as of average intelligence and mildly depressed. Dr. Laswell felt that the defendant experiences low self-esteem and has difficulty establishing relationships. He recommended counseling.

Statement of Probation Officer:

The defendant is a 24 year-old male appearing before the Court on a charge of Petit Larceny, a Class A Misdemeanor. He stole three shirts valued at $120.00. He has one prior sentence of probation for a charge of Driving While Intoxicated. He successfully completed that term of probation. The County Forensic Clinic recommends counseling for underlying depression. He is employed and has an Honorable Discharge from the military.

Recommendation:

Given the defendant's record of only one prior sentence of probation, it is respectfully recommended that the defendant again be placed on probation. It is also recommended that he be referred to the County Forensic Psychology Clinic for counseling for depression.

Probation Plan: Weekly reporting to the Probation Office. Counseling at the County Forensic Psychology Clinic. Payment of Court Costs. No Restitution requested by the store.

Respectfully submitted,

Paul Skipper
Probation Officer

Sentencing Date: November 1, 2009

Sample Memorandum

TO: ROBERT HERMAN, INSTRUCTOR
FROM: JOAN JAMES, SUPERVISOR
DATE: MARCH 4, 2010
SUBJECT: THE USE OF SIMULATION SKIT ON DRUGS

The skit presented in your classroom on March 2 contained some valuable lessons for your class involving students from different fields of interest. It was good of the advanced class to present this material. A simulation can increase interest and also supplement learning from the text. However, there are some points to consider if this training method is used.

Facts Clearly Presented
- No part of a scene or a suspect's body can be considered free of suspicion in a methodical search for evidence.
- Persons involved in narcotics offenses are prone to commit acts of violence to escape or resist arrest.
- Sufficient force may be used.

Points that Need Clarifying
- It is important to keep a prisoner under constant supervision for reasons of safety, his own and others. (The attempted escape added drama and even humor but the point seemed lost on the class.)
- Possible problems must be considered in advance and specific personnel assigned.

Recommendations
- Skits are valuable but should be used with caution.
- Humor can be good, but sometimes a point is lost. The body search of Suspect 1 became a farce.
- Students should be told ahead of time what to look for and a discussion and test should follow. Please give me a copy of the test if one was given after this skit.

Thank you for the opportunity to view your innovative work in Criminology 201.

Sample Forensic Laboratory Report

**STATE BUREAU OF INVESTIGATION
CRIME LABORATORY**

OFFICIAL FIREARMS REPORT

TO: Joe Smith, Det.   **DATE ISSUED:**   10/1/10
           Yourcity PD   **LAB CASE NO:**   101001201
           800 E. Walton Drive   **COUNTY:**   Washington
           Yourcity, TN 37614   **AGENCY CASE NO:** H10060012

SUBJECT(S):   **VICTIM(S):**

Lance LaRue   John Harrod

Received From: Joe Smith
Received By: Otis Gregg
Date Received: 9/15/10
Time Received: 10:10 am

EXHIBIT(S):

Q-1	Shotgun from 800 Carter Street
Q-2	Shotshell case from 800 Carter Street
Q-3	Shirt from victim
Q-4	Pellets from victim
Q-5	Wad from victim

RESULTS:

Examination of Exhibit Q-1 (Mossberg/Maverick, model 88, 12 gauge pump-action shotgun, SN# MV12345678) revealed it to be in normal operating condition with the safety features functioning.

Test shotshell cases from Exhibit Q-1 were microscopically examined in conjunction with the shotshell case in Exhibit Q-2. Based on these comparative examinations, it was determined that Exhibit Q-2 had been fired in Exhibit Q-1.

Examination of the eight (8) pellets in Exhibit Q-4 revealed them to be consistent with the weight specifications of 00 Buckshot. This is consistent with the load markings on the shotshell case in Exhibit Q-2.

Examination of the wad in Exhibit Q-5 revealed it to be a 12 gauge, one-piece, plastic 'Power Piston' wad, consistent with Remington manufacture. Characteristics present on Exhibit Q-5 indicate it was originally loaded with a buffered shot load, such as buckshot. This is also consistent with the shotshell case in Exhibit Q-2.

OFFICIAL FIREARMS REPORT

LABORATORY CASE NO: 101001201
DATE ISSUED: 10/1/10   Page 2 of 2

Examination of the shirt in Exhibit Q-3 revealed the presence of one (1) hole in the middle-left abdomen. The area surrounding this hole was examined microscopically and processed chemically for the presence of gunpowder and lead residues, and a pattern of residues was found.

Test patterns were produced at various distances using the shotgun in Exhibit Q-1 and ammunition similar to that represented by Exhibits Q-2, Q-4, and Q-5. Based on these test patterns, it was determined that a pattern of residues and physical effects like those present on Exhibit Q-3 could be produced at muzzle-to-garment distances of greater than three (3) feet, but less than ten (10) feet.

DISPOSITION:

All examinations have been completed. Please pick up evidence within thirty days.

Respectfully Submitted,

Franklin E. Scott, M.A., D-ABC
Special Agent/Forensic Scientist

Examples of Agency Instructions for Completing Report Forms

The following pages contain examples of instruction for completing the following:

The Nebraska Department of Roads' "Instructions for Completing Investigator's Motor Vehicle Accident Report Forms." This is used with the permission of the State of Nebraska, Department of Roads, Allan L. Abbott, Director-State Engineer.

The Chicago Police Department's Vehicle Theft Case Report Form and General Instructions, and Recovered Vehicle Supplementary Report and General Instructions. These forms and instructions are used with the permission of the Chicago Police Department, Chicago, Illinois, Matt L. Rodriguez, Superintendent.

The San Diego Police Department's Missing Person Report and Report Writing Instruction Manual are used with the permission of the San Diego Police Department Regional Law Enforcement Training Center, San Diego, California, Fred Moeller, Captain.

The Greensboro Police Department's Investigative Report Manual Directions for Automated Dictation System and Narrative Guide for a Burglary Investigative Report are used with the permission of the Greensboro Police Department, Greensboro, North Carolina, Sylvester Daughtry, Jr., Chief of Police.

The U.S. Probation System Worksheet for Presentence Investigation Reports that is used to help probation officers gather the appropriate information for a Presentence Investigation Report.

The State of Tennessee Board of Probation and Parole Monthly Reporting Form used by probation officers to collect Information during monthly counseling and verification of the probationer following the rules of his/her probation.

Sample Instructions for Completing Investigator's Motor Vehicle Accident Report Forms,
Nebraska Department of Roads

Instruction Manual for Investigators

Introduction

The Traffic Records Improvement Committee acknowledges the many
contributions made by the law enforcement community in the
development of the revised investigator report forms and the
instruction manual. This field manual was prepared by the Nebraska
Department of Roads Highway Safety Division as a means to help
the investigator accurately complete the:

1. Investigator's Motor Vehicle Accident Report with Overlay
2. Investigator's Motor Vehicle Accident Continuation Report
3. Investigator's Supplemental Truck and Bus Accident Report.

State statute requires law enforcement officers to provide an original
report of investigation for any traffic accident resulting in injury, death,
or in which estimated damages to the property of any one person
exceeds $500.00. This report must be submitted to the Department
of Roads within 10 days of the accident.

We realize that it is impossible to collect accurate data and establish
a uniform reporting system without the commitment of our peace
officers. Since the statewide crash data base is the backbone of
accident analysis and contributes to the success of Nebraska's
highway safety program, accurate reporting of motor vehicle accidents
serves to make our roadways a safer place to travel.

Investigator's Motor Vehicle Accident Report With Overlay
(DR Form 40)

This form must be completed for all reportable motor vehicle accidents. An overlay, which asks additional questions about an accident, is attached to each pad of reports. The overlay was designed as a means to help collect as much information as possible on the 8½"×11" accident report. Instructions on how to use the overlay are printed on its reverse side.

Type your responses or print them with black ink. If more than two vehicles were involved or more than three persons were injured in the crash, complete the Investigator's Motor Vehicle Accident Continuation Report (DR Form 40a).

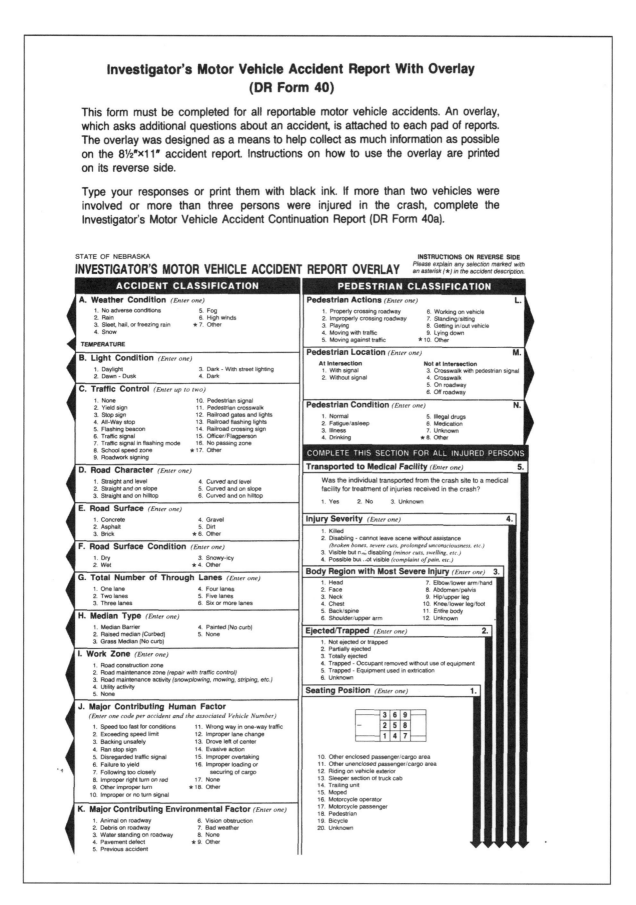

Investigator's Motor Vehicle Accident Report
(DR FOrm 40)

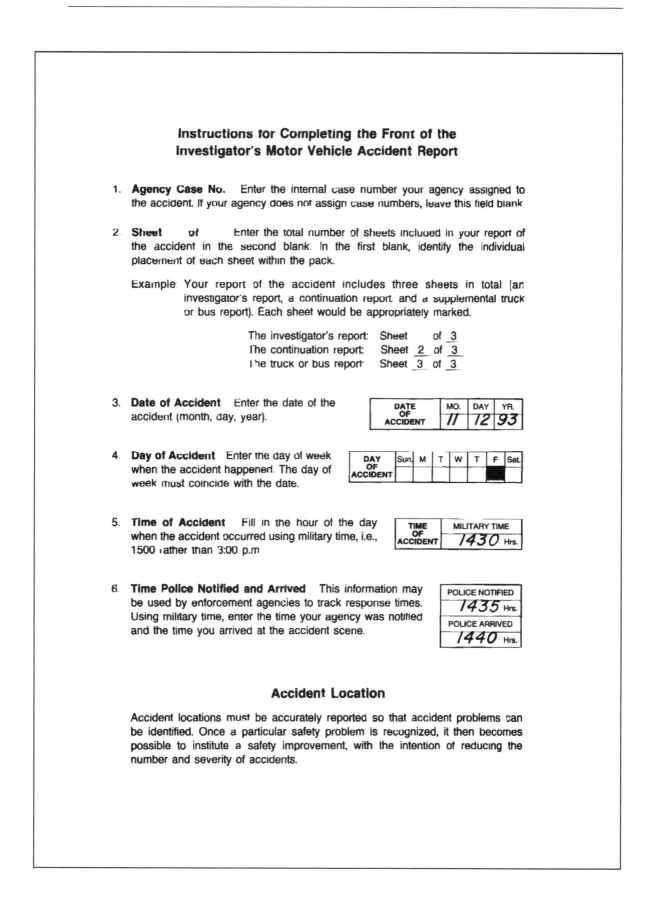

Instructions for Completing the Front of the Investigator's Motor Vehicle Accident Report

1. **Agency Case No.** Enter the internal case number your agency assigned to the accident. If your agency does not assign case numbers, leave this field blank

2. **Sheet   of** Enter the total number of sheets included in your report of the accident in the second blank. In the first blank, identify the individual placement of each sheet within the pack.

   Example: Your report of the accident includes three sheets in total (an investigator's report, a continuation report, and a supplemental truck or bus report). Each sheet would be appropriately marked.

The investigator's report:	Sheet __ of _3_
The continuation report:	Sheet _2_ of _3_
The truck or bus report:	Sheet _3_ of _3_

3. **Date of Accident** Enter the date of the accident (month, day, year).

DATE OF ACCIDENT	MO.	DAY	YR.
	11	12	93

4. **Day of Accident** Enter the day of week when the accident happened. The day of week must coincide with the date.

DAY OF ACCIDENT	Sun.	M	T	W	T	F	Sat.
						■	

5. **Time of Accident** Fill in the hour of the day when the accident occurred using military time, i.e., 1500 rather than 3:00 p.m

TIME OF ACCIDENT	MILITARY TIME
	1430 Hrs.

6. **Time Police Notified and Arrived** This information may be used by enforcement agencies to track response times. Using military time, enter the time your agency was notified and the time you arrived at the accident scene.

POLICE NOTIFIED
1435 Hrs.

POLICE ARRIVED
1440 Hrs.

Accident Location

Accident locations must be accurately reported so that accident problems can be identified. Once a particular safety problem is recognized, it then becomes possible to institute a safety improvement, with the intention of reducing the number and severity of accidents.

Assign the accident to the place where the first injury or damage-producing event occurred.

Example: A motor vehicle ran off the road before hitting a tree. The driver sustained serious injuries and the vehicle was badly damaged in the collision. In this incident, the first damage or injury producing event occurred when the car struck the tree, not when the car ran off the road.

Whenever possible, measure the distance from the crash site to a permanent reference point or landmark (junctions of city streets, county roads, state highways, bridge or railroad identifiers, milepost markers, etc.). The instructions numbered 7-16 explain how to provide complete accident information.

7   **County**   Enter the name of the county where the accident occurred. If the point of impact was on the centerline of a roadway which serves as a boundary line between two counties, enter the name of the county from which the vehicle most at fault was leaving.

PLACE OF ACCIDENT	COUNTY: *Sarpy*

8. **City**   If the accident occurred within the corporate limits of a city or town, enter the appropriate city name.

CITY: *La Vista*

9. **Street or Highway Number**   Enter the name of the roadway on which the accident occurred. If the road has a street name and a highway number, provide both.

ROAD ON WHICH ACCIDENT OCCURRED	STREET OR HIGHWAY NO.: (If No Highway Number, Identify By Name) *4th Street, US-275*

If the accident happened on a county road, include the county road number, if such a road is numbered.

ROAD ON WHICH ACCIDENT OCCURRED	STREET OR HIGHWAY NO.: (If No Highway Number, Identify By Name) *County Road 1352*

If the roadway does not have an official name, show the distance and direction from the nearest named street or road.

ROAD ON WHICH ACCIDENT OCCURRED	STREET OR HIGHWAY NO.: (If No Highway Number, Identify By Name) *City Street (one block south of Lincoln Ave)*

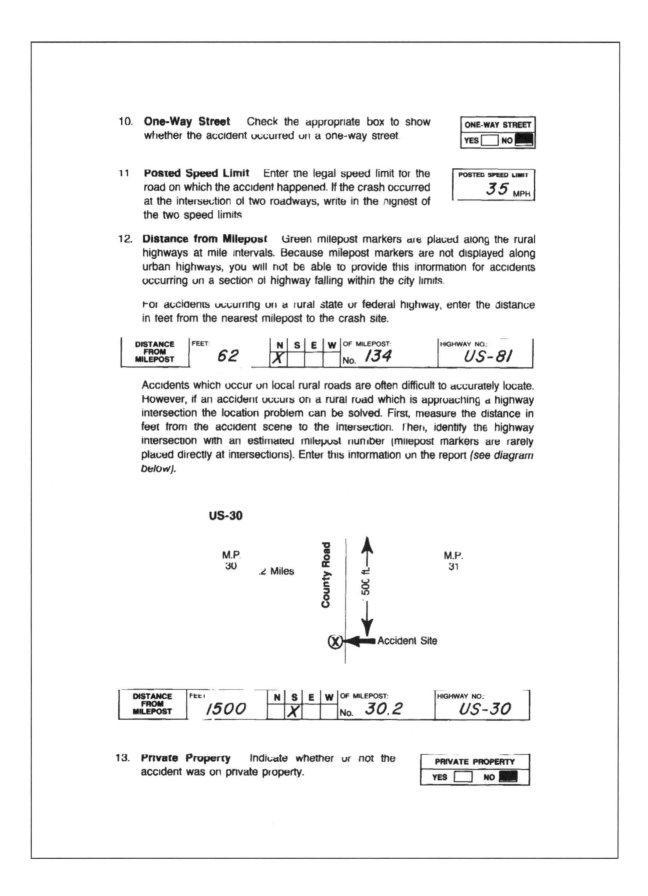

10. **One-Way Street**   Check the appropriate box to show whether the accident occurred on a one-way street.

ONE-WAY STREET
YES [ ] NO ■

11 **Posted Speed Limit**   Enter the legal speed limit for the road on which the accident happened. If the crash occurred at the intersection of two roadways, write in the highest of the two speed limits.

POSTED SPEED LIMIT
35 MPH

12. **Distance from Milepost**   Green milepost markers are placed along the rural highways at mile intervals. Because milepost markers are not displayed along urban highways, you will not be able to provide this information for accidents occurring on a section of highway falling within the city limits.

For accidents occurring on a rural state or federal highway, enter the distance in feet from the nearest milepost to the crash site.

| DISTANCE FROM MILEPOST | FEET: 62 | N X | S | E | W | OF MILEPOST: No. 134 | HIGHWAY NO.: US-81 |

Accidents which occur on local rural roads are often difficult to accurately locate. However, if an accident occurs on a rural road which is approaching a highway intersection the location problem can be solved. First, measure the distance in feet from the accident scene to the intersection. Then, identify the highway intersection with an estimated milepost number (milepost markers are rarely placed directly at intersections). Enter this information on the report *(see diagram below)*.

US-30

M.P. 30   .2 Miles   County Road   ↑ ←500 ft.→   M.P. 31

(X)← Accident Site

| DISTANCE FROM MILEPOST | FEET 1500 | N | S X | E | W | OF MILEPOST: No. 30.2 | HIGHWAY NO.: US-30 |

13. **Private Property**   Indicate whether or not the accident was on private property.

PRIVATE PROPERTY
YES [ ] NO ■

14. **If at Intersection** - When an accident occurs at an intersection, enter the name or highway number of the intersecting street.

IF AT INTERSECTION
NAME OF INTERSECTING ROADWAY:
84th St.

15. **If Not at Intersection** - Accidents which do not occur at intersections are located more accurately when the measurement **from** the nearest intersecting street to the crash scene is provided. Write the number of feet and the direction the accident site is located from the nearest intersecting street.

IF NOT AT INTERSECTION						
FEET:	N	S	E	W	OF NEAREST STREET OR HIGHWAY, BRIDGE, RAILROAD CROSSING OR MILEPOST:
30			*X*		*10th Street*

16. **Accidents Outside the City Limits** - Complete this information when the accident occurs outside the city limits.

The accident happened four miles south of Thedford.

IF ACCIDENT WAS OUTSIDE CITY LIMITS, INDICATE DISTANCE FROM NEAREST TOWN	MILES:	N	S	E	W	AND MILES:	N	S	E	W	OF NEAREST CITY OR TOWN
	4		*X*								*Thedford*

The accident occurred three miles south and two miles east of Wilber.

IF ACCIDENT WAS OUTSIDE CITY LIMITS, INDICATE DISTANCE FROM NEAREST TOWN	MILES:	N	S	E	W	AND MILES:	N	S	E	W	OF NEAREST CITY OR TOWN
	3		*X*			*2*			*X*		*Wilber*

Vehicles and Drivers

17. **Total Number of Vehicles Involved** - Enter the total number of motor vehicles involved in the accident. Include parked vehicles in your count. If more than two vehicles were involved, use a Motor Vehicle Accident Continuation Report (DR Form 40a) to record information about the remaining vehicles.

TOTAL NUMBER OF VEHICLES INVOLVED	2

18. **Driver's Name and Phone Number** - Enter the driver's name exactly as it appears on the license. Some drivers often use a name which is different from that shown on their operator's license. Please indicate the alias on your report by putting it in parentheses, and placing it behind the name found on the driver's license.

DRIVER:	PHONE:
James Public	*481-0090*

19. **Driver's Address** - If the driver of the vehicle is a student, enter his/her permanent mailing address. Otherwise, enter the driver's current street or RFD address.

Do not assume that the address shown on the driver's license is current. Because people often neglect to apply for a replacement license each time they move, it is not uncommon for the address printed on their license to be outdated. The current address is the address needed.

DRIVER'S ADDRESS: *109 S. 12th St.*   CITY, STATE, ZIP: *Parker, NE 68215*

20. **Driver's License** - Enter the driver's license number and the state of its issue. ***Give special attention to accuracy.***

DRIVER'S LICENSE | STATE *NE* | NUMBER: *G02930641*

21. **Driver's Date of Birth and Sex** - Enter the driver's date of birth and indicate male or female by checking the appropriate box.

DATE OF BIRTH *03 12 54* | SEX M ☑ F ☐

22. **Vehicle License Data** - Record the year the vehicle's license will expire, the state which issued the plate, and the license plate number.

LICENSE PLATE | YEAR: *89* | STATE: *NE* | NUMBER: *2-F6556*

23. **Estimated Damage** - Enter a damage estimate which you believe comes close to what it would cost to repair the vehicle. If the vehicle is damaged so severely that it is a total loss, write *"TOTAL."*

ESTIMATED DAMAGE: *$ 750.00*

Try to avoid entering vague estimates, such as $500+. The trouble with this type of an estimate is that we have no way of knowing if you thought the dollar damages were about $500.00; or if you are suggesting that damages are well over the State's $500.00 reportability threshold.

Although we generally accept the estimated damages reported by the driver, there are times when the accuracy of his/her estimate is suspect. Your estimate is very useful in helping us identify questionable estimates provided by individuals. If an individual reports a damage amount which is substantially less than your estimate, we may ask them for a copy of the body shop estimate or a receipt for the repair charges.

24. **Vehicle Year** - Enter the model year of the vehicle.

YEAR: *89*

25. **Vehicle Make** - Enter the make of the vehicle, i.e., Chevrolet, Ford, Honda, Dodge, Geo, etc.

MAKE: *Ford*

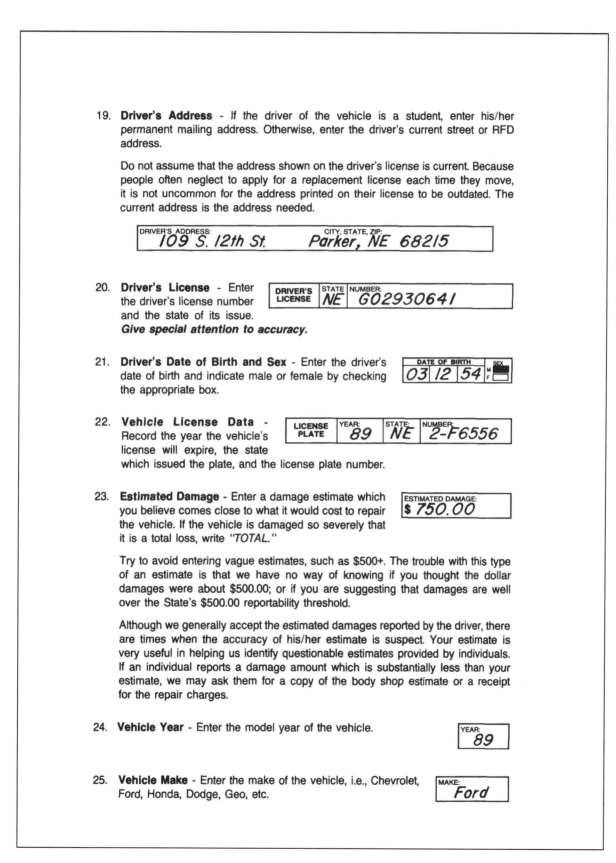

26. **Vehicle Model** - Write out the complete model name of the vehicle, i.e., Accord, Taurus, Voyager, Blazer, etc.

MODEL:
Tempo

27. **Vehicle Body Style** - Enter the body style of the vehicle, i.e., 4-door sedan, pickup truck, station wagon, tractor-trailer, convertible, etc.

BODY STYLE:
4 Door

28. **Vehicle Color** - Enter the color of the vehicle. You may be fairly broad in naming the color, but state if the shade is dark or light, i.e., light blue, dark green, etc.

COLOR:
Beige

29. **Vehicle Identification Number** - Enter the Vehicle Identification Number (VIN).

VEHICLE I.D. NUMBER (VIN):
IFABP0525BWI00065

On passenger cars built from 1968 to date, the number will usually be found on the driver's side of the dash and visible through the windshield from the outside. On passenger cars built in the mid-1950's through 1967 the VIN will usually be found welded or riveted on the doorpost. Passenger cars built before 1956 were identified by the motor number.

30. **Citation** - Indicate whether or not the driver received a citation. If so, enter the citation number.

CITATION:
YES
NO
784678

31. **Owner Name, Phone, Address** - Enter the full name, phone number, and address of the person to whom the vehicle is registered. Be sure to identify the owner of a parked motor vehicle.

If the owner and the driver are the same person, you may write *"SAME"* over this block of information. However, if there is joint ownership of the vehicle and the driver happens to be one of the owners, **DO NOT** write *"SAME."* Instead, list each of the owners.

OWNER:
James and Helen Public   PHONE: *481-0090*
OWNER'S ADDRESS: *109 S. 12th St.*   CITY, STATE, ZIP: *Parker, NE 68215*

32. **Insurance Company and Policy Number** - Enter the name of the insurance company and the policy number.

INSURANCE COMPANY: *Insurance Company Name*
POLICY NUMBER: *197-0497-E02-32*

33. **Towed To and Towed By** - If the vehicle was towed away, enter where it was towed and provide the name of the company or individual that did the towing. Otherwise, if the vehicle was not towed, leave these fields blank.

TOWED TO:	TOWED BY:
3430 West P St.	*Stan's Towing*

34. **Vehicle Movement Before Collision** - For each vehicle involved in the accident, we ask you to:

   - check a box to indicate the direction the front-end of the vehicle *faced* before the accident;

   - enter the name of the road on which the vehicle was moving or parked before the crash; and

   - check a box to indicate the action which best describes the movement of the vehicle immediately before the time of the accident.

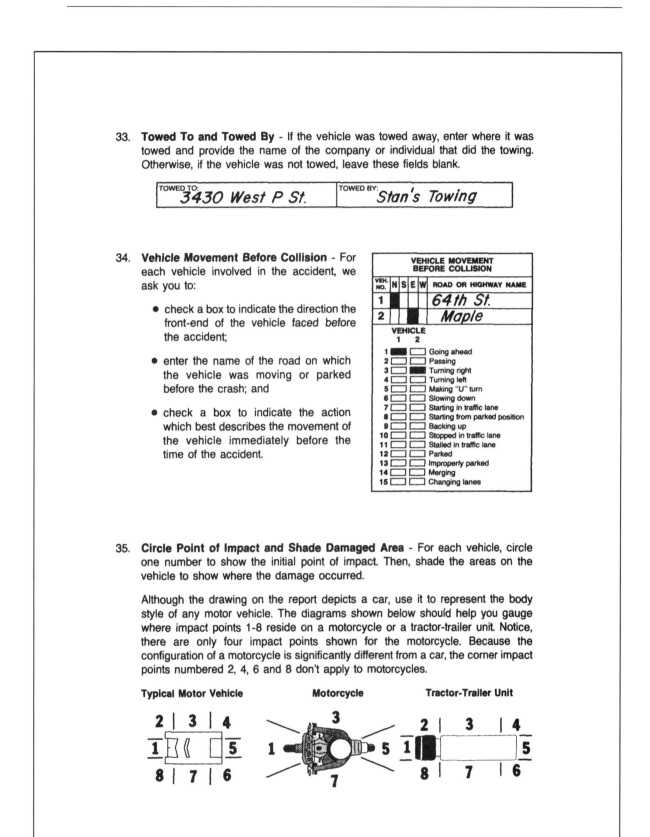

VEHICLE MOVEMENT BEFORE COLLISION

VEH. NO.	N	S	E	W	ROAD OR HIGHWAY NAME
1	■				*64th St.*
2			■		*Maple*

VEHICLE
	1	2	
1	■	☐	Going ahead
2	☐	☐	Passing
3	☐	■	Turning right
4	☐	☐	Turning left
5	☐	☐	Making "U" turn
6	☐	☐	Slowing down
7	☐	☐	Starting in traffic lane
8	☐	☐	Starting from parked position
9	☐	☐	Backing up
10	☐	☐	Stopped in traffic lane
11	☐	☐	Stalled in traffic lane
12	☐	☐	Parked
13	☐	☐	Improperly parked
14	☐	☐	Merging
15	☐	☐	Changing lanes

35. **Circle Point of Impact and Shade Damaged Area** - For each vehicle, circle one number to show the initial point of impact. Then, shade the areas on the vehicle to show where the damage occurred.

Although the drawing on the report depicts a car, use it to represent the body style of any motor vehicle. The diagrams shown below should help you gauge where impact points 1-8 reside on a motorcycle or a tractor-trailer unit. Notice, there are only four impact points shown for the motorcycle. Because the configuration of a motorcycle is significantly different from a car, the corner impact points numbered 2, 4, 6 and 8 don't apply to motorcycles.

Typical Motor Vehicle   **Motorcycle**   **Tractor-Trailer Unit**

Numbers 9-12 refer to vehicle positions which cannot clearly be shown with a two-dimensional drawing. These positions may be circled to show the point of impact, or used along with the drawing to clearly identify the areas of the vehicle that were damaged. Mark "unknown" when a hit-and-run vehicle was involved.

Example: In a two-vehicle collision, one of the vehicles involved was a motorcycle (VEH 1) and the other a car (VEH 2). The front-end of VEH 2 initially struck the right side of the motorcycle's front tire. As a result of the crash all areas of the motorcycle were damaged. Damage to the car was limited to the area shaded on the drawing.

36. **Disposition of Vehicle** - Check the box which best explains what happened to the vehicle after the accident. The choice of "towed-due to damages" refers to a vehicle being towed because of damages received in the collision. If the vehicle was towed for reasons other than disabling damage, check "towed-other reasons."

Example: In a two-vehicle collision, the driver of VEH 1 was arrested for drunk driving. Although damage to VEH 1 was not extensive, the vehicle was towed to an impound lot because of the driver's condition. VEH 2 sustained moderate damage, but was driven away.

37. **Vehicle Condition** - Indicate for each vehicle, whether you observed any defects. If a vehicle has more than one defect, check the defect that contributed most to the accident's occurrence.

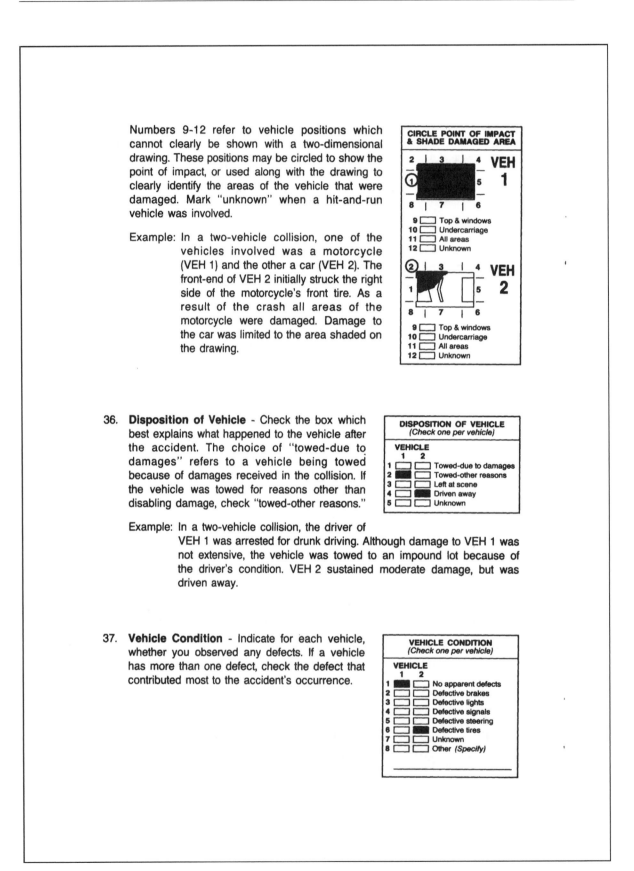

38. **Extent of Vehicle Deformity** - Unfortunately, there is no precise means by which to measure vehicle deformity. Although there are guidelines to help you rate the degree of vehicle damage, to a great extent we are relying on your experience and personal judgement.

The definitions presented below are based on the *"Vehicle Damage Scale for Traffic Accident Investigators,"* National Safety Council, 1984.

Minor Damage: Generally limited to gouges and dents in body sheet metal and trim.

Moderate Damage: Considerable crumpling of body sheet metal, but little or no distortion of the basic structure or frame.

Severe Damage: Sheet metal is severely distorted, torn, or crumpled. The basic structure of the car is distorted somewhat, and there is usually some penetration of the passenger compartment.

Bear in mind that the angle of impact and the concentration of force will influence the amount of crumpling done to a vehicle. To gain consistency in the rating approach, assess vehicle damage with respect to the type of collision, i.e., side impact resulting from sideswipe, side impact due to angular impact, etc.

EXTENT OF VEHICLE DEFORMITY
(Check one per vehicle)

VEHICLE 1 2		VEHICLE 1 2	
1 ☐ ☐	None	4 ☐ ☐	Severe
2 ☐ ☐	Minor	5 ☐ ☐	Unknown
3 ■ ☐	Moderate		

39. **Major Reason for Not Seeing Danger**
For each vehicle, check whether there was something physically obstructing the driver's view.

MAJOR REASON FOR NOT SEEING DANGER *(Check one per vehicle)*

VEHICLE 1 2

1		None
2		Rain, snow, or ice on windows
3		Dirty windows
4		Glare
5		Trees, crops, etc
6		Buildings
7		Embankment
8		Traffic sign
9		Billboard
10		Parked vehicle
11		Moving vehicle
12		Other (specify)

40. **Driver's Condition**   Check the box which best describes each driver's apparent condition at the time of the accident.

DRIVER'S CONDITION *(Check one per vehicle)*

VEHICLE 2

1		Normal
2		Fatigue/Asleep
3		Illness
4		Drinking
5		Illegal drugs
6		Medication
7		Unknown
8		Other (specify)

41. **Alcohol Testing**   Indicate if an alcohol test was given to any of the drivers or pedestrians involved in the accident. Leave the open area on the right side of the box blank.

ALCOHOL TESTING

ALCOHOL LEVEL TESTED	Y	N	
Driver No. 1	✓		
Driver No. 2		✓	
Pedestrian			

42. **Restraint Use**   Restraint information must be provided for **all** the vehicle occupants involved in an accident. The boxes shown on the car graph represent occupant seating positions. Enter a code number, according to seat position, which best describes the type of restraint in use by each occupant.

RESTRAINT USE

VEH 1

1 - No restraint available   5 - Automatic belt
2 - Restraint not used   6 - Child restraint
3 - Lap belt   7 - Unknown
4 - Lap & shoulder belt

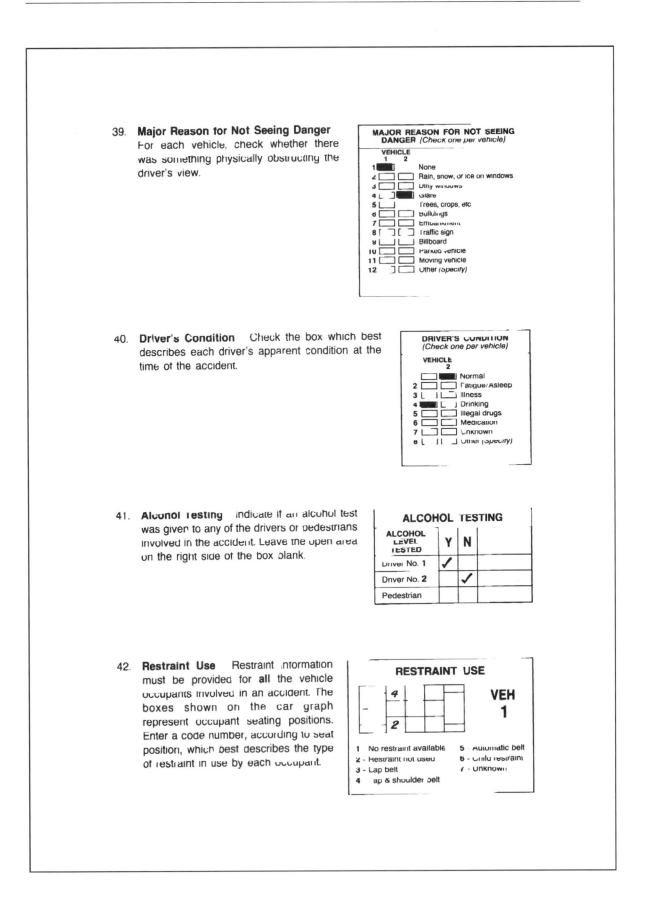

43. **Air Bag** - Air bag information is needed on all vehicles. If a vehicle is not equipped with an air bag, check the "not available" box. For vehicles with an air bag in the driver or front passenger seat position, indicate whether the air bag deployed.

AIR BAG	DID AIR BAG DEPLOY?		(✓) IF NO AIR BAG AVAILABLE
SEAT POSITION	YES	NO	
Driver Seat		✓	
Front Passenger			✓

44. **Helmet Use** - Helmet use is collected for motorcyclists and bicyclists involved in the accident. Check whether the motorcycle operator and his passengers, if any, wore a helmet. Do the same for bicyclists.

HELMET USE	MOTORCYCLE		BICYCLE	
	YES	NO	YES	NO
Operator	✓			
Passenger	✓			

Injured Persons

Information about injured persons is collected on the bottom portion of the accident report. Notice that the boxes numbered 1-5, which are located in the lower right corner, correspond to questions 1-5 asked on the report overlay. If more than three persons were injured in the accident, use the Investigator's Motor Vehicle Accident Continuation Report (DR Form 40a).

COMPLETE THIS SECTION FOR ALL INJURED PERSONS (Complete a continuation report, if more than three were injured).	RESCUE UNITS AT SCENE	1. Sherman Fire Dept. 2.	DATE OF BIRTH	SEX M F	1 Seat Pos.	2 Eject	3 Body Reg	4 Inj Sev	5 Trans
VEH.# 1 NAME Tina Grant ADDRESS 5261 Hancock St., Sherman, NE 68321			7-23-53	F	1	1	6	2	1
VEH.# 1 NAME James Grant ADDRESS 5261 Hancock St., Sherman, NE 68321			5-20-80	M	3	1	1	2	1
VEH.# 2 NAME Alex Mayen ADDRESS 123 Vermot Ave., Lincoln, NE 68503			11-12-61	M	1	1	3	4	2

DR Form 40, Jan 93   THIS FORM REPLACES DR FORM 40, SEP 90. PREVIOUS EDITIONS WILL BE DESTROYED   printed on recycled paper

45. **Rescue Units at Scene** - Give the name of the rescue service(s) which arrived at the accident scene. If the service was commercially owned and operated, give the name of the company. If municipality owned or operated, give the name of the town or county which runs the service.

46. **Vehicle Number** - For each injured occupant, enter the number of the vehicle in which he/she was seated. If a pedestrian or bicyclist was injured leave this box blank.

47. **Injured Person's Name and Address** - Enter the complete name of the injured person and provide his/her current address (street or RFD address, city, state, and zip code).

48. **Injured Person's Date of Birth** - Give the injured person's date of birth. Do not enter his/her age.

49. **Sex of Injured Person** - Enter M or F to indicate male or female.

50. *(Overlay No. 1)* **Injured Person's Seat Position**   For each injured person, enter the number which best describes his/her seat position. Seat positions 1-6 represent the typical seating arrangement found in a passenger car. Positions 7-9 relate to vehicles with a third row of seats. i.e., mini-vans, station wagons.

Numbers 10-20 describe additional seating positions for passengers of motor vehicles as well as identify pedestrians and bicyclists. Examples of seat positions 10-14 are provided below

Description of Seat Position | **Example**

10. Other enclosed passenger or cargo area

Rear cargo area commonly found in utility vehicles, mini-vans, and station wagons

11. Other unenclosed passenger or cargo area

Bed of a pickup truck

12. Riding on vehicle exterior

Hood, running boards, fenders, and bumpers

14. Trailing unit

Towed car or trailer

Seating Position *(Enter one)*   **1.**

```
  3 6 9
  2 5 8
  1 4 7
```

10. Other enclosed passenger/cargo area
11. Other unenclosed passenger/cargo area
12. Riding on vehicle exterior
13. Sleeper section of truck cab
14. Trailing unit
15. Moped
16. Motorcycle operator
17. Motorcycle passenger
18. Pedestrian
19. Bicycle
20. Unknown

RESCUE UNITS AT SCENE	DATE OF BIRTH	SEX M F	1 Seat Pos.	2 Eject.	3 Body Reg.	4 Inj. Sev.	5 Trans
1. Sherman Fire Dept. 2. Sherman, NE 68326	7-23-53	F					1

51. *(Overlay No. 2)* **Ejected/Trapped** - This field does not apply to pedestrians or bicyclists. The term ejected refers to a vehicle occupant being completely or partially thrown from a motor vehicle as a result of the crash. An occupant is considered trapped when damaged vehicle components physically impair his/her removal from the wreckage.

Ejected/Trapped *(Enter one)*   **2.**

1. Not ejected or trapped
2. Partially ejected
3. Totally ejected
4. Trapped - Occupant removed without use of equipment
5. Trapped - Equipment used in extrication
6. Unknown

RESCUE UNITS AT SCENE	1. *Sherman Fire Dept.* 2.	DATE OF BIRTH	SEX M F	1 Seat. Pos.	2 Eject.	3 Body Reg.	4 Inj. Sev.	5 Trans.
;S:	*Sherman, NE 68326*	*7-23-53*	*F*	*1*	*1*			

52. *(Overlay No. 3)* **Body Region with Most Severe Injury** - For each injured person, enter the code which best describes where the person was most severely injured.

Body Region with Most Severe Injury *(Enter one)*   **3.**

1. Head
2. Face
3. Neck
4. Chest
5. Back/spine
6. Shoulder/upper arm
7. Elbow/lower arm/hand
8. Abdomen/pelvis
9. Hip/upper leg
10. Knee/lower leg/foot
11. Entire body
12. Unknown

RESCUE UNITS AT SCENE	1. *Sherman Fire Dept.* 2.	DATE OF BIRTH	SEX M F	1 Seat. Pos.	2 Eject.	3 Body Reg.	4 Inj. Sev.	5 Trans.
;S:	*Sherman, NE 68326*	*7-23-53*	*F*	*1*	*1*	*6*		

53. *(Overlay No. 4)* **Injury Severity**   Enter a code you believe best explains the seriousness of the individual's injury.

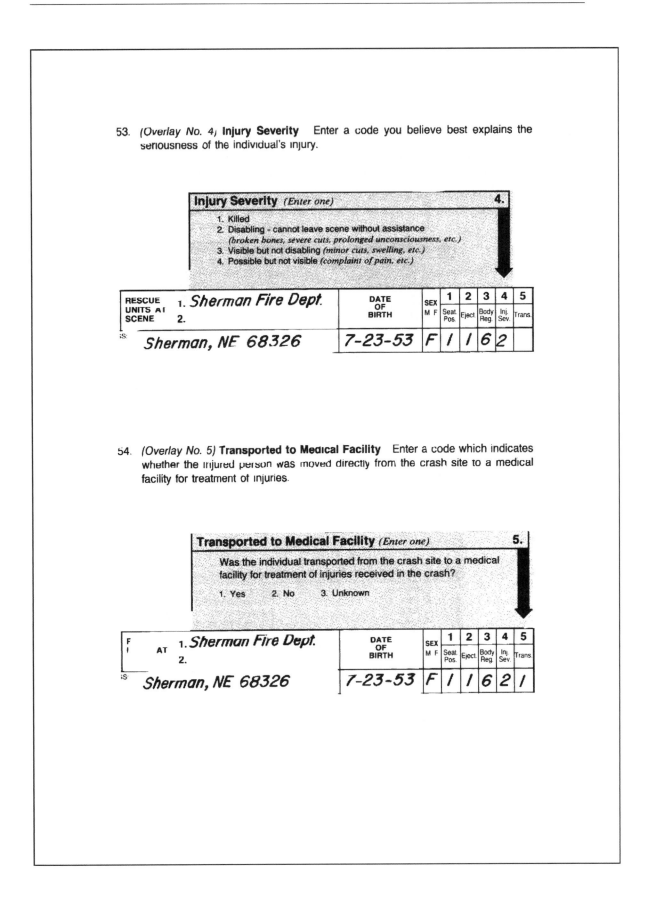

54. *(Overlay No. 5)* **Transported to Medical Facility**   Enter a code which indicates whether the injured person was moved directly from the crash site to a medical facility for treatment of injuries.

Accident Classification

The instructions numbered 55-65 relate to the "Accident Classification" section of the report overlay. Answer questions A-K for all accidents.

55. *(Overlay "A")* **Weather Condition Code**   Enter one code which best describes the weather condition at the time of the accident. If more than one code applies, enter the code which you believe most influenced the accident.

Remember to write the temperature in the box positioned directly below the weather condition code.

```
A|1

75°
```

A. Weather Condition *(Enter one)*
1. No adverse conditions
2. Rain
3. Sleet, hail, or freezing rain
4. Snow

5. Fog
6. High winds
★ 7. Other

TEMPERATURE

56. *(Overlay "B")* **Light Condition**   Enter one code to show what the light condition was at the time of the accident.

```
B|2
```

B. Light Condition *(Enter one)*
1. Daylight
2. Dawn - Dusk

3. Dark - With street lighting
4. Dark

57 *(Overlay "C")* **Traffic Control**   Identify up to two types of traffic control that were present at the accident scene. If an accident occurs at or near an intersection, remember to look for traffic controls present on both legs of the intersection.

The traffic controls relating to pedestrian crossings and railroad crossings are listed according to precedence (most restrictive to least restrictive). In other words, if a pedestrian signal is placed at mid-block to control traffic, it is understood that a pedestrian crosswalk is also present. Because of the pedestrian signal's higher precedence, it is sufficient to code the report with a "10" and not include a code for the crosswalk.

Controls Listed on the Report According to Precedence

10. Pedestrian Signal
     11   Pedestrian Crosswalk

12. Railroad Gates and Lights
     13. Railroad Flashing Lights
          14. Railroad Crossing Sign

Example: An accident occurs at a railroad crossing which is marked with a crossing sign and protected with gates and lights. This crossing is located near an intersection. Traffic signals regulate vehicle movement through the intersection.

In this example, you would enter codes 6 (traffic signal) and 12 (railroad gates and lights) on the report. It is not necessary to enter a code of 13 (railroad flashing lights) or 14 (railroad crossing sign), because these controls are assumed to be present at all crossings protected with gates and lights.

C. Traffic Control *(Enter up to two)*

C 6
C 12

1. None
2. Yield sign
3. Stop sign
4. All-Way stop
5. Flashing beacon
6. Traffic signal
7. Traffic signal in flashing mode
8. School speed zone
9. Roadwork signing
10. Pedestrian signal
11. Pedestrian crosswalk
12. Railroad gates and lights
13. Railroad flashing lights
14. Railroad crossing sign
15. Officer/Flagperson
16. No passing zone
★ 17. Other

58. *(Overlay "D")* **Road Character** - Fill in the code which best describes the character of the road.

D. Road Character *(Enter one)*

D 4

1. Straight and level
2. Straight and on slope
3. Straight and on hilltop
4. Curved and level
5. Curved and on slope
6. Curved and on hilltop

59. *(Overlay "E")* **Road Surface** - Enter a code which identifies the type of material used to surface the road where the accident occurred.

E. Road Surface *(Enter one)*

E 2

1. Concrete
2. Asphalt
3. Brick
4. Gravel
5. Dirt
★ 6. Other

60. *(Overlay "F")* **Road Surface Condition** - Enter one code to describe the condition of the road's surface.

F. Road Surface Condition *(Enter one)*

F 1

1. Dry
2. Wet
3. Snowy-icy
★ 4. Other

61. *(Overlay "G")* **Total Number of Through Lanes** - Count the total number of driving lanes which allow traffic to flow straight ahead. Do not include turning bays, turn lanes, or acceleration and deceleration lanes. If the accident occurred on a divided roadway, be sure to count the number of lanes on both sides of the median in your total.

On some roads the total number of through lanes will change, depending on the time of day. For example, assume roadside parking is permitted on a local road *except* during rush hours (7:00-9:00 a.m. and 4:00-6:00 p.m.). Since these "parking lanes" become through lanes at rush period, there are more through lanes when parking is prohibited.

> **G. Total Number of Through Lanes** *(Enter one)*
>
> [G] **4**
>
> 1. One lane
> 2. Two lanes
> 3. Three lanes
> 4. Four lanes
> 5. Five lanes
> 6. Six or more lanes

62. *(Overlay "H")* **Median Type** - Select one code that best describes the type of median separating the opposing lanes of traffic on a divided roadway.

> **H. Median Type** *(Enter one)*
>
> [H] **2**
>
> 1. Median Barrier
> 2. Raised median (Curbed)
> 3. Grass Median (No curb)
> 4. Painted (No curb)
> 5. None

Median Barrier: A structure normally made of concrete (usually 32" high or higher) which is designed to prevent out-of-control vehicles from entering the opposing lane of traffic.

Raised Median: A raised island with concrete curbing along its outside edge that is built to divide a roadway. The body of a raised median may be composed of either concrete or earth.

Grass Median: A strip of turf used to separate opposing lanes of traffic. Curbing is not used.

Painted Median: When nothing is present to physically divide a roadway, a painted median may be used to guide and warn drivers not to cross over into oncoming traffic.

63. *(Overlay "I")* **Work Zone** - Indicate if the accident occurred in a work zone or if a work activity was being performed on the road at the time of the accident.

> **I. Work Zone** *(Enter one)*
> `3`
>   1. Road construction zone
>   2. Road maintenance zone *(repair with traffic control)*
>   3. Road maintenance activity *(snowplowing, mowing, striping, etc.)*
>   4. Utility activity
>   5. None

Construction Zone: A specific stretch of roadway under construction, generally a long-term project. Construction signs and other traffic control devices are used to inform and direct drivers safely through a construction zone.

Maintenance Zone: A short-term project where road repair is performed along a designated stretch of road. The signing used on such a project is usually mobile and indicative of its short-term nature.

Maintenance Activity: Road maintenance that is performed while the machinery moves along the right-of-way or down the road. Work is not restricted to a particular zone, and there may be no advanced signing to alert drivers.

64. *(Overlay "J")* **Major Contributing Human Factor** - Based on your investigation, enter one code per accident and the associated Vehicle Number. There are two boxes on the report that apply to this field. Enter your code selection in the box labeled "CODE" and fill in the Vehicle Number in the box "VEH NO."

> J CODE `2`
> VEH. NO. `1`
>
> **J. Major Contributing Human Factor**
> *(Enter one code per accident and the associated Vehicle Number)*
>
>   1. Speed too fast for conditions
>   2. Exceeding speed limit
>   3. Backing unsafely
>   4. Ran stop sign
>   5. Disregarded traffic signal
>   6. Failure to yield
>   7. Following too closely
>   8. Improper right turn on red
>   9. Other improper turn
>   10. Improper or no turn signal
>   11. Wrong way in one-way traffic
>   12. Improper lane change
>   13. Drove left of center
>   14. Evasive action
>   15. Improper overtaking
>   16. Improper loading or securing of cargo
>   17. None
> ★18. Other

65. *(Overlay "K")* **Major Contributing Environmental Factor** - Enter the code which best describes an environmental condition or circumstance which contributed to the accident.

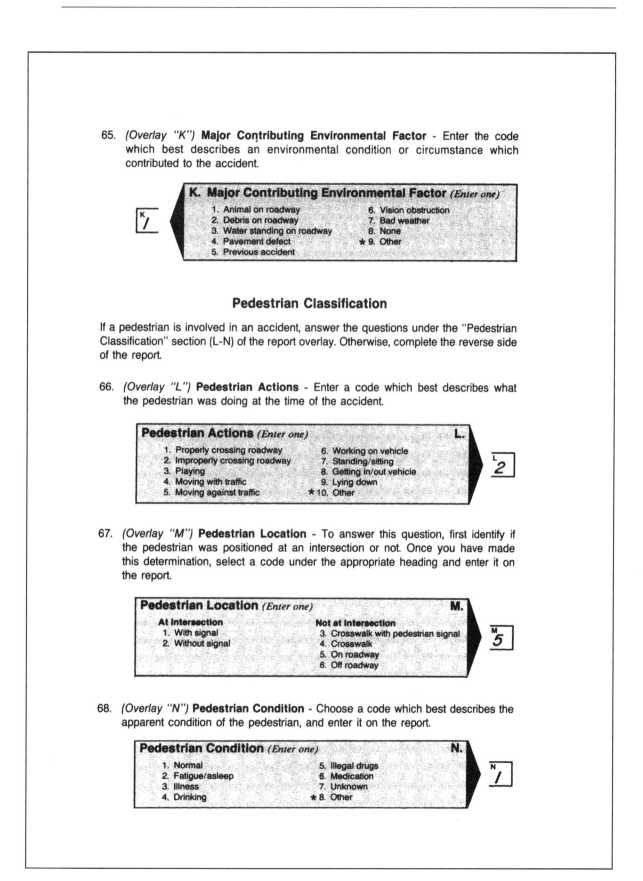

K. Major Contributing Environmental Factor *(Enter one)*

1. Animal on roadway
2. Debris on roadway
3. Water standing on roadway
4. Pavement defect
5. Previous accident
6. Vision obstruction
7. Bad weather
8. None
★ 9. Other

Pedestrian Classification

If a pedestrian is involved in an accident, answer the questions under the "Pedestrian Classification" section (L-N) of the report overlay. Otherwise, complete the reverse side of the report.

66. *(Overlay "L")* **Pedestrian Actions** - Enter a code which best describes what the pedestrian was doing at the time of the accident.

Pedestrian Actions *(Enter one)*   **L.**

1. Properly crossing roadway
2. Improperly crossing roadway
3. Playing
4. Moving with traffic
5. Moving against traffic
6. Working on vehicle
7. Standing/sitting
8. Getting in/out vehicle
9. Lying down
★ 10. Other

67. *(Overlay "M")* **Pedestrian Location** - To answer this question, first identify if the pedestrian was positioned at an intersection or not. Once you have made this determination, select a code under the appropriate heading and enter it on the report.

Pedestrian Location *(Enter one)*   **M.**

At Intersection
1. With signal
2. Without signal

Not at Intersection
3. Crosswalk with pedestrian signal
4. Crosswalk
5. On roadway
6. Off roadway

68. *(Overlay "N")* **Pedestrian Condition** - Choose a code which best describes the apparent condition of the pedestrian, and enter it on the report.

Pedestrian Condition *(Enter one)*   **N.**

1. Normal
2. Fatigue/asleep
3. Illness
4. Drinking
5. Illegal drugs
6. Medication
7. Unknown
★ 8. Other

Back of the Investigator's Motor Vehicle Accident Report

THE FOLLOWING INFORMATION IS REQUIRED FOR ALL ACCIDENTS

INDICATE BY DIAGRAM WHAT HAPPENED

Indicate
North
by Arrow

DESCRIPTION OF ACCIDENT BASED ON OFFICER'S INVESTIGATION

PROPERTY	OBJECT DAMAGED:	NAME OF OWNER:	ADDRESS:	PHONE:	APPROX. COST OF DAMAGE: $
	OBJECT DAMAGED:	NAME OF OWNER:	ADDRESS:	PHONE:	APPROX. COST OF DAMAGE: $

WITNESSES	NAME:	ADDRESS:	PHONE:
	NAME:	ADDRESS:	PHONE:

WAS INVESTIGATION MADE AT SCENE? ☐ YES ☐ NO	IS INVESTIGATION COMPLETE? ☐ YES ☐ NO	DRIVER'S REPORT FORM FURNISHED TO? ☐ 1 ☐ 2	WERE PHOTOGRAPHS TAKEN? ☐ YES ☐ NO	SHOULD LOCATION HAVE AN ENGINEERING STUDY? ☐ YES ☐ NO	OFFICER NO.:	DATE OF REPORT

INVESTIGATOR'S PRINTED OR TYPED NAME:	INVESTIGATOR'S SIGNATURE:	DEPARTMENT:	TROOP:	MO.	DAY	YR.

Instructions on How to Complete the Back of the Report

69. **Indicate by Diagram What Happened** - A diagram is required for all accidents. If the vehicles were moved prior to your arrival at the accident scene, use the information obtained from your investigation to draw the diagram. The State does not require that the diagram be drawn to scale.

    If necessary, the diagram may be drawn on a separate 8½"×11" sheet of paper. Before attaching the diagram to your report, be sure the drivers' names, county of accident, and the accident date is typed or printed on the diagram.

What to Show on the Diagram

1. In the upper left corner, draw an arrow to indicate north.

2. All streets and highways should be properly labeled with their name and/or number.

3. Number each vehicle. Use a solid arrow to show the paths the vehicles or any involved pedestrians were traveling prior to the collision.

4. Draw the vehicle positions at the time of impact.

5. Use a dotted arrow to indicate the post-crash paths of the vehicles, and draw where the vehicles came to rest after the crash.

6. The distance and direction to landmarks (intersections, mileposts, bridges, railroad crossings, etc.) should be indicated and identified by name or number. Choose a landmark that would best help a person unfamiliar with the locality to pinpoint the accident on the map.

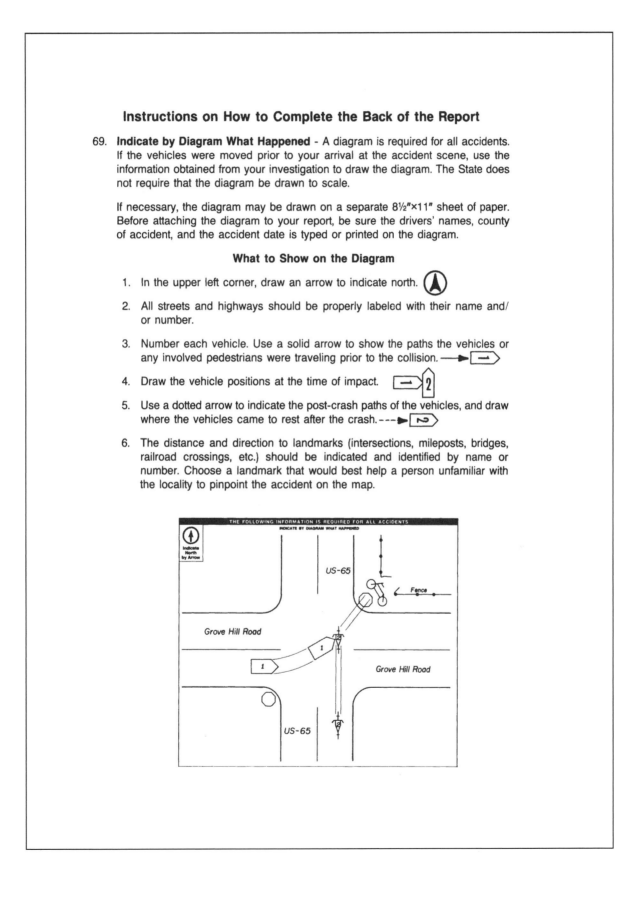

70. **Description of Accident** *(based on investigation)* - Provide a complete description of the accident. Refer to the vehicles by number. Your narrative along with the diagram should describe the main events of the accident.

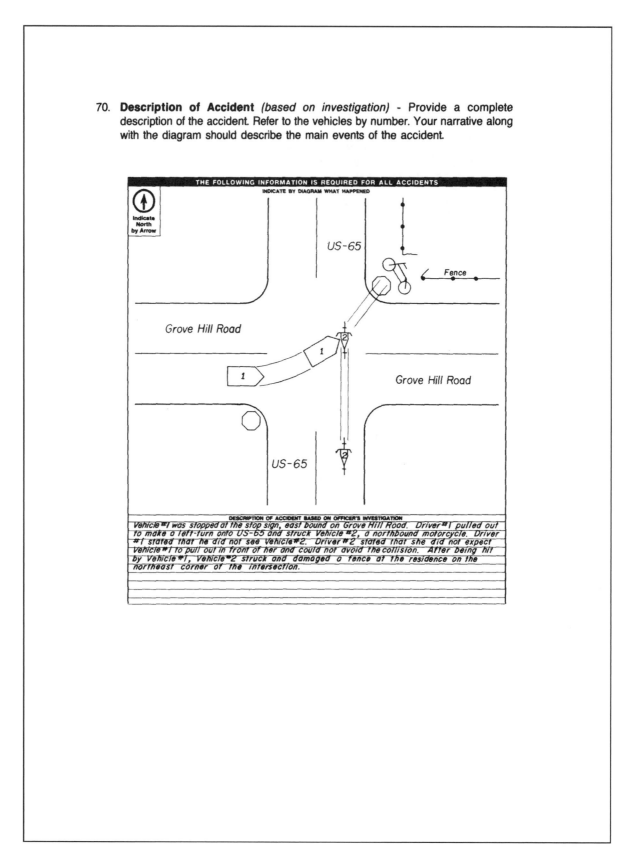

71. **Property** - If property was damaged in the accident, complete this section. Provide the following for each owner whose property was damaged.

    1. Briefly describe the damaged object(s).

    2. Provide the name, address, and phone number of the owner.

    3. Give an approximate cost of the damage.

OBJECT DAMAGED	NAME OF OWNER	ADDRESS	PHONE	APPROX. COST OF DAMAGE
Privacy Fence	John Grisby	742 Elm St. Lincoln, NE	842-2114	$350.00
Mail Box	Samuel Janson	744 Elm St. Lincoln, NE	842-7080	$50.00

72. **Witness** - If there were any witnesses to the accident, enter their name, address, and phone number.

NAME	ADDRESS	PHONE
Rhonda Smith 3210 Adams St.	Roberts City, NE 68085	487-0989
Patrick Smith 3210 Adams St.	Roberts City, NE 68085	487-0989

73. **Investigation Related Information** - Answer each of the questions asked about the investigation by checking the appropriate box. If you believe there may be a problem with the layout of the road, road markings, signing, etc., check "yes" on the Engineering Study box.

| WAS INVESTIGATION MADE AT SCENE? | ■ YES ☐ NO | IS INVESTIGATION COMPLETE? | ■ YES ☐ NO | DRIVER'S REPORT FORM FURNISHED TO? | ■ 1 ■ 2 | WERE PHOTOGRAPHS TAKEN? | ☐ YES ■ NO | SHOULD LOCATION HAVE AN ENGINEERING STUDY? | ☐ YES ■ NO |

74. **Investigator Information** - Complete this information and be sure to *sign your name.*

			OFFICER NO. 27	DATE OF REPORT
INVESTIGATOR'S PRINTED OR TYPED NAME Deputy Roger O'Hara	INVESTIGATOR'S SIGNATURE Roger O'Hara	DEPARTMENT McKenley Co. Sheriff	TROOP:	MO. 04 DAY 30 YR. 93

Investigator's Supplemental Truck and Bus Accident Report
(DR Form 174)

This supplemental report must be completed in addition to the DR Form 40, Investigator's Motor Vehicle Accident Report for any:

1. truck having at least 2 axles and 6 tires;
2. vehicle displaying a hazardous materials placard; or
3. bus designed to transport 16 or more passengers including the driver.

If more than two trucks/buses were involved in the accident, you will need to use additional supplemental forms.

STATE OF NEBRASKA

INVESTIGATOR'S SUPPLEMENTAL TRUCK AND BUS ACCIDENT REPORT

This form must be completed in **addition** to the DR Form 40, "Investigator's Motor Vehicle Accident Report," if any of the vehicles involved meet the criteria listed on the back of this form.

Sheet .... of ....

AGENCY CASE NUMBER	DATE OF ACCIDENT	COUNTY:	FOR STATE USE ONLY
CITY:		OCCURRED ON HIGHWAY/ROAD/STREET:	Dist.

TRUCK / BUS - 1

DRIVER: *(Print or type full name)*

NUMBER OF AXLES *(Including trailer)* ▶

GROSS VEHICLE WEIGHT RATING *(Combined rating for vehicle and trailer)* ▶ lbs.

CARRIER NAME: *(Print or type full name)*

CARRIER NAME SOURCE
1 ☐ Vehicle Side
2 ☐ Shipping Papers
3 ☐ Driver or Logbook

CARRIER ADDRESS: *(Street or R.F.D.)*   CITY, STATE, ZIP:

CARRIER IDENTIFICATION NUMBER
1 U.S. DOT _____
2 ICC MC _____
3 ST _____ No. _____

COMMERCE CLASSIFICATION *(check one)*
1 ☐ Interstate Commerce
2 ☐ Intrastate Commerce
3 ☐ Not Applicable

TRUCK WIDTH *(widest part of truck or trailer)*
1 ☐ 96 inches
2 ☐ 102 inches
3 ☐ Other *(Specify)*

SEQUENCE OF EVENTS *(Indicate the order of events by Code No. for this vehicle)*

SEQUENCE CODE NO.
1st Event ☐
2nd Event ☐
3rd Event ☐
4th Event ☐

CODE NO.
1 Ran off road
2 Jackknife
3 Overturn
4 Downhill runaway
5 Cargo loss or shift
6 Explosion or fire
7 Separation of units
8 Collision with pedestrian
9 Collision with vehicle in transport

CODE NO.
10 Collision with parked vehicle
11 Collision with train
12 Collision with pedalcycle
13 Collision with animal
14 Collision with fixed object
15 Collision with other object
16 Other *(Specify)*

VEHICLE CONFIGURATION *(check one)*
1 ☐ Bus
2 ☐ Single-Unit Truck: 2 axles, 6 tires
3 ☐ Single-Unit Truck: 3 or more axles
4 ☐ Single-Unit Truck tractor (bobtail)
5 ☐ Truck with Trailer
6 ☐ Tractor with Semi-Trailer
7 ☐ Tractor with Doubles
8 ☐ Tractor with Triples
9 ☐ Unknown Heavy Truck

CARGO BODY TYPE *(check one)*
1 ☐ Bus
3 ☐ Van/Enclosed Box
4 ☐ Cargo Tank
5 ☐ Flatbed
6 ☐ Dump
7 ☐ Concrete Mixer
8 ☐ Auto Transporter
9 ☐ Garbage/Refuse
10 ☐ Other *(Specify)*

HAZARDOUS MATERIAL INVOLVED

Did vehicle have a HAZ MAT Placard?   1 ☐ Yes 2 ☐ No

Placard Information:
4-Digit I.D. or Name *(from box or diamond)*
1. _____
2. _____

1-Digit *(from box or diamond)*

Was hazardous cargo released? *(do not count fuel from fuel tank)*   1 ☐ Yes 2 ☐ No

TRUCK / BUS - 2

DRIVER: *(Print or type full name)*

NUMBER OF AXLES *(Including trailer)* ▶

GROSS VEHICLE WEIGHT RATING *(Combined rating for vehicle and trailer)* ▶ lbs.

CARRIER NAME: *(Print or type full name)*

CARRIER NAME SOURCE
1 ☐ Vehicle Side
2 ☐ Shipping Papers
3 ☐ Driver or Logbook

CARRIER ADDRESS: *(Street or R.F.D.)*   CITY, STATE, ZIP:

CARRIER IDENTIFICATION NUMBER
1 U.S. DOT _____
2 ICC MC _____
3 ST _____ No. _____

COMMERCE CLASSIFICATION *(check one)*
1 ☐ Interstate Commerce
2 ☐ Intrastate Commerce
3 ☐ Not Applicable

TRUCK WIDTH *(widest part of truck or trailer)*
1 ☐ 96 inches
2 ☐ 102 inches
3 ☐ Other *(Specify)*

SEQUENCE OF EVENTS *(Indicate the order of events by Code No. for this vehicle)*

SEQUENCE CODE NO.
1st Event ☐
2nd Event ☐
3rd Event ☐
4th Event ☐

CODE NO.
1 Ran off road
2 Jackknife
3 Overturn
4 Downhill runaway
5 Cargo loss or shift
6 Explosion or fire
7 Separation of units
8 Collision with pedestrian
9 Collision with vehicle in transport

CODE NO.
10 Collision with parked vehicle
11 Collision with train
12 Collision with pedalcycle
13 Collision with animal
14 Collision with fixed object
15 Collision with other object
16 Other *(Specify)*

VEHICLE CONFIGURATION *(check one)*
1 ☐ Bus
2 ☐ Single-Unit Truck: 2 axles, 6 tires
3 ☐ Single-Unit Truck: 3 or more axles
4 ☐ Single-Unit Truck tractor (bobtail)
5 ☐ Truck with Trailer
6 ☐ Tractor with Semi-Trailer
7 ☐ Tractor with Doubles
8 ☐ Tractor with Triples
9 ☐ Unknown Heavy Truck

CARGO BODY TYPE *(check one)*
1 ☐ Bus
3 ☐ Van/Enclosed Box
4 ☐ Cargo Tank
5 ☐ Flatbed
6 ☐ Dump
7 ☐ Concrete Mixer
8 ☐ Auto Transporter
9 ☐ Garbage/Refuse
10 ☐ Other *(Specify)*

HAZARDOUS MATERIAL INVOLVED

Did vehicle have a HAZ MAT Placard?   1 ☐ Yes 2 ☐ No

Placard Information:
4-Digit I.D. or Name *(from box or diamond)*
1. _____
2. _____

1-Digit *(from box or diamond)*

Was hazardous cargo released? *(do not count fuel from fuel tank)*   1 ☐ Yes 2 ☐ No

EXAMPLES OF VEHICLE CONFIGURATION CATEGORIES

1 BUS	2 SINGLE-UNIT (2 Axle; 6 Tire)	3 SINGLE-UNIT (3 or more axles)	4 SINGLE-UNIT TRUCK TRACTOR
5 TRUCK WITH TRAILER	6 TRACTOR WITH SEMI-TRAILER	7 TRACTOR WITH DOUBLES	8 TRACTOR WITH TRIPLES

INVESTIGATOR'S PRINTED OR TYPED NAME	INVESTIGATOR'S SIGNATURE:	DEPARTMENT:	OFFICER NO.	DATE OF REPORT

DR Form 174, Jan 95   MAIL TO: Highway Safety Division - Accident Records Bureau, Nebraska Department of Roads, P.O. Box 94669, Lincoln, NE 68509-4669.

Instructions for Completing the Investigator's Supplemental Truck and Bus Report

Refer to the back of the Investigator's Supplemental Truck and Bus Report for general instructions. More detailed directions are provided below.

The data definitions prepared by the National Governor's Association were used as a leading source of information.

1. **Accident Case Information** - This section serves to identify the report as a supplement to an Investigator's Motor Vehicle Accident Report.

   After entering Sheet __ of __, copy the internal case number (if any), accident date, and location information from your yellow investigator's report.

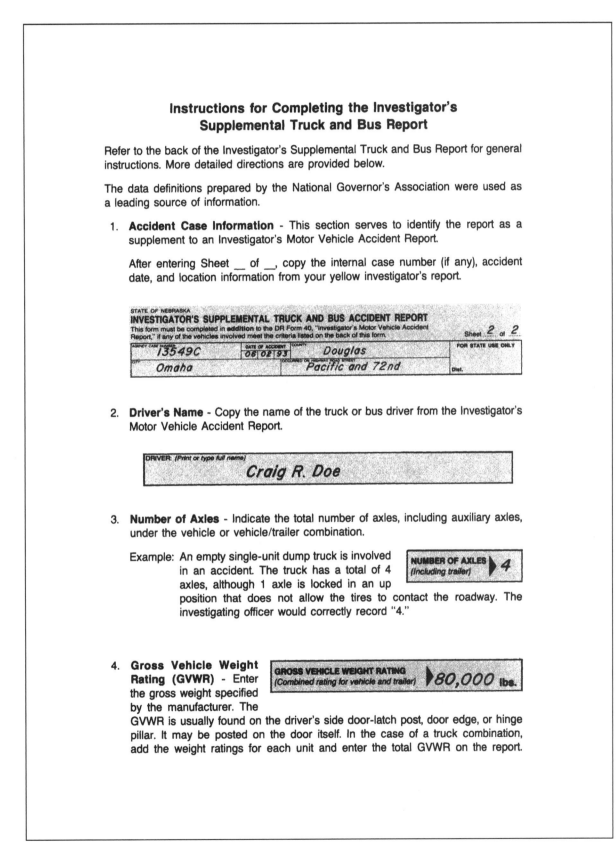

2. **Driver's Name** - Copy the name of the truck or bus driver from the Investigator's Motor Vehicle Accident Report.

3. **Number of Axles** - Indicate the total number of axles, including auxiliary axles, under the vehicle or vehicle/trailer combination.

   Example: An empty single-unit dump truck is involved in an accident. The truck has a total of 4 axles, although 1 axle is locked in an up position that does not allow the tires to contact the roadway. The investigating officer would correctly record "4."

4. **Gross Vehicle Weight Rating (GVWR)** - Enter the gross weight specified by the manufacturer. The GVWR is usually found on the driver's side door-latch post, door edge, or hinge pillar. It may be posted on the door itself. In the case of a truck combination, add the weight ratings for each unit and enter the total GVWR on the report.

5. **Carrier Name** - Determining the motor carrier may be difficult. Although the owner of the vehicle may be the carrier, quite often this is not the case. A motor carrier is defined as the person, company, or organization responsible for directing the transportation of the cargo or persons. The examples below help clarify the definition of a motor carrier.

Example: John Smith owns his bobtail tractor. He contracts with White Manufacturing Company to take one of its trailers loaded with its goods from New York to Los Angeles. John Smith is the motor carrier, because he is the entity that agreed to carry this particular load.

Example: John Smith driving his bobtail, utilizes a cargo broker to obtain goods from Intermodal Co. for his return trip to New York. On his return trip, John Smith is again the motor carrier.

Example: John Smith, driving his bobtail tractor, leases his services to Polyester Chemical Company. Polyester directs Smith to deliver a semi-trailer from New York to St. Louis. In this case Polyester is the motor carrier, because it assigned Mr. Smith to deliver the load.

Example: John Smith is driving a tractor owned by ABC Trucking which has been leased to the XYZ Trucking Co. XYZ uses the tractor to pull XYZ trailers in its regular shipping service. In this case XYZ is the carrier, because XYZ is directing the carrying of the load.

The **first** place an officer should look for the carrier name is on the driver's side door of the cab. On single unit trucks there should only be one carrier name on the vehicle. However, with multi-unit trucks there might be one name on the tractor and other names on the semi-trailer or trailers. The name found on the tractor is a much better indicator of the carrier's name.

The **second** place to look for the motor carrier name is on the driver's shipping papers. A bus driver must carry a "trip manifest" or "charter order" that will give the name of the carrier.

Lastly, ask the driver for the carrier name. The driver may refer to his/her logbook or simply tell you the name of the motor carrier.

CARRIER NAME: (Print or type full name)
Cleaver Enterprise

6. **Carrier Address** - Enter the address of the carrier's principal place of business (street number, city, state, and zip code).

CARRIER ADDRESS: (Street or R.F.D.)	CITY, STATE, ZIP:
2940 Carrington Ave., Knox, MN 56107	

7. **Carrier Name Source** - Check only one box to indicate the source which gave you the carrier's name.

Example: You were unsuccessful in determining the motor carrier name after checking the vehicle side, but did identify the carrier after reviewing the shipping papers. In this case, check the "Shipping Papers" box.

8. **Carrier Identification Number** - More than one carrier identification number may be entered. Interstate vehicles have either a US DOT (United States Department of Transportation) or an ICC MC (Interstate Commerce Commission Motor Carrier) number. An interstate vehicle operates across state lines.

The US DOT number has six digits and is found only on vehicles of interstate private carriers (those operating trucks in furtherance of any commercial enterprise). The number is always preceded by "US DOT," so it can be spotted easily.

ICC MC numbers will be found only on vehicles of interstate for-hire carriers (those in the transportation business). The number is usually preceded by "ICC MC," but may be preceded by just "ICC" or "MC."

State numbers are issued by the public utility commission, public service commission, or other state agency to vehicles that operate in either intrastate (i.e., within the boundaries of that state) or interstate commerce. There is no national standard for the number of digits in state numbers.

Some trucks will not have an identifying number. Although federal regulations require most interstate trucks to have ID numbers, not all do. In addition, many trucks and buses that operate strictly within one state (i.e., intrastate) may not have a number. In some states the motor carrier industry is not regulated, so state agencies have no reason to issue numbers.

9. **Commerce Classification** - Check the "interstate commerce" box if the commercial vehicle can legally trade, traffic, or transport property across state lines. Mark the "intrastate commerce" box when the commercial vehicle is restricted to commerce within one state.

A commerce classification may not apply to some vehicles.

10. **Truck Width** - Measure the widest part of the truck or trailer and then check the appropriate box. If "other" is checked, specify the width in inches.

11. **Sequence of Events** - You are asked to identify and order the events of the accident relating to each truck or bus involved. Determine the events which describe the actions of the vehicle and then enter the proper code numbers in the order in which the events occurred (first, second, third, or fourth). Not all accidents will have more than one event, but indicate all that apply.

    Example: A single-unit truck sideswipes a vehicle in the right lane. The truck leaves the roadway and overturns and loses its cargo. The sequence of events which describe the actions of the truck are indicated below.

12. **Vehicle Configuration** - Check the response that best describes the truck or bus involved in this accident. To help you select the appropriate configuration, refer to the vehicle silhouettes shown at the bottom of the report.

    Example: A single-unit (2 axles, 6 tires) truck towing a passenger car is involved in an accident. The towed car has all 4 wheels touching the ground. Because the car is not a vehicle primarily equipped to carry property, the correct response is code number "2" (Single-Unit Truck: 2 axles, 6 tires).

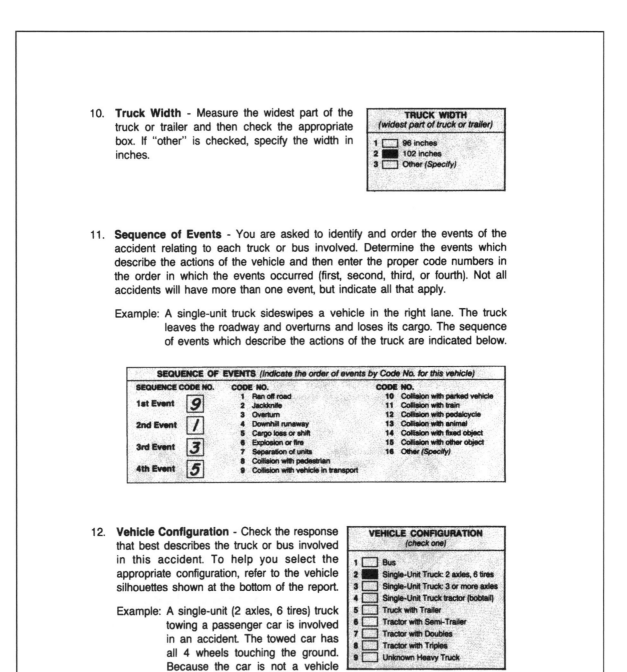

13. **Cargo Body Type** - Check the box which best identifies the cargo body type of the vehicle.

    Example: A tractor with a flatbed semi-trailer picks up a containerized load for transport. Although this body type appears similar to an enclosed box, it is correctly classified as "flatbed" or number "5."

CARGO BODY TYPE (check one)	
1 ☐	Bus
2 ☐	Motor Home
3 ☐	Van/Enclosed Box
4 ☐	Cargo Tank
5 ■	Flatbed
6 ☐	Dump
7 ☐	Concrete Mixer
8 ☐	Auto Transporter
9 ☐	Garbage/Refuse
10 ☐	Other (Specify)

14. **Hazardous Material Involved** - In most cases, vehicles carrying hazardous materials (HAZ MAT) are required by law to conspicuously display a placard indicating the class, type, or the specific name of the hazardous material cargo.

    Vehicles transporting hazardous materials in tank cars, cargo tanks, or portable tanks are required to display the 4-digit hazardous materials identification number on placards or orange panels.

    There are two placard shapes - diamond and rectangular. The diamond shaped placard is the most common variety. Examples of a numbered placard and a placard with an orange panel are shown below.

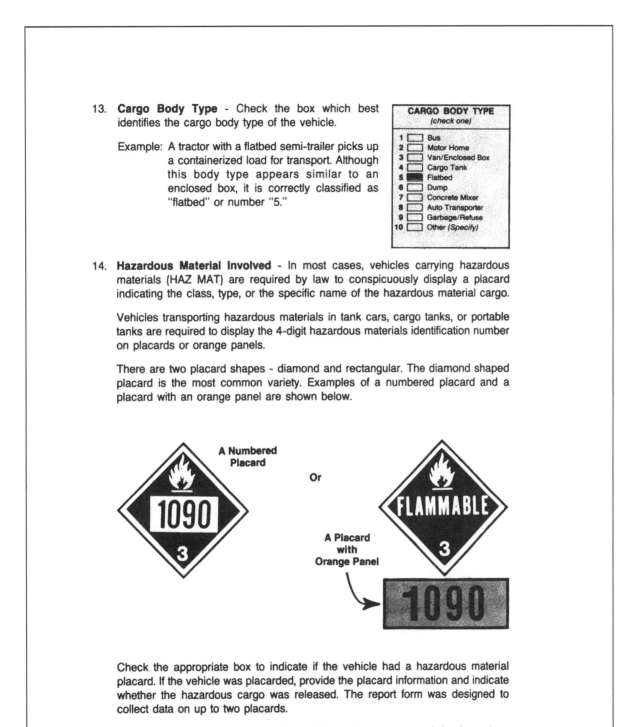

Check the appropriate box to indicate if the vehicle had a hazardous material placard. If the vehicle was placarded, provide the placard information and indicate whether the hazardous cargo was released. The report form was designed to collect data on up to two placards.

On a diamond shaped placard, the 4-digit number or name of the hazardous material is printed in the middle (provide either one). The 1-digit number is located on the bottom tip of the diamond. The rectangular placard displays the 4-digit identification number.

Check "yes" if hazardous cargo was released from the cargo tank or compartment of the truck. Although fuel is regarded as a hazardous material, do not count the fuel spilled from the vehicle's own fuel tank. The intent of this question is to record whether or not the placarded material was released.

HAZARDOUS MATERIAL INVOLVED			
Did vehicle have a HAZ MAT Placard? 1 ■ Yes 2 ☐ No	Placard Information: 4-Digit I.D. or Name (from box or diamond) 1. _1090_____ 2. _____	1-Digit (from box or diamond) _3_	Was hazardous cargo released? (do not count fuel from fuel tank) 1 ☐ Yes 2 ■ No

15. **Investigator Information** - Complete this section and be sure to **sign** the report.

INVESTIGATOR'S PRINTED OR TYPED NAME	INVESTIGATOR'S SIGNATURE	DEPARTMENT:	OFFICER NO:	DATE OF REPORT
Deputy Roger O'Hara	Roger O'Hara	McKenley Co. Sheriff	32	09 10 94

DR Form 174, Jan 93   MAIL TO: Highway Safety Division - Accident Records Bureau, Nebraska Department of Roads, P.O. Box 94669, Lincoln, NE 68509-4669.

Sample Vehicle Theft Case Report Form, Chicago Police Department

Verify all vehicle identifiers (V.I.N., State and City licenses) through owner documentation or a mobile or land based computer terminal, your dispatcher or the Hot Desk. Notify the dispatcher in every instance when the theft appears bona fide, so a preliminary steal card for the Hot File can be completed.
All information, descriptions and statements in this entire report are approximations or summarizations unless indicated otherwise.

VEHICLE THEFT CASE REPORT
CHICAGO POLICE

1. OFFENSE/CLASSIFICATION
☐ THEFT 0910   ☐ ATTEMPT. THEFT 0920   ☐ THEFT & RECOVERY 0930   ☐ RECOVERY 0940   ☐ FOREIGN

2. TYPE OF VEHICLE
☐ 0 AUTO   ☐ 5 TRUCK, BUS   ☐ 7 MOTOR CYCLE, MOTOR SCOOTER, MOTOR BIKE

3. ADDRESS OF THEFT, ATTEMPT. THEFT, RECOVERY-FOREIGN | 4. DATE OF OCCURRENCE–TIME | 5. BEAT OF OCCUR.

6. TYPE OF LOCATION | 7. LOCATION CODE | 8. DATE R.O. ARRIVED – TIME | 9. BEAT/UNIT ASSIGN.

10. VEH. YEAR MAKE | MODEL | BODY STYLE | COLOR Top / Bottom | 11. DOORS LOCKED ☐ 1 YES ☐ 2 NO | 12. IGNITION LOCKED ☐ 1 YES ☐ 2-NO

13. V.I.N. | 14. STATE LICENSE PLATE NO.   STATE   MO/YR. EXPIR. | 15. KEYS IN VEH. ☐ 1 YES ☐ 2 NO | 16. FLASH MESSAGE SENT ☐ 1 YES ☐ 2 NO

17. CITY LICENSE NO.   CITY   EXPIR. YEAR | 18. V.I.N. & LIC. NOS. VERIFIED – IF ANY BOX "YES," C.O.S. MUST BE NOTIFIED   V.I.N. ☐ 1 YES ☐ 2 NO   STATE LIC. NO. ☐ 1 YES ☐ 2 NO   CITY LIC. NO. ☐ 1 YES ☐ 2 NO

19. DAMAGE ON VEHICLE – GIVE LOCATION | 20. SPECIAL ACCESSORIES OR EQUIPMENT | 21. PERSONAL BELONGINGS IN VEHICLE

22. REGISTERED OWNER (VICTIM)–NAME | ADDRESS (INCL. CITY, IF NOT CHICAGO) | ZIP CODE | SEX– RACE–AGE CODE | HOME PHONE | BUSINESS PHONE

23. PERSON REPORTING OFFENSE–NAME | ADDRESS

24. PERSON LAST DRIVING VEHICLE–NAME

25. TEMPORARY LOCAL ADDRESS OF NON-RESIDENT VICTIM & PHONE NO. | 26. WHERE WAS PERSON FROM WHOM VEH. WAS STOLEN AT TIME OF THEFT | 27. SOBRIETY OF THIS PERSON ☐ 1 SOBER ☐ 2 HBD

28. TITLE HOLDER (FINANCING INSTITUTION)–NAME | ADDRESS | PHONE | 29. DATE–LAST PAYMT.

30. INSURANCE CO. FOR VEHICLE–NAME | 31. FROM WHOM WAS VEHICLE PURCHASED –   PHONE | 32. BEST TIME/PLACE TO CONTACT COMPL.

33. OFFENDER'S NAME (OR DESCRIBE CLOTHING) | ADDRESS | SEX– RACE–AGE CODE | HEIGHT | WEIGHT | EYES | HAIR | COMPL. | C.B./Y.D./J.D.A. NO.

NO. OFF. | NAME | ADDRESS

IF RECOVERED VEHICLE

34. LOCATION OF RECOVERY   BEAT OF REC. | 35. EVIDENCE OF STRIPPING–CHECK ONE OR MORE   ☐ 0 NONE   ☐ 9 BODY PARTS OR OTHER (DESCRIBE IN NARRATIVE)
☐ 1 BURNED   ☐ 2 IGN. LOCK PULLED   ☐ 3 STEERING COLUMN PEELED
☐ 4 RADIO   ☐ 5 TIRES, NO.   ☐ 6 INTERIOR   ☐ 7 ENG.   ☐ 8 TRANSMISSION

36. LEADS/N.C.I.C. NO. (FOREIGN STEAL) | 37. CITY/STATE OF THEFT | 38. VEH. DISPOSITION ☐ 2 TOWED   POUND   ☐ 1 RETURNED TO OWNER | 39. VEH. INVENTORY NO. | 40. EVID. TECH. REQUESTED ☐ 1 YES ☐ 2 NO

41. NARRATIVE (Do not duplicate or repeat information – for explanation or additional information only)

IF VEHICLE RECOVERED LEGALLY PARKED (LOCAL STEAL)
☐ 1 OWNER/COMPLAINANT REQUESTS POLICE TOW
☐ 2 OWNER/COMPLAINANT REQUESTS NOTIFICATION
☐ 3 OPTIONS GIVEN–SIGNATURE REFUSED
| OWNER/COMPLAINANT'S SIGNATURE | NARRATIVE ☐ CONTINUED OTHER SIDE

42. REPORTING OFFICER'S NAME (PRINT)   STAR NO.   SIGNATURE | 43. EXTRA COPIES REQUIRED (NO. & RECIPIENT) ☐ NORMAL

44. REPORTING OFFICER'S NAME (PRINT)   STAR NO.   SIGNATURE | 45. DATE INVESTIGATION COMPLETED – TIME

46. SUPERVISOR APPROVING (PRINT NAME)   STAR NO.   SIGNATURE | DATE APPROVED   TIME

FOR DETECTIVE DIVISION USE ONLY | 47. R.D. NO.

I-UCR OFFENSE CODE ☐ 1 CORRECT ☐ 2 REV. | REV. I-UCR CODE | METHOD CODE | SUMMARY DET. STAR NO.   DATE | REASSIGNED ☐ 1 YES ☐ 2 NO | APPROVING SUPV. STAR NO.

FIELD DET. ASSIGNED–STAR – DATE | STATUS ☐ 3 CLEARED CLOSED   ☐ 0 PROGRESS   ☐ 1 SUSPENDED   ☐ 4 CLEARED OPEN   ☐ 2 UNFOUNDED   ☐ 5 EXCEPT. CLEARED CLOSED
☐ 6 EXCEPT. CLEARED OPEN   ☐ 7 CLOSED–NON-CRIMINAL

IF CASE CLEARED, HOW CLEARED (USE THIS BOX FOR SINGLE CLEAR UP OR FIRST CLEAR UP OF MULTIPLE CLEAR UP LIST)
☐ 1 ARREST & PROSECUTION   ☐ 2 DIRECTED TO FAMILY COURT   ☐ 3 COMPL. REFUSED TO PROSECUTE   ☐ 4 COMMUNITY ADJUSTMENT   ☐ 5 OTHER EXCEPTIONAL   ☐ ADULT ☐ JUV.

VICTIM IDENTIFIERS ☐ 1 CORRECT ☐ 2 REV. | REV. NAME | REV. ADDRESS | REV. PHONE ☐ HOME ☐ BUS.

V.I.N.   ☐ 1 VERIFIED   ☐ 2 CORRECTED   ☐ 3 OBTAINED | STATE LIC. NO.   ☐ 1 VERIFIED   STATE   ☐ 2 CORRECTED   ☐ 3 OBTAINED MO/YEAR EXPIR.

CITY LIC. NO.   ☐ 1 VERIFIED   ☐ 2 CORRECTED   CITY   ☐ 3 OBTAINED   EXPIR. YEAR | REMARKS

PREPARED BY–SIGNATURE   STAR NO.   DATE | APPROVED BY–SIGNATURE   STAR NO.   DATE

CPD-11.412 (Rev. 12/83)

LOCATION CODES

096— Abandoned Building	269— Park Property	313— School Property - Private
092— Alley	277— Parking Lot/Garage (Non-Resid.)	314— School Property - Public
095— Airport/Aircraft	123— Parking Lot/Grounds CHA	304— Street
126— Delivery Truck	313— Private School Property	262— Vehicle - Commercial
220— Gas Station	314— Public School Property	126— Vehicle - Delivery Truck
238— Highway/Expressway	317— Railroad Property	259— Vehicle - Non-Commercial
233— Hospital Building/Grounds	290— Residence	327— Warehouse
273— Lake/Waterway/Riverbank	210— Residence - Garage	330— Other - Specify

RACE CODES

1—Black   2—White   3—Black-Hispanic   4—White-Hispanic   5—American Indian/Alaskan National   6—Asian/Pacific Islander

CONTINUATION
OF NARRATIVE

RD
NO.

I HAVE REVIEWED THIS REPORT AND BY MY   SUPERVISOR'S SIGNATURE
SIGNATURE INDICATE THAT IT IS ACCEPTABLE.   DATE (DAY-MO-YR.)

Sample Vehicle Theft Case Report Form General Instructions, Chicago Police Department

VEHICLE THEFT CASE REPORT, CPD-11.412

GENERAL INSTRUCTIONS

PURPOSE OF THE REPORT

The Vehicle Theft Case Report is designed to record an officer's preliminary investigation of a vehicle reported stolen.
Include attempted auto thefts in this category.

WHEN TO PREPARE A VEHICLE THEFT CASE REPORT

A Vehicle Theft Case Report is to be used by any officer making a preliminary investigation of a bona fide vehicle theft, attempted theft, theft and recovery, or the recovery of a vehicle which was stolen outside of Chicago.

The dispatcher will be notified in every instance where the theft is apparently bona fide so that a preliminary steal card with the V.I.N., license and other pertinent information can be made.

This notification should be made immediately on all thefts so the information is entered in the computer and is available to make other officers aware of the theft.

In the event the recovery of a locally stolen vehicle occurs during the preliminary investigation, the fact should be recorded and the classification changed to "Theft and Recovery."

Vehicles taken in other crimes (i.e., robberies, burglaries, deceptive practices) will be reported on the appropriate case report. The dispatcher should be notified as in a normal vehicle theft.

FORM PREPARATION

The numbers below refer to box numbers on the reporting form. If known, include apartment, floor and room number whenever an address is requested.

1. Offense/Classification. Check one square only.
2. Type of Vehicle. Check one square only.

NOTE: The four digit I-UCR offense code is derived from the combination of a checked square in box 1 and a checked square in box 2.

3. If this is a Foreign Recovery, this should be the address of the recovery.
   If this is a Theft & Recovery, insert the address of theft here and address of recovery in box 34.
4. Enter the date(s) of occurrence and time or time span of occurrence.
   If Foreign Recovery, this box should be the date of recovery. In all other cases, this is the date the theft occurred.
5. Enter the correct beat of occurrence using the current beat map. If Foreign Recovery, this should be the beat of recovery.
6. Enter the type and, when applicable, the name of location of occurrence (i.e., street, alley, gas station—Shell).
7. Enter the appropriate Location Code. Codes are listed on the reverse side of the report.
8. Enter the date and time the reporting officer arrived at the scene.
9. Enter the beat or unit assigned to the investigation.
10. Be specific (i.e., '80 Olds Cutlass, 2 door, black/red).
11., 12. Check appropriate square.
13. V.I.N. Insert the vehicle identification (serial) number.

NOTE: On motorcycles, note the identification number present on the frame. Do not enter the engine number.
   Legibility of alpha and numeric digits of the V.I.N. is very important. Do not enter the victim's drivers license number. Start in the first space on the left, enter one character per space.
14. Enter the alpha/numeric state license number and the abbreviated name of the issuing state. When known, include the month and year of the license expiration.
15., 16. Check appropriate square.
17. Enter the alpha/numeric city license number and the name of the issuing city. Include the year of license expiration.
18. Check appropriate squares. A check in the YES square of any one of the three subsections is sufficient to require notification of the dispatcher. Report in the Narrative the document examined to verify the number.

If the victim believes he knows his state license number or V.I.N. but does not have documentation, check the given number with the dispatcher or through a land or mobile terminal for verification. If the information is confirmed, check it as verified in the report.

19. Indicate type and location of damage.
20. Record here accessories which are unusual or extra.
21. Self-explanatory. Use Narrative, if additional space is required.
22. Print last name of registered owner first, then first name and middle initial if any. If registered owner is a business, use the firm name. Enter address of registered owner, including Zip Code. If a business, enter the company address. Be specific with address, include apartment number if applicable.
   Enter sex, race code number and age of registered owner, if not a firm (race codes are listed on reverse side of report).

NOTE: The racial and ethnic categories for victims and offenders are defined as follows:

1—Black: A person having origins in any of the black racial groups of Africa.
2—White: A person having origins in any of the peoples of Europe, North Africa, or the Middle East.
3-4 Black-Hispanic/White-Hispanic: A person who is black or white and, in addition, is of Mexican, Puerto Rican, Cuban, Central or South American or other Spanish culture or origin.
5—American Indian or Alaskan Native: A person having origins in any of the original peoples of North America, and who maintains cultural identification through tribal affiliation or community recognition.
6—Asian or Pacific Islander: A person having origins in any of the original peoples of the Far East, Southeast Asia, the Indian subcontinent, or the Pacific Islands; this area includes, for example, China, India, Japan, Korea, the Philippine Islands, Samoa, etc.

The category which most closely reflects the individual's recognition in his community should be used for purposes of reporting on persons who are of mixed racial and/or ethnic origins. If the individual refuses to answer, it is up to the reporting officer to make a judgment.

   Enter the owner's home and business telephone numbers. If non-resident, obtain local telephone number. Include area code and extension with telephone numbers if applicable.
23. Enter the name, address and telephone numbers of the person who reported the offense. If victim is self-reporting, enter VICTIM in box 23.
24. Enter the name, address and telephone numbers of the person last driving the vehicle. If victim was the person last driving the vehicle, enter VICTIM in box 24.
25. through 31. Self-explanatory. Be specific with address, include apartment number if applicable. If non-resident, obtain local telephone number. Include area code and extension with telephone numbers if applicable.

CPD-63.462 (Rev. 8/84)

32. Be specific, list time, address and/or telephone number if available.

33. Enter alleged offender's name and/or alias; if unknown, give clothing description. If more space is required, identify as Offender and use Narrative.

Enter home address (if known) of the offender.

Enter sex, race code number, age and physical description of the offender.

Enter C.B., Y.D., or J.D.A. if an offender is arrested.

Enter total number of offenders.

34. through 40. To be filled out on all reports in which box 1 is checked as being a "Theft & Recovery" or a "Foreign Recovery."

41. Narrative: List here the results of the preliminary investigation including any information which would assist the detective.

Do not unnecessarily repeat information already contained in the numbered boxes. Otherwise, give a concise statement of the facts of the case. If address of occurrence is different from the address where the report is being made, indicate in the Narrative.

When preparing the report, inform the owner/complainant that, because the vehicle may be legally parked when recovered, he must indicate at the time the original report is being prepared whether he wants to:

a. authorize the police to tow the vehicle when it is recovered.

Explain that authorization for the Department to tow a stolen vehicle upon recovery in Chicago will involve payment of towing and storage fees before the vehicle can be released; or

b. be notified when the vehicle is recovered.

Explain that the owner/complainant will bear all risk of loss, and the Department will make no special effort to protect the vehicle until the owner recovers it.

Request that the owner/complainant sign the report. If the owner/complainant is willing to sign the report and indicates that he wants the vehicle towed by the police, you will:

a. check square 1 entitled "Owner/Complainant requests Police Tow."

b. have the owner/complainant sign his name in the space provided as authorization for the tow of his vehicle.

If the owner/complainant is willing to sign the report and indicates that he wants to be notified of the recovery, you will:

a. check square 2 entitled "Owner/Complainant requests Notification."

b. have the owner/complainant sign his name in the space provided. The signature will serve as notification that the owner/complainant has been informed of his option.

If the owner/complainant refuses to sign the report, you will:

a. check square 3 entitled "Options Given—Signature Refused."

b. report this refusal to the Communication Operations Section dispatcher as "Owner/Complainant requests Notification."

Mark the square to the right, if the narrative is continued on the reverse side.

42. Enter printed name of officer completing the report, star number and signature.

43. Indicate the number and recipient of extra copies required of this report. For normal distribution, check Normal square.

44. Enter printed name, star number and signature of a second officer if applicable.

45. Enter date and time investigation was completed.

46. Approving supervisor enters his printed name, star number and signature when he approves the report. Enter date and time report is approved.

If Narrative is continued on the reverse side, approving supervisor's signature and date is also required on the reverse.

47. Enter the R.D. number assigned to the report. Also record the R.D. number in the space provided on the reverse side of the report ONLY when a Narrative is continued on the reverse.

Preliminary investigators should make no entry in the area of the report headed "FOR DETECTIVE DIVISION USE ONLY."

VICTIM INFORMATION NOTICE: This notice is Part 3 of the formset. Reporting officers will enter the R.D. number in the space provided and mark the appropriate square indicating which unit has follow-up responsibility for the reported offense and leave the notice with the victim.

NOTE: IT SHOULD BE MADE CLEAR TO THE COMPLAINANT THAT DETECTIVES WILL CONTACT HIM ONLY IF ADDITIONAL INFORMATION IS REQUIRED OR HIS FURTHER ASSISTANCE IS NEEDED. COMPLAINANT WILL BE NOTIFIED WHEN THE VEHICLE IS RECOVERED.

Sample Recovered Vehicle Supplementary Report, Chicago Police Department

This report will be used when recording the recovery of a motor vehicle that has been previously reported stolen in Chicago. All boxes must be completed accurately.
All descriptions and statements in this entire report are approximations unless otherwise indicated.

RECOVERED VEHICLE SUPPLEMENTARY REPORT/CHICAGO POLICE

1. OFFENSE/CLASSIFICATION ON PREVIOUS REPORT
2. BEAT OF RECOVERY
3. DATE OF RECOVERY –   TIME
4. BEAT/UNIT ASSIGNED

6. ADDRESS/LOCATION OF RECOVERY
7. TYPE OF LOCATION WHERE RECOVERED
☐ 304 STREET   ☐ 210 RESIDENCE-GARAGE
☐ 092 ALLEY   ☐ OTHER – SPECIFY & ENTER CODE
LOCATION CODE

8. REGISTERED OWNER/VICTIM–NAME (LAST–FIRST–M.I.)
CORRECTION   OWNER'S ADDRESS
☐ YES ☐ NO
HOME PHONE
BUSINESS PHONE

9. V.I.N.
10. STATE LICENSE PLATE NO.   STATE   MO/YR. EXPIR.
11. LICENSE PLATE(S) RECOVERED
☐ YES   ☐ NO

12. VEH. YEAR   MAKE   MODEL   BODY STYLE   COLOR   13. CITY LICENSE NO.   EXPIR. YEAR
TOP   BOTTOM

14. EVIDENCE OF STRIPPING/DAMAGE – CHECK ONE OR MORE   ☐ 0 NONE
☐ 1 BURNED   ☐ 2 IGNITION LOCK PULLED   ☐ 3 STEERING COLUMN PEELED   ☐ 9 BODY PARTS OR OTHER (DESCRIBE IN NARRATIVE)
15. DIRECTION VEH. FACED AT RECOVERY
☐ 4 RADIO   ☐ 5 TIRES, NO.:   ☐ 6 INTERIOR   ☐ 7 ENGINE   ☐ 8 TRANSMISSION   ☐ N ☐ S ☐ E ☐ W

16. VEHICLE LEGALLY PARKED   IF YES, RESULT OF COMPUTER INQUIRY
☐ YES ☐ NO   ☐ YES, BUT HAZARD (SPECIFY IN NARRATIVE)   ☐ TOW   ☐ NOTIFY OWNER   ☐ NO RESULTS
17. OWNER/COMPLAINANT NOTIFIED BY C.O.S.   DATE   TIME
☐ C.O.S. UNABLE TO CONTACT OWNER

18. IF TOWED– POUND NO.   VEHICLE INVENTORY NO.
19. PROPERTY INVENTORY NO.
20. HOT FILE CLEARED   THROUGH WHOM   DATE
☐ C.O.S.
☐ 1 YES ☐ 2 NO   ☐ FIELD INQUIRY
21. EVID. TECH. REQUESTED
☐ 1 YES   ☐ 2 NO

22. OFFENDER/ARRESTEE–NAME   ADDRESS   SEX – RACE –AGE CODE   HEIGHT   WEIGHT   EYES   HAIR   COMPL.   C.B./Y.D./J.D.A. NO.

23. NO. ARRESTED   24. ARRESTING UNIT NO.   25. DATE OF ORIGINAL OCCURRENCE   26. BEAT OF ORIGINAL OCCURRENCE

80. NARRATIVE (Do not duplicate or repeat information -- for explanation or additional information only. If there is an arrest AT THE TIME OF RECOVERY, enter required information above, list court date, branch and charge in Narrative, and a full description of events leading to the arrest.)

SIGNATURE OF PERSON RECEIVING VEHICLE FROM RECOVERING OFFICER
NARRATIVE
☐ CONTINUED OTHER SIDE

90. OFFICER NOTIFYING DETECTIVE DIVISION–   UNIT NOTIFIED – PERSON   ☐ NOTIFIED ☐ ARRIVED   DATE   TIME

91. REPORTING OFFICER (PRINT NAME)   STAR NO.   SIGNATURE   92. EXTRA COPIES REQUIRED (NO. & RECIPIENT)
☐ NORMAL

93. REPORTING OFFICER (PRINT NAME)   STAR NO.   SIGNATURE   94. DATE INVESTIG. COMPLETED–TIME

95. SUPERVISOR APPROVING (PRINT NAME)   STAR NO.   SIGNATURE   DATE APPROVED –   TIME

5. R.D. NO.

FOR DETECTIVE DIVISION USE ONLY

OFFENSE/CLASS. THIS DATE (IF SAME ENTER DNA)   REV. CODE   METHOD CODE   REVIEW DET. STAR NO.   DATE   FIELD DET. STAR NO.

STATUS
☐ 0 PROGRESS   ☐ 1 SUSPENDED   ☐ 2 UNFOUNDED   ☐ 3 CLEARED CLOSED   ☐ 4 CLEARED OPEN   ☐ 5 EXC. CLEARED CLOSED   ☐ 6 EXC. CLEARED OPEN   ☐ 7 CLOSED NON-CRIMINAL

IF CASE CLEARED, HOW CLEARED (USE THIS BOX FOR SINGLE CLEAR UP OR FIRST CLEAR UP OF MULTIPLE CLEAR UP LIST)
☐ 1 ARREST & PROSECUTION   ☐ 2 DIRECTED TO JUV. COURT   ☐ 3 COMPL. REFUSED TO PROSECUTE   ☐ 4 COMMUNITY ADJUSTMENT   ☐ 5 OTHER EXCEPTIONAL   ☐ ADULT   ☐ JUV.

PREPARED BY – SIGNATURE   STAR NO.   DATE   APPROVED BY – SIGNATURE   STAR NO.   DATE

CPD-11.409 (REV. 4/84)   RACE CODES: 1-BLACK, 2-WHITE, 3-BLACK-HISPANIC, 4-WHITE-HISPANIC, 5-AMERICAN INDIAN/ALASKAN NATIONAL, 6-ASIAN/PACIFIC ISLANDER.

LOCATION CODES

Code	Description	Code	Description	Code	Description	Code	Description
)96--	Abandoned Building	233--	Hospital Building/Grounds	314--	Public School Property	304--	Street
)92--	Alley	273--	Lake/Waterway/Riverbank	317--	Railroad Property	262--	Vehicle - Commercial
095--	Airport/Aircraft	269--	Park Property	290--	Residence	126--	Vehicle - Delivery Truck
126--	Delivery Truck	277--	Parking Lot/Garage (non-resid.)	210--	Residence - Garage	259--	Vehicle - Non-Commercial
220--	Gas Station	123--	Parking Lot/Grounds CHA	313--	School Property - Private	327--	Warehouse
238--	Highway/Expressway	313--	Private School Property	314--	School Property - Public	330--	Other - Specify

CONTINUATION OF NARRATIVE

....

....

....

....

....

....

....

....

....

....

....

....

....

....

....

....

....

....

....

....

....

....

R.D. NO.

....

....

....

....

I HAVE REVIEWED THIS REPORT AND BY MY SIGNATURE INDICATE THAT IT IS ACCEPTABLE.	SUPERVISOR'S SIGNATURE	DATE (DAY-MO.-YR.)

Sample Recovered Vehicle Supplementary Report General Instructions, Chicago Police Department

RECOVERED VEHICLE SUPPLEMENTARY REPORT, CPD-11.409

GENERAL INSTRUCTIONS

PURPOSE OF THE REPORT

The Recovered Vehicle Supplementary Report is used to record the circumstances surrounding the recovery of a vehicle which has previously been reported stolen in Chicago.

WHEN TO PREPARE A RECOVERED VEHICLE SUPPLEMENTARY REPORT

The Recovered Vehicle Supplementary Report will be prepared when a vehicle is recovered which was previously reported as stolen in Chicago. This report must be prepared regardless of how the vehicle was stolen (i.e., theft, robbery, burglary or deceptive practice). The recovery of a motor vehicle stolen outside of Chicago requires the preparation of a Vehicle Theft Case Report. (See Vehicle Theft Case Report Instructions.) The recovery of a vehicle other than a motor vehicle (i.e., trailers, snowmobiles, golf carts, motor driven farm or construction equipment, etc.) reported stolen outside of Chicago but recovered in Chicago requires the preparation of a General Offense Case Report. (See Field Reporting Manual General Reporting Instructions.)

FORM PREPARATION

1. Enter offense in which the vehicle was taken.

2. Enter the correct beat of recovery using the current beat map.

3. Enter the date and time of vehicle recovery.

4. Enter the beat or unit assigned to the investigation.

5. Enter the R.D. number assigned to the original case report. Also record the R.D. number in the space provided on the reverse side of the report ONLY if the Narrative is continued on the reverse.

6. Enter street number, direction and street name.

7. Check one square only. If location is not provided in box 7, check the Other square, describe, and enter the appropriate code number for the specific type of location (location/premise codes are printed on the reverse side of the report).

8. Print last name of registered owner first, the first name and middle initial if any. If registered owner is a business, use the firm name. Check appropriate square to indicate whether or not name was corrected.
   Enter address of registered owner, including Zip Code. If a business, enter the company address. Be specific with address, include apartment number if applicable.
   Enter the owner's home and business telephone numbers.

9. V.I.N. obtained from vehicle. If unavailable explain in Narrative.
   NOTE: On motorcycles, note the identification number present on the frame—do not enter the engine number. Legibility of alpha and numeric digits of the V.I.N. is very important. Start in the first space on the left, enter one character per space.

10. State License Number: Enter the alpha/numeric license number and the abbreviated name of the issuing state only if same as when stolen. If different explain in Narrative. When known, include the month and year of the license expiration.

11. Check one square only.

12. Be specific (i.e., '80 Olds Cutlass, 2 door, black/red).

13. Enter the alpha/numeric city license number and the name of the issuing city. Include the year of license expiration.

14. Check one or more if applicable.

15. Self-explanatory.

16. Check appropriate square(s).
    NOTE: No Results square should be checked if, at the time the theft was reported, vehicle owner was not given the option of Tow or Notification at recovery.

17. Enter date and time of notification or check square if appropriate.

18. Enter pound number if applicable and Motor Vehicle Inventory Report (CPD-34.303) number when known. Enter "D.N.A." or "None" if applicable.

19. List all Property Inventory (CPD-34.523) numbers for personal property in the vehicle which is seized, recovered, found, or otherwise taken into custody and inventoried.

20. Check appropriate square(s). Enter date Hot File cleared.

21. Check one square only.

22. Space is provided in the section for a total of two offenders/arrestees. If more space is required, identify as offender or arrestee and use Narrative.
    Enter alleged offender's name and/or alias. Enter home address (if known). Enter sex, race code number, age and physical description of offender/arrestee. As a MINIMUM REQUIREMENT, if offender(s) is named, the sex of the offender(s) must be entered (race code numbers are printed on the bottom margin of the report).
    Enter C.B., Y.D., or J.D.A. number if an offender is arrested.

23. Enter total number of persons arrested.

24. - 26. Self-explanatory.

80. Narrative: Give concise statement of the facts of the case. Do not unnecessarily repeat information already contained in any of the numbered boxes. If the address/location of recovery is different from the address where the report is being made, so indicate in the Narrative.
    Obtain signature of person receiving vehicle. Verify identity through drivers license. Vehicle may be returned to owner or victim as outlined in Department directives.
    Mark the square to the right, if the Narrative is continued on the reverse side.

90. When required, enter the name of the person making the notification, the number of the unit and the name of the person notified. Enter date and time of notification. Indicate presence of personnel at scene by marking Arrived square. If more space is required, use Narrative.

CPD-63.459 (Rev. 12/85)

91. Enter printed name of officer completing the report, star number and signature in the box to the right.

92. Indicate the number and recipient of extra copies required of this report. For normal distribution, check Normal square.

93. Enter printed name, star number and signature of a second officer if applicable.

94. Enter date and time investigation was completed.

95. Approving supervisor enters his printed name, star number and signature when he approves the report. If Narrative is continued on the reverse side, approving supervisor's signature and date are also required on the reverse. Enter date and time the report is approved.

Preliminary investigators should make no entry in the area of the report headed "FOR DETECTIVE DIVISION USE ONLY."

Sample Missing Person Report and Report Writing Instruction Manual, San Diego Police Department

PD-242 MISSING PERSON REPORT

1. CASE NUMBER

   After you take the report, call 555-5555 and get a case number. Write the case number in this block. (NOTE - If a search for a child has been made and the child was found, you still get a case number. In this instance, write the word "LOCATED" at the top and bottom of the report.

2. ADULT

   Check this box if missing person is 18 years of age or older.

3. JUVENILE (12-17 years)

   Check this box if missing person is between the ages of 12-17 years.

4. JUVENILE (under 12 years)

   Check this box if missing person is under the age of 12 years.

5. NCIC NUMBER

   LEAVE BLANK - Teletype will obtain an NCIC number and will write that number in this box.

6. RECORD TYPE

   a. RUNAWAY JUVENILE

       If missing juvenile has left home without the knowledge/ permission of his/her parent or guardian.

   b. VOLUNTARY MISSING ADULT

       If missing adult has left of his/her own free will.

   c. NON-FAMILY ABDUCTION

       If missing juvenile was taken by a known abductor that is not a family member.

MISSING PERSON REPORT (Continued)

    d.   PARENTAL/FAMILY ABDUCTION

        If missing juvenile is taken by a parent/non-parental family member.

    e.   STRANGER ABDUCTION

        If missing juvenile is taken by a stranger or missing under circumstances that may indicate a stranger abduction.

    f.   DEPENDENT ADULT

        If missing adult is 18 years of age or older and has a physical or mental limitation which restricts his or her ability to carry out normal activities (i.e., alzheimer, mentally handicapped, etc.)

    g.   LOST

        Any person, adult or juvenile, who is believed lost.

    h.   CATASTROPHE

        Any person, adult or juvenile, who is missing after a catastrophe (i.e., earthquake, boating accident, fire, airplane crash, etc.)

    i.   UNKNOWN CIRCUMSTANCES

        When the circumstances surrounding missing person's disappearance are unknown.

7.   NAME

Full name of missing person - last, first, middle. If applicable, give the generation of the individual (i.e., Morgan, Archer Raymond, Jr., Sr.)

8.   RACE

Write the one letter code that applies.

W - White	I - American Indian
B - Black	F - Filipino
H - Hispanic	O - All Orientals
	X - Others/unknown

9.   SEX

Check one: M-Male   F-Female

MISSING PERSON REPORT (Continued)

10. HEIGHT

Write the missing person's height in feet and inches. (i.e., 5'11")

11. WEIGHT

Write the missing person's weight in pounds.

12. HAIR

Write the missing person's hair color using the ARJIS abbreviations.

13. EYES

Write the missing person's eye color using the ARJIS abbreviations.

14. AGE

Write in the numeric age of the missing person. For example (16)

15. DATE OF BIRTH

Write the missing person's date of birth. Use the six-digit system. For example (02-08-57)

16. ADDRESS

Write the complete address, including City, State and Zip Code where the missing person currently lives.

17. BEAT

Write in the beat number that corresponds with the missing person's home address.

18. OCCUPATION/SCHOOL

Write the missing person's current occupation. If the missing person currently attends school, write in the name of the school. This includes kindergarten, elementary, junior high, high school, college and trade schools.

19. GRADE

Write the grade level of the missing person (If applicable).

MISSING PERSON REPORT (Continued)

20.   ALIAS(S)/FORMER ADDRESS

       Write in any alias(s) (including maiden name) if applicable. Write
       the complete address of the missing person's last residence.

21.   WHERE EMPLOYED OR PARENT'S EMPLOYER

       Write the name of the business where the missing person is
       employed. If this report is being taken on a missing juvenile,
       then this block should contain a parent's business address.
       (Write "PARENT").

22.   HOME PHONE

       Write the telephone number at the present residence of the miss-
       ing person.

23.   BUSINESS PHONE

       Write the telephone number of the business listed in line #20.
       (If applicable).

24.   EXTENSION

       If the business telephone number has an extension, write it in
       this block.

25.   DATE/TIME MISSING

       Write the date (month/day/year) and time (military) that the
       missing person was last seen.

              Example: 10-01-84   2300 hours

26.   S.S.#/CDL# - SOCIAL SECURITY NUMBER/CALIFORNIA DRIVER'S LICENSE
       NUMBER

       Write in either the missing person's social security number or
       California Driver's license number in this block. If they have
       an out of state driver's license, enter that number and state of
       issuance.

27.   LAST SEEN BY (RELATIONSHIP)

       Write the name of the individual who last saw the missing per-
       son. Include relationship, (i.e., parent, neighbor, co-worker).

MISSING PERSON REPORT (Continued)

28.   CREDIT CARDS CARRIED (Company name)

If the missing person has any credit cards in their possession, list the company name(s) and account number(s), (if known).

29.   LOCATION LAST SEEN

Write the location or the complete address, including City, State and Zip Code where the missing person was last seen.

30.   PROBABLE DESTINATION

If there is a location to which the person might be en route, write it here. If a location is listed, write the reasons why in the narrative.

31.   BANK ACCOUNTS (WHERE)

Check the appropriate box to indicate whether or not the missing person has a bank account.

32.   BANK NAME

If the missing person has a bank account, write in the name of bank and branch, if known.

33.   MARKS, SCARS, PHYSICAL DEFECTS, TATTOOS (LOCATION/DESCRIPTION)

Write a description of any identifying physical "oddities", which might make it easier for officers to identify the missing person.

34.   PHOTO RECEIVED

Check the appropriate box. In all cases you should attempt to get a photograph of the missing person. If the person filing the report requests that the photograph be returned to him/her, the investigating unit will mail the photograph back to them when the case has been closed. Note the missing persons name and case number on the back of the photograph. Attach the photo to the original of the report.

35.   AGE IN PHOTO

If a photograph is obtained, please enter the age of the missing person at the time it was taken.

MISSING PERSON REPORT (Continued)

36.   CATEGORY

Check one or all the boxes that apply. At Risk: At risk includes,
but is not limited to, evidence or indications the missing person is/has.

      A.   The victim of a crime or foul play.
      B.   In need of medical attention.
      C.   No pattern of running away or disappearance.
      D.   The victim of a parental abduction.
      E.   Mentally impaired.

Prior Missing:

      If the missing person has been reported missing prior to
      this occurrence, check box then enter date.

Sexual exploitation:

      Check the box if sexual exploitation/abuse is suspected.

37.   MEDICAL, MENTAL, DENTAL CONDITION (DESCRIBE)

Write in any pertinent information that could assist the investigator in solving the case. (i.e., pacemaker, dentures, mental
illness, etc.) Be specific, if more room is needed, list in the
beginning of the narrative.

38.   X-RAYS AVAILABLE

Check this box to indicate whether dental records are available.

38.   PHOTO/X-RAY WAIVER RELEASE SIGNED?

Indicate whether a photo/x-ray waiver release form (SS 8567) has
been signed by the reporting party.

40.   DOCTOR/DENTIST-NAME/ADDRESS/PHONE#

Write in the missing person's doctor/dentist's name, complete
address, (including zip code) and telephone number, if known.

41.   CLOTHING DESCRIPTION/SIZE

Write a description of the clothing that the missing person was
last known to be wearing. Be as specific as possible and include
size. (From head to toe).

MISSING PERSON REPORT (Continued)

42.   JEWELRY

List and describe in detail the jewelry the missing person was wearing at the time of his/her appearance. (ring, necklace, etc.)

43.   GLASSES/CONTACTS

Check the appropriate box to indicate whether the missing person wears glasses or contact lenses. (If so, describe fully).

44.   VEHICLE USED:

YEAR

Write the last two digits of the year the vehicle was made.

MAKE

Write the ARJIS abbreviation for the name of the vehicle's manufacturer.

BODY TYPE

Write the ARJIS abbreviation for the body type (i.e., hardtop - HT, sedan 4 door - 4D, etc.).

COLOR

Write in the ARJIS abbreviation(s) for the vehicle color(s) from top to bottom or front to back. List no more than two colors

LICENSE NUMBER

Write in the license number of the vehicle used by the missing person.

STATE

Write the state using the two letter code. (i.e., California-CA).

MISSING PERSON REPORT (Continued)

OTHER IDENTIFYING MARKS

Write a description of any other identifying features of the vehicle used by the missing person.

EXAMPLES: Gray primer spots on left rear fender, broken left rear tail light, or large dent in right front fender.

45.   IF ABDUCTION, DID ABDUCTION INVOLVE MOVEMENT OF MISSING PERSON IN THE COMMISSION OF CRIME?

Check the appropriate box to indicate whether missing person was moved during the course of a crime.

46.   SUSPECT NAME

Enter the full or partial name(s) of the suspect(s). If known, (include nicknames).

47.   RELATIONSHIP TO VICTIM

Enter suspect(s) relationship if any to the missing person, (i.e., uncle father, neighbor, co-worker).

48.   DATE OF BIRTH

Write in the date of birth of the suspect (if known), using the six digit system (05-20-90).

49.   FRIENDS/NEIGHBORS/RELATIVES WITH POSSIBLE INFORMATION

Write the name, complete address and relationship of any person who may know the whereabouts of the missing person. There are two lines available in the box area. If more space is needed, continue at the top of the narrative using a similar format.

50.   REPORTING PARTY/FATHER/MOTHER/SPOUSE

Write the last, first and middle names of the person making the missing report. Also give the relationship of the individual to the missing person. (e.g., parent, boyfriend, girlfriend, etc.)

MISSING PERSON REPORT (Continued)

51. FATHER

Write the last, first and middle names of the missing person's father. Also give complete address (including zip code), home telephone number and business telephone number/ext., if applicable.

52. MOTHER

Write the last, first and middle names of the missing person's mother. Also give complete address (including zip code), home telephone number and business telephone number/ext., if applicable.

53. SPOUSE

Write in the last, first and middle names of the missing person's spouse. If applicable, also give complete address (including zip code), home telephone and business telephone number/ext.

54. DETAILS

Write a detailed narrative including all important information regarding the disappearance. Include any useful history or background on the missing person. Officers should include their observations at the time the report was made and any investigative steps they may have taken towards locating the missing person. Include names of any other individuals who may be with the missing person. (If more space is needed, continue on an ARJIS-9).

55. OFFICER

Write in the reporting officer's first initial and last name.

56. ID#

Write your departmental identification number.

57. DIVISION

Write the division and watch you are currently assigned to. (i.e., Northern third watch - N-3, missing person MP).

58. DATE/TIME

Write in the date and time you took the report. (Use military time).

MISSING PERSON REPORT (Continued)

59.   APPROVED

This is an official report, therefore it must be approved/signed
by a Sergeant. The Sergeant must print his/her first initial,
last name and identification number after reading and approving
the report.

SAN DIEGO POLICE DEPARTMENT (619) 531-2277	MISSING PERSON REPORT ORIGINAL to Records, COPY to Area Investigations		CASE NUMBER — 1

ADULT [2]	JUVENILE [3] (12–17 YEARS)	JUVENILE [4] (UNDER 12 YEARS)	ORI CA0371100	NCIC NUMBER 5

MISSING PERSON'S NAME (Last/First/Middle) 7	RACE 3	SEX 9	HEIGHT 10	WEIGHT 11	HAIR 12	EYES 13	AGE 14	DOB 15

ADDRESS 16	BEAT 17	OCCUPATION/SCHOOL 18	GRADE 19

ALIAS(S)/FORMER ADDRESS 20	EMPLOYER OR PARENT'S EMPLOYER 21

HOME PHONE 22	BUSINESS PHONE 23	EXT. 24	DATE/TIME MISSING 25	S.S.#/CDL# 26

LAST SEEN BY (Relationship) 27	CREDIT CARDS CARRIED (Company Name) 28

LOCATION LAST SEEN 29	PROBABLE DESTINATION 30	BANK ACCOUNT 31 YES □ NO □	BANK NAME 32

MARKS, SCARS, PHYSICAL DEFECTS, TATTOOS (Location/Description) 33	34 PHOTO RECEIVED YES □ NO □	AGE IN PHOTO 35

MEDICAL/MENTAL/DENTAL CONDITION (Describe) 37	X-RAYS AVAILABLE 38 YES □ NO □

PHOTO/X-RAY WAIVER RELEASE SIGNED? YES □ NO □ 39	DOCTOR/DENTIST – NAME/ADDRESS/PHONE # 40

CLOTHING DESCRIPTION/SIZE 41	JEWELRY 42	GLASSES/CONTACTS YES □ NO □ 43

36 CATAGORY
□ AT RISK
□ PRIOR MISSING DATE _____
□ SEXUAL EXPLOITATION

44 VEHICLE USED BY MISSING PERSON	YEAR	MAKE	BODY TYPE	COLOR	LICENSE #	STATE	OTHER IDENTIFYING MARKS

45 IF ABDUCTION, DID ABDUCTION INVOLVE MOVEMENT OF MISSING PERSON IN THE COMMISSION OF A CRIME?   YES □   NO □

SUSPECT NAME 46	RELATIONSHIP TO VICTIM 47	DATE OF BIRTH 48

FRIENDS/RELATIVES/NEIGHBORS w/poss. info.	ADDRESS	HOME PHONE	BUS. PHONE/EXT.
49 1. _____	_____	_____	_____
2. _____	_____	_____	_____

	NAME:	ADDRESS	HOME PHONE	BUS. PHONE/EXT.
REPORTING PARTY (Relationship)	50			
FATHER	51			
MOTHER	52			
SPOUSE	53			

DETAILS   54
_____
_____
_____
_____
_____
_____
_____
_____
_____
_____

(Continue on ARJS-0)

OFFICER 55	ID# 56	DIV. 57	DATE/TIME 58	APPROVED 59

PD-242 REV: 9/90

Sample Investigative Report Manual Directions for Automated Dictation System, Greensboro Police Department

GENERAL DIRECTIONS

The Department uses an automated dictation system for preparing certain types of documents. Part of the system consists of recording units which are activated by use of a touch-tone telephone.

Before beginning dictation, organize all necessary notes, rough drafts, and other necessary information. Find a quiet location, remaining aware of distracting background noises.

When dictating, speak directly into the phone, using a clear, normal tone. Do not eat or drink while dictating.

Be sure to spell all proper names, addresses, unusual words, and technical terms. Use the phonetic alphabet for initials, tag numbers, etc. Indicate punctuation, capitalizations, and paragraph breaks.

36

DICTATION DIRECTIONS

1. Dial 555-5555.

2. Enter your **badge number followed by the [#] key**. Do not use leading zeros (for example, if you badge number is 98, do not enter 098).

3. Enter the proper **Work Type Code followed by the [#] key**.

1	Deaths & Attempted Suicides
2	Sex Offenses
3	Robberies & Assaults
4	Burglaries
5	Larcenies
6	Missing Persons
7	All Other Types of Investigative Reports
8	Supplementary Reports & Juvenile Referrals
9	Memos, Letters, & All Other Documents

4. Enter the **case number followed by the [#] key**. Do not use leading zeros. If the document has no case number (such as a memo), enter "9".

5. **Begin dictation by pressing [2].**

6. If the document is on the **Priority List**, press [6].

7. Use the touch-tone keys to control the recording as follows:

1	Places the recorder on **hold** for up to 10 minutes; press [3] to release and then [2] to resume dictation.
2	**Pause and resume** recording; the recording will pause for up to 3 minutes.
3	**Incremental rewind** for several seconds; playback is automatic.
4	**Fast forward**; press [2] to stop.
5	**Disconnect** phone line; use when through with all dictation.
6	Identifies the recording as a **Priority** document.
7	**Rewind**; press [2] to stop; playback is thereafter automatic.
8	Begin a **new document** without redialing.
44	Move to **end of dictation**.
77	Move to **beginning of dictation**.

37

8. To dictate an **additional report, press [8]** and follow the voice prompts. There is no limit to the number of additional reports that may be dictated at one time. **Do not use this feature when dictating related reports that require duplicate narratives.**

9. **When dictation is completed, press [5].**

10. **To dictate related reports that require duplicate narratives,** all dictation must be done at one time. Do not disconnect the line between reports, or use the [8] key to separate the reports. Simply dictate the first report in its entirety, then the block section of the second report, and then request that the first narrative be repeated.

Note that only certain pairings of reports and narratives are possible. These are as follows:

An Investigative Report narrative can be repeated into:
    - Another Investigative Report
    - A Juvenile Referral

A Supplementary Report narrative can be repeated into:
    - Another Supplementary Report
    - A Juvenile Referral

A Juvenile Referral narrative can be repeated into:
    - Another Juvenile Referral

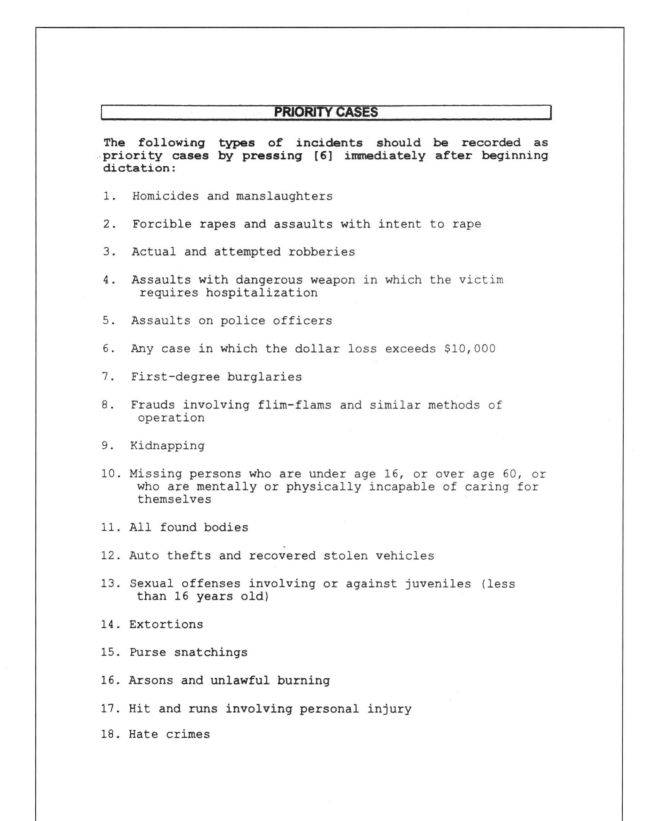

PRIORITY CASES

The following types of incidents should be recorded as priority cases by pressing [6] immediately after beginning dictation:

1. Homicides and manslaughters

2. Forcible rapes and assaults with intent to rape

3. Actual and attempted robberies

4. Assaults with dangerous weapon in which the victim requires hospitalization

5. Assaults on police officers

6. Any case in which the dollar loss exceeds $10,000

7. First-degree burglaries

8. Frauds involving flim-flams and similar methods of operation

9. Kidnapping

10. Missing persons who are under age 16, or over age 60, or who are mentally or physically incapable of caring for themselves

11. All found bodies

12. Auto thefts and recovered stolen vehicles

13. Sexual offenses involving or against juveniles (less than 16 years old)

14. Extortions

15. Purse snatchings

16. Arsons and unlawful burning

17. Hit and runs involving personal injury

18. Hate crimes

39

Sample Investigative Report Manual—Narrative Guide for a Burglary Investigative Report, Greensboro Police Department

Burglary/Forcible Entry (R) (N/R)
Burglary/Unlawful Entry (R) (N/R)
Burglary/Attempt Forcible Entry (R) (N/R)

NARRATIVE GUIDE

The following information should be included in the narrative section of your Investigative Report, although not necessarily in the order listed:

A.   Briefly describe how you became involved in the investigation.

B.   Describe the details of the incident:
    1.   Who secured the structure or was in it last?
    2.   Who discovered the burglary? (Owner, resident, neighbor, etc.)
    3.   Describe the point of entry and how entry was gained.
    4.   If the structure was occupied at the time of the incident, give name, exact location, and what occupants were doing at the time.
    5.   Describe any contact victim had with suspect.
    6.   Describe what was attacked in the structure and how it was attacked.
    7.   Describe any damage to property.
    8.   Describe the point of exit.

C.   Describe the scene of the incident as you found it:
    1.   Include any signs of a struggle, etc.
    2.   Describe any physical conditions, lighting, or other information which might be pertinent to the investigation.

D.   Was a Crime Scene Technician called to the scene and what was done?

E.   List evidence collected:
    1.   Where was it located?
    2.   Who located it?
    3.   What was the disposition of the evidence?

F.   Provide any additional information available:
    1.   Your observations and activities relative to the case.
    2.   Efforts to locate evidence or recover property.
    3.   Efforts to locate suspects and/or witnesses.
    4.   Identify assisting officers.

G.   Include statements obtained from witnesses, suspects, etc.
    1.   Lengthy statements should be recorded separately on supplementary reports and original notes retained or turned in as evidence.

H.   Indicate what, if any, diagrams, sketches, measurements, etc., were made.

I.   Include any other information you consider pertinent to the investigation.

J.   Include any suggestions you may have concerning the best point to begin the follow-up investigation.

103

GREENSBORO POLICE DEPARTMENT • INVESTIGATIVE REPORT
BLOCK SECTION

GENERAL INFORMATION

Initial Case Status: ☑ Active ☐ Inactive

Case Number: 1997-116306

Related Case Numbers: 1996-10391, 1996-179402

Offense/Classification: BURFEN

Location of Occurrence: 2028 WALKER AVE.

Premise Type: FARM EQUIP. DEALER

Date / Time Occurred At / Between: 1/9/1997 at 1730 hours and 1/10/1997 at 0120 hours

How Committed: BY CUTTING PADLOCK ON SHED + REMOVING PROPERTY

M.O. Numbers: 101, 104, 121, 173, 197, 210, 275, 293

Value & Description of Property Lost / Stolen / Found / Recovered: $500.00 CHAINSAWS

Value & Description of Property Damaged: $10.00 PADLOCK

Date/Time Reported: 1/10/1997 at 0120 hours

Badge Number: 391

Investigating Officer: WEBSTER, D.T.

Assignment: IIIC-381

VICTIM

Name (Last Name, First Name, Middle Name, Suffix)	Race	Sex	DOB	Nickname
			/ /	

Home Address / City / State / Zip Code	Home Phone ( )	Relationship to Suspect

Business Name	Business Address / City / State / Zip Code	Business Phone
NASH LAWN + GARDEN Co.	2028 WALKER AVE G'BORO NC 27407	(910) 299-3606

Social Security / Tax I.D. #: 237468263

Extent & Type of Injury: K A B C None

Willing to Prosecute: ☐ Yes ☐ No

Next of Kin	Home Address / City / State / Zip Code	Home Phone ( )

Vehicle Make	Model	Year	VIN Number	Tag Number	State

Top Color	Bottom Color	Foreign Color	TAD Code	Markings

ADDITIONAL PERSONS

Role	Name (Last Name, First Name, Middle Name, Suffix)	Race	Sex	DOB	Nickname
REP	GORDON, JAMES TYLER	W	M	6/18/1949	JIM

Home Address / City / State / Zip Code	Home Phone	Relationship to Suspect
1311 TRENT ST, APT G, G'BORO NC 27405	(910) 299-9694	

Business Name	Business Address / City / State / Zip Code	Business Phone
NASH LAWN + GARDEN Co.	2028 WALKER AVE G'BORO NC 27407	(910) 299-3606

Social Security / Tax I.D. #: 242-31-9774

Extent & Type of Injury: K A B C (None)

Willing to Prosecute: ☑ Yes ☐ No

Next of Kin	Home Address / City / State / Zip Code	Home Phone
GORDON, BETTY	1311 TRENT ST, APT G, G'BORO NC 27405	(910) 299-9694

Role	Name (Last Name, First Name, Middle Name, Suffix)	Race	Sex	DOB	Nickname
				/ /	

Home Address / City / State / Zip Code	Home Phone ( )	Relationship to Suspect

Business Name	Business Address / City / State / Zip Code	Business Phone ( )

Social Security / Tax I.D. #:

Extent & Type of Injury: K A B C None

Willing to Prosecute: ☐ Yes ☐ No

Next of Kin	Home Address / City / State / Zip Code	Home Phone ( )

ROLE CODES.   WIT = Witness   VIC = Victim   PNI = Person Not Interviewed   PWK = Person with Knowledge   REP = Reporting Person

PS POL - 92 565A (Rev 4/97)

104

SUSPECT

Make	Model	Year	Vin Number		Tag Number		State	Top Color	Bottom Color
Foreign Color		Tad Code	Markings		Last Known Location / Direction				

Name (Last Name, First Name, Middle Name, Suffix)		Race	Sex	DOB	Nickname	Social Security Number
Home Address / City / State / Zip Code	Home Phone ( )	Business Name	Business Address / City / State / Zip Code			Business Phone ( )
Personal ID Numbers	Other Description					

Name (Last Name, First Name, Middle Name, Suffix)		Race	Sex	DOB	Nickname	Social Security Number
Home Address / City / State / Zip Code	Home Phone ( )	Business Name	Business Address / City / State / Zip Code			Business Phone ( )
Personal ID Numbers	Other Description					

PROPERTY & EVIDENCE

Enter Below All Lost, Stolen, Found or Recovered Property and All Items of Evidence Except Photos and Latents

Item	Status	Quantity	Item/Description	Brand	Model	VIN Number / Serial Number	Type	Style	Colors	Tag Number Engraving/Markings	Caliber / Size	Value	Other Description	Turned in As Evidence	Retained Victim
1	S	2	CHAINSAWS	STIHL	015	CSC936, CS1120,	GAS		ORANGE WHITE		16"	500	NEW IN BOXES	Y (N)	Y (N)
2														Y N	Y N
3														Y N	Y N
4														Y N	Y N
5														Y N	Y N
6														Y N	Y N
7														Y N	Y N
8														Y N	Y N

Crime Scene Technician Requested   ☑Yes   ☐No

Status Codes: S = Stolen   R = Recovered   F = Found   L = Lost   C = Confiscated   E = Evidence

SOLVABILITY FACTORS

Suspect Identified	Warrant Advised	Warrant Issued	Suspect Arrested	Juvenile (<16) Arrested	NCIC Affected
☐YES ☑NO	☐YES ☑NO	☐YES ☑NO	☐YES ☑NO	☐YES ☑NO	☑YES ☐NO

105

NARRATIVE SECTION

1997-116306

At 0120 hours, today, while patrolling the 2000 block of Walker Avenue, I observed the storage shed doors open behind the Nash Lawn & Garden Company at 2028 Walker Avenue. The shed appeared to have been broken into. Subsequently, I was able to get in contact with Mr. James Gordon, the manager of Nash Lawn & Garden, and he responded to the scene.

According to Mr. Gordon, 2 Stihl brand chain saws were taken from inside the storage shed. These are all new chain saws and were removed from the shelves in the rear of the shed. No other property was taken.

Entry was gained by walking onto the unfenced lot at Nash Lawn & Garden and cutting the padlock off the shed. This padlock was recovered as evidence and was turned in by Crime Scene Technician Maxwell. It appeared to have been cut open with boltcutters or a similar tool. Damage due to forcible entry is $10 for replacement of the padlock.

Mr. Gordon stated he locked up the shed and left the firm at 1730 hours, 1/9/97. He stated he was sure there were 2 chain saws in the shed because they had just recently come in a shipment and he had stored them there until they could be sold.

Crime Scene Technician C. R. Maxwell was summoned to the scene. He attempted to raise latent fingerprints; however, he was unable to do so. He did collect as evidence the above-mentioned padlock.

Mr. Gordon stated his firm had been burglarized twice within the last six months. He stated in each case, small lawn and garden tools or similar items were taken (see Case #1996-10391 and #1996-179402). Follow-up in this matter is therefore recommended.

Sample U.S. Probation System Worksheet for Presentence Investigation Reports:

PROB 1
(Rev. 4/01)

UNITED STATES DISTRICT COURT
Federal Probation System

WORKSHEET FOR PRESENTENCE REPORT
(See Publication 107 for Instruction)

1. FACESHEET DATA

Defendant's Court Name:

Defendant's True Name:

Docket No.:	District:
Judge/Magistrate:	Sentencing Date:
USPO:	Arrest Date:
Assistant U.S. Attorney (Name, address, telephone)	Defense Counsel (Name, address, telephone)

DEFENDANT'S IDENTIFICATION

Defendant's Names: (List every name the defendant has used, e.g., name given at birth, name given at adoption, nickname, alias, names used as a result of marriage, etc.)

Date of Birth:	Age:	Place of Birth:

Race: ☐ White   ☐ Black   ☐ American Indian/Alaskan Native   Hispanic Origin:
          ☐ Asian or Pacific Islander   ☐ Unknown   ☐ Hispanic   ☐ Not Hispanic   ☐ Unknown

Sex:	Country of Citizenship:	Immigration Status:
No. of Dependents:	Education:	SSN:
FBI No.:	U.S. Marshal's No.:	Other ID No.:

Defendant's Legal Address: _____

(Number and Street)   (Apartment)

_____

(City)   (State)   (Zip)

Defendant's Current Address: _____

(Number and Street)   (Apartment)

_____

(City)   (State)   (Zip)

Referral Date: _____

Interview Date: _____

1

PROB 1
(Rev. 4/01)

2. OFFENSE DATA (Presentence Report Part A)

CHARGES AND CONVICTIONS	RELEASE STATUS
Date Information/Indictment Filed: _____ Date of Conviction: _____ Count No.(s): _____ Conviction by (Check one): ☐ Guilty Plea/Plea of Nolo Contendere ☐ Court Trial Verdict ☐ Jury Trial Verdict	Check the Appropriate Box(s): ☐ In federal custody since _____ ☐ In non-federal custody since _____ Released on _____ ☐ Unsecured personal recognizance ☐ $ _____ personal recognizance bond since _____ ☐ $ _____ cash security since _____ ☐ $ _____ corporate security since _____ ☐ $ _____ property bond since _____ ☐ Pretrial services supervision

COUNTS OF CONVICTION

Count Nos.	Offense and Statutes	Offense Classification	Minimum/Maximum Statutory Penalty

DETAINERS

☐ No Detainers

Agency or Court	Type of Detainer	Case Number

CODEFENDANTS

☐ No Codefendants

Codefendant(s) Name(s): _____

_____

RELATED CASES (Co-offenders)

☐ No Related Cases

Docket No.	Defendant(s) Name(s)

2

PROB 1
(Rev. 4/01)

PLEA AGREEMENT	
Check One: ☐ Written ☐ Accepted ☐ Oral ☐ Deferred ☐ No Agreement ☐ Binding Substantial Assistance Motion: ☐ No ☐ Yes	Notes:

OFFENSE CONDUCT

VICTIM IMPACT			
☐ No Loss			
Victim's Name	Financial Loss	Victim's Address	Victim's Phone
	$		
Loss to All Victims:	$		

Describe any social, psychological, or medical impact upon the victim of the offense behavior.

ACCEPTANCE OF RESPONSIBILITY

Defendant's statement regarding offense:

3

PROB 1
(Rev. 4/01)

3. DEFENDANT'S CRIMINAL HISTORY (Presentence Report Part B)

☐ None

Date of Arrest, Prosecution, Referral, or Detention	Charge/ Conviction	Court City/County/State Action No.	Date Sentenced or Case Disposed	Sentence	Defendant Represented by or Waived Counsel (Y) or (N) ↓

PENDING CHARGES AND SUPERVISION STATUS

☐ The defendant has no pending charges.

Charge(s)	Court	Docket/Action No.	Next Appearance Date

☐ The defendant is not currently under supervision.
(division, probation, supervised release, or parole supervision)

☐ The defendant is currently under criminal justice sentence. Type of Supervision:

☐ Diversion   ☐ Probation   ☐ Supervised Release

☐ Parole   ☐ Escape Status   ☐ In Custody

Jurisdiction(s): _____

Supervising Officer's Name and Telephone Number: _____

_____

4

✎PROB 1
(Rev. 4/01)

4. OFFENDER CHARACTERISTICS (Presentence Report Part D)

DEFENDANT

Residential History: (List every town or city where the defendant has lived.)

PARENTS AND SIBLINGS

(List the defendant's biological parents. If defendant was reared by persons other than his natural parents, add the surrogate parent's names immediately below the space allocated to Father and Mother. After the parents, list all siblings, living or dead.)

Name	Relationship and Age		Present Address and Telephone Number	Occupation
	Father			
Current Name: Maiden Name:	Mother			

Notes regarding family history; identify any significant problems:

5

PROB 1
(Rev. 4/01)

MARITAL STATUS

☐ The defendant is presently single and has no marital history.

Spouse or Domestic Partner	Date and Place of Marriage	Status	Date of Separation	Date of Divorce	Court Where Divorce was Granted	Number of Children

Employment status of current spouse:

CHILDREN

☐ The defendant has never had any children.

Child's Name	Name of Other Parent of this Child	Age	Custody/ Support	Child's Address and Telephone Number (If different from defendant)

Note health problems, criminal history, substance abuse, or any other significant information.

6

✎PROB 1
(Rev. 4/01)

DEFENDANT'S PHYSICAL CONDITION

PHYSICAL DESCRIPTION		
Height:	Weight:	Eye Color:
Hair Color:	Tattoos:	Scars:

PHYSICAL HEALTH

☐ The defendant is healthy and has no history of health problems.

List the date(s) and nature(s) of any serious or chronic illnesses and medical conditions.

List all current prescriptions.

Provide the name, address, and telephone number of the defendant's physician.

MENTAL AND EMOTIONAL HEALTH

☐ The defendant has no history of mental or emotional problems, and no history of treatment for such problems.

Describe any past or present mental, emotional, or gambling problems. Include the diagnosis of any problems (if known) and the dates of any treatment. List the name and address of the treatment provider.

7

PROB 1
(Rev. 4/01)

SUBSTANCE ABUSE

☐ The defendant has no history of alcohol or drug use and no history of treatment for substance abuse.

Which of the following substances has the defendant used?

☐ Alcohol   ☐ Heroin/Opiates

☐ Marijuana   ☐ Barbiturates

☐ Cocaine   ☐ Hallucinogens

☐ Crack   ☐ Inhalants

☐ Amphetamine/   ☐ Other: _____
   Methamphetamine

When was alcohol or any controlled substance last used? _____

Which substance does the defendant prefer? _____

Which substance has caused the defendant the most problems? _____

Urine test results:

Describe in detail the defendant's history of substance abuse and treatment.
(Overdose, daily cost to support habit, frequency and quantity of use, treatment programs and dates)

8

PROB 1
(Rev. 4/01)

EDUCATION AND VOCATIONAL SKILLS

Highest grade completed: _____

SCHOLASTIC HISTORY

Name and Location of School (List most recent school first)	Dates Attended	Degree, Diploma, or Certificate Received

Does the defendant have any specialized training or skill(s)?

☐ Yes   ☐ No   If yes, what training or skill(s)?

_____

_____

Does the defendant have any professional license(s)?

☐ Yes   ☐ No   If yes, what license(s)?

_____

_____

☐ None   MILITARY

Branch of Service:	Service Number:	Entered:	Discharged:	Type of Discharge:
Highest Rank:	Rank at Separation:	Decorations and Awards:		VA Claim Number:

Summarize the defendant's military service. Describe any courts martial or non-judicial punishments. Describe any foreign or combat service. Describe any special training or skills acquired in the service. Describe previous VA claims.

9

Sample Probation and Parole Monthly Reporting Form, State of Tennessee Board of Probation and Parole:

State of Tennessee
BOARD OF PROBATION AND PAROLE
FIELD SERVICES DIVISION

MONTHLY REPORTING FORM

OFFICER
NAME: _____   DATE: _____

OFFENDER
NAME: _____   TOMIS #: _____

OFFENDER
ADDRESS: _____   HOME PHONE
NUMBER: ( )_____
   NUMBER   STREET   APT NUMBER

_____CITY_____COUNTY_____State_____ZIP_____

EMPLOYER: _____   PHONE
NUMBER: ( )_____

ADDRESS: _____
   NUMBER   STREET   CITY   COUNTY   STATE   ZIP

SUPERVISOR: _____   NUMBER OF
DAYS WORKED: _____   SALARY: _____

TIME NOW
REPORTING: _____ a.m. _____ p.m.   AMOUNT OF
OTHER INCOME: _____   SOURCE OF
OTHER INCOME: _____

NUMBER OF COMMUNITY
SERVICE HRS WORKED: _____   WERE YOU ARRESTED OR QUESTIONED BY
THE POLICE SINCE YOU LAST REPORTED?   NO ☐ YES ☐   [IF YES EXPLAIN BELOW]

....

OFFENDER DRIVER'S
LICENSE NUMBER: _____

[IDENTIFY VEHICLE OFFENDER TRAVELS IN]
MAKE: _____   MODEL/
YEAR: _____   COLOR: _____   TAG
NUMBER: _____

I AM FAMILIAR WITH ALL THE CONDITIONS OF MY SUPERVISION AND, EXCEPT WHERE NOTED ABOVE, HAVE FULLY COMPLIED WITH THEM.

OFFENDER
SIGNATURE: _____   DATE: _____

RECEIVED BY: _____   DATE: _____

DO NOT WRITE BELOW THIS LINE   TO BE COMPLETED BY OFFICER

Officer Comments

_____ VERIFIED ID CARD	_____ BROUGHT EMPLOYMENT VERIFICATION
_____ NO PROBLEMS OR CHANGES	_____ BROUGHT SUBS ABUSE TRT/SC VERIFICATION
_____ COMPLETED TREATMENT: _____	_____ WARNED ABOUT FEES)
_____ TOLD TO BRING SUBS ABUSE TRT/SC	_____ NEXT REPORT: _____
_____ COMPLETED SEX OFFENDER REGISTRATION	_____ TOLD TO DO FELONY REGISTRATION
_____ ISSUED TRAVEL PERMIT)	_____ DRUG SCREEN RESULT:
_____ RETURNED TRAVEL PERMIT	_____ ATTENDED ADJUSTMENT COUNSELING
_____ BROUGHT IN COURT COST RECEIPT	_____ REFERRED TO ADJUSTMENT COUNSELING
_____ WORK PROJECT HOURS VERIFICATION	_____ OTHER: _____
_____ RESTITUTION PAYMENT VERIFICATION	_____ OTHER: _____

Notes: _____

_____

_____

_____

[over for continued notes]

BP0009 (REV 04/08)   Page 1 of 2   RDA1664

CONTACT _____   DATE: _____   TIME: _____
COMMENTS: _____
_____
_____
_____
_____
_____

                    ENTERED BY: _____

CONTACT _____   DATE: _____   TIME: _____
COMMENTS: _____
_____
_____
_____
_____
_____

                    ENTERED BY: _____

CONTACT _____   DATE: _____   TIME: _____
COMMENTS: _____
_____
_____
_____
_____
_____

                    ENTERED BY: _____

CONTACT _____   DATE: _____   TIME: _____
COMMENTS: _____
_____
_____
_____
_____
_____

                    ENTERED BY: _____

CONTACT _____   DATE: _____   TIME: _____
COMMENTS: _____
_____
_____
_____
_____
_____

                    ENTERED BY: _____

CONTACT _____   DATE: _____   TIME: _____
COMMENTS: _____
_____
_____
_____
_____

                    ENTERED BY: _____

Selected Readings

Barefoot, J. Kirk (1995). *Undercover Investigation*, 3rd ed. Newton, MA: Butterworth-Heinemann.

Bohm, Robert M. & Keith N. Haley (2007). Instructor's annotated edition, *Introduction to Criminal Justice*. New York: McGraw Hill.

Clear, Todd R., Val B. Clear & William D. Burrell (1989). *Offender Assessment and Evaluation: The Presentence Investigation Report*. Cincinnati, OH: Anderson Publishing Co.

Cox, Clarice R. (1995). *Instant Teaching Skills*. Shaftsbury, VT: Professional Training Resources.

Fast, Julius (1992). *Body Language*. New York: Fine Communications.

Funk, Wilfred & Norman Lewis (1991). *30 Days to a More Powerful Vocabulary*. New York: Pocketbooks, Simon & Schuster, Inc.

Garner, Bryan A. (2004). *Black's Law Dictionary*, 8th Edition. New York: Thomson West.

Gibaldi, Joseph (2009). *MLA Handbook for Writers of Research Papers*, 7th ed. New York: Modern Language Association of America.

Glazier, Stephen (1998). *Word Menu*. New York: Random House.

Gordon, Gary R. & Bruce R. McBride (2008). *Criminal Justice Internships*, 6th ed. New Providence, NJ: LexisNexis/Anderson Publishing.

Hall, Edward T. (1973). *The Silent Language*. New York: Fawcett Premier, Ballantine.

Walker, Jeffrey T. & Craig Hemmens (2011). *Legal Guide for Police: Constitutional Issues*, 9th ed. Burlington, MA: Anderson Publishing.

McKeachie, Wilbert (2010). *Teaching Tips: Strategies, Research and Theory for College and University Teachers*, 13th ed. Belmont, CA: Wadsworth.

Mellinkoff, David (2004). *The Language of the Law*. Eugene, OR: Wipf & Stock.

O'Conner, Patricia T. (2004). *Woe Is I*. Penguin Group (USA).

Osterburg, James W. & Richard H. Ward (2010). *Criminal Investigation: A Method for Reconstructing the Past*, 6th ed. New Providence, NJ: LexisNexis/Anderson Publishing.

Shertzer, Margaret (1996). *The Elements of Grammar*. New York: Macmillan, Inc.

Soukhanov, Anna H. (1996). *Word Watch*. New York: Henry Holt and Co.

Stojkovic, Stan & Rick Lovell (1997). *Corrections: An Introduction*, 2nd ed. Cincinnati, OH: Anderson Publishing Co.

Strunk Jr., William & E.B. White (2000). *The Elements of Style*, 4th ed. New York: Longman.

The Chicago Manual of Style, online version: http://www.chicagomanualofstyle.org/home.html.

Travis, Lawrence F. III (2010). *Introduction to Criminal Justice*, 6th ed. New Providence, NJ: LexisNexis/Anderson Publishing.

Turabian, Kate L. (2007). *A Manual for Writers of Term Papers, Theses, and Dissertations*, 7th ed. Revised by Wayne C. Boot, Gregory Colomb, Joseph M. Williams and University of Chicago Press Editorial Staff. Chicago: University of Chicago Press.

Weaver, Richard L. II (1997). *Understanding Interpersonal Communications*, 7th ed. New York: Harper Collins.

INDEX

Note: Page numbers followed by *f* indicate figures.

PERMISSIONS

Figure 1.4 is used with the permission of the Outrigger Hotels and Resorts, Honolulu, HI.

Figures 1.5 and 1.6 are used with the permission of Handy Fender-Bender Corporation, P.O. Box 652506, Miami, FL 33265-2506.

Figure 1.7 is used with the permission of the CAD Zone, Inc., 7950 SW 139th Ave., Beaverton, OR 97008.

Figure 3.1 is taken from National Incident Based Reporting System Vol. 3: Approaches to Implementing an Incident Based Reporting System, United States Department of Justice, Federal Bureau of Investigation.

Figure 3.2 is used with the permission of Philip Arreola, Chief of Police, City of Tacoma, WA.

Figure 3.3 is used with the permission of the Office of the Sheriff, Oakland County Sheriff Department, Pontiac, MI.

Figure 3.4 is used with the permission of the Camden County Sheriff's Department, Camden, NJ.

Figure 3.5 is used with the permission of the Anne Arundel County Police Department, Millersville, MD.

Figure 3.6 is used with the permission of the Honolulu Police Department, Honolulu, HI.

Figure 3.7 is used with the permission of the Louisiana Department of Public Safety and Corrections, Baton Rouge, LA.

Figure 3.8 is used with the permission of Longs Drug Stores, Inc., Walnut Creek, CA.

Figure 3.9 is used with the permission of Al A. Philippus, Chief of Police, San Antonio Police Department, San Antonio, TX.

Figure 3.10 is used with the permission of the Bellevue Police Department, Bellevue, WA.

Figure 3.11 is used with the permission of the St. Paul Police Department, St. Paul, MN.

Figure 3.12 is used with the permission of the Arizona Department of Public Safety, Phoenix, AZ.

Figure 4.1 is used with the permission of the Arizona Department of Public Safety, Phoenix, AZ.

Figure 4.2 is used with the permission of the Anne Arundel County Police Department, Millersville, MD.

Figure 4.3 is used with the permission of the Camden County Sheriff's Department, Camden, NJ.

Figure 4.4 is used with the permission of the Office of the Sheriff, Oakland County Sheriff Department, Pontiac, MI.

Figure 4.5 is used with the permission of the St. Paul Police Department, St. Paul, MN.

Figure 4.6 is used with the permission of the Honolulu Police Department, Honolulu, HI.

Figure 4.7 is used with the permission of the Bellevue Police Department, Bellevue, WA.

Figure 4.8 is used with the permission of the Louisiana Department of Public Safety and Corrections, Baton Rouge, LA.

Figure 4.9 is used with the permission of the Longs Drug Stores, Inc., Walnut Creek, CA.

Figure 5.1 is used with the permission of the Honolulu Police Department, Honolulu, HI.

Figure 5.3 is used with the permission of Carlos Alvarez, director of the Metro-Dade Police Department, Miami, FL.

Figure 7.1 is used with the permission of the Highway Safety Division, Nebraska Department of Roads, Lincoln, NE.

Figure 7.2 is used with the permission of the Oakland County Sheriff's Office, Pontiac, MI.

Figures 7.3 and 7.4 are used with the permission of the Honolulu Police Department, Honolulu, HI.

Figure 7.5 is used with the permission of the Denver Police Department, Denver, CO.

Figure 14.1 is used with the permission of the Arizona Department of Public Safety, Phoenix, AZ.

Figures 14.2 and 14.3 are used with the permission of the Honolulu Police Department, Honolulu, HI.

Figure 14.4 is used with the permission of Jeff Bradford, Point Talk®, Communication by Pointing 774 Mays Blvd., Suite 10, Incline Village, NV 89451.